To God, who allows my life to be Charmed.

This book is lovingly dedicated to the memory
of the most passionate bookworm I've ever known,
my mother, Joanne Tisch.

And,
to my beloved partner: my husband, Mark Sivertsen.
All writers should be so fortunate to be
supported, emotionally and
financially, while they craft their dreams!

D1016169

CONTENTS

ACKNOWLEDGMENTS

So many people to thank and so little room! Thanks to my son, Tosh, who has been asking bookstore clerks for years where *Lives Charmed* was, unable to understand that the book his mom spends so much time on has, until now, been intangible. Endless thanks to my father, Al Tisch, for his constant encouragement and love, and to my sister, Carol Allen, and her husband, Bill, whose humor and friendship are daily gifts. To Joe Parente, my soul brother—your twenty-plus-year friendship means more each day.

Heartfelt thanks go to Health Communications, Inc., my publisher. I had prayed for a conscious publisher to steward this project, but I had no idea that such a vibrant group of souls existed to take this into the marketplace. I am staggered by their huge financial support of the National Arbor Day Foundation, which plants millions of trees. To Peter Vegso and Gary Seidler, who are my champions. And, Matthew Diener, Christine Belleris and Lisa Drucker, who are my dream editors. Thanks to Kim Weiss, Ronni O'Brien and Jodee Blanco, for their enthusiasm and creativity in the publicity realm. And to so many others at HCI who make business a joy, of whom Terry Burke, Kelly Johnson Maragni and Randee Goldsmith are but a few. To my agent, Jeff Herman and his wife, Deborah, for their faith and loyalty. And, to Linda Perlman and Char DeVazquez for their style!

The names of those who have helped me along this path seem endless. Thanks to Deborah Susswein and Erica Orloff for their eagle-eye proofing, Pat Hayman for her graphic talents, Robin Stuart for her laughter and follow-through, Darryl Cherney for his environmental consciousness, Danielle LaPorte and Donna Gianoulis, HRH Princess Elizabeth of Yugoslavia for her detailed historical fact checking and the many skilled photographers who graciously allowed us to print their photographs in this book.

Deep gratitude to Nathan LaBudde at Earth Island Institute, John and Sue Brodie, Hilda Williams, Winifred Palmer, Stephanie Zimbalist, Steve Meadows, Pierce Brosnan, Diane Harrelson, Laura Louie, Stephanie Russell, Doc Giffin, Alastair Johnston, Georgia Viehbeck, IMG, Peggy Parker, Nita Tucker, Janet Gordon, Philip and Mikela Tarlow, Linda Redford, Kirk and Anne Douglas, Eric Douglas, Henry Penner, Dan McDermott, Kathy Schenker, David Michaels, Lauren Tom, Sheryl Lee, Valerie Keegan, Charles Barkley, Danielle Tahos, Sheila DiMarco, Arielle Ford (for so many things), Carol Fields, Buddy Arnold, Mike Venema, Gurmukh Kar, Susan Hecht, Janet Lorenz, Jim Stewart, Joe Luperiello, Paul Hecht, Mariela Bradford, Brian Holt, Leah Teweles, Charlie Jordan, Marlene Wallace, Ram Pravesh Singh, Nancy Martinez, David Van Gilder, and Radha Sloss. I am so grateful for the devoted friendship of Julie and Michael Burkhardt, Gurperkarma Kar, Mike and Shelly Lee, Paul Otero, Terri and Randy Kuykendall and all the kinfolk, Etta Sivertsen, Kim and Jose Vera, and Jerry and Cindy Sivertsen. A special thanks to Richard Lunbery, the entire mountain crew, Denise Thibeau (my Kinko's pal), and Thomas and Sherri, for teaching me how to be a *HazHo*. And, to Gina Turner, Sally Yates, Eugene Whitworth, Bobby Wachsmuth, Kay Grace Beaumont, Pat Johnson and Diane Chandler (my soul sister), for their lifelong friendship.

I send much gratitude to the Bodhi Tree Bookstore, my heavenly haven in the City of Angels. And, to all the four-legged friends who've passed on. Your unconditional love has been one of the greatest joys of my life: Tasha and Ziggy Williams, T. J. Douglas, Obsidian Oxenberg, Sheba Stewart, Socks, Harold, Chipper, Bandit, Kitty, and Leo Tisch, Maggy Brodie, Steed Jaquette, Princess Johnson, Teddy Csimma, Pudgy Yates, Angel and Buddha Allen, Two-Spirits, Cindy and Tiny Kuykendall, Gabi, Trinity, Grizzly, and Lukey.

Most important, profound thanks to all the courageous souls who have allowed their lives to be portrayed so intimately in this book. You mean the world to me.

INTRODUCTION

Talk matters because ideas empower.

BILL MOYERS

How is it that you are so happy?
I have been asked this question repeatedly throughout my
life: in high school on cold, rainy mornings; in college, from drunken
fraternity boys wondering why they weren't happy; even at the check-
out counter at the grocery store. From complete strangers to friends
alike, the question inevitably comes. Each time I am taken aback and
have to catch my breath and remember that my natural state is not
always easily accessed by those around me. In the spring· before I
started writing this book, one woman asked me so many times why
my life was "charmed," that the question itself began to haunt me,
whispering over and over, "Why?" I stopped taking my predominantly
joyous existence for granted and began a rigorous inventory of my life,
what worked and what didn't. So many people had identified my life
as charmed that I felt a necessity, even an urgency, to continue the
positive flow so that my little boy could also experience a healthy,
happy life. I sought out people who seemed to be *as* happy or happier than I was, something I had always done naturally, but now with
conscious intent. I believed, and still do, that there are ways of thinking and modes of living that breed success, and they can be learned.

I write this from my remote forest haven in the Southwest, a locale far more conducive to contemplative creativity than the noisy aura of my past city home, Los Angeles. My husband and I met in the city, and that is where we befriended most of the people interviewed for this book. Our new home is a forest retreat. For four years, we have lived without running water, a telephone line (although we do have a cellular phone that works when the weather's right), or indoor heat, except for what the wood stove produces. My computer runs on solar power, and I marvel at that. Other than having to trek to our outhouse in the freezing snow, life is grand. The only thing I had to do in the forest to make up for the blessed life we led in L.A. was find an assortment of stray dogs for Brodie, our beloved border collie, an all-too-easy endeavor on rambling country roads. Brodie had many dog companions in the city but loves her new pack. She may be slower than she once was, but still herds them into line.

When I started writing this book, the words of Joseph Campbell echoed in my mind: "If you really want to help this world, what you will have to teach is how to live in it." My intention was to find people who were experiencing success in *every* area of life: with strong spiritual faith, healthy families, romantic love lives, creative and meaningful work, harmonious minds and bodies, financial wealth, while living a purposeful and environmentally conscious existence. At first, I found that was an impossible task. With time, however, a collection of people joined on who appeared to "have it all" more than I had ever witnessed. I was fortunate enough to be able to watch many of them carefully, for long periods of time, and I found they possessed sincere fulfillment. And, when they didn't, they often shared with brutal honesty what was missing.

I believe these interviews are unlike the typical magazine piece. My intention is to provide information we don't usually hear: I ask the interviewees about their fears, insecurities and their spiritual disciplines. I want to know how they pray, if they pray, and what they do to continue the flow of good fortune in their lives. I have been surprised that many of them have similar thought processes, making me wonder if there are certain formulas for living a successful life. Because all of the interviewees are well known in their fields, I ask them their views on fame, which are surprisingly personal and different from one another. I ask what inspires them and fosters their creativity, how they get through hard times, what they do to give back, and their thoughts on the future of this planet, which in every case revealed a curious sense of confidence and lack of fear concerning personal safety.

I did not meet these people at star-studded parties or premieres. I was a professional dog-walker in Los Angeles in the late 1980s and early 1990s, pounding the pavement each day with myriad breeds who needed attention because their owners worked long hours. When I started my business, a large portion of my four-legged friends didn't have so much as a patch of grass to lie on; most lived in cramped apartments and cemented side yards. With time, however, my deep enthusiasm for my work endeared me to a wealthy clientele made up mostly of celebrities (although I never stopped working for my original animal friends either). People in the entertainment industry travel frequently, almost always have guard dogs, and have the extra money to hire someone to pamper their pets. And, even when they are home, which can be much of the time, they often experience a genuine guilt if they don't take the time to walk their dogs. That's where I came in.

Brodie was my constant travel companion on my daily rounds. She herded Paul Williams's huskies, Chewy and Tasha, through the winding streets of the Hollywood Hills, and seemed to laugh inside as I lathered up Kiefer Sutherland's dogs, Jack and Dave, for baths as she stood by, warm and dry. Life was simple, full of sun, exercise, and the kind of ever-present joy that only animals can offer.

Being a pet-sitter is a blessed and unique position: Nearly every time you walk in the door, people are happy to see you. One woman told me that her golden retriever would take his leash in his mouth each morning at six o'clock and wait by the door until I arrived three hours later. Needless to say, this kind of behavior ingratiates you to people.

I adored my job, more than any other job I had in my life, even though it was demanding. I was forever covered in dog hair and rarely had a day off. Regular Monday through Friday clients filled the weeks. Weekends and holidays were even busier. When my son, Tosh, was born, I took a week off and then set him in a baby carrier and continued my rounds. As a toddler, he insisted on helping with the smaller dogs, often holding the thin leashes of the pugs, miniature Dobermans or the occasional slow-moving larger breed. When we would return from walking Kirk Douglas's dog, Banshee, in the sweltering summer heat, the maids, FiFi and Concha, would put ice in a bowl for my son. They would call him Dog Boy in gleeful tones as he'd get on his knees and lap the cold water like a puppy. Even as a two-year-old, he knew what made the ladies smile.

Maids and nannies all over Beverly Hills knew us by name; they were usually the only inhabitants visible beyond the confines of the massive homes. I knew I would never get rich living this way because one person can only walk so far, but the day-to-day gifts of peaceful, beautiful environments made for an abundant life. Brodie and Tosh learned to swim in pools all over town. In fact, throwing a tennis ball into a pool every day for a half-hour was my daily task for one happy pup client. The first time I arrived at Kirk Douglas's home, the man himself was swimming with Banshee, his beloved blond Labrador. Swimming together was one of their daily rituals, and he and his wife, Anne, graciously extended an open invitation to enjoy their pool anytime. I had just seen *Spartacus* several weeks before, and I was stunned to find nearly the same bigger-than-life image—over thirty years later—shaking my hand in nothing more than swim trunks.

Then came the dream. Dreams or visions have always shifted my life. I have learned to take the most poignant ones seriously and follow the plans. The results are life changing. Meeting my husband and my pet-sitting business were both results of powerful visions. When I awoke one morning with the title and format of this and several other books, I knew I had to put pen to paper and follow through with my dream. Over several months, I gave my pet business to my sister, a fellow animal lover, and bought a tape recorder from which I could transcribe the stories of those clients who would allow me to interview them.

Most of my clients did *not* lead what I considered charmed lives. For some, tragedy or illness might strike. (For instance, I was taking care of Brandon Lee's cats the night he died from an accidental shooting on the set of *The Crow.*) Others had money and fame, but I was often privy to addictions and personal crises that, in my mind, negated their ability to sincerely help others. I narrowed down the list of interviewees to a few favorites and began. Somehow, they were able to shift their perception of me to this new light and help out with my vision. Interviews led to more interviews, as people suggested others I should include. My husband offered his help, too. Working as an actor for over ten years, he knew his share of fascinating people. What started out as a book about a few of my clients turned into an avenue for me to meet people in all fields, with or without pets, who were leading vibrant lives.

I grew up wanting to be a writer, but it wasn't until I started this book that I realized that it would take a gargantuan effort to find people whose words and actions are congruent. I am grateful that I didn't know how long it would take or how many obstacles I would encounter. I naively went about the daily steps, expecting everything to fall into place. They did, but not nearly as quickly or as easily as I had envisioned. One particular letdown was when Catherine Oxenberg, one of my favorite clients, declined my request to be interviewed. I knew that she had been asked to write her own story and, although I understood that she needed to keep her experiences for that purpose, I was disappointed. Catherine (along with her beautiful cat, Obsidian), had become a dear friend of mine, and I knew she had an incredible tale of healing and personal triumph to share. I continued with my interviewing, trusting in the bigger picture, and two years later, Catherine unexpectedly said, "I tried to write my own story but it's too painful, I'd like your help." Expecting a somber tone, I was surprised by how many funny, crazy stories Catherine revealed (like how she started a food fight with Prince Charles inside a palatial mansion).

I have come to the conclusion that in life a bit of naivete can be a good thing. It may be an essential ingredient to my own charmed experiences because I expect life to be joyful and purposeful. I have faith, as do the people interviewed here, that we can make a difference in individual lives and to the planet as a whole through positive discussion. That outlook has facilitated my befriending the people I've interviewed. It also has allowed them to reveal great depth, over years of interviews and follow-up interviews, for the pages ahead. They trust me to write their stories in the most authentic way because they know my intention: to help readers lead lives that are charmed and, in turn, lighten the stress on our planet.

In retrospect, I'm grateful that I didn't know at the time I'd be writing about my clients. When you see people in their bathrobes day after day, or live in a person's home for months on end while they travel, you become part of the family and relationships are born. Having no idea that I'd be anything but their employee gave our relationships a sort of simplicity. I was there to serve and make hectic lives more peaceful. My clients depended upon me and my husband (who was known to run over in the middle of the night to help with an animal's illness and even to protect one woman from her physically abusive mate). We were given pets, homes, alarm codes and, even on occasion, children for safekeeping. Most importantly, we were trusted with the intimate workings of my clients' emotional lives. Ever since leaving the city, I continue to receive calls from old clients when a beloved cat or dog has passed away. Invariably, we cry together and end up sharing the funny and treasured memories of our loyal friend. They always ask if Brodie is still alive. At ten years old, she's graying but continues to carry a ball in her mouth everywhere, just as they remember.

It is my heartfelt belief that you will encounter much inspiration, entertainment and motivation in the following pages, gaining great insight for your own life. I have watched the people I've interviewed live full and creative lives for years. All encounter challenges like the rest of us, but what continues to intrigue me is not only the way they view their problems, but their ability to get beyond them. Time after time, I have witnessed these individuals create beauty from adversity. Many had tormented childhoods, several have had near-death experiences, but *all* have a persevering, optimistic spirit and humor and knowledge to share. Transcribing their stories has made my life more charmed and, consequently, easier. With sincerity, I can say that these

Photo by Hilda Williams

Linda with Chewy and Tasha Williams.

"mini-autobiographies," as I like to call them, will have the same effect on you.

Following is a brief synopsis of each person, in the order they appear on the back cover.

1. A caring and adored talk-show host who talks candidly about the precarious balancing act of being a wife, mother and career woman simultaneously . . . **Leeza Gibbons.**
2. A seventy-seven-year-old movie and television star "constantly pursued by miracles," even while fighting on the front lines in World War II, where he was wounded . . . **Efrem Zimbalist, Jr.**
3. An Academy-Award-winning composer and songwriter who overcame a forty-year drug and alcohol addiction which enables him to give encouragement and counsel to others . . . **Paul Williams.**
4. An award-winning investigative environmental journalist and television gardening expert and author, who, with the help of her companion Pierce Brosnan, convinced Congress to delay a bill that repeals the Dolphin Protection Acts . . . **Keely Shaye Smith.**
5. A sixty-seven-year-old golf legend who considers his biggest accomplishment not to be the ninety-two titles he has won, but the success of his longtime marriage and the strength of his family . . . **Arnold Palmer.**
6. A passionate movie star who teaches yoga and maintains a strict vegetarian diet in order to access the energy needed for his demanding lifestyle and environmental crusades. As controversial as this man is, he is deeply devoted to the future of our environment, specifically to the trees, who cannot speak for themselves . . . **Woody Harrelson.**
7. The daughter of the princess of Yugoslavia, who went on to soap-opera fame in *Dynasty*, and who inspires with her process of healing a longtime eating disorder, a by-product of a childhood fraught with incest and insecurity . . . **Catherine Oxenberg.**
8. An Academy-Award-winning producer, and one of the foremost talent managers in the world: a man who protects, defends and handles the careers of some of America's biggest superstars. This private man, who has only given four interviews in the last

twenty years, speaks candidly about the challenges of being gay, and credits prayer and meditation with enabling him to overcome terminal cancer . . . **Sandy Gallin.**

9. A 105-year-old woman who said that beyond her famed ceramic and painting career, it was chocolate and dreaming of young men that kept her happy and vibrant. James Cameron used her as the model for Rose, the elderly woman whose flashbacks are the foundation of the movie *Titanic* . . . the late **Beatrice Wood.**

10. A world-renowned Jungian psychologist and best-selling author who almost never does interviews, but was moved to in this case because, like his dear friend the late Joseph Campbell, he believes society is desperate for positive discussion . . . **Robert A. Johnson.**

11. A man who grew up in front of a small black-and-white television, safe inside from the gangs trying to recruit him in his Chicago-ghetto housing project. The voices he mimicked from the box led to a prominent stand-up career and to filmmaking. Crediting his mother's constant affirmations in the power of God to change all things, this man prioritizes his spirituality above all else . . . **Robert Townsend.**

12. The world's leading environmental artist, who has dedicated his life to educating people through his art, worldwide whale murals and coming cartoon series, about the dangers facing our oceans and its inhabitants. This man holds the *Guinness Book*'s record for the largest mural painted in the history of mankind (three acres, painted in Long Beach, California) . . . **Wyland.**

13. An English lord, dedicated to saving endangered animals through a rescue and breeding program on the family estate, Woburn Abbey. Raised with life literally handed to him on silver and gold platters, this man has learned firsthand that wealth and title alone cannot bring true soul fulfillment . . . **Lord Robin Russell.**

14. A European-born supermodel who gave up living in the fast lane to find genuine peace through spiritual disciplines and working with dolphins. Her life story is powerful for anyone who believes that wealth and beauty automatically bring happiness and confidence . . . **Tatjana Patitz.**

15. The man whom Mike Ditka calls "the most underrated quarterback in the NFL." This top-rated, albeit media-shy, athlete grew up with an alcoholic father and nine brothers and sisters. The young boy learned to visualize, focusing his physical talents toward eventual freedom, and now enjoys with his wife and two little girls a safe haven of family that he once could only dream about . . . **Chris Chandler.**

16. A spiritual counselor and Kundalini Yoga instructor (named the 1995 "Best Guru in L.A." by *Los Angeles* magazine), who sees the goodness in each religion and the greatness within all people . . . **Guru Singh.**

17. An Emmy- and Golden Globe-winning producer who left her position as the president of Ixtlan (Oliver Stone's production company) to partner with Lisa Henson (president of Columbia Pictures) to make films that will entertain and uplift humanity—bringing hope, through her work and example, to those limited by discrimination based on race and gender . . . **Janet Yang.**

Catherine Oxenberg

Photo by Michael Greco

Introduction

S ometimes in life, we find ourselves in situations where *"chance" meetings feel like they are guided by a predetermined force. We are chosen to fulfill a plan about which we have little or no knowledge. Such was the origin of my friendship with Catherine, a woman I had admired from afar on magazine covers and the television screen, unaware that in the early 1990s she would prove to be my most influential real-life model of femininity.*

Catherine was a model for countless women in the 1980s, perhaps representing the beauty and glamour many felt they lacked. When she rose to soap-opera fame on the top-rated nighttime television series Dynasty, *Catherine seemed to embody the feminine ideal, which is ironic considering that the very essence she portrayed subsequently became the most challenging accomplishment of her life: feeling worthy as a woman despite a childhood marred by incest and insecurity, resulting in a longtime eating disorder.*

To those of us admiring Catherine, there was never a hint of the personal trauma she had endured. All we knew was that Catherine was wealthy, gorgeous and the daughter of Yugoslavian royalty. What more could a young woman ask for during America's most opulent decade? Playing the role of Princess Diana in two television movies and receiving widespread critical acclaim for the second, Charles and Diana: A Palace Divided, *only enhanced her charmed persona. Life and art seemed inexorably intertwined.*

As with so many fairytale bubbles of the 1980s, Catherine's "perfect" world proved to be yet another royal item for the tabloids. When she gave birth to her daughter, India, the infant became a powerful force of innocence that would jar Catherine out of her prison of blocked memories. As a single mother, her protective maternal instincts kicked in, and, in the process, Catherine discovered she had been denying her own childhood pain. In spite of fervent denial on the part of her relatives, she has chosen to speak out and shatter the illusion of a perfect facade, in hopes that some may be helped by her story.

Having watched Catherine for years, I've seen a certain magical quality I've never known in anyone before. I've had associations with many people touched by incredible fortune and beauty, but with Catherine it's different. She seems to be—and I risk sounding a bit touched here—otherworldly. In her presence, I feel that she has access to an intangible world—home to mysterious realms—that most of us will never encounter, except maybe in the dream state. If the scientific universe is a multidimensional reality, as Einstein and others have suggested that it is, my guess is that Catherine is able to access more than one dimension simultaneously. She may not, therefore, have any world completely mastered, but gives a gallant (and fun, I might add) effort. For those lucky enough to be a part of the magic, it's an enchanting ride.

Catherine's family is the stuff of legend: royalty converged from many European countries to make up her genetic heritage. As one religious scholar told me, she is theorized to be a direct descendant from the lineage of King David, before the time of Jesus Christ. That supposed greatness, combined with the rumor that some of her relatives bordered on insanity because of inbreeding within the royal families of Europe, makes for a mythical soup.

In spite of, or maybe because of, a childhood fraught with fear, Catherine possesses an extraordinary personal power. In her Beverly Hills home—a secluded haven reminiscent of a villa in the south of France—where she is the most comfortable, Catherine is the ruler of a strange and fanciful wonderland. People are instantly taken with the loveliness of her estate and the uniqueness of her personal treasures. Tribal drums and artifacts sit alongside antiquated memorabilia from the Russian and English royal families, also in her lineage. [My son accidentally threw a tennis ball toward the mantle one day and, in horror, I watched as a porcelain egg from Imperial Russia, embossed in gold with the royal emblem, shattered to the ground. Catherine, with her live-for-the-moment attitude, didn't flinch . . . not a care. In fact, in all of the years I've known Catherine, she's never even mentioned her royal heritage until pressed to for this interview.] Gallery-quality crystals frame Asian and East Indian statues of gods and goddesses. The heavenly scent of jasmine fills the air as the blooms billow above the windows and doors, and a radiant seven-year-old India, in Catherine's likeness, joyously plays in a fountain surrounded by a luxuriant tropical paradise.

Interestingly, people have been known to find Catherine's world impossible to identify. I have witnessed several acquaintances become shaken around her potent energy. Her eclectic home has an awesome presence of its own. One born-again Christian friend of my husband, who came to visit Catherine's house when we were living there years ago, felt such a strong energetic presence in the living room that he feverishly invoked a blessing to save her from demons and literally scurried out the side door, never to return. Had he actually met Catherine, I'm sure that he would have been charmed by her kindness, but the mysticism associated with her belongings was foreign and menacing to his strongly held convictions.

My husband and I have been immeasurably altered by our association with Catherine, our lives becoming increasingly blessed and abundant since living with her and witnessing her view of the world. She is like a midwife in the way she brings new life into old belief systems, helping others out of their lack-filled thinking. Her bountiful and generous nature forces people to expand beyond the confines of who they think they are and what they believe is possible for their lives. That is, perhaps, her greatest gift to those closest to her. We noticed over time that people influenced by their relationship with Catherine either catapult into their own magical destiny or experience a crash of sorts, possibly from the weight of seeing her world and not being able to either attain their own beauty or grasp the meaning of hers. In these instances, people have been known to run out of her life, much like our dear Christian friend, spouting libelous gossip about this complex beauty. There seems to be a sort of madness to it, as if the brunt of not being able to pin Catherine down drives people to their worst.

What is striking to me, and others who love Catherine, is her indefatigable nature. She is a survivor in the truest sense. The amount of trauma she experienced as a child fueled her keen wit and wisdom, for humor and her intellect became the only forms of self-expression she felt she could control. After graduating first in her private high school class of nearly six hundred students, Catherine was accepted to Harvard University before being diverted to model and act. Unfortunately, a genius IQ doesn't spare one from experiencing the pains of life. But whether or not time heals all wounds, Catherine is an example of how pain lessens with faith and hard work. This courageous woman is now transforming her experience and talents into writing and producing projects for children, and she hopes that with public discussion, people of all ages will learn that it is never too late to face the past, no matter how daunting, and to find the reserve of inner beauty we all possess.

*   *   *   *

Before we start with the topic at hand, I'd like to say that Linda asked me to speak about my incest recovery for the purpose of helping others, and because of that, and our close friendship, I agreed. It is tricky, however, because this is a chapter of my life that I consider closed. It is hard for me, even at this stage in my healing, to revisit this aspect of my childhood. A crucial part of healing *is* sharing one's story; however, I've felt in the past that I had reached a point of saturation, where I had talked about my abuse so many times that I risked becoming so identified and attached to it that it would forever be "my story." An important part of my healing at this point has become, "Forget the story, let go of the past and move on." The story itself, at a certain point, can become an obstacle to moving forward.

In other words, I'm at a place where my need to identify with the victimization is gone. I feel healed in my psyche and grateful for all of my life experiences. In taking gratitude to the deepest levels, people often ask me, "How can you feel gratitude for having been molested?" I feel, as perverse as this may sound, that my wound has become my teacher. And, the depth to which I've been able to heal my own pain has given me the capacity to heal equal depths of pain in other people. It has given me a value as a human being that maybe I wouldn't have had if this pain had not been inflicted. I don't believe, certainly, that pain is the only way to knowledge, but pain is a great motivator. When I gave birth, in fact, I finally saw that there is healthy pain. There is pain for a reason . . . to create growth. To create life. The amount of physical pain I experienced during childbirth felt as if the scars were literally being washed away so that I could feel equal joy in my heart. It cleansed my heart pain, but now I'm getting ahead of myself.

Happiness

Many times in my life, I've experienced such a deep sense of joy that the event or moment left a lasting impression. One incident that stands out, etched indelibly into my memory, occurred in 1987. I was in Portugal, filming a remake of *Roman Holiday*. On my day off, I found myself exploring the coastline, ending up on a beach in a little fishing village called Cais Cais. (Coincidentally, I found out later that my uncle was married on the same beach.) I sat down on the sand alone and took in the beauty of my surroundings. As I breathed in the sweet warmth of the sun and the sea air, I was flooded by the deepest sense of serenity and complete contentment. I felt totally fulfilled. I wanted for nothing. I was happy to be in the present and in the moment. I was at one with myself.

Relaxing, I opened the book I had brought, *The Way of the Peaceful Warrior*, by Dan Millman, and I picked up where I had left off the previous day. To my amazement, the chapter opened with, "I had traveled the whole world over, looking for what it meant to be a spiritual warrior. I ended up on a beach in Cais Cais, Portugal." And I was sitting on the same beach! Dan went on to describe the exact experience of the "precious present" that I had just experienced. I couldn't believe it. That, for me, epitomized the culmination of the work I had done on myself and the grace that accompanied the feeling of profound union with the universe—being so synchronous, in the right place in the right time, connected with everyone and everything, which was reflected back to me in the book. The moment was so perfect, so simple and so nothing, but it felt so profound. That is the blessing that joy brings. The joyful condition reflects a universe which responds with joy, leaving us welcome signs that we are on the right track and in complete alignment with our destiny.

Discipline

I live by a simple, practical equation which is: Discipline + Faith = Grace. A joyful existence doesn't just happen, it's something that takes tremendous commitment and responsibility. And you have to work on it constantly, at least I do because it's extremely easy for me to fall into the glass-is-half-empty mentality. I constantly have to work at the things that will keep me in a joyful state. I do believe that to be joyful is our essential nature, but it's the ultimate challenge of our life experience to be joyful no matter what. If I'm disciplined in my spiritual practices on a daily basis, I am able to tap into that place within myself where there is an infinite abundance of joy, so one of the means by which I attempt that is through meditation.

Meditation and joy are synonymous to me. I started meditating in the 1980s, and it is the way I open myself to my femininity and to my receptiveness, demonstrating to the God force that I am there to listen and to be silent. Prayer is the way I talk to God. When I find real peace, my ability to manifest everything increases. Meditation releases stress, which automatically increases your ability to access your intelligence. Stress makes you stupid because it inhibits your ability to make intelligent choices. For me to realize that I could generate an incredibly wonderful sensation of well-being, without any external stimuli, without anybody else validating me, simply through my own stillness and breath, was the most empowering thing I have ever discovered.

It took about a year of meditating before I was able to grasp what I felt: I sat and breathed in one morning, surrendering to the stillness and the silence. Suddenly I felt texture to my breath: a consciousness and intelligence seemed to accompany the process. I felt the sweetness of bliss permeate my being; it almost tickled as it filtered through me. I felt my whole body smile as I fed myself with my own essence. The knowledge that I had the power to create a sensation of well-being gave me a new license on life. I was so used to causing myself and others pain through unconscious behavior, that I had begun to believe, on the deepest level, that I was dysfunctional and inappropriate. Now I understood that my only crime was my lack of insight and lack of awareness. The ultimate joy was the realization that the further I plunged into my own psyche, the more beauty I found within.

I have a funny story about meditation that involves another person interviewed for this book. It was around 1987, and I had just been introduced to transcendental meditation [referred to as TM throughout this book] by Deepak Chopra at his Ayurvedic center in Massachusetts. I was flying home on the MGM Grand plane (which was nice for privacy because it was a whole first-class plane that took off from private terminals so you could drive right onto the tarmac without going through the airport). Sandy Gallin [chapter 10] and I were the only ones sitting in what was called a "train compartment" (consisting of four seats, two facing each other). We started talking, and Sandy suggested that we meditate together. He started doing this breath-of-fire type of meditation, an extremely agitated meditation. When we finished, about twenty minutes later, I looked at him and said, "Gosh, I don't mean to sound judgmental or anything, but your meditation seemed awfully stressful." He looked at me and said, "Well, yours seemed really powerful." Two weeks later, he booked himself into Deepak's center, where he spent three weeks. I joined him there, and we had a great time. Ever since, Sandy has called me the "Guru of Beverly Hills."

Another way I access joy is through physical exercise. I believe that negative thinking is mostly from chemical toxicity, a chemical phenomenon. When I'm able to oxygenate my system through exercise of some form, I feel stronger mentally as well as physically, and I am able to reconnect with a sense of balance and harmony, which leaves me better equipped to take on life's challenges with optimism. My father, Howard Oxenberg, encouraged us tremendously as kids in the athletic realm, teaching us tennis, swimming, snorkeling and skiing. Physical discipline was natural for him because he was an Olympic swimmer. My father's self-confidence, and what he thought set him apart from others—in terms of being an achiever—was based upon his physical excellence. He then used these same skills in business and in all areas of his life.

I know this sounds corny, but my attitude of gratitude is my lifeline to God. And it requires discipline, too, because sometimes feeling grateful seems like work. Without gratitude I could never experience joy. In every challenging situation, I pray that the gift of the experience be revealed to me. Being able to shift my perception from one of adversity to gratitude ensures me a constant state of serenity and acceptance. Part of this process is taking responsibility that I am a co-creator in my universe and everything that happens to me, I am somehow responsible for. So, I ask, "How can this situation be beneficial in my process of growth and evolution?" What keeps me in gratitude is a firm belief that every aspect of life is sacred, down to the very breath I take. And, last but not least, maintaining a sense of humor is crucial to this whole process. After all, angels fly because they take themselves lightly.

Early Years

Most people think that I had a privileged lifestyle as a child. The truth is that I suffered a lot of neglect and emotional deprivation. The pain that I carried was never validated because my scars didn't show on the outside. In retrospect, I often wished that I *had* carried my scars on the outside. At least no one could have denied their existence. To hold a reality all by yourself causes you to question your sanity because no one else responds to what has happened to you.

At this juncture, I would like to clarify that the incest I experienced was not perpetrated by my mother or father. On the other hand, they've never validated it. As far as they're concerned, I'm nuts. And that's okay because they come from a generation that believed therapy and self-awareness were forms of self-obsession and self-indulgence. This is not how they feel today (my father has actually joined me in some of my therapy, and I am close to both of my parents), but they still view self-disclosure with extreme disdain. As much as I love them both, I've gotten beyond the need for their approval. So, if I can help one other person who's in pain and on a downward spiral of self-destructive behavior, then exposing my past is worthwhile. I really believe that my parents did the best they could, and as I said, I've reached a place of gratitude and acceptance toward my upbringing. There is no point in blaming anyone.

A lot of people ask me about my family lineage. Because I want to be accurate, I've done a lot of research lately. My mother, Princess Elizabeth of Yugoslavia, has been a big help sorting out the many details. I happen to be related to all of the European royal families through repeated arranged marriages. According to an article published in the *New York Times* a few days after my birth, I was named after Catherine the Great, who would have been my great-great-great—oh, whatever—grandmother. I'm going to get the greats wrong because I'm not so identified with this part of my life. But let's just say that although I'm named after her, all similarities end there! [Catherine laughs as we speak of the rumor that this most beloved Empress of Russia was said to have died having sex with a horse.] All the royal families intermarried, and consequently, I am related to all of them: Danish, Russian, Greek, English, Hapsburg and so on. For instance, my grandmother (my mother's mother) was Princess Olga of Greece, who died in 1997, and her mother was the Grand Duchess Helen of Russia (granddaughter of Czar Alexander III, father of Nicholas II, the last Czar of Russia). My grandmother Olga's first cousin is the duke of Edinburgh, who is Queen Elizabeth's husband. Families ensured the sanctity of their lineage through arranged marriages to other royal houses. Ironically, my grandmother, who had previously been engaged to the crown prince of Denmark, ended up marrying my grandfather for love! The same arranged-marriage fate may have awaited my mother, who they hoped would marry the King of Belgium, but when she met my father, she, too, married for love. Unfortunately, repeated inbreeding causes problems ranging from mild eccentricities to total mental insanity, which history has shown. I'm eccentric enough as it is . . . thank God for my father's fresh blood-line! Who knows how wacky I'd be otherwise?

An interesting point is that the Yugoslav royal family was truly a grassroots royal family. Most European royal families were imported from other countries. It was extremely rare that the actual bloodlines of the royal families were indigenous to the countries over which they ruled. The founder of the family was George Petrovic, known as Karageorge, or Black George, to the Turks. He started the first upris-ing in 1804 against the Ottoman Empire, who had occupied Serbia for five hundred years. He became a national hero and his son was crown prince of Serbia.

People ask me what happened to my mother's family, and it's a long story, and not an easy one to talk about because the politics of war are complex and conspiratorial. The gist of it is this: My grand-father, Prince Paul, became the Regent [ruler] of Yugoslavia when his cousin, King Alexander, was murdered in a plot masterminded by Mussolini in 1934. It was stipulated in King Alexander's will that Prince Paul take over as ruler while his son, King Peter, was too young to do so. My grandfather had always maintained strong ties with Britain through blood and friendship: King George VI had been best man at his wedding in Belgrade in 1923, and his sister-in-law, the duchess of Kent, was married to King George's brother. My grandfather had been awarded the Knight of the Garter, which is the highest honor the British crown can confer. But, with the onset of World War II, my grandfather was precariously placed and under constant threat of being overrun by Italy and Germany. His country was ill-equipped to fight off any invasion and he repeatedly asked Britain for military aid and ammunition, which was promised, but never arrived.

Yugoslavia had only been formed in 1919, and Prince Paul was left with the difficult task of creating and maintaining a strong sense of solidarity between the Serbs and Croats in an arena of suspicion involving many different factions. All you have to do is look at what has happened in recent years to see how much skill that required. In an attempt to avoid the inevitable destruction of his country, and to preserve its unity for Peter, Prince Paul worked out a neutrality pact with Hitler, which stipulated, among other things, that no German troops were allowed to cross the country. This part of the pact was never published, and one of the reasons he was later vilified was that people in Yugoslavia didn't know the terms. Prince Paul's predicament was summed up by the head of the opposing party in Yugoslavia, who told him that if he signed the pact he would be declared pro-German and if he didn't, "We'll say that you plunged us into war on account of that Greek wife of yours." It appeared as if he couldn't win, regardless of what he did. The neutrality pact had been a delaying tactic to win Yugoslavia time to get the support they were expecting from England. My grandfather, who became increasingly anxious, also reached out to the United States of America, France and Russia, but was rejected by all. What he didn't know at the time was that in 1939, the Soviet dictator, Joseph Stalin, had also forged a nonaggression pact with Hitler, carving up the countries of Europe between them. Unfortunately for Yugoslavia, it had already been promised to Soviet Russia.

In 1941, Churchill suddenly decided that mere neutrality was not enough. The British were going to send a mechanized force to Greece and proposed to form a united Balkan front. Prince Paul was horrified. He considered the plan impetuous and doomed to failure. The landing of British troops in Greece would provoke Hitler into a Balkan offensive, so basically Britain was calling for a Yugoslav act of suicide, which London referred to as a "side show in a Mediterranean theater of war." When my grandfather protested, Churchill's response was, "Prince Paul's attitude looks like that of an unfortunate man in a cage with a tiger, hoping not to provoke him, while steadily dinnertime approaches." I'm quoting from my stepfather, Neil Balfour's book, entitled, *Paul of Yugoslavia, Britain's Maligned Friend*. As a consequence of the appalling responsibilities and exigencies of war, Churchill was driven to the conclusion that it was the right of a great power to sacrifice a smaller neutral state for the sake of ultimate victory. Prince Paul was well aware that if he went to war unprepared, he'd risk sacrificing his people. In the final act of betrayal, the British sanctioned and funded a coup d'etat in Belgrade, which overthrew the Regency. The British had been behind the scenes funding willing communist conspirators to help organize the coup.

As a child, I remember my mother speaking of being four years old and seeing soldiers running through the palace, as she and her family evacuated, leaving all of her family's belongings behind. Her parents were given four hours to leave the country and were sent into exile in Kenya and South Africa. Prince Paul started the art museum in Belgrade in 1939, and at the time of the evacuation, he had one of the most impressive private art collections in the world and had to leave everything behind. Hitler, suspicious of the sudden change of leadership in Yugoslavia, refused to continue to honor the neutrality pact. Hitler ordered the Nazi destruction of Yugoslavia, which he called "Operation Punishment." The invasion began on April 6, 1941. Within a week, just as my grandfather had foreseen, Yugoslavia was destroyed. For the remainder of the war, and for many years after that, British propaganda used my grandfather as a scapegoat by portraying him as a traitor. He was kept with his family under house arrest in Kenya by the British for two years until they went to South Africa at the request of General Smuts, who was quite a formidable character in South Africa at the time and helped my family. The propaganda was England's way of justifying that the coup had been the right move, rather than having to admit that their interference had resulted in a hideous tragedy.

Catherine with her father, Howard Oxenberg, at three years old.

Courtesy of Princess Elizabeth

Portrait of Prince Paul of Yugoslavia, painted by Sorine, 1937.

As a result of being labeled a Nazi collaborator by Britain, a country he had so admired, my grandfather suffered tremendously, and I don't think he ever recovered from the blow. It was such a painful betrayal. Interestingly, toward the end of his life, Churchill admitted that he had made some terrible mistakes, the treatment of my grandfather being one of them.

My grandparents were in exile in Africa for eight years until they moved to Paris, where they remained until their deaths. My grandfather was very resourceful and was able to build up a successful art collection again with time, and this was how he supported himself and his family. My mother, who had never been allowed to vacation without a chaperone, somehow finagled a skiing trip to St. Anton, Austria, by herself and there, at the ski resort, she met my father. He was a very successful clothing manufacturer from New York. They fell in love and eloped. My mother showed tremendous courage by defying convention and tradition, and in a way, I suppose, my father became her ticket to freedom from that whole royal lifestyle.

My mother returned to Yugoslavia in 1987, two years before the fall of communism. She was the only member of the family to do so, thanks to the help of her husband, Manuel Ulloa, who was the former prime minister of Peru, and his political connections in Yugoslavia. However, my mother was still subject to a law against the family that was passed in 1946, which forbade any of the royal family from ever returning to the country or claiming any nationalism, passport or property. It was like being a nonperson. The royal family had been deleted from the history books, so there were people, particularly children, who didn't even know they had existed. My mother has subsequently dedicated most of her efforts to helping Yugoslav orphans and war victims. She had been raised with a heritage of service, but she had never been allowed the opportunity to fulfill her destiny until recent years. In fact, my mother started a foundation called the Princess Elizabeth Foundation, whose motto is "Service is Love in Action."

I went to Yugoslavia for the first time last year. I was hired by Zepter Cosmetics, an extremely popular, multibillion dollar European company, as their spokesperson. I had never heard of Zepter before, but I discovered their cosmetics in Eastern Europe are tantamount to Estée Lauder in the United States. I was invited to Belgrade because Zepter was opening a new building for the company, and they asked me to make an appearance. I was surprised to find that huge billboards of my face had been displayed all over the city. We were taken to the Opera House, which had previously been restored by my grandfather. Standing on the balcony at night, we overlooked the main square, the same square where all the violent student demonstrations had previously been held against the new government after the fall of communism. About two hundred thousand students were now gathered because Zepter had donated a concert to the city, with a very well-known Yugoslavian singer performing. It was the first peaceful public event in this square in a very long time, and it was also the first time in many years that so many people were allowed to gather. It was amazing to me because as I opened the show from the stage, I could see in the square below a large statue of my ancestor—the first prince of Serbia—signifying the consummate war hero.

The whole experience felt like a historical and healing event. I did a lot of interviews and there was a lot of press response, but the effect for me was much more internal. I was able to own a part of me that I had never been encouraged to own, which was a sense of nationalism as a Yugoslav. Any time there were galleries of people waiting, old women would come up to me and hold my hands and look at me with tears in their eyes and say, "You are our princess." It was the wildest thing. I had intellectualized my role there and thought that because I had never been to Yugoslavia before, I wouldn't be affected too strongly, but I was wrong. It was a very moving experience and it touched me on a deep level. Just looking at the land, I felt a part of it. As I drove around, I was mesmerized by the landscapes, hungrily taking in every view as if I was filling a part of my being. I could feel the emotion in the land; it resonated in my soul.

Prince Paul's living room at his estate, Villa Pratolino, Florence, Italy, 1960.

The whole experience hit me in a way I was emotionally unprepared for, catching me completely off-guard. The devotion of these people toward me, as a figurehead and for what I represented, was staggering. Up until that time, I almost felt as if the historical aspect of my family didn't apply to me, that it wasn't part of me. I was taken to the mayor's palace for an event and didn't know at the time that my grandfather had lived there. As I sat in one of the rooms, I was overcome with a sense that my grandfather was there with me. I looked up at the paintings and there was something profoundly familiar about all of them. I later found out that they were his.

I was born in New York City, and my parents divorced soon after my sister's birth. My mother, my sister and I moved to London when I was five, and my mother remarried when I was seven, and she had another child. We lived primarily in England. However, we moved around a lot because my stepfather had a job at a merchant bank, so we lived in Spain for a year, New York for another year and so on.

I didn't think at the time that my parents' divorce was hard on me. I remember my mother asking me if I minded her getting a divorce from my father and marrying her boyfriend, and I said something to the effect of, "No, I'd rather you be apart and happy than together and unhappy for our sake." I am struck by the precociousness of that statement, and I wonder, "Where is the six-year-old girl?" About that same time, I became much more introverted and depressed. I can see now that I was going through the grieving process of their separation, but no one understood that, least of all me. People would say to me, "Stop moping around and feeling sorry for yourself." No one around me knew how to deal with emotions, and therefore they were in no position to interpret mine, or how my parents' breakup affected me.

I learned early on to shut down; because my sensitivity wasn't acknowledged, I didn't feel I had the right to be sorrowful. When your emotional reality is not validated as a child, you easily lose your sense of self and self-worth and end up not trusting what you feel. My parents' responses weren't malicious, but now that I'm a parent, I realize how damaging it can be for a child not to have her emotions valued and understood. All along, I received messages about my emotional responses that made me feel completely abnormal. Whatever I felt seemed to be constantly inappropriate. My sister would cry her eyes out every time my father left after visiting us, and I'd just stand there without emoting. He'd say, "See, you don't love me like your sister does because you don't cry when I leave." My sadness wasn't appropriate, my anger wasn't appropriate, nothing seemed appropriate. I became extremely mistrustful of my own emotional responses and lived basically in my intellect, because it seemed that was the only sanctuary I had. Reasoning everything through gave me the illusion of control, but really I had no understanding of my emotional truth. I became very disconnected. Anytime I felt threatened, whether it was physically, emotionally or spiritually, I checked out and left my body. That became my automatic response.

I was a solitary child. As is common with most abused children, my ability to disconnect helped me suppress those memories until I was ready to handle them as an adult. My loss of innocence, however, left me as a strange, lost, confused, lonely little girl who always felt misunderstood and incapable of healthy human interaction. I preferred to live in my room, where I lost myself in a world of books, homework, drawing and painting.

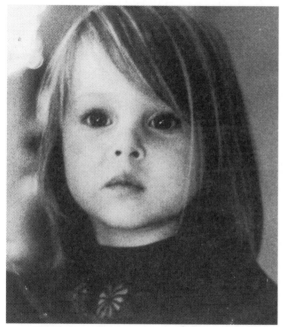

Photo by Alex Lieberman

Catherine at her third birthday party.

There is a model for dysfunctional families where the oldest child is the hero child, the second is the scapegoat child, the third is the lost child, and the fourth is the family mascot. I tried all the roles to see which shoe fit because different roles worked with different parents. My basic personality was the hero child: I was an overachiever, trying to get love and validation through academic achievements, which only worked part of the time. I also identified closely with the lost child because after my sexual abuse started, I became highly introverted. Few photos exist of me smiling in my childhood after the first year or two, which is around the time my abuse started. There is such sadness and confusion in my face after that time.

People who meet me now often think I am extroverted. That is only because I have healed a lot of the part of me that wanted to wither away and disappear into myself. With that came a sort of blossoming, even though shyness is still my basic nature. For me to act for a living is the ultimate challenge because of how badly I had shut down emotionally. But, I've always tried to get beyond the shyness and not let it keep me from my goals. Absolutely one of the best traits I received from my mother is not only her rebelliousness, but her spontaneous nature and her ability to adapt and go with the wind.

A good example of that was in 1976, when my mother and I went on a trip to Iran, right before the Shah was overthrown. The trip was set up by the Persian ambassador to England, and we had been flown around the country in the prime minister's airplane, visiting many different sites. [I asked her, "Did you and your mother receive that privilege just because you're important?" and Catherine replied, "Beats me!" with a laugh.] It was a magical and hilarious trip. We were probably the last people ever to visit the Imperial Tennis Club in Teheran, where they had four ball boys per court and served freshly squeezed melon juice on the court. Then we were flown to the shore of the Caspian Sea, where a man arrived with ten pots containing ten pounds each of freshly harvested caviar. The man handed me a golden spoon and told me to test each pot to see which one we liked best and wanted to take back with us to give as gifts. These pots of caviar were bigger than any caviar container you've ever seen, as big as beer barrels!

On our way home, we had a layover in Athens and my mother, on the spur of the moment, said, "All right, let's just get off the plane." We had no prior plans, but spent a couple of weeks roaming around the Greek Islands. It was a blast. I remember meeting Mick Jagger on his sailboat. I was young and thought I'd have some fun, so I found some makeup and painted a moustache on his face. He seemed to think that was a terrific idea. He was so down-to-earth and funny.

Another great influence my mother had on me was her open-mindedness in discovering new forms of thought. When I was only ten years old, she gave me the life-changing gift of taking my sister and me to a two-day Silva Mind Control seminar in the countryside. We learned about goal setting and intention and how to establish "a peaceful place within from which to create and visualize." It taught me that the thought process, applied with intention, was the precursor to manifestation. The first time I consciously remember applying these tools was when I was fourteen. I decided that I wanted to go to Harvard and, fueled by a burning desire, I devised a plan. I would apply to prep schools known for their high-level entries into the Ivy League. I chose St. Paul's and was soon accepted. I will never know where I got my certainty and sense of destiny from; it was assuredly evidence of a basic, essential nature which was finally emerging. It was a miracle that I followed through at the time. My mother, with whom I was very close, didn't want me to leave. I was very dependent on her love and approval, and this was the first time that I dared , risk losing her love in order to fulfill my own needs. I had never defied her and did not fully comprehend the power of this force that propelled me in another direction.

I knew when I was thirteen years old that I wanted to become an actress. My mother was engaged to Richard Burton and he was the most profound male influence in my life—the most involved male in a healthy way. He spent hours and hours teaching me Shakespeare and inventing crossword puzzles with me. We even invented a six-foot crossword puzzle, filled it out together, and rolled it up into a scroll. Richard also taught me how to drive his new Mercedes. I was so little that he had to prop me up on six pillows so I could see over the steering wheel. One of the best times we had together was when he took me gambling in Switzerland for my first time. I was not allowed in the casino, obviously, so the owners put up a screen and hid me behind it. I gave Richard my bets, and then he went off and placed them. He came back, his shirt loaded full of chips. I guess I had beginner's luck because I won a huge amount of money.

I adored Richard; he never talked down to me or patronized me. He was so loving and sweet and attentive and his influence shaped my whole desire to act. Unfortunately, Richard and my mother didn't last long; she couldn't handle his alcoholism. I remember his constant struggle with booze. He took me to lunch in the mountains of Switzerland, and I had warned him that if he drank, I wouldn't talk to him. He drank a bottle of wine anyway, and the only way I agreed to communicate with him was by passing him notes written on the tablecloth. Richard passed me a note asking me if I would like to drive

Princess Elizabeth and India, 1996.

home. I declined, horrified, because not only was I just thirteen, but the road home was a series of icy hairpin turns from the top of the mountain, where we were having lunch, to the bottom. I probably should have driven home because it would have been safer. I prayed to God the whole way home as I closed my eyes and tensed every muscle in my body because we almost crashed four or five times into oncoming traffic. We nearly slid off a cliff. It was a total miracle that we got home intact.

The impact of knowing Richard has lasted a lifetime. It was my dream to follow in his footsteps, and I remember wondering when I was with him if it was possible to be a great artist, like he was, and not be consumed by one's neuroses. It was such a profound thought that I never forgot it. Regrettably, he wasn't alive when I became a professional actor. The last time I saw him I was sixteen years old. He was playing in *Equus* on Broadway, and they had bleachers up on stage where some of the members of the audience sat. Richard sat me up there and at the end of the play he pulled me down from the bleachers when he was getting his bows and kissed me good-bye on stage. That's the last time I ever saw him.

My experiences with Richard remind me of a wonderful book called *The Power of One,* where a boy's life is completely changed by a chance meeting with a boxer on a train. The effect of the meeting, however brief, shaped his destiny forever and he became a boxer himself. Sometimes just one moment of being related to with love and understanding can shape a child's whole life.

Vision

I was a strange teenager and never fit in at school. Again, I sought out approval through good grades. School was co-ed, and I started getting a lot of attention from boys and that freaked me out completely. I never felt beautiful, probably because the only feelings I ever had about my body were ones of shame, contempt and hatred. This negative body-image is a big clue for incest survivors, and speaking of clues, so is developing an eating disorder immediately after a first failed sexual experience. I was curious and had toyed with the idea of sex, until I was faced with the stark nakedness of going through with it. One half-assed fumble with my boyfriend was enough to put me off for two years. I ran to the cafeteria, and within weeks gained twenty pounds. The weight was protection from a lot of uncomfortable feelings I wasn't ready to deal with. And it worked—male attention subsided considerably! However, I was soon bombarded with shameful remarks concerning my weight again. I was horrified and humiliated by the negative attention, and, when I saw my girlfriends throwing up in a school bathroom, that seemed like the perfect solution. It was really the beginning of a nightmare.

At eighteen, I had my first boyfriend. After making love for the first time, he made a very strange remark. He said, "You know, you don't feel like a virgin." I was totally shocked because I had never slept with anyone else. It wasn't until many years later that I understood the cryptic relevance of what he had said.

I want to add that for a long time I was adamant about not having been molested. In my early-twenties, I started taking therapy seriously. My life was a mess, and I couldn't figure out what the hell was wrong with me. Certain friends of mine would talk about the symptoms they had from being sexually abused, and I would say, "You know, it's so ironic that I have all the same symptoms, but I know that is the one thing that never happened to me." These symptoms grew progressively worse, so bad at a certain point that I became incapable of functioning in all areas of my life. I experienced chronic, persistent depression and an overwhelming sense of hopelessness. When I was in auditions or in front of a camera, tetany would set in. This is a form of paralysis that would spread throughout my upper body. My hands and mouth would seize up as if I were crippled, making it impossible to talk. It was both devastating and humiliating. I had severe anxiety attacks and often felt like I was going to pass out. I lost interest in sex, opting for celibacy for years. I never got my periods and couldn't swallow food without gagging. I thought I was going insane, that I was falling apart.

Actually, what was really happening was that I was coming together. All of the frozen parts of my body were beginning to thaw and I was getting "pins and needles" as the sensations returned. During this period, I had persistent nightmares. I would wake up at night, panic-stricken, heart pounding, sweating, feeling like there was an intruder in the house, feeling that "my space" was being violated. I believe these dreams were the warning signals of my psyche, that my subconscious was readying itself to unleash a full onslaught of forgotten information. Last, I had full-body memories. I was in an inner-child workshop doing holotropic breathing—a form of deep breathing (similar to rebirthing) often used in therapy. Deep breathing is a powerful way to reconnect people with emotional truth. I had always been a shallow breather; it was my way of shutting down and remaining emotionally disconnected. (I continue to practice Kundalini yoga and yogic breathing as a discipline to help me stay open.) Suddenly, without any prompting or manipulation, I relived one of the most horrific incidents of my abuse, in front of twenty gaping strangers. The physical memory of having a penis forced down my throat as a young child overwhelmed me and I couldn't stop myself from reliving the whole experience. It was beyond my control. My physical responses were so graphic that everyone in the room clearly evidenced the same picture and experienced it along with me. As well as going through the choking sensations all over again, and the memory of my nose being pinched shut so I was forced to open my mouth, I felt the absolute powerlessness of my young body, and the revulsion, as I tried to throw up what had been forced into me so long ago. It is no coincidence that throwing up became my coping mechanism in later life.

After the shock of that experience, I checked myself into a rehab. I had started losing weight at an alarming rate and didn't feel I could cope until I underwent further healing in a protected environment. For the first part of my healing, I walked alone. Many of those I had counted on as friends took a backseat when my life took a downward spiral. I don't feel any bitterness toward them. I recognize individual limitations and know how challenging it is to support someone through their dark night of the soul. If someone has not already confronted and resolved those same issues, then the person in pain becomes an excruciating mirror. Most people would do anything to avoid delving into their dark side and will run a mile at the first sign of another's torment.

A critical part of my healing process was going to Twelve Step meetings. The credo of those meetings was anonymity. Mine was violated hideously. A girl who had seen me in a meeting sold a story to a tabloid. I was devastated when I saw the front-page headline of the *Star*—which was a complete lie—stating that I had taken diet pills and laxatives during my pregnancy. I went to the paper and threatened to sue, demanding to know their source. When they realized that they had printed a complete fabrication, they immediately divulged their contact. I went to the girl, who had been paid a huge amount of money, and told her that she had robbed me of a threshold of healing that was available to anyone else. By the time I finished with her, she was groveling with apologies, but the damage she had done was irrevocable and I never felt safe going back to those meetings. My consolation was that the *Star* printed a microscopic retraction on page twelve.

Anyone who believes that they do not have a shadow, a dark side, is in serious denial. And self-righteous to boot! I think I have the potential to be as light as I am dark. Pure physics. As long as we're wearing a body, we're bound by dualistic reality: Light/dark, man/woman, yin/yang, etc. It seems that the dilemma plaguing every human being alive is the constant battle between the light and dark within themselves. I have to consciously choose, in every moment, to live in the light, because there is always that negative thought hanging out there telling me I'm a piece of shit and wanting me to wallow in it. That option is always there, grinning. And it is hard not to succumb to that because there is a lot of familiar pain in there that I can beat myself up with.

I reached critical mass when my daughter was one year old. Having a child was a powerful trigger for my memories. As she reached the ages of my own abuse, she became a mirror for me and stimulated my subconscious. This is the reason childhood sexual abuse is generational and the reason so many victims of abuse become perpetrators. Children become mirrors for their parents' unresolved childhoods. They become a reflection of their parents' own powerlessness. Parents are so disturbed by the feelings their children unleash, when they haven't dealt with their own abuse, that they unconsciously end up acting out the destructive patterns all over again. It is behavior the computer learned when the ego was forming. Human beings are not programmed to self-destruct unless something is introduced into the system of growth that disrupts it. And that is abuse. It is an element of negative programming that, when introduced, results in the breakdown of the healthy growth process. That is the origin of sabotage. I was lucky enough to figure out what was happening to me, and I chose to get help and break the insidious cycle of abuse. I wanted my daughter to be healthy.

I believe the body is a computer and has the ability to record every single experience on a cellular level. A child's psyche is not able to incorporate the sensations or experience of sexual abuse. It is too overwhelming, too incomprehensible. The abusive experience creates a sensory overload, the psyche splits, and the trauma is compartmentalized and stored in various parts of the body. This process is referred to as dissociation. Later, the psyche releases these cellular memories when it is ready and equipped psychologically to process them. It takes an enormous amount of energy to suppress anything in the subconscious. I find I have so much more energy than I used to have. I feel like a large portion of my life force was returned to me when I relived and released my memories. Carrying emotional baggage literally weighs you down. Life becomes a drag.

The topic of suppressed memory is very controversial, and I am sure there have been instances of therapeutic manipulation. Where I am concerned, it doesn't really matter. What *does* matter is how I have changed as a result of owning those memories. Today, I am no longer plagued by debilitating symptoms, and I am able to enjoy a healthy attitude about sex. Sex is sacred; it is an exaltation of the human spirit. That is a far cry from the distorted, degrading view I used to have! I am no longer afraid of physical intimacy, I am no longer ashamed of my body, and not only am I able to remain present in my body during sex, I am actually able to enjoy it and experience pleasure. Inability to orgasm during intercourse is another result of sexual abuse because letting go, completely surrendering, being totally vulnerable with another human being, becomes far too dangerous. Also, the intensity of orgasm releases unresolved emotions that remain stored in the traumatized parts of the body.

Photo by Cesare Bonazza, 1996.
Catherine and India.

I am lucky enough to have been with a man who was willing to go through all the stages of healing with me. I went through all the pain and humiliation of my abuse during our lovemaking, and had violent emotional outbursts, sobbing and shaking. Instead of running away, which was my greatest fear, he held me in his arms. He didn't reject me for exposing him to the part of me that felt so ugly and contaminated. Instead, he felt the experience bonded him to me in a way he could never be bonded with anyone else. He experienced a simultaneous healing, as my vulnerability took him to a place of innocence and understanding and compassion within himself. The trust we developed took me to the other side of all this turmoil, where I was able to experience pleasure without guilt, without pain, without shame. Freedom, at last!

During this unraveling process, I confided in a friend of mine, Deepak Chopra, that I had been molested. His response surprised me.

I had worked with him quite closely at his healing center and, as I said, he had taught me how to meditate several years before. "I always knew you had been molested," he said, "but I didn't feel it was my place to tell you."

One point of interest for other survivors is that Freud's original theory stated that children never lie or fantasize about being abused. He further concluded that 95 percent of all mental illness is a result of childhood molestation. A wonderful book called *The Assault on Truth*, by Jeffrey Moussaieff Masson, explores Freud's original work and the reasons why Freud was forced to suppress his evidence.

Spirituality

I didn't feel protected as a child at all, but I feel protected now. I think God is supremely loving and benefic, desiring for each and every one of us to reach a self-realized state. I only wish God could interfere more in our process! Sometimes free will really sucks. I feel that my responsibility on this planet as a spiritual being is to maintain my spiritual consciousness while I'm in a dense dimension, in a physical body. That is hard. It is so hard.

What constantly throws me off is the pettiness of daily living, with the stresses we get caught up in. I become myopic, easily losing all perspective. I think it is the hardest thing to live a life in a metropolis, having relationships, being a mother, having a profession and being spiritual. You are constantly challenged. I believe that I have had many lifetimes in monastic settings where it was easy to have a constant relationship, uninterrupted, with God because there were no distractions. The hardest thing is to be totally in our bodies and remember that we are spirit. Society does everything to lull us into a state of complacency, apathy and deadness.

Cultural doctrine bombards us with messages that tell us that to be spiritual we cannot have wealth. "It is easier for a camel to pass through the eye of a needle, than for a rich man to pass through the gates of heaven"—or something to that effect. Sayings like these have left many of us somewhat ambivalent about accruing vast fortunes. As far as I'm concerned, real wealth is an inner condition, it has nothing to do with money. To me, the universe is abundant; there is enough for everybody. I call this prosperity consciousness. Why should there be a stigma attached to an external condition mirroring a healthy inner condition? After all, we created money in the first place as a resource, a bartering tool. Aren't there all sorts of mystical symbols engraved on the dollar bill, including "In God We Trust"? Money isn't evil; how we choose to use it determines whether it is empowered for good or for evil. Unfortunately, more often than not, we see evidence of people using money for the wrong reasons: as a means to control and dominate others. I see money as a gift from God. In the right hands, money can do so much good; it can help so many people. I have been able to help others through my own resource, and I'm a strong believer in the philosophy of tithing. Every time I've had the privilege to give, I've been gifted back with so much more. Through God's grace, I've been able to support myself since I was seventeen. I've never asked for money from my parents or anyone else for that matter. I believe that we are here to create heaven on earth: an abundant, prosperous environment for all. If money can help us toward that goal, why not put it to good use?

Fear

I seem to operate on two levels. One is on a deep level of Knowingness, with a capital *K,* where I experience a place of total acceptance, peace and trust, where, as a child of God, I feel deserving of all the wonderful things that life has to offer. That is my true nature, my essential self and, I believe, everyone's true nature. Then there is the part of me that is always fearful. The part of me that feels that my hand is going to be slapped for asking, that I shouldn't have any needs, that I will always be disappointed, alone and unloved. A nothing.

All of those fears represent the wounded child aspect of me. I sometimes lovingly refer to her as "Damage Girl." I constantly have to nurture that part of me in order to diminish its hold. If I try to deny the existence of these unwanted feelings, I inevitably end up abusing myself in some form or another. As long as I honor my feelings, process them, and ultimately release them, I am gifted with a deeper place of understanding, beyond emotion, a higher self. The technique

I use is called *self-parenting*. It involves dialoguing with these different, fractured aspects of my psyche that split off because of past trauma. It sounds corny, but it works: The inner parent initiates a dialogue with the inner child. This communication helped me diagnose and resolve my feelings far more effectively. Abuse victims have a hard time identifying feelings because a frequently used coping mechanism is dissociation, whereby they disconnect from their emotions. The result is frozen feelings. For me, this way of "leaving my body" was a reaction to not being able to prevent the abuse from happening. Residual consequences have been a complete lack of trust in my body and a feeling that my body betrayed me. Through healing my relationship with my body, I have come to realize that the body never lies, it has total integrity and an innate intelligence that dwarfs my mind by comparison. After all, my mind could never have fostered another life!

Obstacles

Part of my discipline and one of my ultimate life challenges—a real humbler, I might add!—is to be conscious with food. Eating disorders, whether in the form of overeating, starving or purging are often symptoms of childhood abuse. Manifesting addiction can be a way of recreating the original abuse cycle, over and over again, in an unsuccessful attempt to resolve it. Except, in this case, you become your own perpetrator. I find it hard to believe that people are capable of taking on self-destructive patterns unless they witnessed or experienced them in some form earlier in their lives. They are, quite simply, perpetuating the self-hatred they felt as children. When we are abused by those we respect and trust, we always blame ourselves as bad and unlovable. I remember crying as a baby, repeating over and over again that I was a "bad baby." Often the abuser will tell us that we deserve to be punished because we are bad, only reinforcing the negative self-image.

The whole issue of abuse is too complex to go into thoroughly, but I'll try to outline the basic elements: Food is a form of love and nurturing for all of us, but my relationship with food became confused. Food became my way of substituting love. It became comfort and nourishment. It felt safer than human interaction. It gave me the illusion of the control I so desperately craved. It never rejected me. How I related to food became a substitute for intimacy, as a result of how I experienced toxic love as a child. Toxic love is how we interpret experiences and messages that we are told are loving but are very harmful to our well-being. "I'm doing this because I love you," is a perfect example. Whether it was food or love, I had no boundaries, no guidelines. I didn't know how much to put in my body and keep in before it didn't feel safe anymore. How much was too much? What was unhealthy? What was safe? How much to take in before I got hurt? And inevitably, how to get rid of it when it became too much?

I have the most peace with food when I'm at peace with myself. This peace is generated through feeling connected to a Higher Power and when I can give myself nurturing and nourishment that is not contingent on eating. It's when I feel deprived that I go for food, so I have to be careful about how I set myself up to feel deprived. As long as I'm not dependent on external validation, and my happiness is not contingent on any external source or stimulus over which I have no control (like love from someone else), then I am fine. So really, my eating disorder is my teacher. I am forced to be aware because when I am not centered, my urge to eat controls me. It is the ultimate challenge for me to relate to food healthily; sometimes I liken it to having to walk a tiger three times a day, with reference to three meals! I have to live my spirituality in order to overcome my compulsive behavior.

Lifework

After being admitted to Harvard, I wanted to pay for my education on my own, so I deferred for a year and decided to start modeling. My mother was old friends with Alex Lieberman, the editor in chief of Condé Nast publications, who incidentally took the lonely little picture of me as a child that is in this book. They had a meeting, and my mother thought that because I was trying to get into modeling, it couldn't hurt to bring me along. When we got there, Alex took one look at me and called in the other editors: Grace Mirabella and Polly Mellon. I was struck by how theatrical they were. With great fanfare, Polly looked at me with what appeared to be tears in her eyes and said, "Look at that face," hiring me on the spot to do the ten-page opening spread for *Vogue*. It seemed so over the top. The next thing I knew, I was shooting with Patrick DeMarchelier and Denis Piel, two of their top photographers. I was an unknown at the time, but the response to the layout was huge. *Vogue* sent me to Ford Models, and I signed with the agency. From there I got a lot of work and was able to support myself like I had hoped.

My father tried to discourage me from modeling because I was only five feet, five-and-a-half inches tall, a midget by modeling standards. But I was undaunted and found a place inside of myself that didn't believe that I could fail. I refused to welcome defeat. I understand that my father was trying to protect me from failure, but I've always been one to challenge the odds. In fact, in his later years, he has come to see how similar to him I am.

Not long after I started modeling and taking acting classes, I was picked to play Princess Diana in a television movie entitled *Charles and Diana*. I had already met the Princess, on the night of her wedding, at the ball given at Buckingham Palace. [That same night, Prince Andrew asked me to marry him on the balcony. He had been courting me at that time, sending me huge buckets of roses. Obviously, this was before Fergie came along. I thanked the Prince, but I told him that I preferred to be an actress.] I have to tell you that after playing Princess Diana in the movie, I was never again invited back to Buckingham Palace! Even so, I was caught very off-guard by her tragic and untimely death. As it did with so many other people, her death struck a personal chord. I suppose I had identified with her on such a deep level, having played her twice. In a way, through the enormous outpouring of grief, her wish to be the Queen of Hearts was fulfilled through her death.

I know this is veering off the point a bit, but I just remembered a funny thing that happened with me and Prince Charles. He is a second-cousin to my mother and they are good friends, so I had seen him many times throughout my life. When I was seventeen, we sat next to each other at dinner at a very beautiful country estate called Wilton, which is owned by the earl of Penbroke. I didn't make much of an impression on the prince because he knew far more about my family history than I did. He was trying to make conversation with me and was shocked that I was so ignorant about my genealogy, so in order to redeem myself, I started a food fight. We spent the rest of the evening flinging giant prawns across the room of this palatial mansion, aiming them at the other formally attired guests. No one got upset by our food fight because the future king can do whatever he wants. And anyway, the British aristocracy has always been famous for loving a good food fight. After that evening, my photograph ended up in the newspaper with the caption: "Is this Charles's secret love? This sultry filly could be the dark horse in the race to be the favorite girl in the life of Prince Charles," and, "The secret love of the Romeo Prince . . ." I don't think he was ever interested in me, it was just the press that concocted this stuff. At that time, the press linked anyone thought to be eligible to him.

I resumed college studies at Columbia, but because my acting career took off, my life path steered in a different direction. I soon became engaged to a man living in Spain, whom I loved very much. [Catherine is fluent in three languages, including Spanish. Her mother speaks eight languages fluently, and so did her grandfather.] Eventually, the engagement became priority, and I took several years off from work to be with him. But, in time, I decided that I wanted to go back to acting, and my fiancé told me I'd have to choose between marriage and career. Even though I loved him with all of my heart, I knew that I would resent him for the rest of my life if I didn't give myself the chance. I knew it meant loss of security for me to leave him, but I couldn't live with a lack of contentment with such a strong sense of my own destiny. Again, my vision made me feel insane because my decision wasn't supported by anyone around me. My father was telling me, "There are no good roles for actresses; you'll never make it. You should just get married." Again, that was his way of protecting me. But when my father told me I couldn't do something, it always pushed me to prove that I could. I used the world's negativity and pessimism as my motivating force.

Any time I've taken a risk in my life where I felt that I was walking out on everything conventionally secure and appropriate, with the faith that something more appropriate was out there for me, I've been rewarded. I left Spain, and on my twenty-second birthday on the twenty-second of September, I was having lunch at Gino's in New York with Sir Gordon White, an old family friend, who happened to invite

George Hamilton. I thought George's behavior was a little strange, certainly not indicative of any great interest, as he got up and disappeared for half an hour. When he returned, he presented me with a birthday present: a diamond ring. I was overwhelmed; nothing like this had ever happened to me. Gordon said to George, "Hey George, Catherine wants to get back into acting, why don't you help her?" George said okay and quite nonchalantly invited me to meet him at the Polo Lounge at the Carlysle Hotel at six o'clock the following evening.

So I sat in the Polo Lounge, in a pair of worn-out blue jeans. Without much ado, George looked at his watch and asked me if I could be packed and ready to leave for the airport in half an hour. His offer came out of left field, it seemed so outlandish. But before I had recovered my composure, I could hear the words coming out of my mouth, "No problem." Eight hours later, still in a daze, I was in Los Angeles, living on George's boat in the marina, ready to embrace a whole new adventure.

At that time our relationship was platonic. He was my mentor. But I fell in love with him and our relationship *evolved* over the next two years. During the time he was helping me, he was very gentlemanly and respectful. George used to drive me around in his Rolls Royce to auditions and wait in the parking lot. This is not a side of George too many people know about! He introduced me to Aaron Spelling, who said, "Gee honey, what great windows you have." I was perturbed because I didn't know that he was talking about my eyes. Then he said, "I'm going to make you a star." I thought he was just mouthing typical Hollywood clichés. I was sure I had just walked straight into the shark-infested waters of deceitfulness, but he did what he said.

Aaron called me in for three screen tests for three different shows. The first one was a ridiculous show about undercover aerobic teachers. I didn't know what aerobics was. I went to Jane Fonda's class, but I was too embarrassed because I had never done aerobics in my life, so I went home and hired a teacher to come to my little apartment for a private class. The next day I walked into the audition stiff as if I had a full-body cast on because I was so sore. They said to me, "What the hell happened to you?" I couldn't move and was supposed to dance for the audition. This was a reoccurring pattern in my life: When the stakes were high, I had a way of unconsciously sabotaging myself. Needless to say I didn't get that one. I didn't get the next one, either, but the third audition was for *Dynasty*, and I hit the jackpot.

After I got the series, around December of 1983, Aaron wanted me to do a *Love Boat* special in Paris in the spring because shooting for *Dynasty* didn't begin until August. I was in New York, about to fly back to shoot the special, and the gas oven had been turned on without my knowing. I went to light the pilot and the whole thing blew up in my face. I had no eyebrows, no eyelashes, and the front of my hair was singed off. It was not a pretty sight. Then, a day later, I was moving a bed and it fell on top of me and damaged my Achilles' heel, so when George came to pick me up at the airport, I was on crutches with no hair. He said, "Shit, I leave you alone for one week and look what happens!" That was my sabotage. Anytime anything great happened to me, I messed myself up. Here was my big break, and I was trying subconsciously to destroy myself. Thank God I don't do that anymore. It was like a bad comedy showing up for the *Love Boat* job wearing a wig and false eyelashes.

Miracles

On numerous occasions, I have witnessed circumstances that I can only term miraculous. One day, George and I took his boat to Catalina Island. I was wearing beautiful ruby and diamond earrings that had been an engagement present from the Spanish man I mentioned earlier, who had told me to keep them. George and I were goofing around on the pier at night, waiting for the ferry to pick us up. When we boarded the ferry, I felt my ear and the earring was gone. I was devastated and figured it might have fallen off when we were on the pier. Six months later, George and I were back in Catalina having dinner in a restaurant. A woman came up to us with an envelope and handed it to me saying, "I found your earring." She mentioned that she had found it on the pier, which was amazing to me because if you've ever been to the Catalina pier, it is made up of these large, old beams of wood with spaces in between the slats. I have no idea how she knew it was mine, or how she happened to see us in the restaurant. I felt at the time that she was an angel, that she *had* to be an angel. It was unbelievable because I had never been seen in the press with the earrings and had never publicized losing them.

There have been times in my life when I have been struck with a vision of something I feel I am supposed to accomplish. It usually sounds nuts, even to myself. In 1988, I voiced a strong desire to tithe [give 10 percent of] a million dollars to charity. I was very specific in projecting a particular outcome. I wanted to be put in charge of someone's foundation and I wanted my emphasis to be children and the environment. Then, following the principle "Do the footwork, and leave the results in God's hands," I proceeded to collect information on hundreds of different charities, as if I already had the money. I was told that I was insane, that no one in their right mind would give me one hundred thousand dollars for any reason, but I persevered! Exactly three months later, an acquaintance of mine took me out for my birthday. He knew nothing about my wish. Over the course of dinner, he put me in charge of his foundation, offering me the sum of one hundred thousand dollars a year to give away, carte blanche, to any organization I chose. He said, "I feel like I'm giving this money to an angel; I trust your judgment completely." I was stunned and profoundly grateful. Never have I so enjoyed a task as much as I enjoyed distributing those funds. It was such a gift. Over the course of the next few years, I was privileged to help so many worthy causes. To me, *that* was a miracle!

When I first arrived in L.A., I used to drive around and spy on houses that looked good to me, and one day I found my dream home. I walked onto the property and there was something so profoundly magical about the house that I immediately fell in love with it. I wrote down the address and asked a realtor to see if it was available, but it wasn't. I ended up buying another house soon afterward that came about in a miraculous way: I asked for the second house by telling my real estate woman, "I want a house in Beverly Hills, off Coldwater Canyon, on a dead-end street with an acre of land, a pool, and I want the house to be in foreclosure for under $450,000." She said, "You'll never find that." The next week, we found it. Being specific is definitely an important part of manifestation.

I put a lot of money into the house because it needed remodeling. But after several years I left *Dynasty* and decided to let go of everything in my life at that point, including the house. But it would not sell, and I was scared that I wasn't going to be able to support myself.

I had the house on the market for two years and it finally sold when the market peaked, for more than two hundred thousand dollars over the asking price two years before—the asking price I couldn't even get one offer on. I sold it for almost $1 million—so much money that I was able to afford my present home. It was as if some protective force wouldn't allow me to sell the house until I had made the maximum profit possible. And meanwhile, I had no idea that this was a blessing. I was biting my fingernails, fretting, worrying, banging my head against the walls, kicking and screaming, with no trust whatsoever that I was being taken care of.

Escrow was closing and I thought, "Where am I going to live now?" I remembered my original dream house from years before and drove there and knocked on the door. A woman answered and I said, "Hi, I just wanted to drop by and tell you that I really love your house." She said, with sarcasm, "That's really great." She obviously wanted me to leave and I said, "You know, if you ever decide you want to rent or sell this house, please keep me in mind because I just love it." She said, "I don't have any intention of moving, but I'll keep your number." It was a little unusual for me to be so forward, especially because I'm really shy, but I felt compelled, again driven by a burning desire. I knew that I wanted the house, and I had a very clear image of owning it as my goal. This was my dream house, so I set an intent by planting a thought into the universe: "I would love nothing more than to live in this house, if it's for my highest good and for the highest good of everyone involved."

Soon after I had a dream: The woman was smiling and handing me the keys to the house and saying, "You can rent it for three thousand dollars a month." She called me the next morning and said: "You're not going to believe this but my entire life has changed. I'm leaving L.A.—would you like to rent the house for three thousand dollars a month?" So I moved in. When my six-month lease was up, I was miserable thinking that I was going to have to move out of this house, and I had another dream that she was going to sell me the house. The next day, her secretary came over and said, "All my boss has been talking about this weekend is selling the house." So I bought it.

I think this incident demonstrates the power of intention combined with faith. Simply my heart's desire. And it worked out for the highest good of all because the owner had her dream awaiting her—an incredible horse ranch in Kentucky. A win-win reality. I'm not a believer in winning at someone else's expense.

In closing, as I chose to champion my own process, I went from being my own worst enemy to my own best friend. The decision to commit to inner exploration heralded the end of my living to meet other people's expectations and the beginning of living for myself. I recognized my potential as a conscious being and that I was the only valid judge of how I chose to evolve into that full potential. I was living by a new paradigm, no longer believing that I was rotten to the core. Instead, I could recognize the essence of life and the essence within myself as the same divine energy. Every layer I peeled away left me, not barren and empty, but closer to my own source. Every part of me that had split off, that I have been able to retrieve and merge with myself, left me whole, complete and fulfilled. Like pieces of a puzzle, I now feel like I fit. Today I see my scars as the battle wounds of a warrior. I remain a work in process.

2

Paul Williams

Photo by Deborah Wald

Introduction

Paul Williams is blessed to embody an infinite wellspring of creativity, with talents in comedy, acting, writing and singing, to name a few. Most acclaimed in the songwriting arena, Paul's work has reached worldwide record sales in the hundreds of millions. Not bad for a man who has no formal musical training, and who, in his entire life, has never listened to much music, preferring talk radio instead. Paul even went through a period of years where he did not own a stereo system. Upon visiting his estate for the first time, I expected to find a grand piano and state-of-the-art technology. Instead, I uncovered a small, weathered piano and a boom box. Over the years, when Paul wanted to share a new song, we went down to the garage and sat in the car. The speakers in his BMW were better than those on the box.

What this showed me was that real genius isn't reflected in showy paraphernalia. Paul never did need the many accoutrements of technology to prove his creativity. In fact, when he started writing and didn't yet know how to play music, Paul just sang the melody in his head to the band he was working with. Creativity is so intrinsic to his being that it sets him apart and makes him, in my biased opinion, truly one of the world's great eccentrics. I don't think it would matter where he was or what he was doing, the songs would continue to play in his brain, demanding to be written down. The list of Paul's creations seems never-ending. He has had such a prolific career that I couldn't list all of his hit songs here, but a portion of his musical standards include "We've Only Just Begun," "Just an Old-Fashioned Love Song," "Rainy Days and Mondays," "You and Me Against the World," "Won't Last a Day Without You" and "Evergreen," for which he and Barbra Streisand won the 1976 Oscar for Best Song of the Year from A Star Is Born. Though this is an impressive list, I'm most amused by the fact that it's the royalties from the old Love Boat theme song that still pays the rent.

Despite Paul's outward success, his biggest triumph came in 1989 when he took a break from his career to check himself into recovery for drug and alcohol addiction. Nine sober years later, as a certified drug and alcohol counselor, Paul is on a new course of creativity. The 1993 *movie* The Muppet Christmas Carol, *for which he composed the music and lyrics, was his first sober song score. Once fearful that creativity would cease to exist without the use of substances, it was a welcomed validation when the soundtrack was nominated for a Grammy.*

This introduction has been the hardest for me to write, regardless of Paul's many achievements. How do I express the deepest of feelings on paper without sounding trite or redundant? I adore all of the people in this book, and my respect for them fuels my creativity. With Paul, however, a man who has been like a second father, an only brother and a guardian angel to me all at once, I'm left a little tongue-tied. So I shall start at the beginning.

I'll never forget the voice. I had just started my pet-sitting business and took a minimum-wage job at a pet store on the border of Beverly Hills in an effort to meet potential clients. One afternoon, as I stood in my itchy polyester smock, hanging dog collars, I heard the voice. I turned to see Paul Williams talking to Lenny, the head salesman. Their talk was familiar and I felt a touch of envy that he wasn't my client. I was too shy to introduce myself, but I had adored Paul's music throughout my childhood and teenage years and wished that I had been the one to wait on him. "Do you have any dogs?" I wanted to ask. Oh, if only I could take care of his dogs! Paul left quickly and I told myself that the next time I would have more luck. In Los Angeles it is common to find yourself standing so close to a celebrity in a store or restaurant that you can smell their perfume or cologne. Often you feel that you know these public personalities, only to remember that they do not know you. Unless you want to be one of a multitude of interruptions in their day, it is usually more courteous to let them be.

The following day, again on the floor of the pet store, the phone rang. There were four of us working that morning, but I was moved to walk across the large warehouse-style building to answer it. I heard the familiar voice.

"Hi, this is Paul Williams. I can't seem to find my address book with my kennel information in it. I'm going out of town and I need a place to board my two huskies. Do you know of a good place?"

"Didn't you just lose your wallet the other day?" I asked, teasingly.

"Yes. Who is this?" He sounded amused and playful.

I explained that I had overheard him talking to Lenny the day before. I gave him a kennel number and before hanging up I added, "By the way, if you ever need a professional dog walker, I'm one and I love huskies!"

"How soon can you be here?"

"Two hours."

I got directions to his home and hung up. I had been expecting miracles with my new business and here was my first one. I went to my manager, Kevin Ryan, and told him why I wanted to leave early. He was excited and he encouraged me to "get moving." I raced home, grabbed Mark, and off we went.

Mark and I found Paul's gated home high in the Hollywood Hills. I had never been to this part of town and the view from the small and winding road was so mesmerizing that we nearly drove off a cliff in our state of wonderment. Paul's business manager handed us the two elated fluffballs, Chewy and Tasha, and we ran and ran. I was overwhelmed to be making four hours pay—pet store time—for one-half hour of fun exercise. Afterward, Paul invited us into his home. We began conversing like long-lost friends, and an hour later we were sitting on the tiled kitchen floor with the dogs in our laps, talking about God, miracles and healing. Paul informed us that he had to take a lengthy last-minute trip the following day and that he wanted us to take care of his house, property and animals. Thankfully, he felt that we would do a better job than the person he had hired.

For the next six weeks, Mark and I kept our little apartment, but spent most of our time at Paul's estate. We lounged on the porch during balmy evenings, losing ourselves in the sea of tiny, shimmering lights below. In the early morning hours, I took walks in the garden, letting the fragrance from the old lemon tree take me back to the smells of my childhood streets in Northern California. When Paul returned to find his home more organized and more "lived in," he asked us to please stay. He knew that his highly energetic Alaskan sled dogs needed more attention, and Brodie had become their new best friend. The nurturing aromas of my homemade soups cooking on his stove probably didn't hurt either. Having recently split with his fiancée, Paul was in need of a family. We, too, felt isolated in the city and found his essence wonderfully assuring. I had some hefty student loans to pay off and other debt accumulated since college, and Paul was offering us the chance of a lifetime: to live in his gorgeous home, rent free, with all the food we could eat. We could finally clear our credit and think about having a baby. Paul gave us our own quarters and unlimited use of the house, pool and gardens. All of that, just to take care of some pups. It was unbelievable.

Paul and I shared countless heart-to-heart talks on the carpeted stairs. We cried to each other about lost loves and broken hearts, coaching one another to forgive the past and move on. I was newly married and knew it was time to get over old victimization, and ironically, the man who had written "the most codependent songs of the 1970s" was just the person to help me get through it. Paul was a sounding board for Mark to bounce off acting ideas, and Mark and I had open ears to listen to any new songs or lyrics Paul wanted to share. Mostly Paul made us laugh, with the quickest wit we had ever known. His endless creativity was astonishing, as we'd watch him write songs in minutes, constantly affirming for us that God uses people as an instrument for His eternal handiwork.

Our son must have been hovering above because we conceived less than a year after moving in. Paul let me slack off considerably on my animal-care duties as my pregnancy progressed, and our healthy baby was born in the house. An attending midwife kept the King of the Castle abreast of the details as he anxiously paced the stairs during my grueling thirty-six-hour labor. It was an experience that brought a deeper sense of family to our already special friendship. Six months later, with a newfound strength that came from having lived together, we came to the mutual decision that it was time for Mark and I to find a home of our own. We had not only paid off all of our debt, but we had saved a significant amount of money for the first time in our marriage. Because of that, we were able to move several hours out of town to a honeymoon cottage in the country, which was precisely the environment in which I wanted to raise our baby. And Paul found the love of his life, Hilda Keenan Wynn, and got married. Chewy and Tasha immediately welcomed Hilda's beautiful Ziggy, an elderly terrier mix.

Paul recently recorded two new albums and his latest love songs, inspired by the joy he has found with his bride (and menagerie), are as beautiful and sensitive as some of his best-known works. As of this writing, two of his songs are on the country charts ["You're Gone," cowritten with John Vezner, and sung by Diamond Rio; and "Party On," cowritten with Karen Taylor Good, sung by Neil McCoy.] Recently, Paul was nominated to be inducted into the Songwriters' Hall of Fame, along with Bruce Springsteen, James Taylor, Michael Jackson and Diane Warren. Paul has been a regular actor on The Bold and the Beautiful [seen daily by 350 million people worldwide, making it the most popular television show ever according to the Guinness Book of World Records], where he played a recovering alcoholic. Paul and Hilda's home is an oasis of warmth and comfort. Hilda is a gourmet cook and a phenomenal decorator and gardener, and there are always scrumptious and inviting smells coming from the kitchen, and fragrances of blooming flowers throughout the house and property. Their marriage seems to be a blessing from the universe to Paul for overcoming his addictions. I can't help but wonder if his immense generosity toward us and so many others is also part of that equation. For the first time in his life, Paul is truly able to accept the gifts of peace and ease.

Perhaps the greatest contributions our society gains from this man are the quiet acts you do not hear about: the way he drives through dangerous parts of town picking up addicts who need help; inspiring rooms full of people, laughing, then crying, at recovery meetings; or the vast amounts of time and money he gives every year helping to heal tangled lives. As a recovery counselor, Paul inspires healing on a daily basis in his community, and also on the national level as a member of the board of directors for the National Council on Alcoholism and Drug Dependency. When Paul was using, he lived an isolated life. Now sobriety affords him the ability to venture out and embrace others who need his help. I wonder how many other people out there see Paul as their guardian angel?

One of the greatest lessons for me surrounding this friendship is that I never assume that I know where a seemingly dead-end job may lead. I pray that if my son ever ends up broke and missing home in some big city, that he will be so lucky to meet an angel like Paul. It seems too good to be true to have happened at all, much less to happen again. But, angels come in all shapes and sizes, and chances are there are more than a few out there. If you find one, just don't expect him or her to be so talented. Now that would be asking a lot! Even of God.

Happiness

To be at peace with my own emotions is the beginning of happiness. To do so, I have to let go of a lot of things: all of my angers and all of my fears. I subdivide life into two states: fear and faith. The more that faith is working in my life, the more I am free to dabble at whatever emotions are rolling by. The changing of emotions is constant. In the course of a day, I'm going to go through all kinds of feelings, but I have a home base to return to in faith, or one to return to in fear. It's my choice.

To stay happy, I have to fight certain natural instincts. History can be both an ally or an enemy. If we have a personal history that includes a great success or joy at one place, it's the natural human instinct to try to turn the cosmos around and head back to that place. One of the ways I've found to keep experiencing life to its fullest is to try and let go of what has been. For me that means not trying to recreate the success I've had as a songwriter, an actor, or anything else. The goal is to leave myself wide open to what the new day is going to bring. Just as the notes after death will be more beautiful than those within the context of this life span, I'd also like to believe there's a beauty ahead of me here that I haven't yet experienced.

Early Years

I was raised in an alcoholic household where there was great fear and no consistency. As a construction brat, I was constantly moving from state to state. Always the new kid in school and always the littlest—only four feet, six inches tall when I got out of high school. My childhood frightened me so badly that I ran through those years rather than experience them. If someone wanted to talk to me in junior high, I would tap my watch and keep walking as if I had someplace else to go. But I had nowhere else to go. I just couldn't bear sitting down and confronting another human being—someone who might hurt me. It was a difficult time.

My father was killed in a car wreck when I was thirteen. He was drinking. I was busy trying to be a parent when I was a kid and had to grow up fast, so I acted out my childhood in my thirties.

My mother was very nurturing and loving, but let me go when I needed to be with her most. When my father passed away, my little brother was only eight years old, and my mother was overwhelmed with the responsibility of raising two kids by herself, so she shipped me off to Long Beach, California, to live with my aunt and uncle, who were quite abusive. I guess you could say that the "woman" who cared for me constantly and unconditionally for a long period of my life was my drugs. Self-medicating allowed me to shove the fears down to where they didn't speak to me so loudly. Not looking at my pain was all I knew how to do, otherwise I would have been sobbing constantly. Mom, who died in the 1970s, ended up feeling very badly about sending me away, and she frequently said that she had done the wrong thing with me. I'm sure that some of the longing present in various songs I've written comes from that time: When I needed most to be held by my mother, she wasn't there.

One of the positives of living with my relatives was the school they enrolled me in. Aside from hanging out with the punks, who felt safe to me because of their street smarts, there was another group of children that I gravitated toward: the intellectual, theater crowd. I could relate well to these other outcasts who were my own age, and they ended up being great teachers to me. These kids appreciated classic writing, the theater and the best movies. They taught me about the finest artists and painters from history and influenced me to read books instead of comics. As a result, I read voraciously and still do. Reading offered me a wonderful escape, but it was more than I realized. It was an amazing teacher. In hindsight, I got what I needed. A good analogy would be that of a fly on a painting by Seurat, who was a pointillist. Standing on the canvas, all the fly could see would be a bunch of dots. But if it got far enough away, it would see that the dots go together to make a beautiful picture. Now that I get far enough away from my past, I see that my childhood was exactly what I needed for me to be who I am today. Yes, it was painful, but what history has shown me, at least at this point, is that I'm always going to get what I need.

Drives

Unable to handle the fear in my family, I consciously replaced my anxiety with thoughts of grandiosity. I came to believe that I was so special that one day I'd be able to do things nobody else could do. You know, because we manifest destiny for ourselves, I managed to do that in some ways. I had two choices: Either I could continue to be this little guy who was afraid of everybody, or I could be a force that would not be deterred from whatever it wanted. I created a determination that took me toward fulfilling a lot of goals. I think more than creating anything of value though, my goal was to be famous. I saw famous people getting respect, and I wanted that.

When I was twenty-one, I decided to become an actor. I was such a strange type because I looked like a kid, until you put me next to real kids, and then I looked like a kid with a hangover, which was usually the case. As hard as I was to cast, I stayed with it. I knew I would succeed; I had no doubts. My grandiosity was immense. On some level I knew that entertaining people through acting or something else was what I was meant to do. I had always sung. I was one of those kids who sang "Danny Boy," you know, the kind you want to slap. Even so, songwriting was not a talent that was revealed to me early on.

I really wanted to be Montgomery Clift, because inside I felt like a tortured artist and that's what I wanted to project as an actor. But I looked like Haley Mills, so I played children. Somehow, I always managed to stay alive and make a living with limited work.

Paul singing at an Air Force base in Rapid City, South Dakota, 1949, at nine years old.

Creativity

One day when I was twenty-two, a friend of mine invited me to lug equipment to a photo shoot he was doing for a new band called the Chancellors. The night before we went, I wrote two songs—my first ones. It never occurred to me that I couldn't do it. I sat down, wrote the songs, and went out and played them for the band. I didn't know how to play the piano at that time, so I wrote the words and sang them to the melody in my head. They liked what I came up with and years later we wound up making a record together.

Soon after meeting the Chancellors, I started fooling around on a friend's guitar during an acting job. I didn't know the chords had names; I had no clue an E was an E or an F was an F. Eventually, I figured it out and acquired a piano, writing numbers on the keys so that I could remember what the chords were. I used to joke that I couldn't play other people's songs, so I wrote my own. I met a guy named Biff Rose who played me some of his melodies and I was inspired to write words to his music. He later went to A&M Records and played for them everything he'd ever written and they liked the four I'd scripted words to. So I arrived at A&M records with no prospects, no future, and I found a career. I was so broke, my line was that I arrived at the studio in a stolen car. Herb Alpert signed me as a staff writer and there I began.

At A&M I met Roger Nichols, a brilliant composer and trained musician. I watched him like a hawk and learned a lot of the basics about song composition from him. When our long workdays were done and Nichols went home, I'd stay, continuing to write through the night. It seemed I was there around the clock. I adored every minute. To eliminate the need for sleep, I turned to amphetamines.

One day, Roger and I were asked to write a song for a Crocker Bank commercial. Roger wrote the melody and I scripted the lyrics. Because the spot was about a young couple starting out, I wrote:

We've only just begun to live
White lace and promises
A kiss for luck and we're on our way.

This took us through the wedding. As the new couple drive off into the sunset, I added:

Before the rising sun, we ride. . . .

A young singing group saw the commercial and asked us if there was a whole song to it. Thankfully, we had added another verse with the hope that someone would want to record it. We were still shocked, though, especially when it raced up to number one. Our schmaltzy little song, that went on to become one of the highest-playing songs of all time, had all the romantic beginnings of a bank jingle. The song was "We've Only Just Begun." The kids were the Carpenters.

In hindsight, I backed into the right career by not getting work as an actor. It was then that I discovered what I could really do. My mother used to say that God would slam one door so that he could open another. My acting career door had been slammed, and the hallway was scary before the songwriting door opened up. But I knew as soon as I started writing songs that I could script words and put music together. Writing is an easy process for me because I feel the words that are already in the notes. Whether I script them or somebody else does, I hear the emotion in the melody and find the words in that emotion. I think the composer of the music also feels the words and the people who listen to the music do as well. It is that common element that makes a hit. What makes my songs successful is not what's different about me from other people, but what we have in common. It's the sameness and

Photo by Armando Gallo

Paul and Barbra Streisand at the Academy Awards, 1976.

oneness in all of us, that shared bond of emotions and needs. People think, "Yeah, I feel that, too; I sense that, too."

I look back at my twenties, when I didn't have a relationship with a lady, and I remember feeling such longings for romance. I totally idealized love relationships. The good of that was that I was able to write some of the more famous codependent anthems of the 1970s. Looking back, I often wrote with greater accuracy about an emotion I wasn't experiencing at the time. For example, when I was in a relationship that was nurturing and sweet, I could write a song called "Loneliness." When I was heartbroken and alone, desperately needing to be with somebody, I could write about a perfect love. I think I wrote about my fantasy at the time, and in a way, that kept some emotional distance between myself and my work. By intellectualizing my feelings, I put myself in the role of narrator. I also see that I used my writing, too, like a drug: a way to write about my emotions instead of feel them.

What I do now is totally different. Instead of trying to prod the creative process along with substances and endless hours at the keyboard, I just get out of my own way. Drugs didn't make me more creative, they only helped me to stay up longer; with that energy I took on impossible goals—like committing to do an entire song score for a movie in one month. I was a maniac. Now I tell God that I need his help. When I was writing *The Muppet Christmas Carol,* I was told to come up with a song about the first time we see Scrooge. I had no ideas. I picked up a mystery book and began reading, ignoring the task at hand. I had given the assignment of what I needed to God and let it go. All of a sudden I put the book down and thought (singing):

> *When a cold wind blows it chills you, chills you to the bone.*
> *But there's nothin' in nature that freezes your heart like years*
>   *of being alone.*
> *It paints you with indifference, like a lady paints with rouge.*
> *The worst of the worst, the most hated and cursed, is the one*
>   *that we call Scrooge.*

I thought, *Hello! That's it. . . . That's exactly it.* There it was presented to me. I did the work, but the inspiration was a gift. I trusted that my unconscious was tapped into all of the information it had about the subject and once it turned itself into soup, my job was to ladle it up. As long as I can trust like that, I have no fear in my abilities.

For someone who is not a writer or an artist, the best example I can give is when you try to remember somebody's name and can't. It's when you stop trying to remember that it comes. This is exactly what happens in the creative process for me. There is a tension and resistance in effort that interrupts the flow; when I stop trying, the creation appears.

Obstacles

Drugs made me feel good for awhile. Cocaine made me want to shoot basketballs for money. At one point in my life, drugs and alcohol were a tool—the wrong tool, but the first thing I became aware of to get me somewhat out of myself. They fueled the grandiosity and medicated the pain. Along the way, however, I moved down the road from use to abuse to addiction. Once I became addicted, it was all over: I had to ride it out until I had a spiritual awakening. I believe you have to hit your bottom before that can happen. I learned a lot from the depth down there. I wasn't crawling the streets, and I wasn't poor. My bottom was on a beautiful estate, but I was emotionally and spiritually bankrupt. People look at the concept of a charmed life as somebody who is successful, but I believe that the most valuable gifts I've been given, and the greatest lessons I've learned, have not been in my success, but in my failure. By bottoming out as a drunk and being forced to turn within for support (instead of to the recognition that came from my work), my true growth was able to begin.

Robert Bly, in his book *Iron John,* points out that in all of mythology the hero emerges after he's wounded. I had to be wounded. I had to be on my knees in order to look up. There in that quiet moment after I had been knocked down, I glanced up and read a recovery prayer. Part of the prayer said, "relieve me of the bondage of self." These words hit hard because I had taken myself prisoner in trying to invent myself for the world around me, instead of letting God invent me on a daily basis. I had been outlining my life for what people demanded, what an audience demanded, and what the person who was then the love of my life demanded. I had to let go of all that. Life, as I knew it, had to make way for God's constant creations. I had to follow his words and his voice to lead me to what I should be doing.

Because I had written my best work under the influence of drugs, I was terrified that I wouldn't be able to write sober. That fear chased me away from creating for a long time. Ironically, taking a break was exactly what I needed to do. When I went away from the work, I went into the thing that was most important to me—my sobriety. I went to UCLA, got my certificate as a drug and alcohol counselor, and began working every morning with patients. I worked in two hospitals and at a center for dual-diagnosis patients (schizophrenics who also had substance-abuse problems) in a lockdown unit. I went each morning, letting myself in with a key, and had some of the most rewarding experiences of my life. For some of the patients who had seen me in the media, I felt like an old friend. Basically my presence made a blanket statement about addiction like, "Whoa, it can happen to anyone."

My quest now is freedom from fear. How do I feel safe? I have to go inside. I have to trust and have faith. For instance, I still get nervous when I perform, but that feeling of safety quickly washes over me, telling me once more that I am never alone. Now that I am living without medication I turn to my inner self: that source of Christ-consciousness. I am so grateful now. I feel like Lazarus, as if I've been reborn. Each day to me is another miracle.

Because I was raised without healthy guidance, it would be ridiculous for me to feel badly about who I used to be. Regrets are a total waste of energy. If I did things that have had negative results, I focus on what I can do now to right the situations. How can I make amends? How can I go back to somebody I did something inconsiderate to and balance it with something loving now? I wouldn't change my past, but I've had to do some real work at forgiving myself for some of my former actions, especially the jokes that so casually popped out of me. I used to be a frequent guest on the *Tonight Show*, with Johnny Carson. I was so unpredictable that no one knew what was going to fly out of my mouth. Even now, every once in a while I'll remember yet another fragment from that show and sit straight up in bed and say, "Here we go again, another amends needs to be made."

The path I've chosen to walk now, the spiritual path, is narrower. Life has become more black and white. The choices between right and wrong are more obvious and the right one speaks to me in my head. It may not be the easiest choice in the moment, but in the long run it always is. I guess that old wiseass, caustic side of me was really just a defense, part of my armament. I loved looking into the dark side of life and lowering myself into the well. It was exciting. A big show. I've always loved a big show. Drugs were a way to get to a place of non-reality, a greater-than-life experience. I have had the wonderful fortune of being able to travel all over the world and meet some of the most exciting people: presidents, royalty and stars of all fields. When I was a practicing alcoholic, I drank with some amazing celebrities. I won't mention names because we're talking about other alcoholics. People whom I had longed to hang out with, some of the great classic bad boys of Hollywood, wound up being my best buddies. We'd hoot and howl together. Of course the fun didn't last.

At one point, right before I got sober, I was beaten up by a devil of my own making. I was dressed up in a tux, ready to do a show, and was walking to an escalator with my promoter and my road manager. I had been taking Antabuse to keep from drinking, but I was still doing cocaine. I think what happened was that I had a complete psychotic breakdown from the toxicity because something invisible threw me up in the air, higher than my own head. It slammed me into a wall and as I bounced off onto the ground, I was thrown again, this time down the escalator stairs. My ears were being twisted, and I felt like I

Courtesy of Paul Williams

In concert, 1970s.

was being tortured. Everyone around me had seen me being thrown, and they were terrified. I hurried into my car and could see a devil version of myself in the rear-view mirror. It was so weird, but that didn't scare me because there was a part of me that used to invite that energy in. Again, that was the part of me that lowered myself into the well. A line from my song "Beauty and the Beast" says:

Courtesy of Jim Henson Co.

Paul and Kermit, 1970s.

To work them out I let them in
All the good guys and the bad guys that I've been
All the devils that disturbed me and the angels that defeated
*   them somehow*
Come together in me now

Maybe my need to take on such energy was an attempt to feel strong and powerful. You know, people used to tell me that I did dangerous, macho things—like skydiving and race-car driving—because I was compensating for my size, trying to prove I wasn't little. I used to deny this vehemently, saying that I just loved high speeds. After spending thousands of dollars on analysis, I now know they were right. I was absolutely compensating for my size.

Spirituality

I think for all of us, more powerful than the fear of death is fear of life. Life makes me insecure—I think that is the constant battle for people in general. Unconsciously we must know there is more after death, otherwise we'd all be running around screaming, "Oh God, how much time have I got left?" We know on some level that death is an illusion and not reality. Our intellect may question, but our hearts know. After being me in this life there's going to be me in something else. I don't yet know what, but I assume it's going to be even more colorful and beautiful, including notes that haven't been played yet on this level.

Probably the most important word in my life today is trust: I trust there's a perfection in being me, and that it's not an accident that I'm here. I trust that what I'm experiencing is going to be all kinds of things, including painful, but that it's safe to be me. I have always believed in God. Always. When my father died, I'm told I was like a preacher at the funeral: talking to and comforting everyone. The variety of life and experience is an absolute billboard for a God presence to me. Even in my own backyard I can't help but see the unlimitedness of God's creations, especially with the way my wife gardens.

When I think about God, appearances change. When I go running and see a dried and lifeless tree, fighting for its life in the smog, and recognize it as a God presence, suddenly it looks different. By my recognizing the spirit of God manifest on this plane, whatever I'm looking at transforms. All I have to do is stop and acknowledge the divinity. I do my best to see God in everything now, including people. For example, I always had a vision of the type of woman I thought was beautiful. All I have to do is honor the person before me as a part of God and he or she becomes that beautiful. Suddenly I am free of the type.

I think God is loving. I cannot explain the pain in life, although I do believe there must be reasons for it all. Certainly we often choose the pain. When you think about the people who die in earthquakes, for example, you wonder why. The fact is that some of us choose to build our homes in places where the Earth dances. The wonder that she moves is, for me, more immense than my fear of being on her when she decides to do her shaking. And I've got to tell you, my fear of being on her when she does shake is *huge*. My wonderment of this constantly shifting planet is greater than my desire to avoid pain. I trust there is a divine plan in all of this chaos.

When I experience something that frightens me, it always creates more space inside of me. I remove the fear by living it. When I first walked out onstage sober, I was afraid, but I knew I had to do it. I saw what it was like and the fear got used up and went away. All of a sudden, there was more room to play handball inside of myself. When I start stacking fear in the rooms, there isn't room to play.

Discipline

I'm really sweet to myself; after all, I'm coming back from a major disease. It's important for me to be peaceful, so I give myself a lot of time to be alone. Quiet time for me is restorative, it's how I recharge my energy. I meditate, talk to God, let my mind wander, and read my religious books that are stacked next to my bed. I also sleep when I want. My bedroom is my safe place. I take the time I need to be there, and then I am better able to go out and be of service.

As for spiritual disciplines, I don't meditate as much as I'm going to. When I do, which is almost every day, it puts me back on center. All I have to do is sit down and do it. Meditating for me is not a long-term process because I feel such an angelic presence, and such an energy rush from it, that I jump up and start doing things. It's like a battery charge: Instead of sitting there and allowing the battery to charge from zero all the way up to ten, I get a little goose at three and go "whoa" and am off running. It's a miracle that I meditate at all, with what feels like the busiest head in the world. The calming effect is instantaneous, though, so my goal is to get more comfortable with God's healing energy running through me without having to do something with it. I'm working on that one. These are new disciplines for me: to sit down and meditate, jog, or feel my feelings. I'm not nearly as good at them as I will be in a few years. Progress, not perfection.

Life gets better the older I get, and I like myself more and more with each year. I can slap on tapes of myself at thirty-three and see myself arrogant and full of self, which is a gift, but a painful one at that. I was such a baby then, but it got me where I am and for that I'm grateful. I'm really pleased that I'm making healthy choices and I'll get better at them. It's a learning process because basically I'm an energy junkie who is becoming comfortable with an even peacefulness, as opposed to days filled with big highs and lows. My life revolved around drama before my sobriety. It had its fun moments, but there was always a down side. If I find now that I'm experiencing an energy rush, I pull back and calm myself, trying to avoid the immense mood swings. There seems to be an indulgence in them. When I'm feeling really good, I like to get quiet and experience the sensations instead of talking about them and pumping off the energy. I seek to smooth out my life, understanding that there are no big deals. Peace is forever the goal.

Family

I now have with my wife, Hilda, the first solid partnership of my life with a woman. We were introduced by mutual friends—my first blind date. I had been divorced from my first wife for a few years (who is the mother of my two children, Cole and Sarah, ages sixteen and thirteen), and I liked Hilda instantly. We were so comfortable with each other from the beginning. She has a fabulous spark of life about her, and it's a godsend for me that sobriety and spirituality are of equal importance in her own life. Hilda is wonderfully maternal, too. She loves my children and has made our home their home.

Photo by Lisa Stefanson

Paul and Hilda Williams with Cole and Sara Williams.

Hilda's father was a famous character actor, and her grandfather, Ed Wynn, was a vaudeville actor who crossed over into a successful movie career. Hilda was a talent agent herself, so we had a lot in common from the start. We've always felt married, just like we belong together. Our marriage gives me a sense of real security. I feel safe in the love I get from my wife and that I give back to her. Our relationship gives me challenges to let us grow and change, without trying to direct the course.

One of the ways we keep our marriage healthy is through therapy. I go to individual sessions myself and to a counselor once a week with Hilda. Therapy helps me deal with my fears, helps me understand where some of them were born. When you have a point of origin for some of your character defects, it's a little easier to excavate them. Therapy for us as a couple allows our relationship to get stronger by reminding us that we are each individuals and that communication is key to our longevity. I believe that when you're strong, you don't have to prove your strength, which enables me to admit my weaknesses. This is the only way I'm going to get any help with them, or help anyone else. Couple's therapy is an exercise in expression. For some reason, we can sit down with a cofacilitator and be reminded that we don't know each other totally. I have to tell Hilda what I'm thinking and feeling. I can't assume things. We love our sessions together, making them like a date, going out to lunch beforehand. Anything that enhances our communication skills is going to improve who we are together.

Earth

As long as there are people suffering in this world, we have areas of work that are immediately defined for us. The old "Visualize World Peace" slogan is not a bad idea. In terms of the problems facing this planet, I approach them with affirmative prayer. With crime in our cities, I just see the problem as being less. I don't need to carry a gun to protect myself. I believe we will start seeing the reality of divinity more and more. Times have changed so much since I was a child. Back then, I wasn't able to look at my issues at all, not many people could. When my beautiful daughter was nine (four years ago) she would say things to me like, "I think my brother is really getting in touch with his anger," which would have been laughed at when I was growing up. We have evolved so much in a few decades. For all of the dark we read about in the newspapers, there is also a universal healing taking place that may just outrun the darkness. There is a movement afoot that is going to have an effect, and like many other times before we've seen transformation, things will likely get worse before they improve. I have to assume that the world is changing and getting healthier. It sounds a little Pollyanna-ish, but that is where my energy has to go.

I do what I can for the people in front of me. There was a great speech in the film *The Year of Living Dangerously* where a male character named Billy Quan, played by a woman, Linda Hunt, witnesses slum conditions. He takes the money he earns as a photographer and keeps a family alive in a slum area. A journalist says to him, "Why do you bother when there is so much suffering here?" and basically his answer was that if everyone took care of the suffering directly in front of them, there wouldn't be any. The more of a success I am, the more I can help those hurting in front of me. Forums are available to me. That is why I am so open about my recovery. I feel I have a voice that can be heard.

There is a part of me that would like to see something really *big* happen here on Earth, whether it's verification of life on other planets, or the first proven contact with spirit or ghosts. There's a wonderful book called *Childhood's End,* by Arthur C. Clarke, where all life—all history as we know it—changes in a single day, when simultaneously over the cities of Paris, London and New York, huge mother ships appear from outer space. I expect something major like that to happen in my lifetime. Perhaps it will be a great discovery that changes our thinking. For some reason, I think it has something to do with spirit: proving life after death, or that people have been here before from other planets. I don't know what it will be, but I'm waiting. I love a big show.

Fear is a shorter word than faith and
easier to type into our manifest.
With a little more work and dexterity,
we can type in faith every time.

PAUL WILLIAMS

3

Keely Shaye Smith

Photo by Cesare Bonazza

Introduction

T
hree years ago I was approached by a woman who asked me if I
wanted to interview her friend, Pierce Brosnan. My reply brought
an enthusiastic smile to her face. "Actually, I'd rather speak with
his companion, Keely Shaye Smith." Keely* is an award-winning investigative journalist who has explored many environmental issues, from
toxic waste to dolphin slaughter. As a career-oriented woman myself,
also partnered with an actor, I was intrigued by the life of this passionate and intelligent beauty. I wanted to know how a successful
woman stays independent and true to her path while in a relationship
with a man experiencing worldwide success. Perhaps more importantly, I wanted to know what inspired Keely to give up a lucrative
career as an actress to concentrate on burning issues, specifically the
environment.

What I found was a woman on the front lines of global change. A
woman who aligns herself with some of the most innovative, revolutionary and courageous environmentalists in the world. A woman
whose integrity and commitment to the earth is so entrenched that she
was willing, even happy, to give up great money as a model and an
actress for the unsure future of an activist. Once again, I found myself
with a person who chose the road less traveled, with the faith that she
would be rewarded for choosing good.

Keely's illustrious career, which started in her early-twenties, has led
to a myriad of jobs as correspondent for Entertainment Tonight,
Unsolved Mysteries, The Today Show, Good Morning America, and
recently a two-book deal with HarperCollins writing gardening books.
The Weekend Gardener, her first book, will be followed by a TV series
of the same name. Keely is also the creator, producer and host of the
1995 PBS organic gardening series, Home Green Home. Her favorite
assignments are hosting documentaries such as Great Bears and her
latest assignment In the Wild, with Jane Goodall in Tanzania. In the
midst of her work schedule, she and Pierce are raising their child,
Dylan Thomas Brosnan. Keely didn't consciously know during our

[*AUTHOR'S NOTE: Keely is an Irish name, meaning graceful.]

first interview that she had just conceived, and spoke with excitement and certainty about wanting to be a mother: "I'd really like to have one child. It doesn't matter if it's a boy or a girl, I would just like to go through the process. How can I be a gardener and not bear fruit?" In spite of the beautiful and detailed account she gave me of how she and Pierce met, and how they have grown together in their mutual support, Keely's independent nature surprised me several times during our meetings. I have very rarely come across a woman this grounded, centered and complete within herself, or so sure of her life mission.

Keely's personal history clearly illustrates the underlying philosophy of this book: There are specific reasons why people succeed. Put simply, Keely works hard to manifest her dreams. She also has a golden touch that makes things happen in the most remarkable ways. I don't know if Keely was born under a magical star (although my astrologer sister would give a good argument to the affirmative), but one thing is for sure: Keely makes things happen. She writes her goals each year on her birthday, and almost always achieves them. I wonder if this is because she uses her time, energy, talents and money for good. I wonder if her constant dialogue with God has something to do with her good fortune. Maybe she's just lucky. Whatever the reason, Keely embodies so many of the attitudes and beliefs that make up a healthy, happy life, that I cannot imagine writing this book without her.

In case you haven't already guessed, this woman has a fiery personality, as the natural red highlights in her chestnut hair suggest. Heaven help anyone who intends to victimize women, children, animals or the earth in her presence. She is blatantly fearless, and bound to expose, on national television, whatever she finds. Above all, Keely is an earth mother in the truest sense: She is happiest working in the garden, with her hands in the earth. The climate in Southern California allows her to plant and nurture her childhood favorites (from living in Hawaii until she was five): various perfumed flowers, herbs and fruits like oranges, bananas, figs and guavas. One might guess that Keely has a bevy of gardeners planting and designing her landscapes, but with the exception of when she travels, she sees to the implementation and maintenance herself. I imagine that the thumbs of those she would hire could scarcely be greener.

Now, years after our introduction, Dylan happily nuzzles into Mom. Keely gracefully carries him through a dense thicket of sunflowers that she had planted months before. They sway many feet above her head, seeming to celebrate their life-giving caretaker, as she and baby traipse among their mighty stems. This summer afternoon, Pierce is in London filming the latest Bond adventure, so I take a woman-and-child-and-flower photo to send overseas.

Keely seems to exist without physical insecurities, although some would suggest that is an easy task for a woman who looks so good. But in my experience, it is often the most beautiful who live with the deadliest self-doubt. Each time we meet she is completely devoid of makeup, and her hair, usually blown straight for photos, is wavy and a bit wild. She comments on how lucky she is to be with a man who actually prefers her in her natural state of slight disarray. Keely doesn't appear to think twice about changing in front of me to go swimming, no effort to hide the extra pounds remaining from her pregnancy. I am refreshed by her uncommon self-assurance and find her an unusual breed: a mixture of earth protector, tribal mother, career woman, international jet-setter and brainiac. Like one woman she admires, Barbara Walters (who shares the same birthday), Keely has no qualms about being a trail-blazer. The December 1997 issue of Redbook *magazine featured Keely, Pierce and baby Dylan in a close embrace while Dylan is clearly being breast-fed. A contented Keely looked confidently into the camera. She says that everywhere she goes, including other countries, women thank her for taking a stand for nursing mothers. Some have said that because of the* Redbook *cover, their husbands have been more supportive of them breast-feeding their children. Hundreds of letters were sent to* Redbook, *including many from birthing centers, to express thanks and appreciation for such a conscious cover choice.*

Keely didn't know she'd be on the cover of a magazine nursing her child. During a family photo shoot, which she had arranged beforehand to be scheduled on "baby time," Keely took a break to nurse Dylan. The two-hour shoot was nearly complete, and the last three shots of the day were taken spontaneously during this intimate family moment. The photographer, who is Keely's dear friend, told her that one of those last shots had resulted in the most beautiful picture of the session and asked if it could be used for the inside of the magazine,

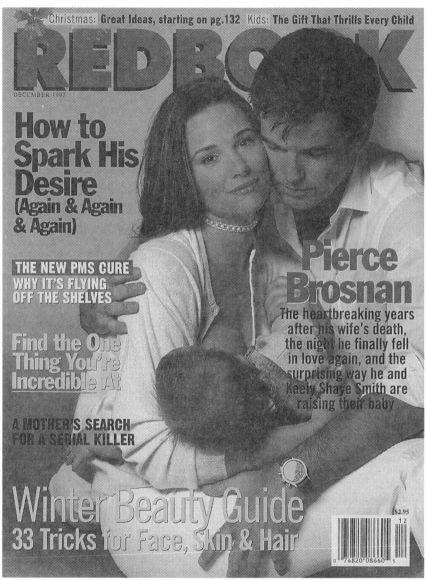

Photo by Greg Gorman, a courtesy of *Redbook Magazine*

saying that the normally conservative Redbook *would surely never use it for the cover. But not too long afterward, Keely was awakened by an early phone call from a girlfriend. "Quick, turn on the TV, you're in the middle of a controversy." Throughout the morning, Keely watched as Katie Couric of the* Today Show *and Barbara Walters of the* View *covered the story. Tabloid shows picked up the scoop and comments ranged from calling the cover "a courageous triumph for nursing mothers," to "not the place to make that statement." Newspapers printed stories about the cover. Even in Rome, where Pierce was working, newspapers carried the "news." Keely laughs, calling the response "a storm in a teacup compared to the world issues presently plaguing humanity," but is honored to represent such a blessed practice. She strongly recommends breast-feeding to any woman who has the opportunity, calling it "one of the most beautiful gifts you can give to your child."*

Keely has always seen herself as a highly motivated career woman and laughs at how fulfilled she is in her new role as a "human jungle gym" to baby Dylan. This is the first time in her life she has been a full-time homemaker and she is in awe of how fulfilling the "hardest job I've ever loved" is. Living with Pierce has given her an instant family (he has three other children, one of whom is still in his teens). She relishes sending Easter baskets to London (to his children) and flowers to his mother. These are the things that mean the most to Keely now. She'll never stop fighting for the environment, or creating her dreams, but her pace is slower now. Keely's rhythm now ticks to a different clock: baby time.

*   *   *   *

Happiness

I am happier now than I've ever been. Happiness to me is to be free of desire, to be at peace and to have harmony. The birth of my child has made me feel complete. I'm deeply, truly happy. I have always been very happy with Pierce, but I don't think either of us knew how much happier we would be with a baby. We are a family now. Pierce's children love Dylan, which is truly wonderful. They bring out a really loving energy in each other. Sean is very tender with him and perhaps he likes the fact that someone is going to grow up and look up to him. Pierce is always saying, "What a great idea, thank you for this beautiful gift. I'm so in love with this baby," which is food for my soul. I feel so blessed.

My work, especially for the environment, the animals and the dolphins, brings me a lot of happiness, too. Occasionally my accountant will say, "Keely, your bank account is . . ." And I say, "Yeah, well there are two kinds of bank accounts and my psychic account is really rich right now so I'm sure the other one will catch up any day." I'm mixing my vocation with my avocation, doing the things I really want to do, and I'm making money. At present, I sit in the garden or at my desk overlooking the ocean and write my book almost every day. It's a wonderfully creative place to work, to write, to dream. I believe that if you do good work, you will be rewarded. That brings true happiness. And it doesn't always come from the source you think it's going to come from. True happiness comes from within.

Family

It's amazing having a child. My heart has opened up in a fashion that I never knew was possible. You think you love your mate. You think there's nothing you could love more. And then along comes your child and you know you'd throw yourself in front of a speeding car to protect him. It's a love like no other, I'm sure it's the deepest, most unconditional love you can have.

As much as we give to our children, we also get so much back from them, their purity and authenticity. There is something about a child's natural state that is incredibly dreamlike. It's as though they're in a club, and as you grow up, you grow out of it. It's as if they have a secret key or window into all that matters. I hope that I remain open to what it is that Dylan has to teach me because I have a feeling those lessons are as much a part of the process as me teaching him about our world. Right after Dylan was born, I said to him, "Will you tell me about God because I've almost forgotten?" God was still fresh in his mind. Having a child is so life-affirming. Dylan definitely defines my life on a time line in terms of my mortality, but motherhood is also wonderfully refreshing because he has revived everything that's important: my sense of awe, my sense of wonder, my sense of humor and beauty.

I believe that two successful people can be in a loving, rewarding union, while maintaining their independence in the outside world.

Pierce and I are two individual energy fields, two circles of energy spinning independently. When we come together, the synergy of our energy makes us stronger. Then we go off and do our work until we come back together again. I think the very element that brought us together is the same quality that keeps us together: We have a tremendous amount of respect for each other. Neither of us is trying to dominate the other and there are no control issues or fear factors.

I'm so proud of Pierce. Wherever we go in the world, he brings such immense joy to people. It's touching to watch. I've seen four-year-old girls shake with excitement near him and a ninety-four-year-old woman drive eight hours across Ireland to stand outside a theater to say hello to him. Pierce takes the time to be there for all of them. He's a really special person and has an unusually eclectic background that's made him tremendously compassionate.

I like the idea of marriage and contrary to what's been written, I'm not opposed to marriage. I just think that sometimes people get married for the wrong reasons. I never wanted to do that. I wanted to make sure that if I did get married, it would be the one and only . . . forever. That's very important to me. Do I want to spend the rest of my life with Pierce? Yes. Does he say he wants to spend the rest of his life with me? Yes. He fulfills my idea of the perfect partner, he nurtures me and my dreams. I love him dearly.

Early Years

When I was eight or nine, my mother and I were folding laundry and I said, "Someday when I grow up, I'm going to be on TV, I'm going to live on the ocean, I'm going to have a lot of animals, and I'm going to be really happy." I just knew.

I was born in California, but shortly afterward, my parents and I moved to Hawaii. Being young and growing up on an island had a big impact on me. Parts of my childhood were incredible. Having mango trees and beautiful groves and grottoes to play in, while breathing clean air and swimming in the ocean every day, was priceless. I don't know how I'd replace it. That's probably why I have such a deep respect and affinity for the environment.

When I was five years old, we moved from Hawaii back to Southern

California and my younger sister was born. We have always been very close. She's quite ethereal and extraordinary. I adore her. I'm thirty-four years old, so imagine growing up in Newport Beach [and later in nearby Huntington Beach] twenty-nine years ago: There were wheat fields, lima bean fields and strawberry fields. There were drive-through dairies and people rode their horses on beaches and in the streets. It was beautiful, earthy, organic, not a yuppie town yet. There was

Keely at three years old.

affluence; people from the film community had second homes there, but all of the industrial parks and skyscrapers are new since my childhood. Recently I saw a new freeway being built through a pristine canyon. I thought, "Where do you go, where do you run, where do you hide?"

As much as I love to have fun, I have always had a very serious side. I used to write children's stories when I was a kid. The first book I ever wrote, *My Side of the Story,* was highly accepted within my academic community. I was nine years old and I guess all of my lessons about black American history deeply affected me because I wrote a story about a little slave girl and the injustice from her own point of view, with a Tracy Chapman-type voice. I put myself in the mind of this young girl who went to a farm to pick cotton in the fields and who worked her way up to the inside of the main house. The story followed her life all the way to being ninety years old and peacefully dying. I illustrated it and the school bound it, laminated it and put it on display.

From the time I was nine years old I knew I wanted to be in television commercials. I used to sit in front of the television and say, "I'm going to do that." Of course I wanted to be a newscaster, too. I'd write stories and perform in school plays. One day a talent scout came to my school. I said, "Mom, let's go. They said I can come to Hollywood, they want me to come!" My father, however, was against it. He said, "No, you're going to have a normal childhood. When you're old enough to decide for yourself you can go, but not now." I bugged my mother for a whole year. They never took me.

Lifework

I moved out of my parents' home when I was seventeen and found a place of my own. I lied about my age and started waiting tables. I used to get one-hundred-dollar bills on my tip tray pretty regularly, which put me through school. One evening I waited on a man who said, "You should be on television."

My goal before I turned thirty was to travel the world so I could experience how different people live, integrating that knowledge, wisdom and experience into my own life. Living in Newport as a child gave me a certain lifestyle. But I didn't want to marry and spend the rest of my life in that town. About a month after I met the man in the restaurant, I rented out my house, gave my car to my sister, and went to New York. I had about three hundred dollars in my pocket and I didn't know anybody.

When I arrived in the city, I went to the Elite modeling agency, but they weren't sure they wanted me. I thought, "Okay, now what? I'm here, I might as well make the rounds." I went to J. Michael Bloom, which was the talent agency for the television division within Elite. I walked in and met two women who handed me some copy to read. I read the copy and they asked, "You've never been on television before? No formal training?" I said no and they basically said, "It doesn't matter, sign here." Within the first ten days, I booked a national commercial, and from then on I booked an average of one national commercial a month. Everything from Coca-Cola to Keri lotion. My mother said, "I should have let you act when you were nine!" My first job was a dream: ten thousand dollars to lay around on the gorgeous beaches of St. Croix to get a tan so that I would look good walking out of a pool for the commercial.

My commercial career was very successful. Often commercials had print campaigns that coincided, so I'd do those as well. That's how I became an Elite model. Suddenly I had a lot of cash. I had enrolled in commercial classes, only to find I could hardly ever attend because I was always booked. I felt a bit guilty because I'd come into the class and people would say, "I had an audition last week," and I had just booked three commercials. It was unbelievable! I did forty national commercials in three years, and all kinds of smaller regional spots. My dream as a

nine-year-old had come true. I was having a
great adventure.

I think I was successful because I didn't
have the androgynous look that was big in
the 1980s. Girls were really tall, thin and flat-
chested, with boyish haircuts. I had longer
hair and a womanly body. I stood out. One
day I woke up and thought, "I'm lying for a
living: I don't drink Coke, I don't eat
Pringles, I don't use Keri, and I don't advocate or recommend using any of these products I'm helping to sell, so what am I doing?
This is terrible!" I had a real spiritual crisis
and decided I couldn't do it any longer.

Photo by Cesare Bonazza

Modeling didn't make me happy, either. It
can be a brutal industry. On some level, I became very uncomfortable
propagating the beauty myth. Women compare themselves to highly
glamorized versions of models and sit at home feeling badly about
themselves because they don't look like that. There are exceptions,
but most models don't look perfect in person. And we haven't even
discussed airbrushing yet! Modeling felt competitive and superficial. It
didn't matter who I was, what I thought or felt, or what I had to contribute. It felt very impersonal, like big business, not like an art. The
truly great models are very artistic: They have great style, great walks,
great looks and they know how to make love to the camera. I started
out late—at twenty-one—and I knew it wasn't something I was going
to grow into, but out of. By the time I was twenty-five I left the industry altogether.

I made the decision to be an actress. I wanted to touch people's
lives, move, and inspire them. I thought I could take all of my experiences and life lessons and bring them out through great characters
and stories. But the only roles I was offered in the early 1980s were
of ornament, fantasy or victim. I decided I needed some good, solid
training and knew I could get that working for a year on a soap opera.
I began to audition for the daytime shows and immediately got a part
on *General Hospital*. I believe that whatever you think you have to
have, you get.

My role, Valerie, on *General Hospital* was in a love triangle with the characters played by Jackie Zeeman and Brad Maule. *General Hospital* had a great group of people to work with, but I'd come home and say, "Is this it? This can't be it! I've got to have more." Soon after, the *Home Show* called my manager and said, "We're featuring *General Hospital* stars all week and we want Keely to come visit our set. We have a segment about cooking in microwaves for her." I said, "I love to cook but I don't believe in microwaves. Let me talk about something I really know about. I'll grow sprouts."

So my first segment was how to grow sprouts in the kitchen. They liked what I did so much that they called me back a few days later and asked me to do another gardening spot. I said, "Sure, how about gardens under glass, little terrariums, or maybe Ten House Plants You Can't Kill." I ended up doing both ideas for them. They called me back the next week and pretty soon I had Post-It notes on my dressing room door at *General Hospital* saying, "*Home Show* wants you on Wednesday. *Home Show* wants you this Friday. . . ." I started juggling the two and *General Hospital* became annoyed because I wasn't able to attend all of my morning blocking. (When you're an actor, the first thing you do at seven in the morning is go through the day's script with the other actors so you know who stands where.) A lot of talented people have come out of soaps, and it's certainly a great discipline for a young actor, but I wasn't excited about the material I was working with. The *Home Show* offered a better atmosphere. It was more creative and interesting to me. I was able to talk about things I knew about. Soon after, *General Hospital* and I came to a mutual agreement that it was time for me to move on.

The timing was miraculous. I was on the stage of the *Home Show,* waiting to present my segment and there was this older man moving a cord and kind of standing behind a camera. I was thinking out loud as I was watching the show live on air and said to him: "You know what they need on this show? They need somebody young. Somebody earthy to talk about plants and flowers and animals and the environment. It is obvious that they're missing a whole audience here." The man looked at me and said, "Oh yeah, what else do they need, kid?" "Well, they need something outdoorsy, organic and fresh," and I started rattling off the fact that gardening is America's number-one outdoor hobby.

It turned out that the man was Woody Fraiser, the executive producer and creator of the *Home Show*. Woody had a long history in television. He had started *Good Morning America, Real People, That's Incredible* and the *Mike Douglas Show* thirty years ago. Had I known all of that and been in a meeting with him, I may have been more subdued, but because I didn't know who he was, my expression was natural. Several months later, he said, "What do you want because I want you to give up being an actress and work for me." I had always wanted to work in television and I thought, "This is television. This is good television, and I'm not endorsing a product that I don't believe in and I don't have to run around in some love triangle." These were the kinds of things that I didn't want to glamorize or portray any longer. I didn't think being a vixen exemplified a healthy role model for women. As an actress, I found that often there were a lot of parallels, where life imitates art and vice versa, even down to characters' names. We've seen it over and over again with various artists. Life does imitate art: You cannot drum up certain emotions in yourself and not experience some of that internally. It affects your psyche.

In 1989, I went to work full-time for the *Home Show*. At first I was covering light and creative topics. Then I started thinking, "Wait, this is powerful." I was driving into work looking at the ABC logo and I thought, "I'm definitely in the right place." As a kid, ABC was my favorite network. I saw these huge satellites, the size of my house and I thought, "I'm going to be a guest in people's homes today. What am I bringing to these people?" I started thinking of the issues that were important to me. I am deeply passionate about a healthy environment—which I consider a basic human right—and about animal advocacy. All of my animals are rescues. I started thinking, "We have this horrible, deep, dirty secret about what we do to animals in the United States and nobody's talking about it." Nearly twenty million dogs and cats are gassed annually in the United States because of pet overpopulation. Their only crime is that nobody wants them. We as a country are not being responsible about our breeding programs. So my first exposé was discussing the issue with innovative politicians who suggested an unprecedented breeding moratorium, which of course sent all of the breeders upside down.

Then I produced a segment about the real life of a circus animal

that expressed my belief that animals don't belong in the circus, traveling for months at a time in cages or chained in cars and trucks that
are not heated in winter or cooled in the summer. Next, I did an
exposé on dog racing, which led to a public outcry against greyhound
racing. We helped thousands of abandoned dogs (ex-racers) find new
homes. I produced a story about factory farming, how animals are
raised for human consumption, which was inspired by the book *Diet
for a New America* by John Robbins. My reporting and producing
gained recognition. Shortly afterward, I started winning awards for my
work, and was honored with two Genesis Awards. I followed kids to
the rainforest, to stress the importance of biodiversity. People would
say, "Why do we need the rainforest?" and I'd say, "Because in addition to it producing about 20 percent of our oxygen, your bananas,
chocolate, coffee, vanilla, orchids, cashew nuts and medicine come
from there," which brought it home on a very basic level. Then I did
a piece that was exceptionally important to me about children's rights
in the classroom. Why should a student be given a failing grade
because he or she has a different philosophy about dissecting animals?
There are other ways to teach using models, books and computers, so
kids don't have to cut a frog or rabbit open for biology class. I
profiled a girl who received a lot of attention over this issue. She
stated that children should be able to choose not to dissect a living
being without being penalized for it. Shortly after that the laws were
changed so that children can use models, computer-generated images,
write alternative reports and use other teaching methods to further
their education.

My new work was all about awareness. I loved finding special
people and profiling their stories. I was carrying a little torch for them.
I would wake up in the mornings and know just what I wanted to do
next. In all the time that I went to Woody to approve my stories, there
was only one he wouldn't let me produce, and I understood why. But
everything else was like, "Okay kid, what's next?" We would have our
pitch meetings in the commissary over breakfast, usually bagels and
coffee, and I'd tell him what I wanted to do, which was really irking
some people at work. They were like, "Who the fuck is this twenty-
four-year-old kid?" And not only that, I accompanied my stories into
the editing room. I didn't get paid for that. But I knew how powerful

crafting these little jewels would be and I wanted to make sure that my work stood up years later. They still stand up when I watch them today. I earned while I learned. That's how I made a name for myself as a journalist.

One of the best stories I produced (which was nominated for an EMA, or Environmental Media Award) profiled a woman named Carla Roberson, who had a chemical spill on her property. No one would help her—not the EPA, the Texas Wildlife Board or government officials who had jurisdiction over her property. She wrote to me and said, "I know your work, please help me. You are my last chance." I believed her because she sent me compelling documentation and photographs. Her horses looked so ill, in a most unusual way, and intuitively I knew something really serious was happening to her. Initially, the *Home Show* didn't want to do the story, so I said, "If it gets out in the press that this woman wrote to us for help and we ignored her, it's going to look really bad." By doing that, I got the story on the air.

We crafted Carla's story like a *60 Minutes* investigative piece. I had never done anything like it before. I went to the oil companies and they didn't want to talk to me. I said, "That's fine, but I'm going to have to go on camera and say that you declined comment." One company finally granted me an interview, the other one, however, did not. We put Carla on tape explaining how her situation was too unnatural, how the spill was poisoning the land, water and horses. She discussed being petrified about her three-year-old child growing up on contaminated land. She showed us her mares who were aborting their foals, and the babies that were born blind and crippled. We also spoke to her community, her neighbors and her family.

Our first story was about her horses. We ended the piece with her swinging her child saying, "I'm petrified for his safety, that he's growing up on contaminated property." Six months later, he was diagnosed with a rare nongenetic terminal cancer and a year later he died. I did everything I could to help her. We found specialists and doctors (like Dr. Michael Klapper). Carla put him on a juicing regime that enabled him to live through all kinds of chemotherapies and other things that most people wouldn't have lived through. Sadly, he died three years ago on Thanksgiving. That was the update or second half to her story.

I'm hoping to help Carla make a movie about it. The point of telling Carla's tragic story is to help her get her message out about protecting children. She wants to prevent this from happening to even one other child and family. No one believed her or would help her. The truth is that if you smell a rat and see a rat, then there's a rat. Nobody was legitimizing her, and she felt like she was going crazy. Carla wasn't an environmentalist. She was a young housewife who became a stronger woman through this incredibly painful situation. It's a beautiful, truly touching story. Selling it at a network has not been easy because they wanted to wait until she won her case. I put her in touch with some of the best scientists and lawyers in the country and eventually Carla wound up winning a huge, multimillion-dollar settlement. Thank God, because at least on some level she was validated and able to move on with her life. I feel that if there was even one reason I was put here on earth, helping her would be enough.

I continued to do these kinds of stories. It didn't matter to me that they weren't very commercial because, in my heart, I was so inspired. I'd go to bed at night and wake up with a dozen new ideas. I knew where to go and just how to get them done. I kept saying, "Okay God, clear the path, clear the path." Woody had told me that he wanted me to give up my acting career and now there was no looking back. I was so much more intrigued and excited than I had ever been while acting and I thought, "I have so much more to contribute to the real world than to the world of make-believe." I was dazzled with people's responses to my stories. And I was bringing accolades and recognition to the *Home Show*, so if I needed any kind of an affirmation, that was it. I was twenty-six years old, and I was producing work that added value to human existence.

In April of 1994, the *Home Show* was taken off the air and I was hired as an entertainment reporter for the *Today Show*. [Keely also did a show for HBO at the same time called *The World Entertainment Report*.] Before taking the job, I said, "If I'm going to do this, then I need to talk about more than just a person's latest movie because that's prepackaged by the studios. I want the people I interview to reveal themselves, to divulge their wish lists and to inspire us. I also want them to explain what they do to help the environment and their community." Everything this book [*Lives Charmed*] does, only I chose the medium of television. They went, "Oh." And I said, "If you want me, that's the package you get." On my first assignment, they sent me to Cabo San Lucus to cover the American Oceans Campaign yearly fund-raiser. "While I'm there," I told them, "I'm going to produce a package called 'Eco Tips from the Stars' for you." They said, "Where's that going to air?" and I said, "On the Entertainment Satellite News Reel for Earth Day." They agreed.

I flew to Mexico, missing the wrap party for the *Home Show*. A job that had changed my life. For me not to be able to go to the wrap party to say good-bye and to immediately have to be in Mexico that same day was fate. Early the next morning, Ted Danson, Lorenzo Lamas, Jason Priestly and I were on a boat. The paparazzi, who thought I was some mystery girl, were chasing us. They didn't know I was just a journalist interviewing them. The boat was rocking wildly and Ted said, "I think I'm going to get sick." The minute he said that, the power of suggestion got the best of me and I did get sick. I felt so ill and I said, "Would you mind waiting fifteen minutes for me while I go to shore, brush my teeth and change my clothes?" I went back to my room, brushed my teeth, put on a clean suit and T-shirt, and ran back out to meet Ted. I walked right by Pierce, who was reading a script. He looked up and followed me with his eyes. He thought I was an actress. I conducted the interview with Ted, and, shortly afterward, I noticed that Pierce was still looking in my direction. I thought, "Maybe he's friends with Ted," but Ted was already gone. Then I thought: "He's looking at me. Now I've got to walk back the same way I came. Okay that's cool, I need to get interviews for my Earth Day special." So I walked up and said, "Hi, my name is Keely, I work for the *Today Show* and I'm producing a piece called 'Eco Tips from the Stars.' Do you do anything to help the environment?" He said, "Well, yeah, I recycle glass, plastic and cans at home." "Great," I said. "Will you tell me that on camera tomorrow?" I wasn't being paid to do the special, so I had to fulfill other obligations first before I could concentrate on filming for Earth Day. For two days, I saw Pierce around the hotel but I was always busy working. On the third day, we talked and he asked me if I was still working. I replied, "I'll be off in an hour." He invited me to join him that night for dinner. We've been together ever since. It was and continues to this day to be so magical and romantic.

Miracle

It's ironic that the job I'm most often recognized for, *Unsolved Mysteries*, was the easiest to do. People ask me how I got that job and all I can say is that I wanted a vehicle to help people. I went to the audition, told them who I was, what I did, and what I wanted to do, and after auditioning, I got the job. People often say, "Why did you choose that show? It isn't environmental." The answer is because it made a difference. Approximately 40 percent of the fugitives profiled on that show were apprehended and about 64 percent of the lost loves and 5 percent of the missing children were found. There were so many stories that made me feel good about that job. It accomplished what I hoped it would, and it affirmed for me that I was in the right place at the right time to be part of an important process. I used to come home from work and want to celebrate, only it would be one o'clock in the morning. There were so many times I wanted to go out and drink champagne and just yell, "YES!"

Some stories made me weep. One of my favorites was a story about a man who was madly in love with a woman thirty years ago. She was pregnant, and they were to be married, but being a young soldier, he was suddenly sent to war. They corresponded and shortly afterward, she sent photographs of his new baby boy. He was so excited to come home to them, but something happened and he wasn't able to return as scheduled. By this time, the woman's frustrated family had moved her to another place and had convinced her that he wasn't ever coming home and forced her to marry another man. She went on with her life, had a new relationship and another child. Then one day he showed up. Her family, protective and upset, told him to stop coming around or they would have him arrested and deported. (He was an immigrant.) So, for thirty years this man ached and wondered where his son was, what he looked like, and where the woman, who was the love of his life, was. He needed closure. He was now married and had children, but he never stopped thinking about his first-born child. Within five minutes of this story airing, all three of them were talking on the phone. The show, as always, paid for their reunion. I drove home that night thinking, "I have the greatest job in the world."

Another evening, we aired a story about a woman who had been in a terrible accident when she was five years old. Her mother's car had stalled on railroad tracks and her two younger sisters and mother were killed instantly by a train. To this day, she has guilt over why she lived and they didn't. Her face was completely disfigured. Her father was so upset that, once she had completed several reconstructive surgeries on her face, he moved them both far away to another state to escape his past. This young woman never knew anything about her past—her mother, sisters, or the maternal side of her family, her grand-mother, aunts, uncles, etc. She contacted us because at thirty-five years old, she had a desperate need to find them. We put her story on the air and within ten minutes we had her maternal grandmother, grand-father and aunt on the phone. That's powerful television, bringing goodness into people's lives. I have been graced by the miracle of good television.

Spirituality

We as human beings live on a planet, a ball that hangs in the sky. And, there is only one in the entire universe that will support life as we know it. I marvel at living on a planet. If that's not a miracle, what is? Every day, when we get caught up in our bills, the traffic or some other small issue that seems like the biggest problem in the world, we need to remember where we are. If we are in awe, we won't be so caught up in the marginal details. I try my best to apply this philoso-phy to my daily life.

My mother is a Buddhist, and I think I was able to adopt some pro-found fundamental Buddhist principles through her practice. Spiritually I tune in to God whenever I need him. I tune in to express my gratitude or my humility. I tune in for guidance, to say thank you, or to share something great. It makes me feel centered, focused and calm. My spiritual beliefs are not something I want regimented. I do not carry with me the limitations of some religious practices. I know God's love is unconditional.

I believe in humility. It's okay to pray. I give thanks and ask for blessings for my family, my friends and the world. I don't know why some people see prayer as a weakness. I see it as a strength. I see humility as a strength. If we see ourselves as a part of something much greater than who we are as individuals, we can achieve a certain level of confidence from that understanding. We don't have to be afraid of dying or anything else because it's all a part of our spiritual journey.

Even when I was young, I felt that God was accessible to me anywhere: in the garden, in the bathtub, in my bed, looking at the moon. God was always a loving energy. I was baptized Catholic and occasionally I go to church with Pierce, who is also Catholic. He enjoys the tradition, and I especially like going with him on holidays such as Christmas and Easter. I find it uplifting for the most part, but I'm always astonished when the service begins with something like, "You sinners. . . ." I'm looking at these tiny tots and I think, "That's not a sinner, that's not a sinner, and I don't even know that I'm a sinner on some level." I feel, and always have, that I'm a spirit having human experiences. I do not confuse the two—that I'm human having spiritual experiences. There will come a time when my spirit will be free from this human package, and I'm going to travel to other places. My concept about spirituality is so personal that it's not easy to describe.

I have an open dialogue with God. I ask for insight and then I am very still so I can hear the answers. It took me a while to learn to meditate, to slow down, to be still. I think meditation can take different forms; there isn't one way to meditate. Just like there isn't one way to eat, sleep or live your life. Gardening is my meditation. Yoga is another form of meditation for me. And, the seashore is one of the places I feel the most connected, focused and in tune. Meditation is all about breath; we have no life without our breath. The ebb and flow of the ocean coming in and going out is a powerful force of nature and is symbolic of breathing to me. Wherever I go, I feel in touch with the intuitive voice inside of myself that says, "Yes, go here," or "No, don't do that." Strangely we're not always taught to trust that voice as we grow up. I've learned over the years to go with the flow. To trust that when I don't get something that I think I want, there's a reason for it.

Passion

The most basic human pleasures to me are good company and gardening. Gardening is one of the most spiritual, meditative, fruitful activities that any of us can do. And if we're really connected to ourselves and our spirituality, we understand that gardening is our connection to this planet. Without tilling the soil of the Earth, we'd have no means for feeding ourselves, clothing ourselves or building our homes. As a society, we miss something as basic as the life-death-life cycle when we simply shop at the grocery store.

I enjoy gardening more when I'm really doing it than when I'm demonstrating it on television. But by doing it on television, an amazing thing happens: People stop me on the street or write to me and tell me that because of my shows they have grown a rose garden, or they began a garden with their children, or they teach horticulture to their students in grade school. Recently a porter in an airport stopped me and said, "I saw your piece on houseplants that remove pollution from the air, and now my sister and I have a house full of plants." I liken my role to that of being a modern-day Johnny Appleseed on television.

I didn't find gardening; it found me. My mother and father are both gifted gardeners and I grew up with lots of beautiful flowers and plants. When I was little, I used to pull the weeds in our garden. My mother is also a talented and artistic florist. She does a good deal of designing with flowers and plants, even though she has an entirely different career at present. Throughout my adult life I have always had my own gardens. They have always brought me tremendous joy. As a teenager I used to garden in my bikini. That was the way I got my tan.

Gardening is a richly rewarding activity that helps to establish our connection and bond to the seasons and to the cycle of life. Eating is a spiritual act to nourish our bodies. By growing your own food with your own two hands, you are assured of its purity and it doesn't get any better than that. You know nothing has been sprayed on it. What I can't grow myself, I buy from local health food stores. My diet is nearly vegetarian, except for small amounts of fish. I'm raising my son on a vegetarian diet, and he is thriving.

The Weekend Gardener, which I'm almost finished writing, is a book I was asked to write by the thousands of fans who watched my work weekly. They wrote to me requesting more information, instructions and so on. I thought, "If they can take the time to write to me, I can take the time to write this book for them." *The Weekend Gardener* features specific activities like creating a butterfly garden, a hummingbird garden or an edible flower garden. If you want an herbal tea garden, or a kitchen garden with organic greens and heirloom produce, it explains how to do it. I'm also working on a children's version of *The Weekend Gardener* to help children appreciate our mother earth. I don't want my son and children in general thinking that food comes from a building. It's no wonder kids don't like to eat vegetables—commercially grown produce cannot compare to the flavor of homegrown produce. I'm a big advocate of organic gardening. Personally, I don't want to eat anything grown with the millions of pounds of pesticides that are sprayed on U.S. crops every year.

Earth

Young people embrace the concept of taking care of our Earth. Recycling, however, is not going to save the planet. We, as a society, are going to have to completely shift our consciousness and stop looking at everything as just a resource, a commodity. We all have a lot of work to do on a wide variety of issues, from clean air and oceans, to the protection of the rainforests and biodiversity. It's not too late. Nature is so optimistic!

The protection of dolphins and whales is my focus at present. Pierce and I are passionate about saving a place called San Ignacio Lagoon in Baja, Mexico. San Ignacio Lagoon is one of the last unspoiled places where gray whales can birth and raise their newborn calves. It's truly unique, as gray whales and calves seek out pangas (little boats) in order to interact with humans and be rubbed by them. This is the only place in the world I know of where gray whales exhibit this sort of friendly behavior. A salt company owned by the Mexican government, ESSA, and Mitsubishi International Corporation have plans to build a huge industrial salt factory at this pristine lagoon. Two other lagoons have already been affected by the construction of one of these industrial salt factories. In essence, their plan is no different than building an oil refinery in the middle of Yellowstone National Park. People who want to get involved with the campaign to save San Ignacio Lagoon should contact Earth Island Institute.

Equally as dangerous is the "The Dolphin Death Act" (The DDA). The DDA was a bill before Congress in 1996 that threatened to repeal portions of the Marine Mammal Protection Act (MMPA) that had been put in place over the last decade to protect dolphins from tuna fishermen. Last year it passed, even though over eighty environmental groups [and the big American tuna companies, who had invested huge sums of money in dolphin-safe practices] fought against it. There are different theories, but for scientifically unknown reasons, yellowfin tuna in the eastern tropical Pacific swim underneath schools of dolphins in the open ocean. Some fishermen, rather than fishing for tuna on the open seas, target dolphins. The DDA sanctions the practice of purposely setting nets on dolphins and allows the chasing, encirclement, injuring, harassment and killing of dolphins while catching tuna. The DDA will very likely change the federal definition of the "dolphin-safe" label on tuna cans, resulting in consumer fraud.

To give you some background, in the 1950s, the United States developed a form of fishing with purse seine nets (when dolphins and other marine life are encircled in the net, the bottom of the net is then drawn up and closed like a purse). It's horrific to watch as fishermen spot dolphins and dispatch speed boats to chase them down for hours until they are too tired to escape. Mothers leave their young and abort their fetuses in the panic and terror of being chased and rounded up. The fishermen corral the dolphins with exploding seal bombs, which are very loud. Dolphins are audible animals and use sonar as their method of moving through their world. The sounds of the overhead choppers, combined with the explosives, make the whole situation warlike and very frightening. Once the dolphins are tired and unable to escape, mile-long nets—a football field deep—are dispatched around the entire pod, which is usually made up of hundreds of dolphins, and the nets are pulled together and hoisted up like a big drawstring pouch. Some dolphins die a terrible death being crushed in the wench. Dolphins are mammals and need to breathe, like we do. If they are not brought up to the surface every five minutes, they drown. When tangled or trapped in nets, their rostrums are broken, and their fins rip and tear. Panicked, they're looking for their babies, they're looking for their mates, and shrieking and squealing as they lose the battle for their lives. Nearly 75 percent of some species of dolphins have been depleted, as over 6 million dolphins have been killed this way.

The dolphin-safe label came about in the late 1980s, because millions of mothers and children found out about the practice of fishing on dolphins to catch tuna and, as a result, boycotted tuna, creating the largest consumer boycott in world history. A man named Sam LaBudde was instrumental in the boycott. In 1989, Sam got on a Panamanian tuna fishing boat in Ensenada, Mexico. He was working undercover as a speed boat driver, but he couldn't shoot video footage that way, so after a month when the cook quit, Sam took over as the chef. The chef is the captain of the galley, so Sam was able to lock up his video camera there. The first mate loved Sam's rolls and coffee in the morning and looked after Sam, but the captain was really suspicious. Once they started fishing, Sam would bring out his video camera and film them killing dolphins. The crew thought he was just some gringo making home movies. He eventually got away with filming the fishermen reeling in thousands of dolphins in the nets. Sometimes they'd kill a hundred dolphins just to get one tuna. If the fishermen had found out what he was doing, he would have been thrown overboard.

No one had ever gotten footage of dolphins dying in tuna nets, and it visually brought home just how heinous the whole practice of setting nets on dolphins is. When the footage aired on the evening network news, Americans were outraged to see dolphins being slaughtered in this manner—sacrificed for the selfish motive of profit. Sam spent three years on the road campaigning, speaking at colleges throughout the United States, going to Washington, D.C. to lobby Congress and traveling to Europe to talk with government leaders, environmentalists and trade officials. It was one thing for Sam to get the amazing footage in the first place, but perhaps even more important was how he went out and told the story to so many different people and made it mean something. We can all point to injustices around us, but it doesn't mean anything until we do something about them. Sam has a saying, "Knowing and not doing is not knowing." Personally I think knowing and not doing something about it is worse.

Millions of Americans said that they didn't want to buy tuna if dolphins were killed in the process, so an embargo was enforced on tuna caught in Mexico, Venezuela and Colombia (portions of their fleets still fish this way). For the first time, "dolphin-unsafe" tuna was not allowed on U.S. supermarket shelves. The United States is a major market because we account for 55 percent of the world market share of tuna consumption. U.S. ships were no longer able to fish dolphin-unsafe. Americans were happy and buying tuna again.

The successor to the Global Agreement on Tariffs and Trade (GATT) is a body called the World Trade Organization (WTO). The WTO is an international "free and fair trade" court that doesn't care about environmental laws or whether or not Americans want to eat only "dolphin-safe" tuna. Their primary agenda is trade for trade's sake. We've heard the Clinton administration say: "Above all, we need free and fair trade." In free trade circles, the U.S. embargo against "dolphin-unsafe" tuna coming from Mexico, Venezuela and Colombia was a real embarrassment for those countries. Especially Mexico, as they kept suing the United States and our "dolphin-safe" laws in GATT trade court in Geneva.

Those nations still killing dolphins would say, "These laws and the U.S. embargoes are unfair." The trade court judges, studying the case in a closed-room session, decided, "You're right, these laws are unfair because free trade is more important than dolphins." These rulings were of no consequence until 1997 when all subsequent GATT (now the WTO) rulings became financially and legally binding. The United States would most likely have been obligated to pay Mexico, Venezuela and Colombia financial reparations unless we allowed their "dolphin-unsafe" tuna to be sold in U.S. supermarkets. The United States had just bailed out the Mexican economy with huge billion-dollar loans, courtesy of the American taxpayers. Then Mexico threatened to sue the Clinton administration and the strong U.S. dolphin protection laws in World Trade Court. As a result, the administration decided to weaken the Marine Mammal Protection Act concerning dolphins and tuna fishing to avoid the embarrassment of paying millions of dollars in reparations to Mexico, whose economy we had just rescued.

"Free trade before the environment" officials in the White House scouted around Washington, D.C. and found five huge environmental groups, who were not connected to the tuna/dolphin issue, to endorse the Dolphin Death Act. When the DDA went before Congress, it was put forth as an internationally binding agreement of cooperation reached by all the tuna fishing nations in the eastern tropical Pacific.

It was really a plan to sacrifice the dolphins on the altar of "free trade." We fought it for three years. Pierce and I helped several environmental groups work toward publicly defeating the DDA. It's been a long haul, and it isn't over yet. It began with producing a one-minute PSA [public service announcement] starring Pierce. We produced it in the middle of the 1995 *GoldenEye* Bond tour in Australia, and it aired on the *Today Show, Entertainment Tonight, Extra,* the Discovery Channel, and several local news programs. It became a powerful message that people responded to. People love dolphins. They symbolize freedom, purity and harmony.

We have also done several fund-raising benefits for the dolphins and have worked closely with Nathan LaBudde at Earth Island Institute. Nathan, Sam and I penned a letter to President Clinton that was sent to a lot of celebrities like Jack Nicholson, Nick Cage, Melanie Griffith, Richard Gere, Robin Williams and Sean Connery. The Hollywood community responded by showing their support for the dolphins by signing that letter. Pierce and I also met with Newt Gingrich and discussed the fact that we didn't want the DDA to pass. This temporarily got the House vote in Congress delayed. We also had Barbara Boxer on our side. Senator Boxer stood alone before the entire U.S. Senate and defiantly stated, "I will not let you weaken our dolphin protection laws, which millions of school children and their mothers fought for." When you see such a person, who just happens to be a political leader, something happens to you both as an animal advocate and as a member of the world's largest leading democracy. In your heart, you begin to believe one person can make a difference. By meeting with Newt Gingrich, the bill was actually delayed long enough for Senator Boxer to defeat it in that session of Congress. However, during the next congressional session, the DDA did pass.

Currently, a study is being done on the three dolphin populations affected by purse-seine fishing to see if this continuing practice on dolphins has any effect on their populations and their recovery rate. Based on these studies, a determination ruling will be made in 1999 to decide whether or not other countries can sell dolphin-unsafe tuna under a weakened dolphin-safe label. The DDA lifts the embargo, so by the end of 1998, Mexico and other countries may be allowed to import tuna caught by killing dolphins. Consumers will go to the supermarket and if tuna cans don't have a label on it, they will know that dolphins were killed. What can consumers do? They can refuse to buy dolphin-unsafe tuna and be aware that it could make a return via inconspicuous sales to hotels, schools and restaurant chains. They can also contact Earth Island Institute in San Francisco for more information.

Those countries fishing on dolphins will be allowed to police themselves, even dividing tuna into separate holds on the boats between those caught killing dolphins, and those caught more humanely. It's a self-regulated industry and the American people are going to be really angry when they learn about this. When the millions of mothers and children, who said that they would not eat tuna caught by killing dolphins, learn of this they will say, "Wait a minute, we don't want dolphins dying in nets to get tuna. We told you this before! Why aren't you listening to us?"

My first experience swimming with a wild dolphin was initiated by a friend of Pierce's named Kim Kindersley. He's a filmmaker who made an amazing film about a wild dolphin named Funghi, who swam into the Ring of Carrey in Ireland about twelve years ago. Some say Funghi lost his mate, some say he just loves contact with people, women especially. Pierce and I were going to Ireland for a vacation after he wrapped his first Bond picture, and I said, "I don't care what we do or where we stay, but the one thing we have to do before we leave Ireland is swim with this dolphin because it's going to be magical for both of us." We got up at 6:30 A.M. and put on our wet suits. It was a glorious clear day, just like those in summer when I was a teenager. The sun rose golden-orange, and the water was flat and still and glassy. It was so beautiful. We chartered a boat without any guarantee that the wild dolphin would show up, although I knew intuitively that he would be there. I packed a basket of Irish soda bread, jam, coffee and tea, and Pierce was laughing at me saying, "What are you carrying all this for?" Of course, later, when he got out of the water and was freezing, we had toast and tea, and he was comfortable and happy.

We churned the water with a paddle and soon the dolphin came leaping out of the water. We dove in and swam with this huge dolphin for about two hours. His display of trust was incredible. In fact, all over the world these animals befriend humans, making contact with strangers who pose a threat. Their fear is obviously overshadowed by their inherent trust. To look at these beings, or tuna for that matter, as just a commodity is insane because they are all part of the entire ecosystem. Forget about rainforests for a second, which generate about 20 percent of our oxygen. Nearly 80 percent of our oxygen comes from the sea, and so too do most of our weather conditions. Unless you don't believe in the theory of evolution, everything at one time came out of the ocean. We will not survive without it. The current decline of coral reefs, fisheries and of the health of our estuaries (nurseries where 80 percent of fish are hatched before they go out into the ocean) is a frightening and urgent warning. Dolphins have been around for thirty to sixty million years. They have a wisdom that we don't, and we may not be sophisticated enough yet to understand what their true role is.

Dolphins aren't a commodity to be used for tuna fishing. In many ways, they are our mirror-image in the sea, and they are one of the only wild animals who value human life. Dolphins have repeatedly rescued people throughout history: fisherman, boaters, swimmers, people who've been lost at sea or who are threatened with shark attacks. It's a mystery why dolphins rescue people. Rescuing someone who is drowning is a hard job. The water is a hostile place to bear your young and to spend your life. I don't think it's an easy, whimsical place to live, so again, they have knowledge we don't. We don't have to kill dolphins to get our tuna.

Influences

Sam and Nathan LaBudde are two of my heroes. Their courage to fight for the environment is staggering. Both Sam and Nathan are unusual because they never pat themselves on the back or seek the spotlight. They talk about the issues without talking about themselves. The PSA we all produced, of dolphins dying in the tuna nets, wound up at the White House in front of members of the Senate and the House. The dolphins you see swimming off the coast of Malibu or Santa Monica wouldn't be out there if it hadn't been for Sam, Nathan, their supporters and the millions of mothers and schoolchildren who wrote letters. You can't kill a significant number of dolphins and expect that species to thrive. Extinction is a strong word, but you never know what can happen in nature. You simply cannot significantly deplete a species because when natural catastrophes occur, the population may not survive. There are tens of thousands of dolphins left, but this is less than 40 percent of their original numbers, which is dangerous from a biological standpoint.

I'm proud of the work that's been done, but in many ways we're back to where we were in the late 1980s. The baby harp seal issue, for example, is almost nowhere in the consciousness of the American people. Other than the fact that Captain Paul Watson goes up to Canada every year and fights for them, few are paying attention to the seals. I don't want to see that happen with dolphins. It could, if the public doesn't know what's happening.

Other organizations I have worked with are The Sea Shepherd (Captain Paul Watson's organization), the NRDC (National Resource Defense Council), Earth Communications Office (ECO), Global Green and the American Oceans Campaign. People like David Brower (at Earth Island Institute), Captain Paul Watson, President Mikhail Gorbachev (who started Green Cross International, which Global Green is an affiliate of) and Jacques Cousteau have all inspired me.

Photo by Barry E. Levine

Pierce Brosnan, Keely and Mikhail Gorbachev, Global Green U.S.A.'s second annual Green Cross Millennium Awards, 17 October 1997, Beverly Hills, California.

Fame

Pierce and I went to Bora Bora [a small island off the coast of Tahiti, which the author James Michener described as the most beautiful island on the face of the Earth] for a vacation after he finished *GoldenEye,* his first Bond film. When we arrived, we found the island in turmoil over a not-yet publicized nuclear testing series about to be done by the French government. We were saddened to see how this insane action would threaten such a sacred place. The French government had provided major military equipment for *GoldenEye* and a big premiere was scheduled to take place in Paris at the end of the year. In light of the nuclear testing being done in the South Pacific, Pierce decided to boycott his own premiere. Despite a last-minute meeting in Paris with the French Minister of Defense and top military representatives, the premiere was cancelled. Many French citizens were against testing the bombs. Ultimately, six bombs (ten times the size of the bomb dropped on Hiroshima, according to experts) were detonated.

Pierce and I participated in an antinuclear press conference for Greenpeace in Washington, D.C. at the beginning of 1996. The positive side of fame is that it can be a tool for effecting change.

Future

I see my future as peaceful, happy and tranquil. I'd like to live on an island, close to the ocean, with a really beautiful garden. I need to live near the sea. I want to live somewhere where I can swim every day, grow my own food and shower with rainwater that I've collected. Somewhere that's far away from freeways, telephone wires, pollution and smog. I'll still want to come back and tap into the energy of great cities like Paris, London, Rome and Venice, to experience people and the artistic communities. That's always great fun. But in my heart I'm a beach kid. I hope to fully experience my life's mission and the roles of lover, companion, friend, mother, child, sister and parent, because at the end of your life what really matters is who you loved, how you loved them and how they loved you.

I've always seen my most valuable work in terms of the animals and my environmental work for children. They are holding in their tiny hands the life that I won't live—the future. We experience the future through children. In essence, Dylan is my future and everything that I do for him benefits others as well. He is always my priority.

I feel that we do ourselves a disservice saying that we're younger than we are, denying the life experience that we've had because there is beauty to be had in each year. We all need to find that part of ourselves that shines and radiates each month and every year of the calendar. A calendar is man-made anyway. It's sad that age isn't respected anymore. Our culture is one of the few that doesn't look up to old age and experience. We think the younger are more beautiful, and although they have their youth and beauty, real beauty comes from inside. No one escapes the aging process. In reality, we're only here for a blink. It's so short and so sweet, and that's why wherever I am, I look for the best. For love. The best things in life really are free.

As a lark, I used to say that I wanted to host *Good Morning, Tahiti* when I left L.A., but after the nuclear testing, that idea is probably out. Tahiti was my place. I've been there seven times and probably lived there six months out of my life. I feel a deep affinity with that physical part of this universe. When I go there, my passion for the area is so intense that it makes me ask, "Was I Tahitian? Did I live here before?" I love the people, their food, their culture, their history, their priorities.

I was in Bora Bora for two of the biggest hurricanes in thirty years. People's homes were blown out to sea and nearly everything they owned was ruined. The next day they were happy, laughing and driving around with their children. Being a journalist, I had to pose the question: "Why?" or even better yet, "How?" And they replied, "Hey, I've got my wife, I've got my kid, I've got

Photo by Casare Bonazza

Keely in Bora Bora.

Photo by Casare Bonazza

Pierce and Keely in Bora Bora.

my dog, I've got everything—I'm happy." How many of us could lose every material thing we own, and I mean everything, and the next day be laughing, smiling and singing? I watched as villagers had a great time helping each other rebuild, knowing that when they were through, their house would be the next group effort. There is a lot to be learned from that, which is why I always wanted to experience other cultures.

My mission is to do the best work I can, to effect positive change, and then, one day I can go find my little place in the sun. I am young and have a lot of creative energy inside that still has to come out. Whenever I get frustrated with the traffic or the smog, all I have to do is remember that I live on a ball that hangs in the sky. What a miracle!

If you fear what's happening to our planet, do something. Action alleviates fear.

KEELY SHAYE SMITH

4

Guru Singh

Photo by Carolyn Hugo

Introduction

G uru Singh's life exemplifies a rare balance of family commitment
and spiritual devotion. His disciplines and universal knowledge are
more intrinsic to the saintly wealth of India than to the bustling
activity of his West Hollywood, California, home. But Guru* and his wife of
twenty-two years, together with their two children, flower in their city locale
like native cactus to the desert sand.

Guru Singh is a spiritual therapist and an enormously popular Kundalini
yoga instructor. Named the "Best Guru in L.A." by Los Angeles magazine,
people joke that his yoga classes, packed for years, are now nearly impossible
to join unless one can levitate for space. His counseling practice, a form of
Sahaj Shabd therapy (an ancient art of healing, or spiritual technology, as
Guru calls it), has been developed over eons to bring people "in union with
ease," the opposite of which is dis-ease. Many regard Guru as a true healer,
although he claims no powers as his own, believing God to be the source of
all blessings. The healing world in which he operates is one of subtle energies
deeply affected by tone, music, rhythm and other sensory stimuli. It is in
magical chambers, surrounded by grounds populated by precious rescued
cats and dogs, that this loving man has been of service for the last twenty-five
years.

Upon entering Guru's secluded establishment, the tranquil energy present
is instantly calming. The peace is essential for him to be able to facilitate in
the transformation of lives; his approach to mental and physical health is so
effective that people come from all over the United States and Europe to work
with him. Frequently referred to by clients as a personal achievement coach,
Guru has a wonderful way of seeing the greatness in every person, and motivating even the doubters to take action. I know because I was one of them. I
went to Guru with what I thought to be a healthy case of skeptical curiosity.
My sister had been raving about his work, and I wanted to see what all the
fuss was about. At the time I was happily ensconced in my life as a dog
walker, so when Guru took one hard look at me and asked why I wasn't a
writer, my defenses surfaced. He seemed to be looking into my very soul with
emphatic scrutiny, and he proceeded to rail me with accusations that I was

[*AUTHOR'S NOTE: The word Guru in this case is used as both a name and a title.]

not only "missing out on my calling," but "hiding behind my dogs in the process." I was not comfortable during our session, but I returned again and again because something inside me felt liberated. It was no surprise to me that when I had the dream of this book, only a few months later, it was in the early morning hours following my first yoga class with him.

Dozens of major celebrities, including several in this book, attribute Guru's work with helping them enhance both their public and private realities. With a profound understanding of what it means to be a well-known personality, Guru is able to assist others dealing with the inherent problems that often accompany success. This is the primary reason Guru lives in Los Angeles. It seems to be where he is most needed.

Guru's chapter is one of the longest of the book, simply because of his vast knowledge. Each time we talk he reveals more, and I accept that I will never have room for all of his insights. Appearances can be so deceiving: It is tempting for some to think that a man who wears all-white clothing, never cuts his hair, and dons a turban would know little of the world in which most of us live. Perhaps that is why Guru is so influential. He has an uncanny understanding of most things. Professional athletes are dumbfounded when Guru passionately talks about the ins-and-outs of their chosen game; musicians relish hearing his firsthand accounts as a rock-and-roll performer (who played with and was a dear friend of Janis Joplin); and parents are comforted, by his example, that family life can be a haven of peace in the chaos of the modern world. Guru's life story is so adventurous that a movie of his shamanic training is in the works; and for anyone who wants further understandings, his own book, Buried Treasure, *is presently being written. Enjoy this man; he is a rare jewel to uncover—one who prefers to glitter inwardly.*

* * * *

Happiness

Happiness for me is extensiveness. A neverending process of accelerating forward. To keep happy, I do countless things—basically monitoring each moment of my life. I ask myself, "Am I accelerating, or resting on my laurels?" Unhappiness comes when I try to filter back through what I've already done, returning to what has previously been achieved.

If the head of an arrow were to decide that it didn't like being in the front position, it would be a blunt arrow. If it began to change its position, the feathers, which are the guidance system of the arrow, would throw it off course. In this physical world, our lives are akin to an arrow propelling forward in time and space. If I want to be in charge of my goals and their outcome, I have to be at the tip of the arrow. Happiness is not a goal, but a condition by which I reach other goals. If I am not happy, I haven't learned how to speak. If I cannot speak, how can I express myself? Happiness is one of the first stages to evolution. A birthright. An absolute prerequisite to living a charmed life.

Unless we are willing to release the ego of its control, we can see as much happiness as we want, but we will never achieve it. Happiness, like love, has to be unconditional. We cannot be happy *because* of something and expect to stay that way. In other words, it cannot come from outside of ourselves because all outside conditions change. Space changes . . . guaranteed. When people think the house and the family will make them happy, they are missing the point. Get happy first. The rest will fall into place.

Early Years

I came here knowing myself consciously. We all do. But there have been diversions in my life in which I strayed from that knowledge. I teach from the standpoint that we are born knowing everything and die knowing nothing. When we arrive into this world, not yet hung up on language, we know everything. We see everything. For the most part, all of our glands and chakras are working. What upsets us and makes us cry is that we're taken away from our mothers and put in a room full of baskets. If you're a boy, chances are a piece of your penis is cut off. These are the things that hurt, and it's through the process of pain that we start looking for ways out of our sensitivity. As we desensitize, we stop knowing who we are because it's only through incredible sensitivity that we can know ourselves. In our retreat, we chase the good job, the perfect relationship and so on. These are sideshows, a dance in front of our eyes we create so we won't have to feel vulnerable again. But in order to get back to knowingness, we have to go back through the monsters.

In my youth, I was sort of caught. I, like innumerable others, found that I never really fit in. I vacillated between trying to fit and being glad I didn't fit. I went through life as a misfit, doing the things that misfits do: mischief, mistakes and other misses. Misfits can't quite hit the mark because the mark has been set up by the flimsy fabric society has woven over the centuries, filled with rules and conditions. Eventually misfits make a little way in the world, or say, "This is not reality," struggling through the rock pile to get back to what they once had. Even though they end up with a lot of bruised knuckles and skinned knees, true happiness is found.

Although I felt out of place as a boy, I thought I was special. I thought everyone was special. I was a curious child and a lone child, even though people were all around me. One of my personal attitudes, even then, was to step out of line. I got in a lot of trouble being a cutup in school, but at the same time, I succeeded with hands tied because I was a straight-A student. I finished schoolwork quickly, eating it up, but there was not enough of it.

My birth name was Gerald Herbert Pond. I grew up in Seattle, which felt like a wonderful hick town to me, even amongst three quarters of a million people. My environment had many softer qualities of small-town existence, and our family life was simple and peaceful. We lived a healthy, middle class, abundant life. My mother was a musician and my father a commercial artist, and Mom didn't have to work until she wanted to. Thankfully, she stayed home with my older sister and me until I was fourteen years old, making our home a place to come into, touch base with, and go out from with love.

I have vivid recollections of waiting for my father to come home from work, watching his car drive up, and running to the door to jump in his arms. The kinesthetic imprint of his cold face with its five-o'clock shadow rubbing against my cheeks will stay with me always. Dad lived to be eighty-four and was active until the last year. We had a lot of fun, the four of us, living an involved life with the Earth. Every weekend in the summer we went camping, on outings or hiked together in the mountains. Dad played sports with me, encouraging me without a great deal of pressure. Knowing how to motivate without pushing is an important balance my parents implemented well.

Mom and Dad celebrated fifty years of marriage before Dad died.

They had a happy life together, with occasional disputes, but no arguments. My sister and I could tell when our parents did not agree on something, but emotional fights didn't happen because they each had outlets that enabled them to work out their psychic debris.

As a family, we ate all our meals together. The food was simple, with a lot of things like wheat bread and fresh vegetables, which I thought was boring because I didn't get the sugar and junk food my friends got. I thank God now that my diet was limited, even though I was too young to realize how fortunate I was. When a body is forming, it is the most crucial time to feed it healthy food.

Even though I didn't like meat, often feeling sick afterward, I was eighteen before I became a full vegetarian. Mom read *Autobiography of a Yogi* by Paramahansa Yogananda when I was a toddler, marking the end of her interest in meat. Her godmother, Edith, a dear friend of hers who helped raise her, had traveled around the world and studied many different cultures. Aunt Edith was influenced by Madame Blavatsky and the early Theosophical Society, which looked at spirituality from a scientific and cosmic perspective. Most theosophists adopted a vegetarian diet. In the 1920s, Edith lived in an area of Los Angeles that was an avant-garde melting pot for the new spiritual ideas; many magicians, including Houdini, made this area their home. Mom was raised and schooled with this unique kind of spiritualist-theosophical-yogic attitude, and naturally that influenced the way she dealt with me.

I still have healthy eating habits. Three meals a day are not enough for me because, though I get hungry, I will not eat too much at a time. I am inclined to have four to five smaller meals a day. It's hard to get up from a lot of food and hit the road running; more meals with less food in them is better for me. I keep my intake at about 3,000 calories a day because I exercise heavily with weights and do yoga, so my metabolism is quick.

Drives

From the age of seven, I wanted to be a rock-and-roll star. My parents started me at five on the piano, at eight on the violin and stand-up bass, and at twelve on the guitar. From there, one instrument followed the other. I felt that one day I would be famous, either from music, which has always been a huge part of my life, or something else. I wanted that because I understood the constructive power of fame. I saw the destructive side, too, but knew I would use it to better the world.

I knew as a child that my future would be prosperous and happy. You cannot have anything unless you *know* you can have it. I knew that I would have a beautiful wife, terrific children and abundance in many ways. It was clear to me, early on, that my purpose was to reach people, teach people and be a part of changing the way things were moving at the time I was put on this planet. Anytime I ever attempted to make a difference, it worked like a charm. The only thing that ever stopped me was my fear of the responsibility that came with that posture. Rising quickly in music, that fear altered my life in an interesting way. With hindsight, I see that sometimes a life course can change as a result of fear in a positive way. Fear does not have to have a negative result, but I am grateful that at this point in my life, I have run out of positive opportunities to use my fears.

The relationship with God has been the driving force of my life. My family and I attended Episcopalian services growing up, which were far more regimented than we would have liked, but I had some profound experiences while attending church. Often I would go into trance, experiencing a tremendous sense of spirit. I liked church because regardless of what people's lives were like outside of the building, they were there to create a sanctity for themselves during those two hours. That much energy focused on a divine purpose used to get me high.

When I was nineteen, I traveled through Europe. My dream since childhood was to visit the cathedrals; I knew that the vast amount of time people have been worshiping in them would make for intense energy experiences. I went to Westminster Abbey, sat down and couldn't move for hours. The feeling was supernatural. Recently, while working on scientifically identifying healing energy with medical doctors in England, I returned to the Abbey and gained more of a perspective of what I had felt years ago. Inside the basilica, it dawned on me that I was surrounded by the remains of famous and powerful individuals buried within the Abbey's walls: Isaac Newton, Winston Churchill, kings and queens, and the like; all made this structure their final physical residence. Suddenly, the whole concept of spirit guidance was illuminated for me. By immersing myself in the spirit of these rooms, I sensed that I was tapping into eons of divine knowledge.

Many people have played a part in my growth, including some who have passed on. Every person is a facet of the infinite, and throughout history, the abundance of wisdom is never lost. I access the subtle nature of these entities to guide me, and at this time in my life, I have some main players in my hierarchy, my *spirit guidance committee,* so to speak. It is those beings I work with at this time. The key to successful living is to be middle management: Get your subconscious to work for you while you go to work for your higher conscious mind. To a devout Christian, Jesus is that; to a Buddhist, Buddha is that. I have a handful of powerful relationships that guide me.

Most of humanity is ignorant to their higher conscious mind, except that they have a vague, often impersonal relationship with an avatar (Jesus, Buddha or someone else). If I have a relationship with somebody, I had better be able to sit on their lap, whisper in their ear and express my feelings. It is not enough for me to have an intellectual sense of a being somewhere off in a distant realm; spirituality must be felt from the heart, like in African-American churches. You want some good music? These people will show you how to sing to God! These congregations enjoy their relationship with the Creator, and more than any other race, they have been least affected by the modern process of desensitization. If you want to see a puny relationship between man and Maker, go to a prudent church where you are intellectually told all about God. I would rather be celebrating the Union.

Obstacles

I am a believer in experience, walking through many lessons that could have been dangerous to me. I've had three near-death experiences in my life, all of them rewarding. I would not trade any of the experiences of my life; they all make up the weave of the fabric. In the 1960s, I used peyote, without any painful experiences. It was really the spiritual experience I was into. This was a time when LSD was still legal. My goal was to expand my limits by breaking down the patterns of the way society had assembled its bricks. Each time was a vision quest.

I was performing with my backup band in San Francisco, playing folk rock. Janis Joplin was one of my closest friends, and we hung out with all the other rising stars of the time. Once an extremely fulfilling life for me, the business end of performing was becoming riddled with problems. People were trying to get more done in shorter periods of time, taking speed and cocaine as a means of producing beyond their normal limits.

An executive at a San Francisco-based production company came to one of my shows and asked me to send him a tape. I did, and within a week he flew me to L.A. to negotiate a contract with the Warner Brothers Reprise label. It wasn't long before I had songs playing on the radio, and was featured on television programs like *American Bandstand* and the *Lloyd Thaxton Show*. All you needed back then was five or six singles to put together an album.

A crisis soon erupted nationwide. Because of lyric content and the consciousness of the time, my first singles were banned in major radio markets. References to "walkin' high" in one of my new songs, by the same name, was being taken literally to be promoting drugs. The radio program directors chose to withdraw this, and other fast-rising singles, from their play lists. Not wanting to lose the money invested in promoting it, the record label was challenged to release and publicize more material and immediately control the damage. Special promotional events were staged to connect with the radio industry.

Radio executives were flown in from around the country to a large country estate in Forest Knolls, Marin County, rented for this last-ditch effort. I felt a little like a hero and a lot like a criminal entering the main room to the waiting eyes. There was more money in the room than I had expected, but then there was a lot to be made as music was taking off for the first time since Elvis. They began introducing me around the room.

A total stranger approached me who was obviously not one of the radio bunch. This man looked more like a clothing designer, dressed in silks, his long, black hair hanging over the dark skin of his cheeks. He congratulated me for having created such an uproar at this very young age, and he handed me what looked like an expensive box of candy. I thanked him, put a piece of candy in my mouth at Janis's insistence, and went about the introductions. Just before they called me to play, not wanting the candy to get in the way, I washed it down with a glass of punch and stepped to the microphone. The songs went over fantastically. At the end of the final song, they showed their appreciation with a huge ovation and the job was done. But I soon felt sick to my stomach, dizzy, and started vomiting. I thought it might be the adrenaline from the show, but within a short period of time I was unconscious and Janis was frantically taking uncertain charge of the situation. They say that I died and was revived, and I know for a fact that I went to the other side several times during the ordeal. I heard and saw sounds and visions more enchanting than I had ever imagined, and I saw Janis standing at the end of this tunnel, not letting me pass. This was long before the time of 911, and the house was extremely remote. It was taking the paramedics forever to get to us, so my friends acted quickly and put me into a bathtub of cold water and party ice from the bar; pinching, slapping and squeezing my body to revive me. When the paramedics arrived later, the episode was finally under control, and I ended up in the hospital for a few days.

At first, when I regained consciousness, I was in a complete fog for days because I had lost a lot of mind/body connection. My thinking process was foreign, and my thoughts did not string together like they had before. I wouldn't say that I was scared, but more curious as to how this could have happened. Janis told me later that she had been joking when she told me to eat the candy, which turned out to be opium. We were crazy kids and I just did it.

At the start of the party, I had thought my life was under control. When I faced my death under that controlled system, I said to myself, "If I could see death and be *that* unprepared, then perhaps before I do anything else, I better prepare." From then on, I was determined to discover what my life was about. Whatever happened back at the party, my path changed forever. I told my management that I was going away for a couple of weeks and took what I thought would be a short break from this lifestyle. An adventure.

Healing

I planned to drive to New Mexico, get some land, and relax. I was traveling north of Albuquerque, on the highway, when I ran into a town called Placitas: an incredible place with geodesic dome structures all over it. Among the outstanding people I met there was a Native American Indian man. We became good friends and spoke in-depth about our visions of a healthy life. I revealed my interest in out-of-body work, explaining that I wanted to gain knowledge without the use of any substances, and he told me about a Yaqui Indian shaman, out in the Senora Desert of Mexico, who would be able to assist me in my quest. The beauty of this man, he said, was that he used no herbs or drugs in his teachings. All attainment was done with an intense enchantment and entrancement, combined with deep levels of work.

The shaman's name was Pablo Ramon Diego Dias. I was determined to find him. I was told he did not like being a teacher and would be reluctant, but I would not be deterred. Two days later, a buddy and I jumped into a Volkswagen van and drove to Mexico. Our directions were hilarious: We had to find a colored gate, measure x number of miles, and follow many dirt roads. Eventually we wound up at a village of roughly three hundred people, and sat outside for two weeks waiting for Pablo to relent to instruct us. I think he kept hoping we would go away.

Pablo was a magician—a sorcerer—from a long lineage of magic men, and he possessed outstanding abilities. In six hundred years, Pablo's tribe had never used any herbs, making them masters of the physical realm. No one claimed any powers as their own, as they knew all originated from a Universal Source, but as individuals they were comforted that nothing needed to be ingested to access those powers. This created a strong people who never looked outside of themselves for answers.

Despite what is currently shown in children's videos, a sorcerer is not evil at all. Sorcerer is a word, like many ancient words, that lost its meaning through the modern process of representation. A sorcerer is a seer of the source. In Christianity, they claim the only true seer is the prophet. All others who profess to see are condemned: they've been burned, hanged, tortured, poisoned and shot. The word *witch* originally meant wise woman; the word *wizard* meant wise man. What amazes me is that Jesus himself said, "You will do far greater things than I," so how can we be fearful when others perform miracles? Every true teacher must claim that the student, or the fruit, is greater than the tree. Jesus knew that people who followed his ways would have the same results. That was the whole point of teaching his message. When followers deny the greatness that can be, identifying only with the greatness that was, they limit their own future growth.

For eighteen months I studied with Pablo, every word in Spanish. Even to this day, when I teach class, words come through in Spanish and I have to catch myself. I have experienced so much magic in my life as a result of the lessons Pablo and I shared together. We did sweat lodges and fasts. At night, he took me on walks where my ears were muffled with a headband and I walked barefoot in rhythm to the beat of my own heart, straight through the night. We did blind walks where I couldn't see a thing. The severest process we went through was to be buried in the ground. As barbaric as it sounds, it was done in a special and sacred way. Digging our own graves, that were just big enough for us to fit into, we lay down in them. Although my friend went through this procedure as well, we always went through it alone. Once in the ground, Pablo covered me in such a way that I could breathe, but not move an inch. I won't get into it exactly because I would never want anyone to try this. Pablo knew what he was doing, but it is extremely dangerous.

Lying in this hole, sealed in such a way that I had air, but was in total darkness, I had no ability to move or hear the outside world. All I could feel was the vibration of Mother Earth and her rhythms. I started out in this space for thirty minutes, then an hour, two hours and so on, until I worked up to over half a day. Sometimes I was down there so long, I peed in my pants. The level of intensity was such that it could be done for that length only once a month. Once per full moon. Not being able to see, hear, or move, I would go crazy—hysterically screaming and crying—begging to be let out. After the first couple of hours, I actually never knew if I would ever be released. It was terrifying. My fears escalated to their absolute maximum volume. I went more frantic than ever before, reaching the extent of my ability to be berserk. Every time I went down, I experienced the same thing. At a certain point in the experience, it would all snap, moving clear through my rage to an incredible peace. By realizing that I could not challenge the universe, it suddenly dawned on me there was nothing to be angry about. That was the point where

I began to move through all of my issues in virtual time without time.

Through this procedure, I reached the end of my ego, thinking that it was so powerful. I went from thinking that I was going to emerge breaking the world in half, to just letting go. I simply quit. Suddenly, I was sitting next to my teacher. I mentioned a few things to him, and he spoke back to me. I leaned my arm on his shoulder, and it went right through his body. My body was still in the ground, but there was such a manifestation of my consciousness that my spirit was set free. I heard myself say, "Let's dig me up now." And he did. Obviously, to get to that state, I had to let go completely.

When we move out of our bodies in meditation, into the space that is connecting our soul with the universe, mystery and mastery appear. If we dwell in that space, we must stay grounded. There are plenty of nuts walking around with their heads in the clouds, which is so often a by-product of New-Age thinking. That is why I owned a factory (making brass beds) for twenty-five years, in addition to my healing practice, to teach me to maintain my capacity for these magical realms while keeping my head in the world of the world. We live on such an absurd planet, that business has brought me down many times, but eventually I became comfortable in my center.

One day, while working with Pablo, I had a vision that Janis [Joplin] died of an overdose. I was so foolishly proud of this ability at the time. The image haunted me, so I told Pablo that I would go warn her. He told me not to. "There will be no power in your words for almost thirty years," he said. This sounded absurd to me, so I went anyway, but he was right. When I told Janis, who by this time was becoming a star, she laughed and essentially told me that I had gone mad. When she died, in the same way in which I almost did [when she saved my life], and in the same way I had seen in my vision, she and I had lost touch with each other, even though she died only blocks from where I lived at the time.

Going to Pablo, enduring these difficult lessons, was something I did for one reason only: to get beyond the absurdity of all that I had lived through. I was born into a great family, but the ludicrousness of this world was unbearable to me. I saw that humanity lives under a blanket of its entire emotional system and enslaves itself therein. When we touch our fears, we react. When we touch our anger, jealousy or envy, we react. Even when we touch our joy, we react. Humans live in cages of their own making and every bar is a different emotion. I wanted out of this prison because I knew I was trapped. Like so many others, I had experienced brief moments of life outside of the cage, and I knew there was a realm in which I could live beyond the ridiculousness. Soon my life experiences with Pablo became so potent that the psychedelic influence seemed silly. Through my new awareness, my goal was to maintain this level of clarity in the outside world.

After completing my work with Pablo, I made my home in Los Angeles. I had lost touch with everybody. I had fallen off of the face of the earth. Almost instantly, I met Yogi Bhajan, a spiritual master, who introduced me to the Sikh way of life and Kundalini yoga. I found that by engaging in these yogic practices, which I instantly felt at home with, I could sustain the Spirit I had worked so hard to develop with Pablo.

Influences

The word *Sikh* means student. In India, the word for teacher is *guru*, so I consider myself both a student and a teacher. The Sikhs were born out of hypocrisy, just like the Christian and Jewish religions before them. Abraham, with Moses really crystallizing his idea, was the first of the Hebrews to say that there was one Almighty God. By the time Jesus came along, the Jewish people were losing their power—they had been dealt a terrible blow in Egypt and were being overrun by the Romans. As you know, Jesus was condemned for teaching his message. The psychological lesson we all get from this is that anyone who starts to teach truth is going to run into some heavy opposition. Truth tends to change the people it touches and new knowledge is often contrary to accepted views.

Five hundred years ago in India, a similar circumstance was happening with the Hindus and the Muslims. Out of the hypocrisy of the time came a man called Nanak who, like Jesus, had a message. He said, "There is no Muslim, there is no Hindu, there is only human . . . mankind." He taught that it does not matter what religious path or creative force is taken to the one God. Whether it is acknowledged or not, we are all energized by the one Universal Force. We can go through our whole life saying it does not exist, spitting on it or yelling at it, but nevertheless, it is what is giving us breath. The key is, if we relate to this one God, we get more joy out of the energy we breathe. That is the beauty of being a devoted person.

Following Nanak, a succession of nine men continued the teachings. In the 1700s, during the time of the tenth guru in the lineage, the Sikhs compiled their scriptures because the gurus wanted to stay away from people worshiping them, which in their mind would constitute a cult. They decided to stop the external show of having a leader and create a scripture of guidance for people of the religion to turn to. This same concept must have been in the making of the Bible, the Koran and the Torah. Gathered together was knowledge from Muslims, Hindus, Sikhs and other holy spiritual leaders, which was important because what spiritual leaders reveal is always very elevating.

The Sikh religion, like any other religion, has devoted followers, and not so devoted ones. As in all religions, there are members who behave differently from what the scriptures advise. The interesting thing in my life was that nothing needed to change that much. I was already wearing white consistently, as it has a powerful vibration being the combination of all colors. I had never shaved in my life, so letting my hair grow was easy. I didn't drink or smoke either; the life change was minimal. In church, it was normal for me to go flying like a kite with energy, so the visions that came as a result of my disciplines were natural. Wearing a turban was the only new practice. Turbans were considered to be royal in Nanak's day, and only royalty wore them. It was important to him that Sikhs wear them because he felt that all people were kings and queens in their own right. There are technical reasons to wear them as well: We let our hair grow, tying it up above the tenth gate, or crown chakra, where it helps to focus energy, much like an antenna. The yogis of ancient time knew to do this as they, like Samson in the Bible (and the Native American Indians), believed there is tremendous strength in hair.

The physical benefit of wearing a turban is that it locks the cranial bones and pulls the skin of the scalp, much like a good massage will do, helping to focus the energy at the crown. Unlike a massage, however, its effect is all day long. This is why the Native Americans wear the headband. In the time of Moses, the yarmulke was a full turban. There was a time when the Jewish people never cut their hair. This technology has been known for thousands of years; Sikhs just have an ability to package ancient wisdom.

Family

My wife is a wonderfully devoted person. Our meeting was one of the most blessed encounters of my life. I was twenty-nine years old and single. One day I was looking through a Sikh magazine and saw a picture of a 200-year-old painting of a Sikh woman in India. Instantly I got a sense that this was what my wife was to look like, so I cut out the photo, put it in a frame, and hung it on the wall of my apartment. Every time I looked at it, I got the same feeling: my wife would resemble this image.

A year and a half later, with the photo still on my wall, I attended a yoga gathering for the winter solstice in Florida. Walking around, I saw a woman in the exact posture and dress as the one in my picture. I could tell, even from a distance, that she had sparkling eyes. I stood there and stared at her for awhile.

About thirty minutes later, I got a message that some people wanted to see me in a nearby cabin. When I got there, Yogi Bhajan said, "Guru Singh, how old are you now?" I told him I was thirty and he said, "That's too old to be a bachelor, isn't it?" and the group started laughing, as if they had been discussing my love life before I got there. The next question was, "Well, haven't you seen or met anyone lately?"

About two weeks later, it dawned on me what had happened. I called up Yogi Bhajan and said, "When you asked me about marriage, I had just seen somebody, but I didn't think of it then because it was all so new." He asked who, and when I told him that I had found out her name was Gurperkarma from Toronto, he told me to give her a call, like it was no problem.

I called up to Toronto and she answered the phone. I said I was calling for her boss, which was actually true. The next time I called, I flat-out told her, "By the way, I've talked to Yogi Bhajan about the possibility of us marrying." We had never said anything more than hello to each other before this moment, so it was pretty wild. She said, "Well, what did he say?" I told her that he was in agreement, and she just sort of said, "Ah, okay." Interestingly enough, we found out later that in Florida when we had sat near each other a few times, both of our hearts had beaten very rapidly.

I had business in New York a few weeks after our phone conversation, so I flew up to Toronto to see her. It was so natural being around each other that we just figured we were supposed to be together. From there, we flew north to meet her parents, and that was it. We were married three months later. She stayed in Toronto until the wedding, and one day before we were married, I flew her to a concert I was doing in Detroit. We hadn't so much as kissed, but we had held hands and hugged. The night before we married, we had one kiss.

There has never been a time that I haven't been committed to our marriage. Both of us have been from the start. Commitment is the key to overriding any of the underlying emotions that can disrupt relationships. You can feel all sorts of things, but as long as the commiment is there, nothing will change. That is what a marriage is all about. I have performed a lot of wedding ceremonies, and "for better or worse" is said because marriage is great in the beginning, but it always gets worse. It gets better, too, and worse again. The North Star (that sailors use to guide them through the storms) of marriage is commitment. It enables you to ride through all of the storms.

Guru and his wife, Gurperkarma Kar.

Miracles

When I think of the charmed events of my life, I remember an abundance of spirit in each moment, where the presence of divinity was unmistakable. Not every minute of driving our car, or conversing with friends, for example, has that thickness. When I first saw my wife, and during the birth of our children, the rooms were filled with spirit. Many times, too, in working with clients, doing meditations and training in shamanism, that essence has been there.

Two of the three death experiences I've had were filled with that thickness. In hindsight, all three were attempts for me to bail out of my destiny. I already knew what I was supposed to be doing. Like I said before, I understood from a young age that I was meant to reach many people and help lift their awareness in the process. For me to die before I was fully engaged in that course of action was a cop-out. Each time I have gone through the infamous tunnel and seen the white light ahead, I have received the powerful question, "Okay, what are you doing here?" It was clear that it was not my time to die, even though I wanted out of the responsibility of my life. Everybody creates every experience they have, whether it's to achieve or avoid their ability to respond. I was clearly choosing avoidance.

I had a remarkable blessing surrounding my last near-death experience. I was twenty-eight, and as a member of a musical group called "The Khalsa String Band," we were scheduled to play all over India for a four-month tour. Before we left Beverly Hills, I had been given a cholera vaccination for the trip and came down with a full-blown case of cholera. The disease is morbid, causing a high temperature for long periods of time until a person's brain cells are destroyed under the heat. Dehydration causes the body to eliminate its fluids, and my body began to dry up. I traveled to India while still extremely ill because my teacher, Yogi Bhajan, felt that I should go. He later told me he believed I might die and thought it would have been better to do so in India than in Los Angeles. By the time our plane landed, I was in and out of coma states.

An Indian homeopathic doctor in a local hospital brought me a glass of the dirtiest water I had ever seen. He instructed me to drink it with a couple of little white tablets. I did as he said, every drop, and the next morning I was well. I later found him on the streets of Amritsar and asked him how my healing took place. He told me that there was nothing in the tablets but milk and sugar (the blank tablets of homeopathic remedies), and that my psyche would not have accepted a miracle healing without the belief that it came from the pills. The reality of what had happened, he told me, was that the dirty water had made me healthy.

Photo by Guru Kaur/Amritvela

Guru in front of the Golden Temple, Amritsar, India.

The water I had ingested was from the foot-washing tank of the Golden Temple. This temple, also in the town of Amritsar, is visited daily by ten thousand people who walk through a tank of water on their way inside to pray. This sacred structure, built in the middle of a big lake, is surrounded by marble and is designed to work with the four earth elements: A golden top represents the masculine sun energy, a marble base represents the femininity of the moon, all sitting in the element of water with an eternal flame, the fire element, surrounded by earth and sky. The result is a magical place people have flocked to for hundreds of years in order to be healed. There is so much the West can learn from the immense ancient knowledge of the East. The scientific reason the water heals is that, as humans, we have approximately seventy-two thousand nerves in the bottom of our feet and whenever we intend to do something—walking to our goal— those intentions and aspirations register in our nerves. Anyone who goes into this temple transmits their intent to heal right into the water. Knowing this, the doctor took the water directly from the tank. It was muddy, but it saved my life. That's the miracle of reality.

Several weeks later, Yogi Bhajan asked me how I felt. I told him I was still weak from losing thirty pounds. Cholera ravages the body. He looked at me and said, "There is a hairline difference between being sick and being Sikh; draw the line and step on the side you want to be." Truth can be blunt. Sometimes it has to be.

Fame

Originally, I started the practices of yoga and meditation as a way to re-create my consciousness on a daily basis. Breathing deeply into the diaphragm, as is required in yoga, literally says to the subconsciousness, "I'm awake." No matter what is done until that time, the subconscious believed you were sleeping. For people who use a lot of deep breathing in order to exert themselves physically (like athletes and singers), the breath will bring up things that people in other areas of work may never have to deal with. By waking up the subconscious, life is accelerated to a greater extent than most people experience.

Because of this extended state, people who do a lot of deep breathing also face more of their fears: Whatever blocks remain in the system come to the forefront to be burst through. The more the breath is used, the more the subconscious is cleansed, bringing the obstructions to the surface. It is as if the subconscious says, "If you want to accelerate your life, we don't just accelerate the good stuff, you have to deal with the whole ball of wax." This can be a difficult road, and people often attempt to deaden the effects with drugs. Rock stars are notorious for drug use, in part because they accelerate to such a fanatic degree on stage that the slow pace of life offstage, in comparison, is just too much to handle. In reference to the arrow I spoke of earlier: If you get off the tip of the arrow and slow yourself down, the energy billows up around you, and you have to deal with your sludge.

For a musician to keep up the acceleration once they get off stage (or an athlete once the game is over) takes action—spiritual discipline—that furthers the forward momentum. Then follows the knowledge that they are not responsible for their success; things happen in magical moments that cannot be attributed to anything that has been taught. A person becomes a master at what they are doing.

When people attain fame, they step into a courageous way of life because of the amount of energy they will have to deal with. In order for someone to accelerate their life in such a way as to be well known, most experiences are heightened, positive and negative. Unless the work of clearing inner demons is accomplished, problems will arise in some way. Many celebrities have to deal with public humiliation, in the form of tabloids, scandals or something else, and for those who don't create an outer manifestation of their inner turmoil, the ridicule comes from the inside. Look at the trauma so many famous people admit to. The ones who manifest it on the outside have the greatest fear. When our fears are not dealt with, they manifest outside through our influence, resulting in public problems.

The powers right now of the media are clear; there are more opportunities than ever for being discredited. People have to be able to accelerate through those discredits without dwelling on them. Those sitting focusing on them will be left way behind. If someone is attracting public humiliation, it is because of an internal causation. If they want out of it, they have to get *it* out of themselves. For someone who does not have a healthy self-image, getting admiration from millions of people can be a devastating inner torture. The bigger the audience, the more intense the experience. If you open your sail in a gale-force wind, by using drugs to recapture the high, the result is a life that speeds out of control. It's a never-ending cycle.

Fear

If I have any fear, I would say it has always been aloneness: that my path would be so advanced I would be all alone. I have been reconstructing that by the realization that if I don't fulfill my destiny now, I will have to do it sometime. Everybody does. We all have to achieve and accelerate to our absolute epitome, otherwise our life is a waste. That holds true for any profession or role we have in life. In doing so, fear will surface, because with acceleration there is always wind in our face. We must use the resistance as energy, staying away from playing the role of victim. A sailor learns that if he has to get to his destination while there is wind in his face, he must tack. It is possible to use the wind to propel us forward, even though it's blowing against us.

Lao-tzu said a profound thing: "The tallest tree catches the most wind." A little tree hiding in the forest gets no wind, but also misses out on the sunlight and the view. In being the tallest tree with the most sunlight, we grow the fastest. Isn't that what it's all about—growth? The problem for most people is that growth is not easy. Once the average person accelerates and experiences the abundance of obstacles that come with acceleration, that person is deterred from going toward his or her own personal greatness. You cannot get through the blocks unless you are ready to get through. When you are, the obstacles are just energy. I have learned many things the hard way; sometimes the easy way doesn't get it done. When we take short-cuts, we move away from that which we have to move through. We must get beyond those things that tend to keep us outside ourselves, otherwise we continue reincarnating over and over.

In order to get out of any trap, we have to be able to go in and change the roots. Imagine going down to the base of a cherry tree and attaching apple roots to it. With time and focus, this is the effect of healing work on the human condition. We can all surpass our pain. It's just a matter of doing it. Yoga and meditation are the best tools I know of.

Discipline

I meditate every day. I figure that if I want to make a law in a country, I had better be able to sit on the desk of the ruler. I get up every morning before dawn, from 3:00 to 5:00 A.M., to meditate, do yoga and set my intentions. After thirty years, it's a natural part of my everyday life. The yogis call this time the *ambrosial hours* because it's when the atmosphere is most cleansed of vibrations. The sun's infrared rays precede the white rays of the visual spectrum by two and a half hours; these long rays sweep across the atmosphere of the planet before the sun comes up, erasing all of the erratic debris and thought waves from the previous day's hustling and bustling activity. Once the day gets going, it's easy to feel the bombardment of thoughts from a variety of places, especially in the cities. This is why so many creative people work late at night or early in the morning. It's much easier to access creativity when the majority of people's thought waves are asleep.

Meditation allows me to center myself. As a society, we are out of our center. This stems from the consumer condition that has been sweeping the planet for the last two hundred years—since mass production created the need for mass consumption. If we as a populace were in our center, we wouldn't need to consume. If we didn't consume, who would support the industries? The whole economy is trying to shift, and we're pumping life into a dying body. Even so, we are gradually making the transformation from a consumer-oriented system to one that is more reality-based. People are feeling the desire to produce the right foods, feed the whole planet, and get ourselves healthy in the process. We need to get beyond the need for constant titillation and entertainment; we must educate ourselves. The more I meditate, the more I see the bigger picture and my place in it.

Meditation allows me to understand what I already know. It enables me to be conscious of the fact that we all know everything. All universal wisdom is encoded in our beings; there is nothing we cannot access. That is why it is said that humanity was created in the image of God, who has all knowledge. Everyone is created equal, but what we understand, and how well our lives flow, comes from our hard work. The computer has all of the data, but the operator has to know how to access the information. In this case, the computer is the internal DNA, and the operator is the conscious mind. Because I want mastery while operating my computer, I make a lot of time for my spiritual disciplines.

Photo by Nick Fleming

Yoga pose.

Do I have all the time I want? I am working on that because that's what it takes to be able to accomplish my dreams. As time transmits from the center point of the universe, and we attach our intentions to time, space is created. All of this spacious world around us is a by-product of time. This is why people like Anthony Robbins advise us to write down our future now, because what we envision today will happen ten years down the road. The rooms we are presently in manifested from visions that we transmitted in moments past. Moments in time are momentum and momentous, rippling out in multidimensional space.

Everyone needs to have a routine that centers them on a daily basis. This brings more time. To think there is not enough time to meditate, exercise or engage in some activity that centers and calms, is backward thinking. By taking the time for our higher natures, everything else gets done in less time. The right people, circumstances and conditions come into our life. Our days become easier and more charmed.

Earth

The civilization of man is one big family; men and women are in the same boat. Often men want to think our boats are separate and keep women out, but because women are paddling just as hard, it's only going to help us all get where we're going faster. The strongest people are gentle. They understand that strength is both constructive and destructive; in its constructive state, actions are harmonious. That which takes eons to construct can be destroyed in a moment. Men need to use their destructive force sparingly. We have much to learn from the nurturing ways of women.

Men have constructed a fake world in order to wall and cage women out. We know that if women enter our world of male-oriented business, it's all over: What we've been doing for the last few centuries would be exposed as ridiculous, and the competition of the male world would give way to compatibility. This is why the Japanese have been so powerful in business: They work with compatibility rather than competition. By enabling one another to gain ground in the bigger marketplace, they all make their fortunes. This is a woman's way.

According to the ancient yogis, humanity is now in the form of the fifth root race (the fifth time humans have evolved to this extent on the planet). Cave people were initially like us, but went underground to protect themselves from the previous annihilations. Living without light, they had no use for the frontal lobe, hence, the Neanderthal look. There have been all kinds of untold disasters on this planet, including nuclear wars. Mother Earth has been around five billion years. Scientists will come to the conclusion that humankind has been around for more than a million years, just this time around. But a million years is only one-thousandth of a billion. The yogis, who have viewed it, say that the cycle (in one way or another) will happen two more times. And this is one planet in an infinite universe. So when you think about what life really is, you see why happiness is only the first step. Living a charmed life is a necessity.

The yogis can see the past because they go out of body and read it in the Earth's history. Each moment is still happening; they see, hear, feel or sense them all. In doing so, they know where we are from a perspective of what has gone before us. Obviously, you have to work a long time to get to that capability. Being able to see that vast a horizon is a rare and potent experience most people would never want to have. Many people cannot see beyond their own lives.

The Earth has greater power than we do. We won't destroy her, but we will destroy ourselves if that is what we choose to do. The challenge is being stated clearly. The need for change will only get stronger because we are in the early stages of this awareness. The profiteering that has been rendered across the planet is making the change difficult. Those who are benefiting from the destruction of the rain forests, the oil extraction systems and the like are having a difficult time accepting the fact that they've got to alter their ways. They are trying to disprove the statistics, but enough will happen in the next fifteen years to give the ecologically minded peoples of the planet tremendous power. It will be done in a way in which a mother would do it because the Earth is our mother. This doesn't mean people won't lose their lives as the Earth changes, but it means that it will all take place with a particular message in mind. Lost lives are never lost, they recycle over and over.

Souls have no problem with dying and going through life again; egos do. Understanding that not everyone on this planet is of the same evolutionary status is a relief because we don't have to persuade all of humanity to accept the bigger reality. Only the appropriate people have to see that the larger picture is the way to go. The rest will follow like happy children. This is why so many people feel a compelling urge to educate, and it is working. Many people now are gladly changing. Look at how certain brands of batteries have pictures of tiny green trees on them. The companies who make these batteries are trying to convince us that disposing of them is not going to be harmful to the environment. They didn't have to do that seven years ago, but they are now driven to because of the shift in consciousness of consumers. We are only in the first few years of this consumer awareness. Imagine in five or ten more years what products are going to have to do.

The consciousness of this planet is going to be so accelerated that people are going to be clear on what they will and won't accept from the destruction of our mother. It's similar to a child or a teen feeling that he can abuse his mom, but when he gets to be twenty-eight or thirty, he may think to himself, "Well, Mom wasn't right on, but she wasn't *that* bad either." As each of us becomes older and wiser, the movement of consciousness becomes older and wiser. All people will eventually know what it feels like to be at the tip of the arrow, leading charmed lives. Thank God.

A leap of faith is a fall from grace,
according to those who would
keep you in place.

GURU SINGH

5

Beatrice Wood

Photo by Marlene Wallace

Introduction

A few months before this book went to print, I awoke to the L.A. Times front-page news that Beatrice Wood had passed away. She was 105, after all, and this day had been looming on the horizon for the many who loved Beatrice [or Beato, as she was fondly called]. Her age didn't make the headline easy to accept, but I was consoled by the fact that Beato had lived such a full and creative life. Beatrice was a rare and wonderful example of someone who walked her talk. Her honesty, self-discipline, creative success and outstanding wit were all powerful models of a vibrant soul. She had attained and maintained many of the goals generally aspired for in life. Her vision was global while her hands remained in the substance of Mother Earth—clay. In the award-winning documentary of Beatrice Wood entitled The Mama of Dada, it is said, "If Beatrice were Japanese and we were Japanese, she would automatically be acclaimed a living national treasure." Governor Pete Wilson must have agreed with that when he named her a "California Living Treasure," in 1994. The same year the Smithsonian Institution granted her its "Esteemed American Artist" award.

Although Beatrice was quite famous in the contemporary art scene as a world-class ceramicist and draftsman, publicity was something she rarely sought. People, driven by their fascination with this woman, found her. The movie director, James Cameron, was delighted to find Beatrice in his search for a centenarian model of an elderly woman for his movie, Titanic. James was so taken with Beatrice that he patterned the lead character, Rose, after her. The opening of the movie finds Rose at a potting wheel. [Gloria Stuart was nominated for an Oscar for the role.] Beatrice and the elderly Rose were so alike, in fact, that while my husband and I watched the movie, unaware of the purposeful resemblances, we couldn't get over how much Rose reminded us of Beato, even down to her bare feet.

Years before I met Beatrice, my family and I lived briefly in Ojai, California, where she resided. I heard time and again of a little woman (she stood just under five feet tall) who lived nearby in the surrounding hills. She was rumored to have special powers, although what those qualities were was not clear. No one I spoke with had even met

Beatrice, but it was accepted that she was uncommonly gifted in her artistic and spiritual abilities, extraordinary in many ways. Her training in art and the ways of spirit were from a bygone era, and people were forever drawn to her perceived "secrets" of life and longevity. Some called her a living goddess; others said she was a witch—a good witch—a woman who could conjure magic in a world of the ordinary.

Spending time and corresponding with Beatrice greatly expanded my consciousness of the word "elder." Her talents and outlook were ever-expanding, as if the longevity and exposure to life she had been given had magically united her consciousness with eternal wisdom. Most noticeable, however, was her flair for having a good time: When Beato spoke, she frequently teased relentlessly, laughing openly with glee. Upon telling her that I would need photographs from her life, she exclaimed, "Show me what you write. If I like it, you can have any that you wish. If I do not, I will give you pictures of another woman." One afternoon she warned my husband, "If you ever cheat on this woman, I will personally find you, cut you up in little pieces and bury you under the mustard plants." Witnessing this elfin woman threaten and revel in a deep belly laugh, Mark knew he was in the presence of mischievousness at its best.

Beatrice had no fear of any man and knew there was little time left in her incarnation, therefore her expressions were candid and sometimes delightfully shocking. More than a few people have been taken aback by her straightforward remarks like, "celibacy is exhausting" (a quote from Marlene Wallace's beautiful photographic book of Beatrice at 100). The uninhibited twinkle in her deep blue eyes appeared to have a life all its own. When Beato and I started this interview, she was 102. Over the years, after I left California, Beatrice wrote humorous letters to me in her own script with follow-up information. She seemed to love the process of going back in time. She told me that the questions she was asked for this book were the most enjoyable she had ever been asked. I could never have expected such a blessing; just being able to talk with her intimately was an honor I will forever treasure. On that first meeting, I was invited to visit with the then only living remaining friend from Beato's young life, Rosalind Rajagopal, who was in her nineties. Rosalind was someone I had read about and admired as well—the woman who had captured the lifelong romantic love of the famous spiritual teacher Krishnamurti. To say that I was filled with reverence by the company of these beautiful women—role models unequaled in my experience—is a definitive understatement.

Included in this introduction is more detailed background information than in the other chapters. So much has been filmed and written about Beatrice that, out of respect, I refrained from asking her to rehash too many known details. I knew all along that her moments were precious. I highly recommend Beatrice's autobiography, I Shock Myself, *from Chronicle Books, or the aforementioned documentary for further insights into her unique life story.*

Beatrice Wood was born in 1893 to a well-to-do family in New York City. The atmosphere of her childhood was one of tradition: She was expected to behave properly, *which Beatrice deplored. At eighteen, she informed her mother that she was going to run away and become an actress. Threatening suicide at the thought (not an uncommon occurrence), her mother reluctantly escorted Beatrice to Paris, where she studied acting at the Comedie Française. While in Paris, Beato found immense pleasure in spying through a fence at the great painter Monet (an old man at that time), as he worked on canvases in his garden. With a growing passion to create her own art, Beato attended drawing classes at the Julien Academy, where her renowned career as a draftsman began.*

During Beatrice's stay in France, World War I broke out, and although she found the sound of cannons exciting, the young American rebel was forced to return to America. Back in New York, Beato performed in over sixty plays with the French Repertory Company, and traveled briefly with a vaudevillian tour. The turn of the twentieth century brought the avant-garde, Dadaist movement into existence, and people were looking to the new century to redefine for them what art was all about. With the conclusion of the first world war, a considerable number of people wanted nothing to do with the past, or bourgeoisie notions of what was right or wrong. Beatrice says of that time: "Modern art was an expression of revolt against the first time that masses of people were killed by airplanes in war." She found herself drawn to new forms of expression, especially modern art, because of the way it opposed long-held traditions.

In 1916, at twenty-three, Beatrice met and became inseparable from Marcel Duchamp, the most famous modern artist of the day. Marcel adored Beatrice's ability to sketch and paint, as well as her humorous way of viewing life, and introduced her to the Arensbergs, who owned the first large modern art collection in America. Included in their home were works by Picasso, Matisse, Rousseau and Miro, and as Beato's interest in modern art grew, a lifelong friendship was born. Eloquently portrayed in The Mama of Dada *were the many social evenings at the Arensbergs, where some of the most influential people of the art and theater world—writers, poets, dancers, painters and actors—gathered for long and playful discussions. Freudian psychology was becoming popular and conversations were said to be eyeopening and enriching. During games of chess or twenty questions, psychoanalysis and dream interpretation philosophies were discussed. The group was described as "a band of cultural renegades that were trying to redefine art—a major overthrow of tradition." Beatrice found what she had always missed in the overprotective and sheltered grasp of her family. And her own art was influenced by the notion that creativity should have no restraints from the surrounding society.*

When Beatrice turned thirty, she was introduced to the Theosophical Society—an organization dedicated to world religions and occult sciences. The Russian founder, Madam Blavatsky, spent years training with masters in the Himalayas of India and worked diligently to transmit their wisdom from East to West. Beatrice became a member of this spiritual group and was to form a friendship with Krishnamurti, the most celebrated member. Later, when Beatrice made her home in Ojai, California, she was to be present at Krishnamurti's renowned camps and helped much with the Happy Valley School that he and her close friend, Rosalind [the woman at Beatrice's studio on the day we started this interview], founded there in the 1950s.

It was not until the age of forty that Beato's passion for pottery blossomed. In a fruitless attempt to find a teapot to match a set of ceramic plates she owned, Beatrice decided to make one herself. Suddenly, it seemed that all of her artistic endeavors throughout her life had been the preparation for this craft, and she soon became known as one with supreme ability. Garth Clark, an art and ceramic historian, says: "By 1950 Beatrice was beginning to create extraordinary luster surfaces. In fact, the works were so unique that there is no real comparison that can be made within the ceramic tradition. In aesthetic terms, the work resembles most closely the exquisite glass antiquities of Egypt, with their lustrous patina (the result of centuries of being buried)." Mr. Clark explains that Beatrice is famous for her reduction glazes. In the process of firing her pieces, oxygen is sucked out of the kiln, driving the metallic salts into a beautiful iridescent glaze. "There have been relatively few masters of this through the history of time," explains Clark. "Beatrice is basically an alchemist: she takes mud and turns it into golden vessels that could grace the table of a maharaja."

Training with the Dadaists gave Beatrice courage to allow imperfection, even though there have been times when her work has hit the mainstream in such stores as Bullocks, Neiman-Marcus and Gumps. Nowadays, a small fortune is needed to purchase her creations. Even before her death, Beato's chalices and vessels sold for as much as forty thousand dollars apiece.

How is it that Beatrice was over a century old and still able to create fantastic works of art, write several books, and be happier than she had ever been in her life? Research into health and longevity mentions repeatedly certain elements of living that, if followed, may sustain people through long and vibrant lives. Beato's life exemplified more of those traits than anyone of whom I am aware. For example, her work was extremely fulfilling, and many believe that in her nineties, she created the most adventurous works of her life. Some think that Beato's strict vegetarian diet of seventy-plus years was responsible for her energetic nature, while others regarded her equally long daily discipline of meditation as the most significant factor. Maybe it was the rolling hills of majestic beauty Beatrice woke up to each day that brought her vitality. Seldom have I seen more stunning and secluded landscapes than those surrounding Beatrice's home for nearly half a century, where the stress of city life seemed like a concept out of a science-fiction novel. Perhaps it was the combination of these factors that retarded so many of the normal effects of aging from entering this woman's life. Whatever the reasons, there were no signs of apathy present, just a wonderful little lady with the heart and imagination of a fairy godmother, who happened to indulge in the use of occasional brash words and lascivious fantasies.

*   *   *   *

Happiness

I am happier now than at any time in my life. I feel very free and have a lot of fun. When young men enter the door to my studio, I have a ball pretending and flirting, which gives me a great sense of freedom, even though it is just hot air. Also, I love to eat chocolate every day. Doing so gives me immense joy. Though true happiness, I believe, comes when the mind is quiet and free of desire.

Early Years

I wrote in my autobiography that, as a child, I always thought my life would be difficult. Life was hard emotionally because I did not agree with my mother. We were really enemies, although we made peace just before she died in my forties. My mother never understood my longing to be artistically free. Instead, she wanted me to marry a stockbroker and live a conventional life. She forced me to make a social debut—to be a debutante, of all things. I refused to talk that evening and ran away from the line and locked the door to my room. My mother came up to the door and said, "You come back to that line." I was in tears. She couldn't force me to be a successful debutante; I was the biggest flop in all of New York City. I was in great revolt against the conventionality of how I was raised.

Not being much of a social person, I always preferred reading and being with animals to talking. I read a great deal when I was young, teaching me that there was another way of life than the one my family led. Even now I am not a social being. I get uncomfortable in the spotlight. For my ninetieth birthday party, my dealer—who I could shoot—had me carried on a canopy into the party by four men, as Lily Tomlin hosted the affair. For my one-hundredth birthday party, there was a band and sixty or seventy people. I had to put on an act of being in the limelight. I have to do certain things for my profession, but I'm not interested in fame, nor am I too aware of my well-known status. I don't think it has much meaning for me. I am happy to be known in the art world, but with publicity I become kind of a *red-hot mama* . . . which really I am not.

I was exposed to art at an early age. During my childhood summer vacations, my family often went to Europe, where I was dragged by my governesses through museums. My brother, too, went to these museums, but he had no interest in art. Fortunately for me, my life went into creative directions. I think people are born with different gifts, but most children are interested in drawing. My interest grew as I did.

Many forms of artistic expression interested me in my youth. I used to do quite a good deal of dancing. I was fortunate enough to meet Anna Pavlova and work with her choreographer, Ivan Clustine, who taught me Russian dances. My mother thought that dancers were even lower than actors, which of course is what I wanted to be, but I enjoyed dancing so much. I especially loved doing the tango. Such passion.

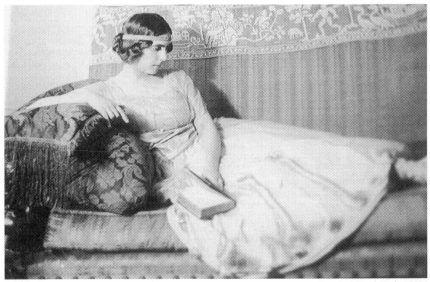

Beatrice Wood Studio, 1995

Beatrice in New York City apartment, 1917.

I lived in New York City just after World War I. The City was very different then. There were horse-drawn carriages. A chariot used to drive by every afternoon, also drawn by horses. The streets were clean, and it was much smaller than it is today, but it was still not entirely safe, even then. So many European artists and writers came to New York. It was an exciting place to live. There were the Walter Arensbergs, with their collections of modern art, who entertained continually with open houses. I was a dear friend of theirs, so I met many of the great artists of the day. Their influence brought much culture to my life. In the beginning I did not get modern art; in fact, I disliked it. I couldn't understand what these lovely people could see in it, but I came to understand it. I love all art now, from primitive to modern.

Discipline

I never thought about pottery before my thirties. I am not a craftsman naturally, so I took classes at the University of Southern California as an adult. I was the worst student in college, but I worked and worked and became a potter accidentally. Many people have talent, but if they don't work hard, nothing is going to happen. Each one of us has the ability to create a charmed life. I began looking at things in museums and getting art magazines to learn by. My sense of form and color slowly developed. I have since made museums that other students in the class, who were much more talented than I, have not made.

For most people who have achieved anything, I think you will find it's due, yes, to talent, but mainly to hard work and organization. In the end, hard work is everything. Not all people want to work for it, but everybody has talent. This is something I witnessed when I used to teach pottery at the Happy Valley School here in Ojai. A great teacher releases talent. When I taught, just for two years, I knew nothing about teaching. I brought art books to the school, and I'd show the children an illustration and ask, "What do you think about it?" If they were not interested, I'd say, "No. You can hate it, you can love it, but you have to express." I got all of the children to express. I thought they did very well. I was surprised and so were some other people. I say, why don't we use our computers to see that round children are in round holes and not square holes? We pay no attention to the fact that we all have different talents. My real talent, I think, is an interest in the world.

Creativity

Photo by Marlene Wallace

Beatrice in her studio, 1993.

If you're sensitive, you can feel the difference between handmade things and those made with machines. There is a vibration in things that are made with the hands. One of my teachers, a great potter, showed me two similar pots. She said, "You see which one is better?" I said, "No." I was a beginner. Now I would know which one is better. The eyes get exposed with experience. Just as an interviewer would know which interview is preferable, or which writing.

In life, you have to love what you do, otherwise your creations have no life. There is nothing more exciting to me than opening a glaze kiln. I generally wake up early to peek (as it cooks all night), even though I cannot really see in. I am madly curious to see what is coming out. I don't think that the rarest of jewels for a woman can touch the joy and excitement of opening a kiln.

The only vocation I would like better than what I do is to be president, so that I could change the world.

Vision

If I were president, I would let all men have vasectomies. Honestly, the first thing I would do is go at right education because it is crazy that we are paying millions to athletes and actors and not to teachers. We are closing so many libraries, and this is doing something to understanding and education. With right education, I would have conferences, inviting all of the most intelligent people, supposedly, of the world and see where it goes from there.

Second, as president, I would never allow people to peek into other people's private lives. I think it is an insanity because few people are virtuous. Very few. If they are, it is generally from a lack of temptation. For instance, a person's sexual life is private. It is crazy that in politics we bring this up. I don't understand it. Perhaps I am jaded where virtues are concerned, because in my experience, men were often unfaithful to me.

Drives

I have always been driven first by love, and then by artistic expression. Never by money. I don't think of my work in terms of money and fortunately do not have to worry now, the last four or five years, since I've gotten a good dealer. I'm not interested in money. When I finally left home, I only took fifteen dollars with me. I fear, however, that I was born romantic and that love has been my major motivator. I went to private all-girls schools where the absence of boys was a fact of life. I think separating boys from girls causes kids to become more sex-conscious.

I was raised on fairytales and was so innocent and romantic growing up. My naive notions had to be crushed, ultimately, but it's still a beautiful dream to be swept up on a horse, only to live happily ever after.

My ceramic figures always deal with unfaithful men. I do think that

Beatrice Wood Studio, 1995

"He Couldn't Wait" (1986), hand-painted etching.

men can be faithful to a great degree, but often temptation becomes overwhelming. When I create these unfaithful figures, I'm just facing the world the way it is, unfortunately.

The best thing about being my age is that you can pretend to break up the marriages of all your girlfriends and everybody knows it's hot air. I've actually been very good. Honesty is vital. But where love is concerned, man plays ball. With my friends, I have been correct

Photo by Jack Case, Beatrice Wood Studio, 1995

Work entitled "Point of no Return."

never to flirt in a bad way with their husbands. One day, after eight years of wonderful friendship, Walter Arensberg was driving me to my hotel and put his arms around me. He wanted to have intimate relations. I struggled out of his embrace and told him that having an affair with my best friend's husband was out of the question. He never said another word to me about it.

I've said that I have lived an upside-down experience: never making love to the men I married and not marrying the men I loved. I was married two times. The first, in my early twenties, was to a friend. We were married strictly to get my mother to leave me alone. There was no love in our relationship; in fact, we never consummated it. My second marriage, to a man I was living with, came from a desire to be honest to the Red Cross. We had just lost our home and my studio to a flood and knew the Red Cross would not give us a grant to rebuild while we were *living in sin*. So, rather than lie to the organization, we married—in name only, once again. It's a good thing I never had children, with such a crazy love life. Interestingly, I allowed both men to talk me into the marriages. I think my biggest lesson in this life has been that I haven't been hard-boiled enough. I should have been more direct by saying, "No!"

My parents had an unhappy marriage, and I am sure their relationship affected my attitudes toward men. If I could change anything about my life, I would have liked to have had a happy and monogamous marriage. I have said that opening a kiln is one of life's greatest pleasures, but if I had the choice, I would prefer love, the man, rather than the art. It is fun to be a woman because we have been given the cunning to ensnare men, and if we use it properly, we can have a very good time in life. I have not lived what I preach, as most of my life in the romantic arena has been a sordid mistake.

When I heard that my friend Rosalind was getting a divorce, around 1962, I started to wonder what a correct life was. My stubborn romantic fantasies about marriage in general were crumbling fast. I had been careful throughout the years to behave and was now free from my second marriage. For the moment, Rosalind's divorce altered my way of viewing relationships. I said to myself, "No use, no use." I was on my way to India and was open to a new way of viewing things. Two men attracted me, and one man I fell very much in love with. But he was Indian, with a strict background, and our love could not go on. I was in love with him for four or five years until I accepted that it was impossible. Love has always been so important to me. Why? Because I'm just a crazy bitch. But don't write that because you'll have me arrested.

I still think about love; age makes no difference in the matters of the heart. I think I could fall in love as quickly now as when I was thirty, except that I don't want to any longer. I am not willing to put up with so much anymore. I don't know if this is age or intelligence. Also, I know that I'm going to float off soon, and I just don't want to let myself become involved. But I haven't been tempted, except by my doctor. Oh goodness, there was another man. . . . A Japanese designer was here three days ago. The most beautiful Japanese man I've ever seen. I even forgot about my doctor. Oh my God. So you see, I am just as promiscuous as any man. Both men are just darling—wonderful human beings. It is not the handsomeness of any man, but their essence I find most attractive.

I don't think most women dress to interest men anymore, and that's a great mistake. When I went to India, I was impressed by the beauty and ease of the clothing worn by the women. From that trip to this day (over thirty years), I have worn nothing but saris. I got rid of every other kind of clothing I had, making up my mind that if people didn't like to look at me, they didn't have to invite me anywhere. Despite the way the world is going, encouraged by television, I like women to be women and dress and wear their hair so I don't have to take a breath thinking, "Oh, are they men or women?" Sometimes people come here to my studio, and it's hard to tell the difference.

Spirituality

Long ago when I lost everything to the flood, I learned something valuable about myself. I felt so free without my possessions. Everything but a row of flowers from the yard was washed away. At times, when I have freed myself from gentlemen's infidelity, I have felt that free. When I touch moments of stillness, I feel free. I meditate every day for twenty-five minutes: I have done it for years, even before I met Krishnamurti. I don't know if it helps still my mind, but I believe it is a wise thing to do, so I do it. I don't think it has added to my longevity, though, because other people meditate and don't necessarily live so long. We don't know what makes for my long life.

Do I feel protected? That's a difficult answer. I feel we are all protected and that there is such a thing as karma. But when we make mistakes, I don't think God is there to say, "All right dearie, I love you. . . . Your mistake is gone." I don't believe in that. I think we learn through our mistakes and grow through hardships. If everything were easy, there would be no expanding of desire.

Am I detached yet? Damn no. Certainly not. I'd be on a cloud if I were, but I think about it and would like to be detached. My friendship with Krishnamurti helped me to glimpse detachment in some areas. He said some tremendously profound things and had a great impact on me. From what I understood from Krishnamurti one day, it is important to drop the negative things, whatever they are. Because of being hurt in the past, I am jealous when I am in love; but where my art is concerned, I am rarely jealous. However, I was once envious of a glaze that I saw. I talked about it with Krishnamurti and he helped me by saying: "Jealousy exists. Do not try *not* to be jealous because you will give false energy to it. Drop it. If you are jealous, drop it and go on to some other dimension of thinking." This has helped me a great deal, whether it was concerning fear, greed, jealousy or something else. Not that I always live at that level, but it has helped.

We cannot measure the senses; there is no such thing as keeping love, fear or greed in a box. Thought is everywhere, so it's best to let go of negative things.

Earth

I am very literate myself because I have read every book that has ever been printed. Like I said earlier, I am wildly interested in ideas. But I am not sure it is the right thing because you see people in our cities who are literate, who watch television and know what is going on all over the world, but are not better people for it. When I traveled in India, for instance, the people in the villages (who had no schooling or money) were smiling and were happy. How can a man be happy who gets up at 6:00 A.M., works at something he doesn't enjoy for eight hours, and then comes home to watch television or read a book? I just don't know. And yet, right knowledge is wonderful.

I would like to see all people gain more knowledge in one area: in learning about each other. I keep telling people that because we have Olympics, we should have Olympics of ethnic and tribal dances from around the world. People would come in their beautiful costumes, and friendships would be made. It is in friendship that we are going to have peace. When you touch, you don't shoot. I think it's a wonderful idea. I am very concerned over the nuclear situation: The Middle East does not like the West, and they are going toward nuclear technology. This is serious.

I have another idea. A heavy one. What would happen if we sent thirty thousand beautiful young women to the terrorists in other countries, to behave horizontally with the men? I think it would have a great impact on their ways. I say this because when I was in Japan doing a pottery exhibition, I said to the attorney to the armed forces of America, "The Japanese are so friendly to me, but we were just enemies in the war. I don't understand it." He looked at me and said, "Thirty thousand of our men have married Japanese women, and endless thousands have slept with them." Now, this is life. We pretend it doesn't happen, but it is on this level that practically everything takes place. Healing comes in union. I think it would make a wonderful difference, but it is a progressive idea we would never look at.

I have met men of all different cultures. I have flirted with them, had friendships with them, never thinking what their race was. In the Middle East, Korea, India, things are done so differently. When I fell in love with the man in India, he was also in love with me, but with his background, culture and family, he could not take it. I understood that. But if thirty thousand American girls had been sleeping with his friends, he would have gone on with me. You see, our society is hypocritical. I don't say it is right, I have no idea what is right or wrong, except for me. I want to be honest. I want to be compassionate and concerned about other people, but the way the world is going toward economic success and money, before human concerns, calls for drastic measures.

It is absolutely true that if you have a relationship with a man, and it's good, then it is going to soften him on the bang-bang [gun] thing. I think women are stronger than men. If women didn't exist, men would spend all of their time kicking balls and punching each other. But because men seem to have most of the outer control in this world, and our planet is strangely becoming one domain on account of computers and television, why not face it? In other words, I want to be the World Madam. That's what it sounds like, doesn't it? A 104-year-old madam. Actually, for years and years, I have lived a life of a nun. But I see things.

When I was 102, I was put in the hospital for pneumonia. It looked as if it was my time to go, but I recuperated, which was unexpected for a woman of my years. It was wonderful to leave there: The architectural angles of the buildings were unfriendly and the people were impersonal. I figure that a good and tender nurse may be more important than a doctor.

Even after being in the hospital, I don't feel too old. I look so much older than I feel. When I look in the mirror I think, "Oh my God, who is that old witch?" I am vain, but probably I would say I am not too vain. In vain, I prefer to look nice when visitors come. My time, I feel, is almost here. I'm older than thirty-two, a little bit. If I were to live to be 120, I'd have to have my face lifted and I don't want to bother.

In heaven, I'm going to be married to five wonderful men: Gorbachev, Prince Albert, Bill Moyers, Charlie Chaplin and Trader Joe.

BEATRICE WOOD

6

Robert Townsend

Courtesy of Townsend Entertainment Corporation, Inc.

Introduction

I *first met Robert at the Hollywood YMCA, where he is something of a regular fixture. For some reason, this old building in an undesirable part of town is a virtual mecca for successful actors: in this informal setting they can experience some sense of what it feels like to be "one of the guys." Unlike the expensive fitness clubs in town, there is an aura of normalcy about the club that attracts the more down-to-earth celebrity, the kind who prefers to sweat rather than be seen.*

Because of my involvement in the entertainment industry through my business, as well as being married to an actor, I discovered the movie community to be like a small fraternity. Gossip in Los Angeles is as plentiful as smog, and in the ten years I lived in the city, Robert and I had several friends in common—some of whom had plenty to say about him. Rather than the usual celebrity bashing, however, all accounts were exceptionally favorable. Never did I hear anything but affectionate words for this gifted man. I used to think he sounded too kind to be in Hollywood.

Robert is one of the nicest people with whom I have ever been acquainted, and one of the most talented. I had been entertained by his work as a comedian and filmmaker for years, but nothing could prepare me for speaking with him one on one. Robert's impersonations were dead-on imitations of the originals—in one five-minute conversation he perfectly impersonated Humphrey Bogart, Jimmy Stewart, Ed Sullivan, Muhammad Ali and Bill Cosby. The way he mimicked any voice I requested, in exact tone and pitch, made it clear to me that creative limitations are not part of his consciousness. Robert has been deeply influenced by both white and black performers throughout his life and has the wonderful gift of bridging the gaps—gently and humorously—between races.

Once touted as the "new Eddie Murphy," this actor, writer, director and producer lives a quiet life with his wife and two daughters, keeping a comfortable distance from the Hollywood social scene. People who have known him since childhood say that he has not been changed by the wealth and recognition he enjoys. His humble beginnings and constant focus on God help ground him in an environment that threatens even the most genuine soul.

Robert's talents are so varied that it is difficult for him to focus on what projects to choose. Four years ago, while taking a respite from writing his first dramatic screenplay, Robert met with his agents and said, "This work is so serious, I've got to do something funny after this." He told them about an idea for a series, based on things that happen around his home with the kids, and soon afterward found himself pitching it to the network. Without hesitation, Warner Brothers said: "It's on the air, thirteen shows. Do it right away." With barely a moment to regroup, the enthusiasm of the network necessitated his immediate shift into artistic overdrive. The award-winning series, Parent Hood, *is in its fourth season, and continues to offer moralistic and inspirational family entertainment. Robert also has a deep love of working behind the scenes, and finished directing his sixth movie last year, entitled* B.A.P.S. *(Black American Princesses) for New Line Cinema, a comedy starring Halle Berry and Martin Landau.*

Robert has learned over the years not to allow his work to become an obsession—a common by-product in an industry forever focusing on the bottom line. He knows that if he lets his work consume him, he will lose part of who he is: a devoted husband and father. Robert has chosen to make sound and even sacred choices so that his family, friends and those who work with him are not cast aside in the all-consuming struggle to get to the top. Robert has experienced a great measure of success, and although he will not allow his creativity to consume all of his time or energy, the enthusiasm he reserves for his career is bounteous. The world of creativity is his to play in, and when it sends him scurrying in different directions, Robert resembles a child running through his first candy store.

With a commitment of his whole creative being to any project he undertakes, Robert prefers to wear all of the creative hats at once, allowing many outlets for his genius. He has a firm belief in his artistic pursuits and would rather accept less than commercial success in something he sincerely loves than to participate in anything about which he is not completely impassioned. Thoughts of failure don't seem to bother him much; his high aspirations and experience in making lemonade from lemons enable him to live in a state of gratitude for all the goodness in his life. Whether Robert's films earn him two thumbs up or down, he is busy taking grateful pleasure in his joyously charmed days filled with fun, family and spirituality.

*   *   *   *

Happiness

Happiness is freedom. Freedom to be able to work, not to work, play, or be silly, stupid or dramatic. I guess this describes me both onstage and off. I have a certain kind of freedom with my wife and kids that allows for madness to happen. We have a great life. To me, home is the happiest place to be. Our joy together as a family carries over from work to life. My work, too, is total happiness. I love what I do. In terms of fame, money and success, I've never been afraid to soar as an artist—to just let my mind go.

Happiness is something I've always had naturally. I don't really think about it; life is just good. Even when obstacles are in my way, I can never stay depressed. If something negative is dumped on me, I get it off and keep moving. I feel like I have guardian angels around me; my life has always been charmed and it's only getting better.

Early Years

When I think of my childhood, I see that I lived in a fantasy world. My mother raised four kids on her own (I have an older sister and a younger brother and sister) in a little Chicago-ghetto apartment. My father wasn't around from the beginning, but came in and out of my life later on. When I was little, during the crucial years, Mom took care of us by herself.

Robert as a child with his older sister, Beverly.

I was kept in the house most of the time because there were gangs outside trying to recruit me. We had a small black-and-white television, and that is where the world of entertainment and I bonded. I could watch anything on TV and do the characters and voices afterward. My nickname was "TV Guide" because kids would ask me what was on television the previous night and I'd answer in the different character voices. I watched everything from *I Love Lucy*, *The Andy Griffith Show* and *My Favorite Martian*, to *Father Knows Best*. You name it, I watched it. Everyone else would be playing together, and I'd be in the bathroom mirror practicing imitations. I had no idea it would lead to anything, or even that I had talent. I thought everybody could imitate what they heard.

When I watched TV, suddenly I would be Errol Flynn. It wasn't a conscious effort at all. [With a thick English accent] "I will fight for England for the rest of my life." If what I saw was in French, I'd do everything they did [proceeds to speak in fluent French verses]. I'd watch *Oliver Twist* and do everybody's part [Robert switches to a boyish cockney accent]. I watched a lot of PBS and was especially fascinated when they aired Shakespeare. I had no idea what the characters were saying: "There hither is our brother." They'd be talking this stuff, and within five minutes I would have all the dialects down. Mom would be in the other room, hearing these weird sounds through the door, and think I was crazy.

I remember in high school, we had to read *King Lear*. Reading was tough for me because I saw things in images. I went to the library and came home with classical albums of the Royal Shakespeare Company performing *King Lear*. Listening to them on our cheap little stereo was so funny because we were in the ghetto. Such a dichotomy. Instead of reading the book as my teacher had instructed, I sensed what it was about from the records. Later in class, our teacher had us read scenes in front of each other. Imagine, an inner-city class reading *Antigone* out loud. I'd be partnered up with a girl for a scene, and she'd start to read her part like: "Eda-piss, Eda-piss, thou are my broder. I luv thee, Eda-piss." It would be my turn, and I'd put on a low, deep, formal voice and do exactly as I had heard on the record. The whole room would stare at me in disbelief, and I'd say [in jive], "That's the way they do dat shit at the Royal Shakespeare Company." Afterward kids came up to me asking, "How do you do dat?" I was essentially a double agent: talking like a regular kid most of the time, but letting out these different sides to me. People said if I talked "proper," I sounded white. So, I'd say, "Yo, what up? What's happenin', man? How ya doin'?"

My first experience onstage was at a speech contest. I was in the fifth grade. My teacher, Mr. Reed, told me that I could articulate well and should enter with a poem. The audience of seven hundred people seemed like seven thousand because I was such a little tyke. I did a poem by Carl Sandburg called "Me Myself and I." It went: "Isn't it strange that however I change, I still keep on being me. Though I may taste a Tomango, or dance a Fandango, it's still my tongue and my feet." I looked at the trophy the other day; it's on my mantle at home. I remember it so vividly. Although the experience felt good, at no time as a child did I think I would act for a living. I cannot remember having visions of my future when I was young. I was just floating on a natural high, purely entertaining myself and having fun.

What I did want to be when I grew up was a basketball player in the NBA. I was a basketball nut. I went to basketball camp and played as many games as I could. If Tiny Archibald or another player was coming to the Martin Luther King Jr. Boys Club, my friends and I got on the bus and went over there. We'd pay six dollars for nosebleed seats in the Chicago Stadium to see Norm Van Lier, Bob Love or Kareem Abdul-Jabbar. I used to say that Oscar Robertson—"The Big O"—was my father, *my old man,* because I loved the way he played. Even though basketball was my dream, I discovered I was not fast enough.

When I used to play ball, my team would be losing by like twenty points, and I would sit on the bench making all the guys laugh while I did my routine. The coaches had no idea what we were all cracking up about. I'd be doing my heavy English accent, saying things like, "Put me in the game, I've got moves like Wilt Chamberlain, I do. I could take all those bloody, blisterin. . . ." [switches to a Jimmy Stewart stutter] "If Coach wu-wu-would only put me in the game, le-le-let me dribble. . . . Mr. Townsend goes to Washington." I just loved to make the guys laugh. I'd hear them beg, "Don't do it. *Don't* do that character." So, I'd say in a serious snobbish voice, "Hey boys, I really don't belong here in the ghetto. I don't know *why* I'm with you guys." I'd be doing this stuff and my friends would be *dying.* They finally said to me, "Man, you different, cat. You've got to do something with this."

So when I was fifteen, my buddies convinced me to audition for a theater production on the south side of Chicago. I got one line in a play at a community theater and was bitten by the bug. By the time the show opened, people had dropped out for one reason or another, and I ended up doing nine little characters. Of course, those were all the voices I had been doing for years in the bathroom. I got rave reviews right away. Everyone around me was tripping off of it, but for some reason I thought what I did was normal. In the theater world, I was welcomed like I was home. My mother came to the show and said, "This is where you belong."

Influences

Mom encouraged me and forever believed in my talent and my dreams. She always told me I could be whatever I wanted to be. I listened to her and I believed her. Mom worked a lot of different jobs and at one period of our life we were on welfare, until she started working at the post office. My grandmother, who has since passed away, would say to me, "Get a job at the post office, baby," believing I should have stability. Then my mother would counter with: "Go for your dreams. What do you want to be? What do you want to do? You can do it." My mother had always wanted to play the piano and be in show business, and my grandmother kind of snatched her dreams away. I didn't really know as a kid that Mom had not fulfilled her goals, but I remember being aware that she made a sacrifice for us children. She was living her life for us, and I used to think, "Dang, Mom, you got to do that, and that, and *that?* Wow!" I could be in it and look outside of it. I thought she had it hard, but could also see that she was a survivor. Early on, I saw that Mom always kept going.

I think I got my humor from my mom; she's a very funny lady. I don't

Courtesy of Townsend Entertainment Corporation, Inc.

Robert, with his mother, Shirley, and his wife, Cheri.

have her brand though—she's like Richard Pryor. Hard core. I don't ask her anything unless I want to hear the brutal truth. We have such a good time together. Our lives are truly charmed in that we get to do what we love to do. We have a lot of freedom.

Drives

I never thought about wanting to be successful, but after my first theater performance, people started to tell me how much they liked my work. Hanging out with girls mattered to me as I got older, and on some level, I must have known fame would help me get girls. Still, success didn't change me—the only difference was that more people found out I was a lunatic. If anything, I was the guy who would ask a girl to dance and hear, "I'm kind of tired." Then a big, strong, macho guy would ask the same girl, and she'd be a dance queen . . . all over the floor. I didn't think about it much, but as I began to taste success, I noticed how people started to treat me differently, especially women.

Family

As much as I didn't envision my creative future when I was young, I always had a belief in love and being married. It was weird because in the images that I saw, nobody was married, except on TV. Television became my link to imagining alternatives to my surroundings, options to what I had outside of our door. In that box, I saw people treat each other completely differently than what I had around me. I used to look at real life and think, "Why can't it be like that?" I listened intently as Andy [Griffith] talked with Opie about how to deal with bullies. He became one of my surrogate father figures. People on TV had a certain kind of honesty that grounded me (in conjunction with the foundation my mother gave me) because I watched and saw an honest way of doing things. Maybe it was because of the standards and practices of the times, but the hero always won, and the bad guy always lost. Right always won out. I look at television now and see that sometimes the themes do not get back to a moralistic place. Sometimes they leave you with a feeling like, "Hey, life is tough, and that's it." I wonder if kids think, "Maybe I'll never make it, like that character there."

Because of my belief in love, I have been given a beautiful marriage. I have a wonderful wife: She is absolutely incredible. My best friend, Tony, introduced us. They are cousins. We didn't want to meet each other, though, because I thought she was *too* attractive, and she thought I was going to be *too* Hollywood. Usually when I meet beautiful women, they don't have brains. I don't mean to be general, but this has been my experience. I would go to different premieres with gorgeous women and they would be stepping on my toes to get to the camera. It was like, "Da da da . . ." [sings *Entertainment Tonight* theme song]. What is beautiful to me has always been what's inside a person's heart anyway. I see beauty in all people. I've had girlfriends that have looked all kinds of ways. People say, "She's not traditionally beautiful," if a woman is heavy or really skinny. I say, "What's in her spirit? What's in her soul?" The outer is not something that will last. As we age and sag and the body starts to fade, what will matter is spirit. Do you love that spirit?

I've learned so much from my wife; she is such a giving and loving person. I am totally blessed in my marriage. I knew her only six months before we

Photo by Carl McKnight

Robert and his family, 1994.

were married, and now we have two girls. They are *baaaad* and have me wrapped around their fingers. I'm not going to spoil them, though,

because the side of me that wants to make sure they have a healthy
work ethic is bigger than the side that wants to indulge them. I will
give them x, y and z, but demand that things like homework and
cleaning up are done beforehand. I want to pass on to them a sense
of responsibility. It would be easy for them to think, "Daddy will take
care of everything." I have them come to my office at Warner Brothers
two times a week and help me clean up. We have a great time.

Creativity

After high school, I moved to New York City to do stand-up comedy.
It was there, at the Improvisation comedy club, that I met Keenan
Ivory Wayans [creator of *In Living Color*]. We were waiting to perform
together. My act was turning in circles, doing impressions. I remember
a joke Keenan did that night: "There's a bully in my neighborhood
named Calvin. My father said, 'If you don't fight Calvin, you're going
to have to fight me.' So I beat the shit out of my father." Keenan went
away to college while I stayed in New York; I was doing commercials
and living really well. Eventually he decided to drop out of school and
move to California to "go for it." I came out to visit him and do a show
called "Evening at the Improv" and we had such a great time that I
decided to move out there as well. The two of us drove my stuff
across country and damn near killed each other. It was hilarious.

Driving in the rental truck through the South, Keenan wanted to
stop at a girl's house he knew from college. He was hot for this girl.
The problem was that Keenan had allergic reactions to cats and dogs,
and she had a cat. The cat went in the closet, but that didn't change
the fact that its hair was all over the place. Keenan thought he was
going to have this romantic night, while I slept downstairs, and
instead, the cat hair broke him all out. He was so sick, his nose blew
way up. I had to drive us out of there right away while he loaded up
on sinus medicine. Later, as we were driving, Keenan needed more
medicine, so I stopped at a little Southern diner. I parked in an awkward way and Keenan needed to move the truck while I was inside.
As he was backing up, he hit another truck. We were the only black
people there, and I was the only one inside. I heard a bang outside
(which even Keenan didn't hear because he was so stuffed up) and a

man in the diner yells, "Some nigger done hit your car, Phil." All these white people jump up and I'm standing at the counter. "Ah . . . can I get some sinus medicine?" Then, because the windows to the diner were open, everyone heard Keenan yell, "Are you out of your fuckin', mother-fuckin' mind?" So, I said, "He didn't mean anything by it." A man looks at me and says, "Get your ass out of here, *now!*" It was like a scene right out of a movie.

Keenan and I wrote a few projects together. The first one we made was a film called *Hollywood Shuffle*. We are like family, but we work differently now. The direction I'm going and the direction he's going may not be totally different, but they vary. I need my work to give back some of the gifts I've been given. That's who I am. Sometimes I don't want to go for the joke. Sometimes it's important not to. Keenan, however, is a joke machine. He loves to go for the laugh, whatever the consequences. [This part of the interview was done before Keenan's talk show.] He is great at what he does, but we don't always see things the same way.

Lifework

Hollywood Shuffle [the first movie Robert wrote, produced and starred in] had a small budget of one hundred thousand dollars. I used all of the cash I'd saved from acting in a couple of movies *(Soldier's Story, Streets of Fire* and *American Fliers)* to shoot most of the scenes, but toward the end of filming, I ran out of money and didn't know how to progress. I went on the road doing stand-up to earn some money, and when I got home, I had a big stack of mail. Just as I was about to open it, I prayed, "God, if I'm supposed to finish this movie, please give me a sign and let me know what to do." As I opened one envelope after another, there were applications for credit card after credit card. I filled them out, and because I had never asked for increased limits before (up until that time I had only used credit at holiday time), they all said yes. I got forty thousand dollars in credit from Saks Fifth Avenue to The Broadway, Chevron, Shell and Mobil. I bought the wardrobe for the movie from Saks, and the paint and supplies from Montgomery Ward and Sears. When I went to the stock house to pick up film, I felt like I was on an episode of *Mission: Impossible.* I had never charged five thousand dollars worth of film before. A man said to me, "That will be five thousand dollars, please." I handed him my Mastercard [sings *Mission: Impossible* theme song] and after a long pause, it was accepted. "Enjoy yourself, Mr. Townsend." I felt like I was getting away with something *big*.

What was so amazing was that by the time my thirty days were up to pay off the credit cards without incurring interest fees, I had gotten a distribution deal with Samuel Goldwyn. The company wrote me a check and I was able to pay off the bills right away. It was a Cinderella story.

The second movie Keenan and I did, *The Five Heartbeats,* was about a black singing group. Everywhere I go, in terms of all people, all races, this is a film that touches people. The humanity of the characters and what they go through makes this a powerful film. I wrote a scene where Digger, one of the guys in an up-and-coming singing group, tells the members of the group that he has just gotten his girlfriend pregnant and will have to leave the group to get a "real" job. It's an emotional scene. Rather than just go with the stereotype (where the guys would tell him to bail out or convince her to abort), I chose to show another side of friendship. The guys ask him if he really loves this woman and when he says, "More than anything," they respond by pulling out their wallets and giving him all their money. I wanted to discover what it was like to be in a musical group. Some of these people, like the Temptations and the Dells, have been together for thirty or forty years. They must have gone through everything living on the road together.

The first time we showed the movie, I was nervous about how some of the sentimental scenes would be accepted. I heard people in the audience begin to sniffle and cry and knew I had made the right choices. Regardless of how many negative images are portrayed of brothers killing and hurting one another, this is real, too. It is real that a man would want to keep his kid. It is real that his friends would want to help out. I think a lot of people applauded the film because they had never seen such tenderness between black men. But the message is universal. It's about forgiveness and friendship. I like to inform people with my work. I like to teach things that may not be seen on a daily basis. For example, many black artists (including the Dells) had to deal with the issue of *crossovers,* a term that most white people are not familiar with. In the 1950s, it was not considered marketable to show photos of black artists in advertising, so various groups couldn't show their faces on their own albums. Even if a song performed by a black group was at the top of the charts, it was considered offensive to actually see them. The record companies that handled these groups often insisted that the album covers show a bowl of fruit, a mailbox or even cartoon drawings of white people instead.

In this same film, I included a scene where the guys are traveling across country in their car and are pulled over and hassled by two white policeman. When we were filming I wondered, "Does this kind of thing still go on?" assuming it might be outdated. Then, right around the time the film was released, the whole Rodney King incident happened. I thought, "Oh man, what I've shown is real mild."

In my life, I have never viewed things with a prejudiced eye. If I see *Terms of Endearment,* I cry just like anyone else. I'm not going to think, "I just hope that white woman can live; she's such a good white woman." If something touches me, it touches me and I start crying or laughing. It's not based on color. I have also never thought that only white people can succeed.

Spirituality

My mother always said, "Keep God first." She taught me that anything I wanted, I could pray for and have. My grandfather owned a church, and I was practically raised in the Livestone Baptist Church on the west side of Chicago. Anytime I'm unfocused or unsure of what to do, I pray and everything is revealed. From early on, I had this foundation. To be able to soar in this world, you have to have a strong base. For me, God is the source of my strength.

I go out to the beach often and pray out loud for hours and hours— just releasing my dreams. I try never to take for granted what I have. I am totally blessed. Thinking of the millions of people that would love to be able to say, "I have some say in my destiny," I am eternally grateful. God gives me energy. When I am weak or drained, God recharges me. Just by praying, I feel like a new person.

I see life like in the movie *Wings of Desire.* In that film, angels are all around the people in the movie, protecting them, even though they cannot be seen or heard. If a person is going through something painful, there is an angel beside him, holding his hand and telling him everything will be all right. There is a scene where an angel comes to earth and can no longer see the other angels that are his friends, even though he knows they're following him. As he walks along, he says, "The people down here can't hear. It's so noisy, so busy. People here are missing the guidance because they *can't* hear." When I go to the beach and talk to God, I *can* hear. That is my source. My total source. I feel completely protected. Quiet time praying is invaluable for me. When I don't take the time to do it, I feel like I am spinning my wheels.

Fame

I never envisioned criticism, but being in this business has caused my skin to get thicker. In all my work as an artist, I was only thinking of good stuff. I never thought someone would say, "Robert's big peanut head walked on the screen and I felt . . ." or, "What was Robert thinking when he came up with . . . ?" It bothers me to hear the bad stuff, but for the most part I've gotten great reviews. Even so, one negative one causes me to think for a moment, "Oh goodness, maybe they're right." My spirituality makes me pretty solid, though. For instance, I don't get intimidated by someone who may be funnier than I am. I think there is enough for everyone. I'm like a little kid, in that I have a lot of hope for the good of mankind. Maybe I'm stupid or gullible, but I still want to believe in the world. If someone says, "So-and-so is jealous of you," or, "So-and-so wants to hurt you," I have to think, "Why?" I have heard people say that it's not fair I have such fulfillment, and to me that is so strange. All I want to do is good. In all of my work, the message at the core is always to follow your dreams, love your friends and overcome obstacles.

One of the bummers about being a celebrity is that, all of a sudden, you have to deal with people as if you have kid gloves on. I am an honest person and like to be truthful in my feelings. It can be hard because if I see a movie I don't like, I want to be able to tell the truth. People want me to see a play or a movie they've created and say, "That was great; everything was great." But, what if I don't like it? I've tried telling the truth, but I get attitudes like, "Oh, Townsend thinks he's a big shot." Even if I'm just hanging out with friends and I mention that I don't like a certain film, gossip carries. Someone will mention to someone else, "Robert said . . ." and it spreads. I want to be a regular guy and hang out with the fellas, but I have to know that I can never be one completely. My wife tells me to be careful, that people are looking for the hidden agenda. Because I love my family so much, all of this is okay. I was never much of a going-out person anyway. I still don't get to spend enough time with my wife; anytime the kids go to bed early, we just lie in the bed and talk. We love being together. I get tired of functions and like to do my work and come home.

The biggest dilemma in my life seems to be finding out what I want to do—what I want to be when I grow up. Deciding is challenging because I have many choices. For example, I wrote a screenplay that is dark, the opposite of anything I've done before. I suppose in this world of duality, the antithesis of comedy would be sadness. I feel all things, but prefer to live in joy. Because there are a variety of sides to me, it can be hard to focus. Certain people can concentrate on one thing. I look at other filmmakers who just do movies and I think, "But I'm a comedian, too." Some people say to me, "You're a filmmaker." And others will say, "You're an actor." In truth, I'm a vaudevillian: I love singing, dancing and being silly, but even that can be a blessing and a curse. I crack up when people ask, "When are you going to do an album?" I really have to think about all of my options; it can get kind of insane. I have to learn to focus better.

Miracles

The fuel that drives my work is to make a difference. One of the ways I do that is to go against stereotypes. In [The Five] Heartbeats, I included a character named Eddie, who becomes an addict with no ability to take care of himself. Often in movies, the bad guy/junkie gets killed. I have never had a drug problem myself, but have certainly known people who have, and there can be a light at the end of the tunnel. At the end of the film, we see Eddie totally rehabilitated.

The strangest thing happened one day. It was my day off, and I wanted to pick up a sandwich and not see anybody. A private day. This guy comes up to me in the store and says, "I need to talk to you.

Man, I saw *The Five Heartbeats* like twenty times: I used to be a junkie
and that movie got me through it." He told me that he watched the
movie when he needed encouragement and felt like he couldn't go
on. Seeing Eddie survive made him know that he could survive. He
told me he just wanted to thank me. "Mr. Townsend, I don't know if
that movie made a dime or a quarter, but it helped me." *Wow!* That
was amazing. My life was so enriched by television as a child, that I
try to give back some of the hope I was given. When I accomplish
that, I feel like I am coming around full circle.

In a funny way, the 1994 Northridge earthquake had miraculous
effects on my life. My hope in humanity was strengthened by seeing
how everybody worked together, first after the riots and then following the quake. I watched as whites, Asians, Koreans and Hispanics
worked together like multicolored little ants. When the going got
tough, most people turned toward goodness. Driving around, that was
the imagery I saw. I had never seen it before, either. Perhaps people
wouldn't even talk to one another unless there was a quake.

I actually lost my whole office building (where I shot a lot of my
projects) to the shaking. It was a wonderful old brick building on
Hollywood Boulevard and was completely destroyed. Only the land
remains. Life can be so strange: I had just renovated the entire place.
We had a sound stage, editing rooms and bays, rehearsal rooms, conference rooms—the whole nine yards. I've always been such a rebel,
never wanting to be on a studio lot. Doing my own thing was
extremely important to me. Now here I am, with my offices on Warner
Brothers's big old lot. Destiny never ceases to surprise me.

The morning of the quake, my wife was scheduled to visit her
mother in Chicago with the kids. We looked around the house and
saw that everything was fine, so we got in the car to go to the airport.
I had a feeling I needed to check and see if my building was okay, so
I had my friend Anthony drive over there. I got a call in my car, and
Anthony says, "You *don't* want to know. I can see into the second
floor . . . your computers and everything." I said, "What do you mean?"
He goes on, "And the water is really high, about ninety feet off the
ground." I dropped the family off at the airport and went to see for
myself. It was the biggest mess I've ever seen, but it was a gift in dis-
guise. The building was great to encase my companies in, but people

who didn't have the right energy were bombarding the doors to come in. Being a nice guy, it was hard for me to deflect the people who were not good to be around. I had a hard time saying "no," so *other* energy was let into the house, so to speak. The earthquake was perfect because I needed to do some serious cleaning. At first, though, it was comical, like, "What should I feel?"

Now my life is more simple. My offices are on a studio lot, and I'm seeing that that can be a good thing. I have more time to concentrate on my family and my art, instead of dealing with details that take away from the life that I love. I knew that God had a plan for me and, as usual, the plan was better than I could have imagined on my own. Everything in life is perspective. I didn't allow the quake to stop me from just living my life and enjoying myself. I got it off me and kept on moving. No matter what, we are here to make this world a better place and have a great time. Each day, I am so excited to see what's next. . . . What can I do next?

7

Lord Robin Russell

Photo by Stephanie Russell

Introduction

When I was in college, one of my sorority sisters was dating an English lord. She was one of the most beautiful women on campus, and he was known as the mysterious, shy guy with the great accent. Although I was interested in his lineage, especially the rumors that he lived in a haunted castle, I had a preconceived notion that, as an aristocrat, Robin would be too conservative to be sympathetic or empathetic to human suffering or the plight of the planet. Never mind that Robin wore jeans and T-shirts most of the time, or that he exuded a gentle, calming essence. Lord Robin was just too quiet and reserved for me, at least that's what I had decided—until we bumped into each other after college at a mutual friend's going-away party. Both of us felt a little out of place that Friday night, as we found ourselves amongst raucous partyers at the Hard Rock Cafe. The truth is, we were in the stay-at-home-and-read-a-book mood that evening, and in our shared discomfort, Robin and I sat down next to each other. I didn't know what to say, so I blurted out the one thing I really wanted to know: "Is it true that your castle is haunted?"

That small question led to a riveting three-hour conversation and hours of phone calls in the following weeks. Robin talked passionately about his deep affinity for the environment, explaining that his personal hero was John Muir, one of the first great American environmentalists. He spoke about the necessity of living a simple life, and he had a profound understanding of what less fortunate people experience. Robin wasn't the polo-playing type, for sure, and hobnobbing with nobility was the furthest thing from his mind. Metaphysical to boot, we had read the same books and especially loved The Way of the Peaceful Warrior by Dan Millman. Robin had been actively asking all of the big questions of life including, "Why are we here?" and "What is our purpose?"—questions I had begged my boyfriends to ask. We toured spiritual bookstores together—the Bodhi Tree especially—and crystal stores, although I must admit that it was impossible to get him to set foot into health-food stores until just a few years ago. At any rate, I felt as if I had finally met the open-minded, intellectual, spiritual comrade I had always searched for. Hopelessly few of my high school

*or college friends ever seemed to care about the topics I found fasci-
nating. Robin and I became seekers together. I would jokingly call him
stuffy and conservative, and he would call me a nut, but our friendship was refreshing for us both. At the time I was in a relationship with
a man I felt emotionally and intellectually stifled by. Robin's friendship
was a lifeline to a different world: one of infinite possibilities, replete
with magic, haunting ancestors, tragic dramas and bigger-than-life
history.*

*Like most people fresh out of school, I didn't have any money, except
what I could charge on my new credit card and finagle from my parents. I was living in an apartment overlooking a busy thoroughfare
and had gotten used to being jarred awake by colossal trucks barrel-
ing by just outside my bedroom windows. My neighborhood was primarily made up of first- or second-generation Californians. I wanted
Robin to tell me about his castle, with his eight-hundred-plus-year lineage, to take my imagination into a place of grandeur and majesty. But
much like Catherine Oxenberg, as I later found out, Robin didn't want
to identify with his palatial home. His focus was on his new life in
California, and getting information about his past was like pulling
teeth. In time, however, I learned that Robin lived the picture of a fairytale existence. His family-owned estate, Woburn Abbey, was not, in
fact, a castle, but a monastery, constructed in 1145 as a religious
retreat for Cistercian monks. Set on three thousand acres of beautiful
English countryside, Woburn is now one of the most famous and visited homes in Britain. Four hundred years ago, the abbot was found
guilty of treasonable utterances against the king, and the monastery
was confiscated. According to legend, the abbot was hanged from an
oak tree in front of the house by King Henry VIII (no wonder spirits lurk
in lonely wings of the abbey), and nine years later, King Edward VI
granted Woburn Abbey to Sir John Russell, who became the first earl of
Bedford. From then until the present day, the Russells have continued
to thrive in this historic locale.*

*As someone with minimal knowledge of her own family history, I am
spellbound by the in-depth record-keeping at Woburn. I'm certainly
not named after someone in the twelfth century, and I can barely
recall the names of my great-grandparents. The chronicles of Woburn's
past inhabitants are ever-present, as the walls are lined with hundreds*

of family portraits painted by the finest European artists of each century's generation. Robin may not be overwhelmed by the riches he grew up with, but he does carry a strong reverence for the people who preceded him. Their individual tales bring depth and unusual perspective to his life. For instance, the son of the first duke of Bedford, Lord William Russell, was beheaded in the Tower of London in the 1690s, also for treason. In the 1800s, Duchess Anna Maria, wife of the seventh duke, started what is known as teatime *in Britain. Maria's hunger between lunch and dinner impelled her to indulge in a light tea in the midafternoon, a practice that caught on with the surrounding nobility and gradually spread throughout the entire country. Bertrand Russell, the famous mathematician and philosopher of the twentieth century, is also a member of this illustrious family, and the "Flying Duchess" (the eleventh duchess, Mary) was a record-breaking pilot. She had been forced to make an emergency landing in the Sahara during one flight, but on her last outing, the Duchess never returned. Only pieces of her plane were found washed ashore.*

The Abbey structure, too, was the site of significant happenings. During World War I, parts of the main building, riding school and indoor tennis court were converted into a temporary ward for as many as two thousand wounded soldiers. Closest to Robin's heart is Woburn's wild animal park, of which he is now a director. The park is a refuge for many animals, particularly elephants, rhinos, giraffes, the big cats and nine species of deer. Perhaps the greatest success story of the animal park involves a rare species of deer—the Pere David deer—that became extinct in China in the late 1800s. Just before their extinction, the eleventh Duke brought them to live and breed successfully on the grounds of Woburn. Robin's father, Lord Tavistock, realized a lifelong dream when he was able to reintroduce the deer back to their natural habitat, where they now thrive. This is the first time a species has been successfully reintroduced. It is safe to say that Robin is the only person I know who can actually use the excuse that the reason he hasn't gotten back to me is that he has been traveling through India, purchasing abandoned or malnourished elephants.

Never one to be showy with his wealth, Robin was infamous for driving around London in his "old bomber of a Ford" for years and still rents inexpensive mid-size cars when he travels. But even so, there is *an aura of unlimitedness to him. When I first met Robin, I was used to borrowing from Peter to pay Paul, and he seemed to have endless resources. I couldn't believe that cashiers accepted his checks without an address or phone number. The only thing printed at the top was Lord Robin Russell. Knowing that English titles didn't necessarily mean anything on paper anymore (beyond the ease of check cashing), I wondered, "Where the hell does his money come from?" In reality, the Russell family receives no money from the British monarchy or government, though much of their present fortune originates from the kingship of long ago. Some of the current Russell estates were granted to the first earl of Bedford in return for services he performed for King Henry VIII, and other estates came through marriage. Much of the family's wealth now comes from rent paid on these lands, some now known as districts of London. However, the home generates its own income since opening to tourists in 1955. The cost of maintaining an estate such as Woburn is exorbitant, exceeding $1 million per year, so the future of the estate is far from secure. With a living heritage preserved in England's historical estates, hundreds of homes throughout the British countryside are open to the public. Robin accepts that his family, and families like his, now play the custodian role. Their hope is that by welcoming the public to share in their history, they will be able to continue to keep the Abbey in most of its original condition.*

Robin experiences a life of wealth and freedom few will ever know, while encompassing a rare understanding that these attributes sometimes bring little peace or lasting happiness. Recently married, he shares an incredibly romantic engagement story with his wife, Stephanie, and a softer and more vulnerable clarity pervades his already unique outlook. Robin was originally hesitant about having his words put into print because he is markedly open about his feelings toward the society into which he was born. It is not an easy world for Robin to fully disengage from. Choosing to face issues head on, Robin ran for and won a seat in Woburn's Town Council in 1995, which was quite a feat. Historically people who live in the town of Woburn have felt separate from the Russell family. Robin believed that it was time to heal the distance and hear the people, so he knocked on doors and introduced himself, making him the first member of the Russell family to get involved at the town level. Never sensing that he belonged in the domain of material excess, Robin is driven by an inner calling: to help educate about and improve the natural environment we all call home.

I am grateful to say that even with our busy schedules, half a world away from one other, Robin and I still enjoy riveting conversations. Thank God some things in life remain the same.

*   *   *   *

Happiness

Happiness is more a feeling than a state. When we think of happiness, the natural assumption is that one has to be smiling and full of energy. I prefer to think of happiness as a feeling where I can sit anywhere at anytime, completely at peace with my surroundings. For me, it comes from knowing that what I've done in the past I had good reasons for doing, what I'm doing now is a contribution to a better future, and what I'm going to do ahead of me will be worthwhile.

I don't know many people who are truly happy. It is easy to be happy on a weekend, when going out to a concert or to dinner, or even while relaxing and reading a book, but to be happy all of the time is another thing altogether. If I could count five people in that classification, I would be surprised. I have been all over the world and the happiest people I've seen are the ones who live and work in harmony with nature: the kind of relationship the human body was meant to have. These people, who still employ the traditional farming methods, get up with the sun, work on the land with their horses and bare hands, and go to bed at dusk. They eat what they produce and build their own houses. It sounds idealistic, but that to me is the kind of person who seems happy—self-sufficient and able to live in harmony with the land, without wanting the material things we *civilized* people believe make us happy. Perhaps when people focus on survival, without the *luxury* to ponder their situation in relation to the world, they are happiest, because certainly happiness can only come from inner peace.

Early Years

In the world I was born into, I often felt that I did not fit in. As a child, I felt disconnected, never secure in my family's world. Society life did not (and does not) interest me. It's not that I felt like a square peg in a round hole, more like a round peg in a square hole: I could fit with a push, but not comfortably or properly. I don't think my parents or my brothers understood me, and my peers often looked at me as if I were speaking a foreign language when I talked about what interested me. That is why I came to America; I think I fit in here better.

My upbringing was strict. Being the middle child was difficult. I don't want to upset anyone, especially not my parents, but they were maybe too young and overburdened when they had me. My parents already had my older brother and I don't think they were completely prepared for another child. Obviously there were many good things about my childhood, and one of them was moving to Woburn from London. There was so much land on the estate, and I adored the animals. It was a beautiful place to be and grow.

Woburn Abbey.

Courtesy of the Trustees of the Bedford Estates, 1998

I experienced a lot of adventure looking for ghosts as a boy. There were many stories about spirits at Woburn; King Henry VIII, who gave the land to my ancestors, hung a man in front of the Abbey. You always imagine there are great mysteries in a house of this size. My brothers and I used to walk around in the dark of night, looking for ghosts and scaring ourselves. It was great fun. I still do it and get equally frightened. The imagination goes wild. I have only seen one ghost myself, in a downstairs bathroom. It was a lady dressed in a long ornate white dress, like something out of the eighteenth century. Plenty of people have seen her. We all refer to her as "The White Lady," but I don't think anyone has worked out exactly who she was. Unfortunately, when I saw her, I ran away very quickly. I was fourteen and scared, planning to get a better look the next time, but I have never had the opportunity.

Courtesy of the Trustees of the Bedford Estates, 1998

Robin's mother with Walt Disney, his godfather, circa 1949.

When I was a boy, I used to sit up late and watch horror films. I loved the old *Dracula* and *Frankenstein* movies; they aired on Saturday night television at midnight. I watched them, and then I had to go back to my room, which was quite a long way from the television. Of course, I could never go to sleep on those nights. I can't watch the horror films made today— they are so violent.

The old *Dracula* is funny when you look at it now. Perhaps I am nostalgic because my grandmother was a successful actress and dear friends with Mr. Walt Disney. Because of his involvement in my grandmother and mother's lives, he became my godfather when I was a baby. Needless to say, I like the kind of movies he envisioned.

At the age of eleven, I went away to boarding school, which was tough on me. The discipline used by the instructors was harsh and cold. I have no regrets because the school taught me how to discipline myself, and for that I am grateful. I learned to be self-reliant. With the distance to look back, I don't think there is reason to regret anything. Our experiences are all important lessons. If I've gained wisdom, what is there to lament? We have to learn from our mistakes and those of the people around us. Maybe they're not mistakes at all?

Influences

My family has a living history of a thousand years. I feel fortunate to know about the people and events that came before me. Humanity benefits from chronicling its lineage because there are many lessons in history. I feel a sense of security in understanding what motivated the lives that preceded mine, and I consider it a blessing to be able to walk around Woburn and see hundreds of paintings of my relations on the walls, knowing that I am connected to all of them. I don't see a lot of resemblance in some of them, but I feel such respect for these faces staring back at me. What does it all mean in the end? I don't know, but I would not be here if it were not for these people, and my life is important to me.

I feel charmed to be able to stand next to a portrait painted a couple of hundred years ago, knowing that if that person had decided to move or marry into another family, then perhaps I wouldn't be here now. Everything we do causes a reaction; the consequences change lives dramatically. Although we don't see it, each one of us exerts a specific effect on the world. We are all so powerful. If we had the mental capacity to see the past, present and future at the same time, we would know how much difference each person makes in the grand scheme. But because of how big we've allowed our population and consumption to become, we don't realize how significant each one of us is. Technology has only helped alienate us more and more from these truths: Instead of passing down ancestral stories to our children, like traditional peoples have always done, we turn on our televisions.

With the fortunate stories of people in my lineage, there are some tragic ones as well. I assume this is true for most families. For example, one of my ancestors, Lord William Russell, was beheaded in 1694. As the leader of the Whigs in the Commons, he was beheaded for a supposed group plot to keep the Roman Catholic Duke of York from the succession to the throne. William was tried and found guilty, which was grievous because he was innocent. His wife and two children loved him immensely and were devastated. Throughout the rest of his wife's life, she campaigned for his innocence, and in the end, was able to have her husband pardoned by the next king. There is an incredible quote William said to his wife, children and the world (in written text and in person) before he was beheaded. Part of his last words were:

In the words of a dying man, I profess I know of no plot, either against the King's life or the government. But I have now done with this world, and am going to a better. I forgive all the world and I thank God I die in charity with all men; and I wish all sincere Protestants may love one another and not make way for popery by their animosities. I do freely forgive all the world, particularly those concerned in taking away my life, and I desire and conjure my friends to think of no revenge, but to submit to the holy will of God, into whose hands I resign myself entirely. I reckon this as the happiest time of my life, tho others may look upon it as the saddest.

Think how centered he must have been to have said that. Here is a man, sitting in a seventeenth-century dungeon, with the wherewithal to understand so much. It gives me a sense of inner pride knowing that people like him and his wife helped form my past. I imagine we all have heroes within us.

Courtesy of the Trustees of the Bedford Estates, 1998

Lord William Russell and his family. Painted by Sir Geroge Hayter, circa 1820.

Was I aware of my fortunate status as a child? An honest answer would have to be no. I did not read the newspapers, watch the news or have any exposure to a world different than the one I was in. Going to private boarding schools and living in England left me sheltered. It was, therefore, hard to know that the rest of the world lived differently than I. When I realized what the world was like and saw what kind of problems were out there, I remember feeling that my life was sadly insignificant. I have since come to believe there must be a reason for my good fortune: If wealth is used to do good, then it must be worthwhile. Part of me believes that nothing is left to chance.

There are no words to describe what it is like to be a human being who is privileged just by being born. I literally ate off of gold and silver platters, although the world I was born into is disappearing. People tend to resent others who are privileged. Most people have to work tooth and nail, causing a lot of resentment toward those who are handed things from birth. That makes sense, but prejudices are such a waste.

I was endowed with a title, which does not mean much anymore.

A hundred years ago, it still yielded power, but not now. Even the monarchies are no longer rulers; they are simply figureheads. Most people born into great wealth see it as a blessing and a curse. On the negative side, it can be difficult knowing what you desire from life when everything is handed to you. From what I've seen, the majority of people who have achieved great things in life had hunger. So many of them had to fight to their positions, the need to succeed carrying them through to realizing their dreams. It is a strange world. I know many people who have been born into wealth who do nothing with their lives. A fair number of them abuse what they have, mix with the wrong people, and become lost souls who had all of the chances but blew them.

I know that I've had difficulty focusing because I haven't had any physical struggles increasing my drive to create. We only have to look briefly at the great authors and painters of history to see that many of them were totally unrecognized in their lifetimes. Given the choice, I would much rather be passionately creating in my career and misunderstood, than lead an accepted life with no passion. People who go out on a limb, believing in their purpose, sincerely impress me. Frequently we call these people "ahead of their time." The world may not be ready for some of their ideas, but twenty years later, people look back and think, "If only we'd listened." Unfortunately, that happens too often. The fact that someone paid $82.5 million for Van Gogh's *Portrait of Dr. Gachet* is unbelievably ironic. The poor man died mad and penniless; no one appreciated him during his lifetime. Imagine, *the* most expensive painting ever sold at auction and its creator was so unhappy, unrecognized and frustrated that he went mad. I suppose in some small way I can identify with that mind-set because I've been misunderstood most of my life. Materially, I've had everything anybody could want, but in the long run these things do not bring spiritual fulfillment.

If I could have the chance to start my life over, picking between the family I was born into or one that was incredibly free, simple and grounded I don't know which way I would go. Perhaps I did have that choice. Selfishly, it would be nice to have had the second, as it would have been a comforting existence. But perhaps I've been given the chance to effect some change. I see myself doing things on a global level—something to help make a difference on the planet. Perhaps I can talk to people. I believe I have a lot to give to the right organization.

Passion

A passion for animals runs in our family. My great-grandfather, Hastings Russell, who started our deer collection, spent more time with animals than humans. Being at Woburn allows me to be with many wild animals, which is also my favorite pastime.

One day when I was a boy, one of the mother tigers in our park was killing her cubs; animals in captivity do not always behave naturally. We took the rest of her cubs, raising one of them in the nursery with my younger brother. We fed the baby tiger with a bottle whenever my infant brother was fed. The cub stayed in our home until he began to knock us down when he thought he was playing. Even as a baby, he was strong. He made these great noises when he knew a person—happy sounds that were a sort of purring. Later, whenever I went to see him in his cage at the safari park, he made the same noises of recognition, deep in his throat. It was so sad for me that he ended up in a cage. I was told there was no way to reintroduce him to a natural environment.

Robin with baby tiger cub in Woburn nursery, circa 1975.

Family

I love living part-time in America. I met my wife in California, so I'd have to say that coming to the States was a big blessing for me. I decided to go to college on the West Coast because it represented a welcome change from anything I was used to. I received a degree in English literature from the University of Southern California. Living in California did me a world of good: I was in a terrific position because I was English and everyone liked an English accent. People wanted to meet me and I had the benefit of having a title, which opened doors for me that perhaps I wouldn't have had the courage to open myself. I was so shy. The English are renowned for being reserved and do not communicate as much as Americans do. For example, in England it is still considered a bit odd to say that you are seeing a psychiatrist. These matters are kept hush-hush. In contrast, going to therapy and healers is practically an accepted part of normal life in California.

Stephanie has helped me become much happier. We were married four years ago, but have been together for eleven years. She is the person who has taught me how to come out of my shell and love people, although I still have a long way to go. Stephanie showed me not only how to love, but how to be loved, which is harder. I find it easy to love animals, like a dog for instance, but to give it to or receive it from another human was difficult for me until she came into my life. With loving and being loved comes more security. From security comes confidence, and it takes off from there.

I knew it was time to ask Stephanie to marry me while I was on a trip hiking in India. It was January 1994, and I was in Katmandu with two friends. We came home from dinner one night to listen to the BBC World Service on the radio and suddenly heard about an earthquake in Los Angeles, which is where Stephanie was living with her parents. It instantly dawned on me that I was so used to having her in my life that I had not realized she could be taken away from me. What if she were suddenly no longer there? It was about 10:00 P.M. and Katmandu is a primitive place, but I found a phone. I was able to get a call through to her before the lines were cut off, but because she had no power, there was no way to know how badly her surroundings were affected. My friends and I were supposed to go on a ten-day hike the

following day, but I knew Steph and I would have no further communication if I went. I had to get to her.

At 6:00 A.M. the next morning, my friends, who were ready to take
their hike, walked down a dark foggy road with me. They went one
way to the bus stop, and I went the other to the airport. It was eerie.
I turned up at the airport and said: "I'd like the first plane going east.
Anywhere. I just need to get east." Luckily a plane was going to Hong
Kong, and from there to San Francisco. When I got to Stephanie, she
and her family were safe. They had some structural damage to a
restaurant they owned, but all were healthy. After being in Los
Angeles for a week, with its constant aftershocks, I went back to meet
my friends in Nepal. It was the longest flight you can take from Los
Angeles, the longest flight of my life. I had to go from Los Angeles to
Tokyo, Tokyo to Singapore, Singapore to Bangladesh, and from there
to Katmandu. During the trip, hopping around the world lost its allure.
The quake had altered my perspective, and I knew it was time to commit to my relationship.

I asked Stephanie to marry me in England. The Royal Opera House,
that my family built in Covent Garden, is an incredible place to see a
ballet and I knew that *Cinderella* was going to be performed there by
the Royal Ballet Company. When I went to get tickets a box was left,

Photo by Jonathan Farrer

Robin and Stephanie's wedding day, 1994.

so we had fantastic seats. I brought the engagement ring with me and was so nervous that I didn't see much of the performance. I had studied the program beforehand, knowing that the third act of the play was when the glass slipper is found and when the prince asks Cinderella to be his wife. I waited until the exact time, and when the prince was on stage asking Cinderella to marry him, I pulled the ring out of my pocket and gave it to Stephanie, asking her to marry me. She started crying and luckily said yes!

Our wedding was perfect. We're not fans of huge affairs, so it was just family and close friends. The ceremony was held in Southern California, and my family came out from England. It was a wonderful day.

Vision

I feel myself get more aware and conscious every day. Traveling, for example, was once much more fun for me than it is now because of my outlook. I suppose I have become disillusioned, but if I had a magic wand—aside from immediately instilling a fundamental respect for the natural world in every human being—I would also uninvent jet travel. The capacity to move humans and goods anywhere around the world is extremely damaging.

People flock to remote and beautiful places with expectations of how unspoiled they are, but the mere fact that we can get to them means they are no longer pristine. With the access that planes and cars give us, we can go anywhere. Tourism spells inevitable destruction. It all starts when a beautiful location is *discovered;* for the first few years, only highly adventurous people can get there, but then a hotel opens up, then an airport, bringing mass tourism. The original setting is no longer possible. If people were still confined to traveling on foot, or by horse and cart like our ancestors were, the world would still be relatively untouched. Before technology it wasn't a matter of money, travel took tolerance, patience and stamina. Now anyone can get up the Amazon provided they have the cash.

Being a person who sees things on a global scale makes it hard for me to completely enjoy being a free and wealthy man. I have to know that *if* I am going to travel, it will better me and my environment.

There are many ways to visit a place, emotionally speaking. There are people who go to a national park, for example, and take photographs or video of the beautiful scenery in hopes of showing people later; they are not really there. They travel so they can arrive home and say, "I was there. I saw that." To really be there, I am *present* in the moment. Instead of taking a picture of a mountain, I prefer to sit and feel it for half an hour. Then I remember it. I will always have the image inside of me, as opposed to in front of me. I see people travel and change by seeing Mother Nature's incredible gifts, only to come home and consume in their normal ways.

I make sure I learn and take new knowledge home with me when I travel. I make sure my actions change from being influenced by the different things I see. Contrasting cultures and ways of doing things can be valuable learning experiences; what is gained can deeply enrich our lives. I remember the first time I saw a forest of giant redwood trees in Northern California. I was standing underneath the trees, looking up, with a waterfall beside me. It was one of the most spectacular moments of my life and changed me forever. In that moment, being a part of something much bigger than I could have imagined, I grew. I admire Woody Harrelson for his courage to fight for and be arrested for these trees. Someone has to take a stand for them. As a result of that trip, I am more aware of the planet and how, indeed, she deserves to be taken care of. If we could all travel like that, putting what we learn to good use, I don't think we would be so destructive.

Often when I start talking about the environment, I see people sort of shut down. Most of us are not ready to face the truth that the human race is basically a vermin on this earth. We should realize we are such and learn to live harmoniously. I think America is to blame for a lot of dissatisfaction in the world because of the media images that go out. Everyone sees these images. Villagers in third-world countries start to think they need fast food and the latest tennis shoes. So much of television programming shows people leading dramatic lives filled with sex, betrayal, scheming, adultery, consumption and man-against-man behavior. But they are so unrealistic. How many people can live that way? And, if everyone ended up doing so, the earth would be destroyed in a matter of decades. We have been brainwashed to

believe that we need so many things in order to be happy, and television is greatly responsible. The reality is that most of us are slaves
to our possessions: They own us rather than the other way around.

In 1977, Neil Diamond did a concert at Woburn. I was fourteen and
impressionable, especially in the presence of such a big star. We had
something like fifty thousand people in front of the Abbey (the family
uses the proceeds from events like this to help pay for the upkeep of
Woburn). Mr. Diamond stayed in our home, and when he left he gave
me a bag he carried—like a small backpack—on which he wrote, "To
Robin, never own any more worldly goods than you can carry in this
bag and you'll be a happy man." It's true. The more we have, the more
we want and the more dissatisfied we become.

I like to go backpacking with only a few necessities on my back;
that is when I feel most free. I know I could always return to that state
if I had to.

Earth

I'm not sure why humanity is so backward, but we've lost touch
with nature and our spiritual history. Materialism gets to most of us,
much like a disease. Good people try to get ahead so they can have
the new car, clothes, stereo, television and everything else, regardless
of what our consuming does to our real home, Earth. Parents think
they have to send their children to expensive colleges so they in turn
can get good jobs to continue the same life-style. We worry about how
we look to other people, and we want to be successful in our society.
Because so many of these desires are contrary to our higher spirit, I
believe most of us are in a fairly constant state of discontent.

When someone comes along and says, "Please stop using that plastic, make sure you recycle each week, take canvas bags to the market,
don't go to the dry cleaners or use your air conditioner, drive less and
walk more," these disciplines become burdens on top of lives that are
already incredibly strained. People's circuits become overloaded. The
warnings may make sense, but if friends and neighbors aren't doing
these things, people wonder why should they take the initiative—
especially when these responsibilities seem to make life harder. The

reality is that this planet is all we have to live on, and we need to preserve her. If we want to save ourselves, we are going to have to change our ways dramatically and quickly.

At this stage in my life, I feel the most comfortable I ever have, thanks to Stephanie, but also the most frustrated. My frustration comes from the fact that each day I get more of this energy, call it spiritual energy, that seems to come from being in an aware state. I have not yet found a global channel in which to use my environmental passions or concepts, so the feeling I have is like being very hungry and seeing a plate of food in front of me with my hands tied behind my back. Being aware can be difficult, unless you are very centered, which I don't think I am yet. So I do the best environmentally that I can, and I feel good about that.

When Steph and I built our home in England, we installed a catchwater system to water our garden with. When rain falls on our roof, which happens often, it flows from gutters into two huge tanks in the ground. Any overflow goes into an irrigation ditch, and during the summer we water our plants with the rainwater. As long as water is kept far enough underground, algae cannot grow because of the darkness. It's a good advancement of the old ways. Before plumbing, everyone stored rainwater.

Californians make me laugh because they complain about droughts, yet there are so many things that could be done. Rainwater tanks wouldn't solve all water problems, but they would make a difference. In England we have what are called water-butts: a gutter pipe comes down the side of each house to fill barrels, also to water gardens with. I cannot believe Americans, as a rule, do not use this process. These are the benefits of conscious travel: We can pick up and bring home with us the best innovations and ideologies of each culture. Obviously, most people don't have the money to put tanks underground. These are still luxury items, but building laws should be introduced. I am fortunate to be able to fulfill my environmental ideals; it costs money to be "green," and space is needed. People in apartments cannot think about composting or storing huge piles of glass or metal, but they can do the basics. I stopped buying fast food because of the wasted packaging, and whenever possible, I walk, bike or take the train to my destinations. I carry canvas bags with me to the market and if I forget, I come out with armloads of stuff. People look at me like I'm some kind of weirdo, but I feel better about myself.

Spirituality

One of the positive influences my parents had on me was their openness to mysticism. They understood that reality is not always what it appears to be.

If there is a religion to me, it is in nature. I don't have a concept of what God is outside of that. The power of nature is awesome. To me, God is an understanding of the ebb and flow of life and its cycles. Everything has a growing and a dying cycle, the whole world works this way. I look at races and cultures who are in tune with nature and they are content to live their simple lives in harmony. Over and over, when approached by governments to go for progress, these people plead to be left alone so that they may continue living as their ancestors have for thousands of years. Seeing themselves as a continuum of history, their lives are important just by fulfilling the role of living.

I don't adhere to any organized religion because they fail to answer the questions I have about the world. As a child, I was raised amidst the Church of England, which is Protestant. We had church at school with daily chapel, but I never felt any closeness to organized religion. When it comes to the mystical religions of the world, like Buddhism and Taoism, they make sense to me because there is so much feeling involved. Both teach how to appreciate the spirits of nature and ancestors, and seem in touch with tangible things that are easily understood. These ancient religions began respecting the sun, moon, planet, trees, oceans and growing cycles. No rules or scriptures—just life.

I'm sure many people go to church because they feel they ought to be there, a result of how disconnected we have become with the physical world. I find much more spirituality from watching a seed grow into a flower or tree than I've ever received from church on Sunday. The forces present to create life are staggering. There is so much to feel in each moment when planting a seed: from the effort of preparing the soil and its nutrients, physically nurturing it, watering it, watching it grow each day in tune with the seasons, to witnessing buds open in the morning and close at night. These are miracles. I

Courtesy of the Trustees of the Bedford Estates, 1998
Aerial view of the Abbey as it looks today.

choose to feel these processes, as opposed to intellectually under-standing them.

Nature accurately exemplifies life. All of the ingredients that go into making a plant grow are metaphors for our own lives. There are certain things that help us grow and others that stop our growth. Humans are pretty basic, but we try and make more of ourselves than is necessary.

When I'm feeling in need of a spiritual boost, I go for walks with our dogs Ben and Indi, preferably in the forest. I talk to our dogs a lot. If I can't be in a wooded area, I walk in a beautiful garden. Nature brings me back. I like to be alone and go off to be quiet. The trees and the sky are healing and calming to me. That is my church.

We are about to plant a forest for the millennium here at Woburn. One winter about three years ago, I went around the park and col-lected acorns and chestnuts. We planted them in the garden and now we've got about a thousand oak trees and about five hundred chest-nut trees. So, this autumn we'll be planting a forest with the help of the forestry department. I'm getting all of my friends to come up and we're going to spend the weekend planting together. It was fun plant-ing the acorns, and it's going to be even more fun going back in fifty years and seeing the results.

If leading a charmed life is being in the right place at the right time, then I guess my whole life has been one big miracle. The challenge is to find out just how to use the gifts I've been given. There is a side to me that would love to give it all up, sell everything, and live in a log cabin in the woods. I'd love to chop wood, get my water each day, and live with my wife and our dogs. It may sound naive, but having been born into great material comfort, with the education and outlook I've been given, I know I am to give back more than I could by being a hermit in the woods. It would be a wonderful escape, but I think I can do more staying where I am. An answer will come and I will act on it.

I have so many dreams and ideas and am in the position whereby I have the resources available to me to fulfill any of them. Everything has been handed to me; I'm looking at it and piecing it all together. I am so filled with energy. All of the anger I used to feel as a child, long ago capped and stored away, has begun to be redirected. I now have a clearer focus and want to use this energy to better the world. With all of this fuel, I feel like I'm going to pop. I hope I pop positively.

8

Efrem Zimbalist, Jr.

Courtesy of Efrem Zimbalist, Jr.

Introduction

In person, Efrem is striking. At seventy-nine years old, he is the picture of vibrancy and health with a tall, perfectly poised presence, and high energy spirit. Efrem's tanned skin glows in contrast to his thick white hair and bright smile. When he speaks, with his alluringly deep and beautiful voice, his strength and wisdom elegantly coincide with a gentle and calming essence. It is a unique combination in today's world. He conjures up visions of idealism—distant memories of a past when all elders were rumored to be this loving and stable. I have searched for this paradigm throughout my life (perhaps because I lost both grandfathers by my first birthday) and rarely found it. However, getting to know Efrem has been, happily, one of those such discoveries.

Once while visiting a set where Efrem was working, I heard several people remark, "All men want to be Efrem and all women want to be with him." As there is truth in all humor, I readily saw the accuracy of this statement. On this remote Caribbean location, I witnessed women fifty years his junior, most of whom were without their mates, enamored of him. I, too, found myself somewhat awestruck; knowing that Efrem was devoted to his wife for nearly four decades made him all the more intriguing. The initial reverence made way for a desire to know what Efrem was about, and what could be learned from such a distinguished being.

Of the many people I have interviewed, Efrem has felt the blessings of his life more consistently than most. He freely admits his past irresponsibilities and laughs heartily recalling his naive rebellions. Judging from the fact that he has sustained authentic familial happiness while employed regularly as an actor from the time he was discovered in 1947, his early antics seem to have had no ill effects on his life achievements. Efrem has performed in countless plays, movies and television programs, with two long-running television series of his own (77 Sunset Strip and The FBI), each attaining top national ratings. All the while, Efrem has been blessed with a fulfilling family life centered around love and spirituality.

As you read on, imagine the voice: strong, joyous and uncommonly humble.

*   *   *   *

Happiness

I think happiness is the normal state of people and is necessary in order to experience life fully. We're certainly not put here to be miserable; that is a silly way to live. When we're unhappy we have mental and physical problems. Worry and stress cause many troubles in life, perhaps even loss of hair is one of them. I guess I do have more hair than most guys my age; I'm grateful that I do. I think it's largely hereditary, but I've been told that my attitude may contribute to its fullness. It's hard to say. I just know I feel lucky.

I'm enormously thankful to have good health, a lovely family, a beautiful home and work that I love. I'm very happy, very contented. Naturally, happiness is an overall state: There are dips in life where we suffer grief, loss and all kinds of things, but the substance of our life should be joyful. My happiness has pervaded everything, including the terrible and tragic loss of my first wife and serving in World War II, where I was wounded. In spite of that, I have always had a good time. Life is a phenomenal experience, and there is so much to learn.

Early Years

I was born in New York, along with my sister, who is gone now. I had wonderful parents—I loved them dearly, and they loved me. I had a marvelous childhood. When I was young, I never thought about becoming an actor. I didn't think about much of anything. I just drifted along, so much so that I managed to get kicked out of college twice, but that's a story for later.

My parents were both musicians and highly successful. My mother, Alma Gluck, was an opera singer and a concert and recording artist. She was enormously popular: the first recording artist to release an album that sold a million copies. She sang mostly folk songs, with some arias, and immortalized songs like "Carry Me Back to Old Virginny" and "Old Black Joe." My father was a famous violinist, and together they knew almost *everyone* in the world: all of the artists, writers, painters, musicians and so on. These people were constantly in and out of our house. My parents felt that their environment was a little too precious an atmosphere for me to grow up in, fearing I would get spoiled and assume their world was mine by inheritance. In order for me not to take things for granted, I was sent to boarding school. The idea was that I had to earn my own way in life. I understood and agreed with it so completely that I sent my three kids to boarding school as well.

Courtesy of Efrem Zimbalist, Jr.

Efrem with sister and mother, 1923.

I know many children who have grown up with every indulgence who are directionless. People have the idea that sending a kid away to school is some kind of cruelty or medieval torture, but it can be just the opposite. However children are brought up, as long as it's done with love, understanding and full explanations, a child understands such an upbringing and it is healthy. My headmaster and teachers were wonderful people to whom I owe a lot. Being away at school, in the long run, taught me responsibility and how to take care of myself. These things cannot be learned when everything is spoon-fed to us.

I think the lesson of responsibility sunk in after college, though. Like I said, when I was young, I didn't plan for anything. I got booted from Yale for not doing any work—just being a playboy and having a good time. I just didn't think. I mean, what kind of a jerk gets thrown out of school, not once . . . but twice? In those days, we considered college to be like country clubs; the purpose was purely to have fun. I found things I liked better than work, and I bluffed my way through the dispensary with medical excuses until I ran out of cuts. That's really where I became an actor—putting on a tremendous show about all the pains I supposedly had. But the school caught on, and I got kicked out. When I requested to return, I was allowed to come back and repeat the freshman year, but the same thing happened. The doctor wouldn't give me any more excuses, and I was released.

I actually worked very hard at the boarding school I went to before college. I did well there, trying as hard as I could to get the best grades in the school—even skipping the last year to go straight into college. Enrolling in Yale was the beginning of my troubles. The religious boarding school I had gone to was so strict that when I got to Yale I couldn't handle the freedom of it all. I was too immature for the responsibility. There were no rules; I just had to show up at class and collect my marks. With the lack of regimentation, I went wild, doing stupid, idiotic things, like following a girly show with a friend from New Haven to Philadelphia and Chicago. When I got kicked out the second time, I didn't dare go home. I was scared. I came down to New York and wandered around for three months looking for a job. A couple of friends fed me and let me sleep in their apartment. It was hard to get employment before the war.

Finally, I landed a job at NBC, where for a year and a half at fifteen dollars a week, I was a page. Then I became head page on the eighth floor for eighteen dollars a week. This was in the days before television, when radio was big. I lived comfortably on this salary: I had a room for four dollars a week and ate three meals a day at a cafeteria for only one dollar. Laundry was fifty cents and a haircut was a quarter, so I had enough left over for a huge weekend. I could take a date to dinner and a movie and have a marvelous time. I have never been that rich again in my whole life: I had no worries or stress. Whoever heard about income tax? I didn't even make enough to be taxed.

While I was at NBC, radio actors would come in. My job was to take them into the studio and stand there while they did their programs. I wanted to be one of them because I thought, and still do, that acting is the best life there is. I auditioned for all of the parts that came up because of a sweet casting director, Donna Butler, who let me do all different kinds of accents. After months of auditioning, I landed a part on a series—my first acting job. I was on a cloud. After getting my forty dollars pay, my mother died and I left the network. Dad and I moved in together and I went to drama school for a year before the war. I guess you could say that I've come full circle because I'm currently doing voice-over work in the studio as King Arthur for the *Prince Valiant* cartoon, and as Alfred the butler for the *Batman* cartoon. Ironically, Paul Williams [chapter 2] also works on *Batman,* as the voice of the Penguin. Small world.

Miracles

When I look back on serving in World War II, it's an odd thing that if I try to remember the bad times, I can't. I don't know if most people are constituted like this, but for some reason I am. I know there were hideous times where I was scared to death and in misery, but I can't remember them. All I can remember are the good times: the weekends and the jokes. The prism of the memory is so strange. Could be a safety mechanism. It's a good one if it is because there's no room for neurosis or anything like that. I've been asked if I block things out with alcohol or other substances, but I don't have anything to block out.

My job in the infantry had a twenty-minute life expectancy, and the reason I survived was because I was wounded. Had I not been hurt, I wouldn't have stood a chance. There were few platoon leaders who went the distance in the infantry. I lasted in action about six months and then spent the following six months in an English hospital before transferring to a special service unit in Paris. Throughout my tour, I had put down on all of the forms, with great aplomb, that I was an actor, but I hadn't done a damn thing. The terrible part was that for five years I couldn't improve on my resume. Everyone kept asking me, "What have you done?" I'd mumble, "Summer stock . . . a little radio . . . ahy . . . mmm," and then try to change the subject. It was agonizing because it went on the whole length of the war.

When I went into the army, I felt that in addition to the tragedy of a world war, it was the greatest personal tragedy for me. Here I was, ready to conquer the world (or so I thought) as an actor and *boom*— five years were cut right out as if surgically removed from my life. I had wanted to work hard and be a success, and I had no idea what was going to happen to me. The way the finger of fate writes one's life is remarkable. I went to officer-candidate school and as a first lieutenant it worked out that I had routine duties with two captains who were both theatrical men in Paris—very important people in the theater. One was Garson Kanin, whom I met in London, and the other was Joshua Logan. Josh and I happened to sail back to the states together on a troop ship where we shared a stateroom. After I was discharged, my half-sister (from my father's second marriage), Marcia Davenport, gave me a miracle. Marcia was a famous novelist and well connected in New York; for her gratitude to me for fighting in the war, she wanted to give a dinner party in my honor, inviting anyone I wanted—anyone I thought may be able to help me get started. At my request, Marcia asked Gar Kanin and his wife, together with Josh Logan and his wife, and the dinner party took place. Three weeks later, Garson gave me the most wonderful part on Broadway in *A Rugged Path,* with Spencer Tracy. It was a superb play, and I had three big scenes with Spencer, which started my whole life.

Ten years later, still in New York, Josh—whom I'd talked to here and there over the years—called me and said, "I'm going to do a picture out at Warner Brothers. It's all cast, and there's no part in it, but I'd like you to test for it because I want to show Warner some film on you." I made the test in New York, knowing that I didn't have the part. Jimmy [James] Garner had the role—his first one. Josh took the test out to California and as a result, Warner Brothers put me under contract. Within two years, I had completed seven films. It was a dream come true. A truly charmed time for me.

Everything I've had in my life came out of those miserable five years in Europe that I thought were just thrown away. All that I have I owe to that experience. This proves to me that there is no wasted time. Miracles can present themselves in any situation.

Lifework

Being happy and successful is a huge gift, provided that I can give some of that back to the world. My whole feeling about my profession is that if I can give ten minutes of pleasure to someone in a hectic day, then it's worthwhile. I want to make people happy, like a drink of water in their day. For me, that's what it's all about.

I have played some clunker parts, been in some terrible things and been personally awful in other things, but most of the time it's been a lot of fun. Hearing myself talk, I guess the common thread of my life is that I've always been able to have a good time. I've been fortunate in that way.

Drives

I have a strong drive toward excellence that was instilled in me from an early age. Sometimes that drive goes against success; it clashes with it. Big opportunities have come along in my career, but because I've wanted to be true to my vision toward a certain quality, I've had to bypass them, sometimes taking lesser roles. I also like to keep the parts I play even-tempered emotionally. I'm not a screamer or anything like that. In real life, too, I like my emotions to be even. I don't trust the troughs or the crests too much. Extremes, whether high or low, are not for me.

I enjoy playing mean guys occasionally; they can be the best parts. Give me a good heavy anytime, as long as he gets what's coming to him. I know it's old-fashioned, but I believe that all of us who are before and accepted by the public have an enormous responsibility not to betray our fans. It is unthinkable for me to do a part that would lead people into an area that is damaging to them in any way. I just couldn't do it. I could play a murderer, as long as he was punished in the end. But to do something that would teach that wrong is right—I don't have the right. It's just our responsibility to be thoughtful. No big deal. What do you do with a child who trusts in you? You're not going to betray that trust. Same thing.

Affluence has never been a goal for me. My parents instilled in me the dictum that, "A workman is worthy of his hire." Mom and Dad didn't care what I did—I could have put soles on shoes—but whatever my profession, I was to do it as well as I knew how. My parents held to these ideals in their own lives, especially concerning their art. They worked themselves hard: struggled, learned and practiced, striving to bring out the best in themselves that they could. I've always tried to be the best actor I can be. My goal was never to become rich, but rather to be my best. This is the way I approach life. If it doesn't work, then it doesn't, but at least I've tried. I do acting, and always have, because I have a good time.

Fear

Criticism can hurt. I don't like people to badmouth one another, although I don't mind criticism of my work if it's constructive and something I can improve on. I believe that to be a successful actor, you have to think that people like you. If you think people hate you, you won't be able to act. This is one of the things I've never understood about many so-called acting schools. I've visited some of them, where they do nothing but tear down the actors. I couldn't get up and do anything if I felt that people were waiting for me to flop.

I don't know that I'm afraid of many things. Maybe I am, but I don't feel so. If I lost everything and was thrown out on the street, I'm so blessed to have children who love me and would take care of me. If I didn't have them, perhaps I might be afraid of destitution. You think about those things as you get older. When I do feel fearful or insecure, it's for silly things. I played tennis for a number of years before I took up golf, and I remember playing in pro-amateur tournaments feeling terribly insecure because I was doing something I was new at. The first one I took part in was at the Los Angeles Tennis Club, playing with Chuck [Charlton] Heston. I think we were the first two celebrities to play in the pro-ams, and I have never been so scared in my whole life. We were in front of thousands of people, so of course I couldn't play. Tennis crowds are not known for their kindness—they laugh and jeer at you for the slightest thing. Golf galleries are much better. You can only imagine the field day they had with me. I did everything wrong.

I had the same fear when I started playing golf in the pro-ams. Anything in which I'm on display for and don't know how to do very well makes me uncomfortable. When I was a kid, I often accompanied my father to the Lewissohn Stadium in New York. It was a big summer concert venue, and he played there many times. I used to have a recurring dream that when we'd get there my father would turn to me and say, "Son, I don't feel like performing. I'm doing the Mendelssohn. Would you mind going on stage for me?" I'd say, "Of course, Daddy." Then he'd leave. Suddenly, as I'm walking out I realize I don't know the Mendelssohn, or even how to play the violin. Each time, I'd wake up in a cold sweat. I guess that is the actor's nightmare—not knowing the lines. It's interesting to me that I had the dream as a child.

Do I have it all? No. Never will. Never could. What is out there that I don't have is not material in nature. I love pleasant surroundings; I'd be a total hypocrite if I said that I didn't. I love my car, my house, my furniture and so on, but the things I truly want involve growth, which is an ongoing process. I don't despair that I'll never grow; I hope I am always going to, but I know I have a long way to go. There are certain qualities and virtues that I hope will become stronger in me that are on the weaker side now. For example, I am a fiendish driver. I drive fast and am impatient, doing all sorts of silly behaviors in the car until I catch hold of myself. I try to control it, but it's an ongoing thing that I'm far from being proud of.

Discipline

From doctors who I know well and respect enormously, I have come to believe that stress is one of the main causes of disease, including cancer. A stress-ridden life changes the chemistry of the body and things stop working properly. I once read a wonderful gerontology study in *National Geographic* magazine that concentrated on three areas in the world (remote parts of the Himalayas, Russia and Venezuela) where people live to incredible old age, functioning up to 125 years old. The study collated all of the things the different people did—diet, exercise and so forth—to see what similar contributing factors were present. In short, the researchers were able to narrow down two things the groups had in common. First, all were rural people and very much involved with the small area in which they lived, not knowing much about what took place on the other side of the mountains, so to speak. These people had never heard of the atom bomb or the cold war, and had almost no stress of any kind in their lives. What concerned them was their daily work and life, and that was all. The second thing they had in common was that they did hard, drudging, almost slavelike work until they dropped. It was common to have them pulling huge logs through the mud at 110 years old, struggling to get it done. Hard physical work was the norm in each group.

Obviously, neither of these examples applies in our world. Five-year-old children in our schools talk about the possibility of never reaching adulthood. We live under a huge amount of stress and top it off with being largely sedentary. We have to compensate in other ways by watching our dietary intake, keeping away from smoking and drugs, and doing regular exercise. Each of us has to make the choice to stay healthy. Nobody can do that for us.

I believe in practicing moderation with the way I eat, even though I'm a little bit piggish and have to watch myself. I'm not an advocate of any faddish diet—I have tried them. I was a vegetarian for three years, but got bored by vegetables. I think you can eat anything as long as you do it sensibly; it was all given to us to eat.

It does seem, however, that denying ourselves smoking is probably a good idea, although I smoked fiendishly all of my life. I smoked in three media—cigars, pipes and cigarettes—and don't really know how I quit. You know, when I look back on my life there have been so many things that have just happened to me, blessings really, that I didn't dwell on at the time. As I reflect and see how some things were just easy for me, I know they were gifts. The way I was able to stop smoking had to be one of those gifts.

I had previously stopped once before, for ten years, but when I returned to Hollywood (after being away for some time), the first thing I was told on set was to light a cigarette for a scene. That was what you did on stage when you walked into a room. I bought a pack to practice with and was immediately hooked. Just like that, I was a smoker again. I took up the habit for a while, but then just stopped. Suddenly the romance of smoking had worn off. Up to that point, I had been enchanted by the idea of being a smoker. It started when I was fifteen or sixteen, in the days when my friends and I would go out dressed in tails to a party. We'd have a cocktail in one hand and a cigarette in the other. It was all quite impressive to the girls. Smoking was a big part of the image.

There were certain Pavlovian connections also, like the telephone and lighting up. As the phone rang, I'd struggle to light the cigarette and then say, "Hello?" Just couldn't do it without that. When I tried giving it up, the behaviors are what I held on to. I finally realized that in all my attempts to stop smoking, I had never declared that I didn't want to be a smoker. The fact is, I always had. One day, however, I reached the point where the pleasure was gone, and it stopped being attractive. Just like that. A week went by, then a month, even a year, without any cravings. I have never wanted it since, not a moment of struggle. I think God simply took the habit from me because it was so easy it was pathetic. Since then, I have often played golf with someone who has a cigar, and I enjoy the smell. It gives me great pleasure. My father used to smoke cigars and that's what I love—the familiarity and memories it brings up. Smells take me back more quickly than anything else.

Three times since quitting, I've had to smoke a cigar for a role. After six years of abstinence I was acting in *Remington Steele*, my daughter Stephanie's show, and the director wanted me to smoke a cigar in the

Courtesy of 20th Century Fox

Efrem with Pierce Brosnan and daughter Stephanie, *Remington Steele*, 1985.

scene. I thought, "Oh boy, first I'll get sick, and then I'll get hooked." To make matters more difficult, he didn't give me a prop cigar, but one of his: a delicious and fragrant Jamaican cigar. The scene was long, involving many takes and angles. All afternoon, I was smoking and enjoying this thing. That night I wondered, "What's going to happen tomorrow?" I woke up with no desire for it. Thankfully, it no longer has a hold of me.

Passion

Golf is my replacement for acting. I love it so much. People in my profession are odd: When we're not working, we think it's all over, and we'll never work again. Golf for me has been an enormous outlet in idle times because it's given me a goal, something to achieve. I don't play just to get out and talk, I play to be as good as I can, with the lowest handicap possible. I feel wonderful, and I am so grateful for my good health. It must be awful not to feel well, particularly as one gets older. I enjoy my life so: playing golf, being outside and being athletic. I don't feel the same energy as I did when I was younger, but that would be too much. The squirming energy of a child is something I would not want to have.

I work out regularly, but I don't enjoy that. I've worked out for fifty years, exercising before it was common to do so. I do it, even though I hate it. In the army, they taught us a physical fitness program with exercises that I kept doing after the war. When people were busy drinking cocktails, I was doing push-ups. Now, of course, everyone is fitness conscious, most more than I. We have a gym here in our home and have had one for many years, although I've cut way down, working out only two or three days a week. I don't do it on the days I play golf because I get too tight and can't play well.

Spirituality

More than physical drives, however, my life is founded around spirituality. I've always had religion in my life. As a boy, I was taken to church every Sunday, but the first deepening in my life in that direction took place in the high-school equivalent of boarding school.

Being a church school, there was a heavy accent on the religious side.
I sang in the choir and went to chapel every morning, with special services on Sundays. Until recently, though, my religious intensity would
sort of come and go. In the army, I was religious. Everybody was.
There wasn't a person I met who didn't pray to God. When it's all you
have, and you know that any minute may be your last, you do some
serious praying.

Before I left for the war, my first wife and I attended church
together. We loved sharing that part of our life with each other. When
I came home from Europe, she was desperately sick with cancer. The
doctor, who adored her, told me that I must not ever tell her how
grave it was because he knew it would kill her to know the truth. They
operated, and we were able to live a wonderful, happy, normal life
for a year before the cancer returned. Again they operated, and it, too,
was successful. We had another wonderful year and the third year it
jumped and metastasized; there was no more hope. Knowing my
wife's condition, which she did not know, drove me to my knees. The
whole time I prayed my eyes out, and when my wife died, I wasn't
spiritually unprepared. By that time, I had a firm belief in life going
on after death. I felt that any kind of grief would be for myself. How
could I grieve for her when she was in heaven? I quickly decided not
to sit around and cry for my own loss, because doing so would only
hold her back if she was to see that I was miserable. I simply let her
go with love and said to her, "Go on and enjoy yourself."

I have searched a lot and been many places. I even got into TM
with the Maharishi. I was one of the early ones. I was initiated and
dazzled by him; he is a fascinating character whom I got to know
very well. But I would meditate and never experience a thing. I was
given three different mantras, each one supposing to be a higher
one, and I saw nothing. All kinds of people around me had these
fantastic experiences, some very supernatural, and I sat and sat and
every once in a while fell asleep. I kept wondering what was wrong
with me.

I remember going on Merv Griffin's show one night, as a guest with
the Maharishi. Merv had just been initiated that day and had already
had these extraordinary experiences. The head of the movement—a
wonderful man and his wife who were dear friends of mine—would

sit with me and hold my hands, trying to bring me to the level they were at. They'd be off somewhere with their eyes closed and I'd be looking around thinking, "I've got to get some groceries. . . ." Eventually after nine years, I decided I didn't have time to do it anymore. It was just a total waste of energy for me. I quit and floated around spiritually until I was drawn back into the Christian church (Episcopalian). Later I joined a charismatic church for a number of years and left that to be right back where I began, with a quiet kind of worship.

I love the Lord. I love him very, very much. Not as much as a lot of people do, I'm sure, and certainly not as much as he does me, but I don't think it matters a hill of beans in what manner you worship him. That's what my wanderings have taught me. I think that every person who loves him, tries to please him and lives the best life he or she can for him, is on the right track, whether that person is a Buddhist, Hindu, Jewish, Mohammedan, Christian, or whatever. Anger toward or fear of people who practice another faith is dangerous. Most of the acceptance I feel about the faith of others is because of the wandering I've done in my life, all of the searching. I cannot imagine the God I love, worship and adore, sitting up there saying, "Now, who do we have coming up here? A Catholic? No way." I mean, what kind of a God would that be? It's unbelievable to think that he would have all those rules.

Worshiping the Lord in my way feels right for me. It would be wrong for me to do something else because this is my life, my path. It doesn't mean it's anyone else's path. There are many ways to displease God, but as long as you are trying to please him, that has got to be what counts. I know who Jesus is. I've been taught that. I believe in him with all my heart and soul. But take someone who doesn't, say a person in the Himalayas, who has never heard of Jesus. To think that person won't be accepted by God is crazy. If God were like that, who would want to worship him? I mean, *we* could do better than that. I believe God is totally unlimited.

Family

Women have known men a great deal better than men have known women. The reason is simple: because women have changed our diapers and raised us. Men haven't done that with women. Thus, women have a profound understanding of men, and it's been one of the great stabilizing forces of our society. That's not going to be there when women are not doing this job. I am not an authority on the family, but the way it has worked for many millennia has been to have the woman the nurturer and the man the provider. Humans have survived this way throughout time. Today it's not considered necessary, but no one can deny that our society has deteriorated alarmingly.

I happen to believe that the liberating movements of our time are devised and thought up, not for the people they are supposed to champion, but to splinter society. In the case of women's liberation, if the state gets the women out of the house working, they can get to the children and bring them up. I think that has been the game plan all along. Who in their right mind could be against women having every opportunity men have? I am for equality with all my heart. I don't think women should be limited to anything, but someone has got to do the job of bringing up the children.

My marriage to my wife, Stephanie, does everything in the world for me. I love her deeply. She has been an amazing mother and nurturer to us all, animals included. I consider myself so blessed that I was able to fall in love again after losing my first wife so tragically. They really have no similarities, as they were from different periods of my life, except that both were born in Washington. Stephanie is a wonderfully capable and gifted person. Everything she does she does well, whether it's cooking, sculpting, skiing, horseback riding or fishing. I don't do any of those things. I knock silly little balls around big lawns.

Stephanie keeps our house beautifully. Most of all, she takes fabulous care of me. We were married in 1956, so we've been going strong for a long time now. I'd love it if she golfed, but it's not in the cards; she couldn't care less to learn because she's so happy doing what she does. Stephanie's very charitable about my golf and doesn't resent my playing at all. When I come home from a day at the course, after a good or bad game, I know that dinner is ready and she's waiting for me. That's wonderful to come home to.

Efrem and Stephanie's wedding day, 1956.   Courtesy of Efrem Zimbalist, Jr.

My first wife gave birth to my two older children, and Stephanie gave birth to my youngest daughter, whose name is Stephanie as well. The name is handed down from my wife's Austrian mother, making our little Stephanie the fifth in a row. I, too, am a junior—my father's name was also Efrem. I decided to name my son Efrem III and he, in turn, named his son Efrem IV. We have little imagination in our family. We just keep repeating names. Some people say that to name your children after yourself limits their ability to find their own way. I don't agree with that because all three of my children have gone way beyond me. Stephanie has had huge success of her own as an actress; my son is a brilliant businessman—a vice president with the *Times-Mirror*—putting me to shame with a mind like a steel trap and a wonderful life; and my eldest daughter, Nancy, is a fabulous tennis player, who heads up the Virginia Slims tennis tournaments.

Earth

I was in our den, sitting in my easy chair when the January 1994 earthquake hit. My wife was down the hall sleeping. The shaking was so intense that I felt as if I was riding a horse or sitting in a little boat heading into fierce waves. It was an extraordinary feeling. I remember thinking, "There is absolutely no way this house can stand up through this; it's going to be in pieces." It was just *way* too big. I am so proud of the house: We lost some chimneys and every single thing fell, but the walls stood firm.

I'll tell you an ironic thing. We, like everyone else, lost so much. We just swept it up and threw it out. But our bar, with many long-stemmed crystal glasses perched on mirrored glass, was totally un-altered. Not one glass moved an inch. [The same thing happened in Paul and Hilda Williams's bar. Neither couple drinks much, if any, alcohol.] I'd say that if God causes earthquakes, he must be a drunk. Can you imagine, not one thing stirred in the entire bar, but everything else in the whole house fell down? Isn't it strange? I am not a tee-totaler; I have a glass of wine every once in a while, but I don't drink much only because I don't really enjoy it. Some people who come to our home want a drink, so we have a bar. Maybe once in three years, I'll feel like having a margarita and then that's the end of it. It's not because of any virtue; I would be an alcoholic if I loved it.

I wonder if the earthquake and other earth changes are precursors to bigger events? I don't think anything will happen to destroy the planet, or that the entire race will kill itself either, but I do believe in what the Bible's book of Revelations says: We will go through some very difficult times, but how they will manifest I have no way of knowing. As for the year 2000 being the time for Armageddon, Jesus himself said: "Even the son doesn't know. Only the father knows." So if Jesus didn't know, you can be sure I've got no idea. I don't think it's our job to know when it will happen, but we must be ready when it does. It doesn't matter a bit to me, if I'm here when it happens, it will be exciting. If not, I can look down (I hope not up) and watch, or maybe even be a part of it all. Who knows? I'm not going to miss out on anything one way or the other.

Will I come back in another life? I used to believe in reincarnation when I was meditating with the Maharishi. One of the few things that has remained with me from what he taught was, "We accept all things." That was great wisdom. I personally don't think I still believe in reincarnation, but I am the last person in the world to say that it's not true. It may well be a fact; I am open-minded. There is no way for us to know all the answers. I can only go with what I do believe and base my life along those lines. Becoming a bigot, thinking I know everything, would be dangerous and terribly stupid.

Vision

Looking back, I do have a few regrets. One of them is for being such a damned fool in college. I'll always feel that. I know now how hard my parents worked to give me the best, and I was a bitter disappointment. My mother died shortly after I was kicked out of college, so I never had a chance to make up in any way for what I had done. It hurt her terribly that her son would turn out to be so irresponsible. My father was so sweet, he never held it against me. Dad lived to the old age of ninety-five and was able to see my success and my happiness. Even with him, though, I regret the way I repaid him for what he gave me. I can't say that I carry guilt around, I would just do it so differently now. I was young.

During college, I was a clotheshorse. I still like clothes, but I am conservative in my shopping nowadays. Back then, I used to buy all sorts of sport jackets and suits. There were marvelous stores near Yale, in New Haven, with the finest materials (English tweeds and the like). I had opened charge accounts in many of those stores and when I got kicked out of school for good, I estimate I owed maybe five thousand dollars to clothing stores—which would be like fifty thousand dollars today. To restaurants, where I'd also opened accounts, I'd say I owed another two thousand dollars. In today's currency, I probably left Yale owing the equivalent of at least seventy-five thousand dollars. My kind father went up to New Haven after I'd left and without ever mentioning it to me, paid off every account. Can you imagine, not one word? Dad understood how badly I felt about it in subsequent years and knew it wasn't necessary to scold me about it. He was an extraordinary man, really the greatest man I've ever known. We adored each other, with the type of relationship where you don't have to say anything.

There came a time when Dad was eighty-five and on his deathbed with cancer. The end was in sight. The doctors felt that for him to live one or two more days was the most we could hope for. At this point he didn't move, his eyes didn't open, and he was being fed intravenously. A body waiting to die. I was in the hospital with him,

Courtesy of Efrem Zimbalist, Jr.

Efrem and father, home in Los Angeles, circa 1975.

holding his hand, when to my amazement he opened his eyes and said, "Son, that was a terrible thing you did to me in New Haven." This was forty years later. I said: "Daddy, I know it. I'm so terribly sorry. I feel awful about it. Please forgive me if you can." From that moment on, he started to get well. A week later, he was up and being sent home. In the car on the way home from the hospital, I asked him, "Do you remember what you said to me?" He said, "No, what was that?" I told him and he got this embarrassed look on his face and said, "I must have been awfully sick." Dad lived another ten years.

I've heard that when people are dying, or close to it, their life begins to play back. I think Dad was back in time; because I was there holding his hand, he connected with me.

I clearly see the hand of God working miracles all the way throughout my life. I was protected in my childhood in so many ways, and then again in the war I felt watched over. Being given my acting career out of what looked like total disaster in Europe was incredible. There have been endless miracles.

A few years ago, I was in the bathroom removing makeup from a show and I fell reaching for soap. I slipped on the floor, I think one of our little dogs had peed. My feet went flying and I came down with a crash and broke my hip. I can't believe how easily I got through even that trauma. From the day I went to the hospital, until now, I have never had pain. They hooked me up to an I.V. and told me that whenever I needed a shot to relieve the pain to push a button. I never had any pain, so I never pushed it. It was remarkable.

Again, that kind of gift has pursued me my whole life. I'm so conscious of the blessings of God in my life. He has always been there for me. The blessings go on and on and never stop.

Courtesy of Efrem Zimbalist, Jr.
Efrem with daughter Stephanie.

9

Leeza Gibbons

Courtesy of Paramount Studios

Introduction

W*hen Leeza and I met for the first time, it was to commiserate. Our husbands had been out of the country for over a month, acting together in a series for NBC. Even before we met, we felt the bond of women with small children who missed their fathers, but as much as our husbands tried from their distant location to get Leeza and me together, our crazy schedules made the meeting too challenging to arrange—until one afternoon when I turned on Leeza's talk show. Missing my husband, I hoped she had something to say about the shoot. Only the week before, Leeza's husband, Steve, had sent home a joke video of scantily clad women surrounding him on a tropical beach catering to his every whim, which Leeza aired. This particular day, however, the show had a different tone. Leeza was sitting down, sharing intimately with America her sincere longing to see her husband. Leeza was speaking clearly and emotionally about something close to my heart: My three-year-old son was showing signs of anger and distress at the loss of his daily playmate, and no amount of explaining seemed to help. As I listened to Leeza speak of her daughter Lexi's nightmares—a result of Steve's absence—I was instantly comforted. Location jobs can be difficult on a marriage, and certainly the most challenging for young children left at home. I immediately called Leeza at the studio and we arranged a meeting.*

    When a public personality like Leeza allows us to witness her growth on television, freely exposing her vulnerabilities, fears and struggles, we feel close to her. Compound that with the rare ability to make us think that life is basically good, even in the face of trauma, and our loyalty is sealed. Oprah has this gift. Rosie O'Donnell and Kathie Lee do also. No one doubts that Princess Diana had this effect on a global scale. America fell in love with Leeza thirteen years ago when, only in her twenties, she joined the anchor team of Entertainment Tonight. *The unabashed enthusiasm she displayed for her work was refreshing in the 1980s, a decade characterized more by attitude than exuberance. It wasn't long before Leeza was ranked one of Hollywood's most popular and trusted entertainment journalists. Her interviewing skills seemed to be innate, but were hard-earned in the school of journalism at the University of South Carolina—where she graduated the top of her class—and in her subsequent television journalism jobs.*

Although Leeza had always wanted to fashion her career after the more serious Walter Cronkite, Entertainment Tonight *encouraged her light and bubbly personality to remain in the forefront. She seemed to have the most glorious time interviewing celebrities, and stated openly that being around exceptional people all of the time seemed to rub off, allowing her to experience many benefits in her own life.*

Not long after our friendship began, I had a dream instructing me to write this book. I called Leeza to ask for an interview, and she said no. Like most high-profile people, Leeza was being approached about writing her own story. I couldn't let go of the fact that everything she stood for and represented was material for my dream interview; I saw her as the epitome of the type of woman I wanted to write about. Even though an interview was not possible until years later, when this book was almost completed, her generosity from the start amazed me as she offered to endorse and help publicize Lives Charmed. *Her attitude showed me firsthand that the warm and caring personality you see on her television talk show and hear on her daily nationwide radio programs is, in fact, the real thing. No one would have expected her to help a woman she barely knew; God knows she was busy enough with her own career and raising her children. But the humanity and goodness that draws an audience to Leeza doesn't waver in her personal life. Perhaps that is why she experiences so much success. Leeza is, in fact, so humble, that I am quite sure that when she reads this she will be somewhat embarrassed about ever offering to help publicize a book that speaks so highly of her.*

One of the reasons it was so important for me to interview Leeza was the career she had chosen for herself. When my father jokes that he cannot quite understand my generation, I humor him by saying that he didn't have the benefit of growing up in the talk-show era. When Dad was a young adult, men and women were expected to be stable, successful and nurturing without complaint. If a person struggled with an eating disorder, alcoholism or the like, more often than not they were isolated in their pain. Because there was so little information about these disorders, people frequently didn't know what was wrong with them, or even how to get help. Nowadays, the seeds of healing are planted for the millions of viewers who have the luxury of watching talk shows. Certainly not all are done with integrity, but the cream always rises, resulting in tremendous opportunities for education and growth.

Leeza, who at the time of this interview was five weeks from delivering her third baby—a boy—has interviewed hundreds of top celebrities for radio and television (she owns a popular radio show that is heard twice daily on 250 stations nationwide, making her the most frequently heard radio personality on air today). It is with great appreciation that I turn the tables here and focus on the woman who is normally the one asking the questions.

*   *   *   *

Happiness

Happiness is to simply be at peace. I'm happy when I'm productive, giving love, and grateful for all of the abundance in my life, while having the time to enjoy it all. The happiest time in my life is overwhelmingly right this very minute. I have such fullness and richness in my everyday existence. I'm in love with my husband, and our children are constant reminders of God at work in our lives. I have opportunities to make a difference in my career, and I'm healthy, awake and alive throughout the process.

This doesn't mean that my life is without struggles or challenges, or wants and desires. There are plenty of those, but to me, those things are the essence of life. From the time I was a little girl, I've had this need to accomplish.

Courtesy of Leeza Gibbons Enterprises

Leeza at nine years old.

That's okay because that seemed to be the source of happiness for me, and still is. I was an extraordinarily happy little kiddo. I was very fortunate to have two wonderfully supportive and nurturing parents who gave me the great gift of letting me test-drive my own dreams. They allowed me to fail and gave me permission to be happy in spite of it.

Early Years

People ask me why I work so hard. I was brought up with a stay-at-home mom who really sacrificed a lot for her three children. Part of me admired her for that, but the other part of me watched her and recognized that I didn't believe in my heart that it was enough for her. I didn't buy it. She was always there for us, and having an available parent is incredibly valuable. Her choice was an honorable one. But I watched Dad get deep fulfillment from his work. I watched him make a difference and use his associations and access and knowledge, and I wanted that. I watched Mom use her nurturing side and that's what I've tried to emulate in my own life. I hope I have her tenderness and soft touch; she taught me selflessness and the value of family. My father taught me the value of hard work.

Dad worked with the State Education Association in South Carolina, and at one point, he got into the political process and ran unsuccessfully on the Democratic ticket for governor. During that time, integration was still a social experiment. There was a lot of racial tension and lip service being paid to accepting people of other colors, particularly black people, but the reality was that there was a lot of fear. People are still afraid, but this was an especially heated time. Dad was a civil rights leader; from him I learned courage. I watched him put his convictions ahead of his popularity, often making unpopular decisions against popular people, and it was a powerful message for me that he wasn't willing to do whatever was necessary to be elected. He was willing to do what was right according to his own beliefs.

When Dad didn't get the nomination for governor, I was secretly glad because it would have propelled our family into a lifestyle that I didn't feel we were ready for. Intense pressure like that is difficult for the strongest of families. We were so proud of Dad. I never saw his loss as a validation that good would not win out. To me, it was a bigger message, bigger than the local politics. We clearly saw that he was disappointed, even though Daddy and I have never really talked about it. Most of us, when we're young, have dreams and goals. Dad had powerful ones that guided him, but they changed. Many people end up making compromises during the course of their lives, but I never equated Dad leaving politics as trading out his dream. Sometimes life changes our dreams for us. To me as a young girl, I saw my father's loss as noble, and I thought that he could do anything. I loved nothing better than to go to the office with him, watching the phone lines light up and people scurry by. There was a back-door entrance to Daddy's office and I thought it was a secret, exciting world. [Leeza laughs as she points to the back-door entrance to her own office.]

Spirituality

Photo by Bill Hanson

Leeza and her father, Carlos.

I remember always feeling that I was somehow guided, protected, looked over. I had a certain sense that everything would be okay. I felt close to God as a kid, I suppose that was a function of the way I was brought up. I remember many times sitting outside with my mother and looking at the sky and talking about God's plan for my life. I felt there would be wonderful things ahead for me. I remember the violent thunderstorms that we had in the southeast, and while other kids shivered underneath their covers, Mom and I marveled at the majesty and power of it all.

As with most little kids, my concept of God used to be a bearded fatherly figure in flowing robes. He sat around on big white fluffy clouds, looking over us all while angels played harps. Now I most often see God through people on earth.

I learned a lot about God from watching my Aunt Wayne. She is the most loving, gloriously happy individual I have ever known, and yet, to look at her life you have to wonder why. She has been tested in ways that most of us can't even imagine. She lost a son to a heart attack, and he left behind two young children; she also lost a teenage daughter to kidney disease. Her husband died after suffering a long, difficult illness, and she herself has multiple problems with arthritis. Yet, I've never seen a more grateful, loving individual. And I wonder why she's had to endure such pain.

Aunt Wayne was the first person who ever taught me that when God closes the door, somewhere he opens a window. She's always finding those windows, throwing back the curtains and opening them up wide. No trace of resentment, no bitterness, no anger, no pity or questioning, "Why me?" I look at her, and I see God. And when I wonder why someone so good has had to endure so much, all I can hang on to is faith. I have to believe that there is a reason for all of it, even though I don't know and can't know what it is. I believe very strongly in the power of prayer, and I also believe in unanswered prayers. I often fall into the trap of asking for things to turn out a certain way, rather than asking for guidance and the ability to deal with the way God feels they should turn out.

I am now so aware of the God force within each of us. Now that I'm creating a new life, I'm aware of my place on earth and the fact that there is a force protecting me. It's funny that the more I think I advance spiritually, the more I realize that we can't have all the answers. That's why it's called faith. Some people may interpret that as being naive, but for me, it's not that I'm relinquishing control of my life, or that I'm not taking responsibility for my life—I do both of those things—rather I do them better when I know that I'm being guided by my creator. And not only are my decisions better for me when I'm aware of that, but those decisions are also better for the people around me.

I never feel closer to God than when I'm holding my children, or hearing them laugh, or watching them sleep. I've always been quite sure that they are little angels and have so very much to teach us. I pray frequently to be good enough to open them up to their potential and to set them on a path to lead a spiritual life. I love listening to them say their prayers at night. My little five-year-old says, "God bless me and Mommy and Daddy and my sister, and I bless you God," and

I think how beautiful it is that this little boy recognizes that he has within his heart the God force to be a blessing and to *give* blessings.

Kids have such wonderful faith. Whenever we're driving and see a fire truck go by or hear a siren, the kids and I always offer up a little prayer that everything is okay. While we were watching the news one night after an apartment fire, the newscaster reported that there were no injuries, and my kids said, "Good, Mommy, our prayers worked." It made me so warm inside to see them have such wonderful expectations, such hopefulness.

I find myself whispering little prayers throughout the day. More often than not lately, they are prayers of gratitude and thanksgiving. In my work, I am surrounded by stories of people who face seemingly insurmountable odds, and I marvel at the power and resilience of the human spirit. All the while, as I admire their strength and courage, I send up prayers of thanks that I haven't yet been tested in that way. I have my health, I haven't lost a parent, and I've never lost a child. Those are the big tests. I pray that if the time comes when I am tested like that, I will have the grace to endure it.

I do sometimes feel almost guilty that I have such abundance when so many deserving people are struggling with so little. I just hope that I can live my life to the glory of God and be constantly aware that these treasures that I hold are only on loan for this lifetime.

Vision

When my spiritual life gets off track, the chaos begins in my life and nothing seems to fit and nothing makes sense. That's when I recognize that I'm trying to do it by myself, and I don't have to. When I glide through life more effortlessly, I'm usually the closest to God. It's not that there are no difficulties for me to overcome, it's just that I have a peace of mind while facing the struggles.

I've always found it miraculous that I've been given so many second chances in my life, so many opportunities to do it again, to do it better, to change my path. Every time that happens, I count it as a miracle from God, recognizing that forgiveness is available to all of us. There have been lots of times when I've come dangerously close to getting seduced by all of the trappings out there, and something has stopped me right at the precipice. I think those are the miracles because it's very easy to project, *what would happen if?*

The second chances have come in all areas. When I look back at going on the air and how raw and awkward I was, I wonder why on earth I had a chance to literally grow up in front of an audience. I was so naive and unsophisticated. Now I watch kids who are starting out at the same age I was, and they are polished and professional. I'm grateful for that naive quality, though, because it never did occur to me that I couldn't do something.

My hard-working attitude has been with me since I can remember. I always expected to do well in school, and I would have had a hard time personally accepting it if I had received bad marks. My parents impressed upon me that knowledge was power, power was control and access, and power led to autonomy. So that was my pursuit. I was bright, with above-average intelligence, but it was not a cake walk. I worked hard. My brother, who is an attorney, was the smart one. He has an incredible mind for details, and took the SATs and all the standardized tests and scored through the roof, with scholarships waiting for him. I was the kind of student who took the SAT one time and said, "Oh no, I can't get into the school I want with that, let me learn how to test better and take it again."

I think our performance in school does signify some amount of worthiness or marketability or advantage, but that goes away almost immediately. It's like driving a car off the lot: The minute you get the diploma, it gets devalued because then you have to start all over. That's my personal view. A college degree is one trampoline jump into your future, and that's it. You only get one jump out of it. Of the people who

Leeza as a cheerleader in Irmo, S. Carolina.

have achieved great things, some of them are academicians, but most of them aren't. I look at the people who impress me and people I hire, and the last thing I look at is formal education. I find it to be the least insightful thing about them. It's a factor, and implies discipline and potential, but true learning comes from your work experience. Mama always said, "I Will is more important than IQ."

I remember working hard to change my southern accent when I got into the working world. I think accents are charming, and can be really pretty, but I thought I sounded like a redneck. People treated me as though I didn't have much intelligence. It's an interesting study in our society that even those of us who think that we're nonjudgmental and well-rounded and open find ourselves fast-forwarding and assigning a whole bunch of characteristics to people based on the way they sound. I didn't want to be in that box. I love the way Barbra Streisand sings, her enunciation is so beautiful. I could hear the vowel sounds so clearly, and I wanted to sound more like that, so I would record myself and then I would play her records, working on certain words that lingered on. A couple of them are still there, though, and when I go back home they really come out.

Fame

I always knew that I would "make it." I always knew that I would have opportunities if I was smart enough and open enough to pursue them. The public profile portion of my life was not altogether expected, but I've never seen it as anything other than an obligation and an opportunity. Never an encumbrance. I think the opportunities I've been given have come my way for a reason, including the show that I host. It was not something that I sought; it just sort of happened to me [Paramount wanted to expand on Leeza's popularity, creating something for her outside of *Entertainment Tonight*], and every day I get glimpses of why, although the master plan has not yet been revealed.

I knew from the time I was in about fifth or sixth grade that I wanted to be a storyteller, and that I would probably use television as the medium to tell my stories. I started out on radio, which led to news, then to entertainment, and now to talk. All along the way, the person who impressed me most as a little girl, and continues to today, is Walter Cronkite. I've never met him personally, but there was something secure about watching him deliver the news, no matter how bad the news was. You trusted him and believed him. He communicated the news, not with a sense of detachment, but instead he allowed himself to feel emotions, which translated to the intimate medium of television dramatically. From the space walk to the Kennedy assassination, I vividly remember seeing Walter Cronkite's humanity at work on the air. I wanted to be able to affect people in the same way, to have that much compassion.

The *Leeza* show has been nominated every year for multiple Emmys. This past year, we received seven nominations, and I could tell you that it's very gratifying to be recognized for the work that I do, but what really counts to me is my own internal sense of pride and my own gauge of what is good. I know that what we do is responsible and handled with integrity. If winning awards follows, that's wonderful. If they don't, then I know just the same that what I'm doing is worthwhile.

There was a girl on our show who had incredibly low self-esteem. She thought she was worthless. Her family was in crisis, and she was hitting her mother and abusing herself with drugs and alcohol. She was at the lowest of lows when I met her. She came on the show a couple of times, and the third time I said to her, "If you really want to make a difference in your life, I want to be the one to help you get it back together." She told me that she needed a new environment, to get away from her friends and have a fresh start. I provided that for her. She moved across the country to a Christian academy where she was given an opportunity to rebuild herself. Talk about miracles in action, this young lady is poised and confident and full of energy and hopes and dreams, and uses all of her time reaching out to other people. I know for certain that I was supposed to connect with that girl on that day. That's the upside to fame.

The downside is not having the time or the resources to connect individually with as many people as I would like. It's just a reality that I do not have the fulfillment of enough one-on-one personal relationships. I try to organize my time and energy so that I can contribute to the greater good in the most meaningful capacity, but I always wish I could do more. I get so many letters from people who want or need something. Although I know it's not physically possible for me to fulfill all of these requests, I agonize over the ones that go unanswered.

Time and Energy

Ah, the bugaboo area of time and energy! No, I do not have all the time and energy I want. I would like to clone myself so that I could have the efficient Leeza and the leisurely Leeza. The challenge for me, as it is with anyone, is balancing those two forces in my life. I think we should switch our weekly line-up in this country, working two days a week, with five days to be with our families and pursue outside interests that would make us well-rounded people.

If I had more time, I would love to do more personal reading. I would love to take up windsurfing. I would love to learn languages and travel to exotic locations just to take pictures and fill pages in my diary. I would love to learn how to build something. There are so many things I would do if I had more time, yet I feel all of that is still out there. Now is my time to do what I'm doing.

The thing that has been most difficult about this pregnancy is that I don't have all the energy I want. Physically I can run on all cylinders and recharge very quickly, but this little baby has zapped a lot of my strength, and it's been a real lesson in humility for me to recognize that I do not wear a cape, and Superwoman isn't even a distant relative of mine. Sometimes I just can't get it all done, and I think the lesson for me is being okay with that. There are no martyr Olympics, and there are no rewards for trying to do it all yourself—quite the reverse, in fact, is true. There is great value in allowing other people to help you along the way. I wish I had learned that earlier.

Obstacles

In my view, I used to consider myself weak if I asked for help. I was a product of the whole feminist movement, and we had a lot to prove and a lot of trailblazing to do. If I knew then what I know now, I not only would allow people to open doors for me, but I would take advice better. I'm trying to learn to take advice more easily, but unfortunately I think that's a learned skill. I would have listened better earlier, too. I'm trying to recognize that people who come before me have answers, and that I don't have to reinvent the questions. It seems that wisdom so often comes too late for it to do you any good.

Have I learned lessons the hard way? Whoa, is that me! I think I've learned every lesson in my life the hard way. None of them have come easily, although the answers were all there, I was just too bullheaded to listen. As much as I'm aware of that character trait now, it still seems to be true.

There is a lot of discussion about "having it all" these days. I do believe you can have it all, but I don't think you can have it all at the same time. And "it" all comes at a cost. It will be interesting to see what my daughter chooses for herself. The art of compromise is one of the most valuable lessons in life, I think. While I like to have the bar as high as possible, setting the highest standards for myself, I've also come to realize that sometimes life is a negotiation, and that's true with things that we want. I believe you get what you focus on. If you focus on a high-powered career and making lots of money, you can create that. You can get that. If you focus on a loving, secure marriage, with a lot of mutual respect and a lot of intimate sharing, you can get that, too. You can be an available parent, who cooks nutritious meals from scratch and volunteers on every committee at school, but you cannot do all of those things all of the time. The cost is sometimes your sanity.

For me, to be the kind of parent I want to be, I've had to pay the price at work and step back from my show and trust others to control it and trust others to make decisions for me. Sometimes to be the kind of parent that I want to be, the cost has been my vanity. I often relinquish time for exercise to be with the kids, or I won't do my nails and my roots will grow out. These are little examples, but they are some of the daily prices. There are no magic elixirs that allow us to be all things to all people. If we try to do that, we end up being no good to anyone.

I'm quite sure that my anxiousness and ambition early in my career cost me some relationships. I'm quite sure that my desire to have a family and be a mother cost me some opportunities with my career. And, if I'm to be real honest with myself, I'm sure that my choice to be a working mother has taken a toll on my marriage in that it makes

it more difficult for me and my husband to find time to grow the way
we want to as a couple.

The people who I think have it all are the people with balance.
They are the people who feed themselves spiritually, who nurture
themselves with good friends and family, who challenge themselves
with work or volunteering, and who have the recipe to keep it all in
balance. That's really having it all. I think women juggling career and
family feel like they are running out of time in both categories. The
glass ceiling seems like such an oppressive reality, but the need to
accomplish at work is great, and the biological need to have children
is also great. Both of those things have a finite amount of time for
accomplishment.

If I have any advice for other working mothers (and it's pretty arrogant for me to try and give advice), I would say that it's important to
ask for help, to admit when you can't do it all, and to accept that most
days you're not going to be the perfect employee and the perfect
mother.

Fear

My fear of dying has lessened dramatically with age. I really don't
fear dying anymore, and while I hope that I'm allowed to live out a
long life here on earth, I have a sense of serenity about what may
come next. I fully expect it to be even better. I've also become more
secure with who I am over the years. I am much more able now to
announce to the world who I am instead of waiting to hear who it
wants me to be.

Before I had children, I used to have anxiety about being a good
parent, and now with the third one on the way, I'm much more calm
about that. I'm confident in my ability to guide this little life. Being a
working parent has been one of the biggest challenges of my life,
though. I'm very careful with how I present my work to my children,
especially my daughter, Lexi. I want her not to see it as this big bad
cloud in her life. I want her to see that it's rewarding and productive,
that it serves a purpose, and that it's *my* choice, but that it doesn't have
to be hers.

I talk to Lexi every night when I'm rubbing her back and we have these wonderful conversations. In our quiet time, she'll ask me about things. One evening, I said to her, "Honey, do you think that it would be different if I didn't work, would you like having a mommy who stayed home?" And she said, "No, because I know how much your work means to you, and you would disappoint so many people if you didn't work." That's a wise thing coming from a seven-year-old girl. Then I asked her, "But, am I disappointing you because I do work?" and she said, "No, but I need more time with you." I thought to myself, "Okay, open up your ears and listen to this little girl who is allowing you to be who you are and is asking you to be more available."

You know, Steve had been asking me for years to slow down and simplify, but as much as I adore him, Lexi's little voice had a bigger impact. I could hear the message so strongly because it was so unencumbered by anything else, whereas Steve's needs are complicated by his maleness and all of his life experience. But Lexi is this pure little spirit who just said what she needed and I thought, "Oh my gosh," and that's when I took an honest look and asked how much I was lying to myself about my availability. There is a big difference between being home and being *present* with your family. Being home and being on the phone or doing business is not being available.

I have a lot of research to do for the show. It seems like there are endless things I need to know about and understand. One thing that is so easy for me to fall into is wanting to research on weekends and at night in bed. If Steve is watching a football game or a movie that I'm not particularly interested in, it's so tempting to lie next to him with articles or books that may be the topic of Monday's show. But I'm not really present if I do that. And, I'm one of those people who likes to lay paper out all over the bed. Piles of research. It must make him crazy!

I've worked the whole time we've been married. My wish when we met was that I could gear down, and that's still my wish and my fantasy. I'd love to take time off, and that's one thing I pray for: To have the guts to walk a quieter path. I think that takes guts. As long as things are running on all cylinders, you don't have to think about it because it's all happening. That's a trap.

I've never really experienced too much fear about my career. Even in the beginning I always felt like I would somehow make it. The big picture belief never waivers, but the insecurity comes in the daily details. I allow myself to hang on to the minutiae. I can do a really great show, and when the audience is leaving and I'm shaking hands, if one person says, "You know, I think you were biased there. . . ." I obsess over it. I guess somewhere it does get back to that need to be liked and the need for approval. There are those days where I'll get a letter and I'll have to call the person to talk about their complaint. I take very seriously the fact that a lot of people depend on me, and I don't want to let them down.

Family

I marvel at my husband's ability to adapt himself to this high-pressured, high-energy woman that he married. What I love most about him is that he's a safe harbor from the storm. I don't have to be brilliant for him; I don't have to be gorgeous for him. I can be vulnerable. He has pulled off an almost impossible task: He's managed to maintain an incredible amount of masculinity and identity in a situation that easily strips men of both. He generously shares me with causes and with people. He is this devoted father with childlike energy to be mischievous. I'm the stricter parent, more often the disciplinarian.

Steve's like a walking home-entertainment center: tons of fun. He loves to be spontaneous with the kids by sleeping out in the tree house with them at night, or by painting their bodies. I often laugh at him and say it's like having another kid in the house. I cherish that about him.

I don't think there is such a thing as the perfect person out there for anybody. I think we create perfect relationships. Sure, there are characteristics that we're attracted to and qualities that we're attracted to, but I believe you love someone because of how they make you feel about who you are when you're with them. When I'm with Steve, I feel like I count. I feel like I stand for something. I want to feed his soul and nourish his dreams in a way that he has done for me.

I live very spontaneously, and I love that. Most men in general, and Steve is no exception, like to know up front and in advance what the game plan is. I thrive on chaos and things falling apart. I expect them to every day. I don't wake up thinking that it will be an orderly day. I always have a plan, and I always know it's going to be fine, but I expect that things will happen to derail the plan throughout the day. Steve gets thrown off when things derail, so I have to update him on what's going on. We made a deal, which has really been the lifeline connecting my personal and business lives. We negotiated a way to be together with my business commitments. It was like, "I'll give you this if you give me that." I know he doesn't enjoy big social scenes. He doesn't like the glitz.

Photo by Kathy Hutchins

Leeza with husband, Steve Meadows, at the Emmy Awards.

I went to Steve and said, "I want you and need you by my side at some of these functions, so let's negotiate which ones you're okay with." And then, once we've got them down, I give him notice and remind him when they are coming up. He then has the time to let it set in his mind, knowing who will be there, how long it will last, and when we will leave. That way I respect his time and the fact that he prefers a simpler lifestyle. If I just come home from work and say, "Oh, by the way, tonight we're going to do this and this," then I'm not honoring him. Isn't it funny that the thing you fall in love with is most often the thing that becomes a problem in your relationship? That rebelliousness that I found so attractive now makes me say, "Can't you just conform here for a minute?" But ironically, that would not make me happy. I love his strength. I love his independence, and although in certain moments I would appreciate him to abandon his ways, it's only a short-term wish.

After we had Troy, Steve and I decided that the four of us made up our family perfectly, and we were so happy with that. Then about five years down the road, we both started talking about a baby. I'm forty and the chances of getting pregnant with your own eggs after forty diminish because they just aren't as viable. But we conceived our child right away, and it seems to be another symbol in our lives that anything is possible.*

One of the things I love most about our lives is knowing that we're creating a future. I love the trip to tomorrow. It's incredibly exciting to me because it holds so much promise. I guess that's why I'm so emotional about having this baby right now, and our children. They represent tomorrow and I think all of our dreams lie hidden somewhere behind our tomorrows.

Photo by Allison Cane

Baby Nathan, Lexi and Troy.

[*AUTHOR'S NOTE: *Leeza delivered a healthy eight-pound, nine-ounce baby boy—Nathan Daniel —on October 3, 1997.*]

10

Sandy Gallin

Courtesy of Gallin–Morey, 1997

Introduction

U
ntil Sandy's most famous client, Michael Jackson, found himself at
the center of one of the most negative media blitzes in American history, Sandy did fairly well in his efforts to dodge the spotlight. That
was, after all, the arena he reserved for his clients. Even when he won an
Academy Award for producing the documentary Common Threads,
about AIDS, it was the movie that rightfully received the attention.
Because his daily schedule as a talent manager includes making and
receiving over two hundred phone calls on behalf of the stars he represents—Dolly Parton, Neil Diamond, Mariah Carey, Nicole Kidman,
Martin Lawrence, and Renee Zellweger, to name a few—getting this man
to agree to an interview, something he still rarely does, is a comical experience. In the beginning of the interview process, until he trusts that the
line of questioning is unique and indeed spiritually based, the interruptions are sharp and incessant. I see why he has been called intimidating.
With time and perseverance on the part of the interviewer, however,
Sandy settles down to a thoughtful and reflective look at the life of an
insecure and overweight boy who dreamed of one day becoming wealthy
and powerful in Hollywood. The vision included befriending the most
fascinating people in the world and entertaining them in his lavish
homes. He recalls that his family laughed at the youngster who spoke of
the millions he would make in Tinseltown, a reality that seemed further
and further away the poorer his family became.

As destiny would have it, Sandy's childhood dreams have all come
true. His personal wealth has been estimated at a minimum of $30
million and his yearly income has come close to $10 million. When he
started out in the mail room at the General Artists Corporation (G.A.C.),
then a huge talent agency in New York City, and quickly rose to a secretarial position, he had no idea that several of his acquaintances, too,
would be prominent in Hollywood's future. Today Sandy is nearly as
well known for his extended family, including Barry Diller, David
Geffen, Diane Von Furstenberg, Calvin Klein, Kelly Klein, Dolly Parton
and Fran Lebowitz, as he is for his clientele. An April 1996 article about
Sandy, which appeared in Vanity Fair, stated that "Sandy is a member
of a group of people whose longtime association makes Bloomsbury look

dull and unindustrious." Although he resides primarily on the West Coast because of his work, Sandy spends as much time as he can in his favorite city, New York, with this tight-knit group of people.

Sandy is a social being, but his love life was not as easily mapped out as his career. When he fell in love for the first time with a man, he was frightened of the challenges that would encompass, and he rushed into a marriage that he hoped would foster a more normal life. The union lasted only a short time, but to his relief Sandy found that living in California, far from his mother and married brother in New York, made the reality of being gay easier to adapt to. His adult life has not been without heartbreak; several years ago his long-time companion, a man whom Sandy considered to be his life partner, chose to part ways. Faithfully committed to his spirituality, Sandy exudes an uncommon maturity when speaking about their breakup, seeming to know without a doubt that God has a plan for his life that will include happiness on all levels. His confident, commonsense approach to life and his relationship to spirit makes it easy to understand why he has succeeded at so many things. He expects nothing less from himself or from God.

Deeply rooted in this charismatic personality is a childlike enthusiasm accompanied by an honest, often blunt realism. It's as if the dreamer of his youth lives on, having successfully incorporated the lessons from his painful past—the optimist and the realist united. In most of the movies Sandy's company, Sandollar [a company he started with Dolly Parton], has produced, optimistic themes stand out. In Father of the Bride, Fly Away Home *and even in* Common Threads, *to name a few, the audience is reminded of the simple joys of living. Having faced his own mortality when he was diagnosed with terminal cancer almost fifteen years ago (which he miraculously overcame), Sandy's appreciation for living became something he desired to share. Movies offer a profound tool for touching many souls in a short period of time, and creating them appeared to be the natural progression for his life.*

Sandy is not unlike the main character of his box-office hit, Fly Away Home, *an uplifting tale of a girl who loses her mother to an accident only to become the mother of a flock of baby geese. The young girl, played by Anna Paquin, takes her sadness and creates a life of beauty for herself. Sandy, too, has transformed his life, bringing tears of sorrow and joy to the world through his work. I'm grateful that Sandy's initial intimidating presence didn't overshadow my desire to know the person behind the man. Some things are worth the wait.*

*   *   *   *

Happiness

Happiness, for me, is having peace of mind and a very good relationship with the Light, the Love, and God. The happiest time of my life was probably when I had just graduated from college and started working in the world. I was twenty-two years old and was working in the mail room of a big talent agency, which only got more fulfilling when I was promoted to an assistant in that agency. I found it all so exciting, although I don't know if what I was experiencing was true happiness or just exhilaration and energy flowing into a whole new world that seemed so interesting and glamorous.

I have a fantasy that if I had enough money to be able to live in New York, Los Angeles and on an island that I owned somewhere in the middle of the ocean, that I would experience true happiness. But in reality, I'm not sure. I really don't know what my ultimate existence would be, or even what inspires me to keep working so hard, for that matter. It's a struggle for me to try and get the right answers. Sometimes I catch myself thinking: "If I had enough money, I would. . . ." But really, who knows if there is *enough* money, or what that amount would be. If you're afraid of losing everything, which became a real fear for me when my father lost everything, then perhaps nothing is ever enough.

I still love aspects of my life, but I am currently searching for happiness.

Early Years

My parents are both gone now. They fought a lot and did not get along well; consequently, I identified with my mother more than my father when I was young. They wound up getting divorced when I was fifteen, but even before that, my father was not at home much. He was a gambler and a ladies' man. Everybody in town knew that he was running around with other women, and that made me very sad and unhappy for my mother. As a child, you see everything in black and white, and I thought that my mother was the good one and that my father was the evil one. Of course, when you grow up and mature you realize that no one is all good or all bad. It takes two.

I felt special when I was a kid. I wanted to be famous: a singing star and an actor. My family used to laugh at me when I told them of the millions I would make in the entertainment industry. They thought my dreams were cute and humorous, so I was fortunate to have a professional role model I could look to outside of our immediate family. His name was Ray Katz, a third cousin who was a mentor for me. We actually became business partners in 1969. Ray was the general manager of the top radio station in New York and a personal manager at the same time, and because of his connections, he was able to get me a job in the mail room of a radio station when I was still in high school. This was my first exposure to the entertainment world. When I graduated from college, he helped me get a job in the mail room of G.A.C., which in those days was a huge talent agency, now called I.C.M.

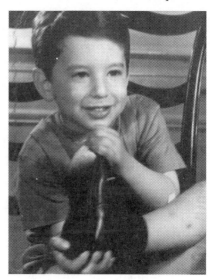

Sandy at five years old, 1945.

Immediately upon getting the second mail-room job, I enrolled in a six-week speed-writing course during the evenings. One of the secretaries at G.A.C. was toying with the idea of quitting her job, so I not only convinced her to quit, but I told her to do me a favor and stay until I had finished my secretarial course. I wanted her position as secretary, but I needed time to learn how to type and take shorthand. She didn't have any expectations or desires to become an agent, so she didn't care if she worked at G.A.C., DuPont or I.B.M. I told her that when she quit, I'd love it if she'd set up a meeting for me to talk to her boss. I asked him to give me a chance, and told him I'd be his work slave. It worked. I had only been in the mail room for maybe six weeks. I was lucky to be in the right place at the right time because a lot of changes were happening within the company, and it wasn't long before I was promoted from a secretary to an assistant agent. Then there were other changes, and within less than nine months I was made an agent. I had my nose to the grindstone and worked all the time, seven days a week. I paid my dues and loved it.

It was the biggest thrill then for me to meet anybody who was talented or famous. Just being around the environment of show business was a dream come true. Six months into my new job, I was already responsible for clients like Richard Pryor, Florence Henderson, Tiny Tim, Dr. Joyce Brothers, Cass Elliot and Virginia Graham, and I also dealt very closely with Paul Anka, Nancy Sinatra, Frankie Avalon and Ricky Nelson.

Two of the agents I worked with went to London and signed the Beatles as clients, and because my boss booked our clients on the *Ed Sullivan Show*, I was able to help book their legendary Sullivan appearance. I serviced the Beatles when they came to America; in other words, I met them at the airport and drove with them to New York City. I knew it was going to be a big night when mobs of fans totally surrounded us and almost turned over our car. We were also mobbed at the hotel; you've never seen such insanity. It was exhilarating. I loved being in the middle of it all, and was aware that something unusual and extraordinary was happening. I didn't know, however, that the show would become one of the most famous shows in the history of television.

I have been so fortunate to work on so many exceptional television programs. At one time I was an executive producer for the *Mac Davis Show*, which I created and sold to NBC, the Osmonds' show, and managing Cher when she and Sonny were doing their comeback show. Being so closely involved with three prime-time, successful variety shows at the same time was incredible. An exciting time for me.

Fame

I feel very lucky and thankful to God to be healthy and wealthy and successful. I don't feel guilty at all about my good fortune. I think if people feel guilty about success, they don't enjoy it and possibly don't even attain it. One aspect of my success, however, that I still wrestle with is that of motivation. The more spiritual disciplines I do, the harder it is to want to strive out in the world because I find so much peace with sitting still. It's a real contradictory situation with me because I love to meditate and do yoga, but I also am addicted to talking and communicating with people, whether in person or on the telephone.

I feel blessed to be able to do both: to have an enjoyable career while maintaining a fulfilling spiritual life. I don't think it is my path to go off to a monastery somewhere because I know that I have worked hard to accomplish all that I have. By the time I was fifteen, I was poor. I worked my way through college, and when I got the mail-room job I really concentrated on working, almost with blinders on. But it paid off. I am so fortunate to have seen the fulfillment of many goals.

I still enjoy working with talented people, but fame is a weird thing. It's surprising to me the way people in the United States treat famous people, particularly movie, television and music stars. They are treated equivalently to the way many royalty are in the rest of the world. It's bizarre. All you have to do is be a big star and you're catered to: You get things for free in stores, you're moved to the front of most lines, your checks are picked up in restaurants and you get reservations when other people cannot get them. "We don't have any room in the hotel," but here comes Marilyn Monroe. "Throw out the people in suite 307." By the way, I'm not criticizing it, but in many cultures around the world, people in the arts are not treated any differently than anybody else.

Americans want fame and gossip. They cannot get enough of it. Look at the popularity of the tabloids. I've had scandalous stories written about me, and I don't consider myself famous! I am fairly well known in my industry, but I certainly don't walk down the street and have people know who I am. Even so, a reporter once wrote a story about me meditating and doing yoga in red underwear. Which is true, by the way, but not the way it was written. The article, which called me "one of the ten scariest people in Hollywood," said that I did yoga and meditation in front of everybody in my office in my red underwear. I had made the mistake of telling a reporter that twenty-two years ago a psychic in New York told me to wear red close to my body whenever I did business. Since then I have always worn red underwear Monday through Friday; and each day, in the privacy of my office, I do yoga and meditate before going home. I do it with my door closed, by *myself*. The way the story was reported made it sound like I called staff meetings to have everybody sit and watch me do yoga and meditation in my underwear. Just for the record, I tend to think there were other elements to my success than just following a psychic's advice. I imagine that some of my hard work, combined with great luck and being in the right place at the right time, held more weight than the red briefs. It may, however, have been one positive element in the whole mix.

Being in the entertainment field, you have to get used to lies told about you, even though they may be cruel. Two years ago, for instance, rumors circulated in the tabloids that Dolly Parton had left her husband, Carl. Dolly is not only a client, I would say that we are soul mates. She is a jewel that I intend to cherish and protect as long as I live, and when rumors like this one take flight, it can be frustrating. That particular rumor was totally, completely, absolutely, 100 percent not true. Not even based on a morsel of truth. Not even based on a disagreement. I don't think the thought of leaving Carl enters her mind. Ever. She's married to him, he's her best friend, and she doesn't want it any differently.

My former client who has had the most lies told about him is Michael Jackson. Michael is probably one of the most talented people on the planet, and the single-most misunderstood and attacked person by the press that I've ever known. But really, I have a fiduciary relationship with my clients, even with my ex-clients, and I don't talk to them about each other, nor do I talk about them to anyone else. Being able to keep things confidential is something I learned the hard way in high school. I don't remember the exact incident, but the lesson has been paramount to the success of my business. Famous individuals need to be able to count on the fact that the people who represent them can be trusted.

Spirituality

When I was young, I didn't understand the whole concept of a Higher Being, nor do I remember feeling protected. I feel protected much more now, and I would say that comes from the amount of praying I do; studying different spiritualities, different religions and improving my relationship with that Higher Being. In other words, the more I put into my spirituality, the more I get back. Whenever I neglect my prayer time, I notice that I become unbalanced, off-center, scattered and insecure. As my relationship with God improves with prayer, I become more centered, less judgmental, less fearful, more content, stronger and happier.

As busy as I am, I consciously schedule time for my prayers. It is part of my morning routine, which also consists of yoga, exercise and meditation. Part of my prayer ritual is putting on tefillin [phylacteries used in Jewish prayer ritual]. Shortly after I was operated on for malignant melanoma, three different friends said to me, "Do you have any idea how lucky you are? You should put tefillin on every day." When the third person said it, I thought, "There are no accidents, everything happens for a reason," and I got a rabbi and learned the procedure.

I don't think of myself as a religious person, and I don't know much about tefillin, but what I do know is that it is an old traditional ritual, mostly practiced by religious Jewish people. Tefillin is used every day except the Sabbath or holidays, and is worn in conjunction with the yarmulke and the tallis. A small Torah in a box is strapped around your left arm and another on your head with the Torah box at the third eye. After a few other steps, I say four short prayers in Hebrew and then add my own prayers. That connection with God or a Higher Being makes me feel good.

Before I got cancer, I used to pray for things. Most nights I prayed, "Now I lay me down to sleep, pray the Lord my soul to take. . . ." and then I blessed everybody I ever met. I would fall asleep saying, "Bless this one, bless that one, bless everyone that that one ever met, and everyone that that one ever met," and so on. Then I would just pick somebody and bless everyone that they knew. Nowadays, I thank God more when I pray, and I apply more ritual, like with the tefillin. I would say honestly that aside from being cured of the cancer, the greatest benefit of being ill was learning to put on the tefillin every day, and embracing the daily prayer that not only goes with the ritual, but that evolved over the last fifteen years.

Another benefit of being sick was an increasing ability to go into deeper meditative states. I started meditating around 1973, way before my cancer, but I became more disciplined with the threat of an early death. Originally, I learned how to meditate at the TM center in Los Angeles, where I was taught to meditate with a mantra. A mantra is a word you repeat over and over to push away any thoughts you have so that you're just there sitting with yourself, not thinking about anything. The goal is to become free from thought. I've been told by various teachers of different forms of meditation that you cannot judge or compare your meditations with other people, or even your own meditations. They just are what they are. There is a cumulative effect; the more years you meditate, the more it benefits your mind and body.

People who do not meditate often assume that there are supernatural experiences that take place, but I don't find meditation to be a mystical, voodoo or an occult experience. The feeling can be magical, but it's not mysterious. For me, it has never been filled with any of the woo-woo things that are sometimes associated with it. Meditation is simply a tool to relax the mind and body. It centers you and brings your energy and focus to peace. Twenty minutes spent meditating should be equal to several hours of sleep, like a good nap that allows you to pick up the pieces of your scattered mind and body and put them together so that you're refreshed and energized. Thinking becomes easier and clearer. But, let's face it: It's not going to make you three inches taller, or give you blond hair if you're a brunette. It will, however, help you to be more peaceful about those things you cannot change because you experience peace on a deep level, regardless of what is going on around you.

I'm also studying the Kabbalah, and part of that is looking at the Hebrew letters and reading the Hebrew scriptures without knowing what they are saying. I'm told this enlightens and blesses you, and I am trusting my teachers. We'll see what happens. I may never know in this life, although there may be something to the fact that the sacredness of the scriptures cannot help but rub off. So you see, I do whatever I can that may benefit my life, regardless of what religion it stems from.

I am not nearly as disciplined with my diet as I am with my spiritual practices, but when I was diagnosed with cancer, I became diligently disciplined with food for a year, eating only raw uncooked fruits, vegetables, nuts and seeds. I started drinking wheat grass every day, and that is the main dietary discipline that is still with me. Wheat grass cleanses and purifies the body and the blood. I have flats of the grass delivered to my home and then make it with a special juicer. Even so, the impact of having cancer has been more of a spiritual influence than a dietary one, for sure.

Creativity

I've been proud of some of the film projects I've produced. From *Father of the Bride* to *Fly Away Home*, but the movie I'm most proud of is *Common Threads*. My goal as an executive producer is to make movies that inspire the audience, make people laugh, scare them or make them cry—anything that provokes real emotion.

When we started out making the film *Common Threads*, which is a deeply emotional film about the making of the AIDS quilt, I had no idea that it would end up being such a powerful piece of work. Howard Rosenman, who worked at Sandollar, brought it to me with two filmmakers from San Francisco, and I was impressed with the people. I thought that we could help raise the awareness of AIDS and what AIDS really is, and what problems it is to individuals and to our society as a whole. I had no idea at the beginning that it would be released as a feature, because it was made for television. HBO decided to release it as a feature, and when it won the Academy Award for best documentary, I think it was the single thing that raised the awareness of AIDS more than anything during the late 1980s.

There is definitely more of an understanding nowadays that it is not dangerous to be close to someone with AIDS. We've had fifteen years to learn about the disease, and people are becoming more compassionate as they see how devastating it is. I have a close girlfriend in New York who has lost all of her male friends to AIDS. All of them. I've lost many acquaintances, and two very, very close friends. Most of my closest friends and I, however, have been lucky and blessed enough not to have contracted or died from the disease.

I think another reason people are becoming more compassionate is that there is increasing acceptance that being gay is not a choice, but possibly a fact of genetics. I believe, and many scientists have agreed, that you are born with your sexuality. I personally never felt that I didn't want to be with women, but I do remember when I started fantasizing in my mind about wanting to be with men. I was about twelve or thirteen, but I still ended up getting married. It was 1965, and things were different. I was moving to California by myself, and I didn't know anybody. I was dating a woman who I liked a lot and was having good sex with, and when she wanted to get married I thought,

"Hmm, this is probably going to be an easier and better life." Being gay then was much more complicated than it is today. And, living in New York with my mother and my brother, who was older than I and married, made it more difficult.

When I told my family that I was gay, I must have been around thirty-two years old. It wasn't too much of a challenge for me because I believe that keeping secrets about your sexuality is dangerous, leading to all sorts of lies. Honesty, for me, has always been the preferable policy. It's so much easier. The catalyst was one of my programs, like est, the Forum or Life Spring. I've done self-help programs, taking pieces from each, learning a little more each time. I don't become a cult member of anything, nor do I believe there are any save-all or end-all practices, but I always learn something new. After I did est and advanced est, I did something called the Advocate Experience, which was, if I remember correctly, sort of a gay est. One of the processes was to write your family and tell them of your sexuality. I wrote my mother and explained to her that I was homosexual and that I had a very full life. I told her that I did not want her to think that I was a drag queen, or that I dressed up in women's clothes, or that I had some bizarre lifestyle. I explained to her that I simply preferred sex with my own sex, rather than with the other sex. Period. It was important to me that she knew I wasn't living a weird existence.

Her reaction was what you would expect. For a short time, she wanted to know what she had done wrong. She was surprised by the news, which is unusual because I thought every mother knows when her child is gay. Mothers typically just know. But, I honestly believe my mother didn't because I had been married, and when I was young, I was girl crazy, with lots of girlfriends.

Mom came to understand that, for me, being gay is not a lifestyle, but just a sexual preference. I have as many or more women friends as I do men, and definitely as many heterosexual friends as I do homosexual. Just right now in my life, sexually, I'm attracted to men.

Fears

Being gay is not easy, but ironically my greatest fears have nothing to do with my sexuality. I thought my fears would disappear with maturity. It would seem logical that the older people get, the less fears they have, but I have not yet found that to be the case. I was an overweight boy, and the fear of being heavy has been with me ever since. I'm working on releasing my fears, however, and I hope I will accomplish that sometime in this life.

When I was fifteen, and my father declared bankruptcy, we lived in the Five Towns of Long Island in New York. When you were fifteen there, everybody got a car. Not only wasn't I going to get a car, but we had to move out of our house into a little apartment. The peer pressure, which was totally in my head, was scary. I was devastated, but when I look back I see that it motivated me in a forward direction. I decided that I was not going to be poor and that I would work very hard in the entertainment business. My mother instilled in me the importance of getting a good education and making an honest success of myself. I knew that I would become successful, and as funny as it now sounds, it was a goal for me to have a big house in Hollywood and have everyone in town know who I was and respect me. I imagine that this mind-set was a result of losing my childhood residence. [Sandy ended up building the big mansion, but immediately upon completion he knew that it was far too large and eventually sold it.]

Passion

As I get older, the material trappings are less and less important. Now I prefer to live in smaller, cozier and warmer surroundings. I have three homes, and I love all of them. I keep an apartment in New York, a home in the Hollywood Hills and a Malibu beach house, but I know as clear as can be that within a year I will get the bug to do something new because I am a construction-aholic. So help me, it's true. I will be absolutely itching to do another environment, although I have no idea where. Almost everybody hates this process, but I love all of it, from designing the architecture to the interior furnishings. You have no idea how many people say to me, "Would you please do it for me, just take it over, finish it, move into it." This creative trait must have been handed down to me by my father, who was a builder. When I find a piece of land, I love imagining what I could have there. It's also a pleasure to find a really awful, horrible house and turn

Photo by David Michalek

Sandy and his Boston terriers in his Malibu screening room.

it into something great. I don't have a favorite style. It changes all the time. Right now, I love old, old European eclectic, cluttered, antique mishmash. I've been into modern, too. Dolly and I share the apartment in New York, and it is contemporary, with antiques and white walls and white damask slipcovers. Dolly left the designing up to me. She says that if I left it up to her, she would probably have jars of Kool-Aid in the windows and it wouldn't look very elegant.

I spend most of my time in L.A. because that is what my business dictates, but I really prefer being in New York. L.A. is an easier place to live; the weather is nicer, and it's easier to get around. It is right near the mountains and the ocean, and you can live in bigger spaces. But for me, New York is more exciting. There is a pulse to the city, and there is infinitely more going on. I have no idea why it is, but in L.A., it never occurs to me to go to the theater. People don't walk on the streets in Los Angeles. I get entertained just walking through Central Park, or up Madison Avenue, and looking at the people and in the store windows. L.A. is basically inhabited by people in the entertainment business. In New York, I have friends who are lawyers, artists, painters, fashion people, political people, old friends from high school and college, restaurateurs and hotel owners. It is more diverse, and I have a more well-rounded lifestyle there.

Sometimes I wish I had more time in the day to do all the things I like to do on both coasts, but the reality is that I have only as much time as we're all given. In truth, if I had more time, I would certainly do more of nothing, like lying in bed or sitting. I'd probably be talking, though.

Basically I'm enormously grateful for my life. It's not a perfect life by any means, but I don't think it's possible to have it all all the time. I do think it's possible to have it all in life. . . . sometimes, but not always. The person who comes the closest to having it all, that I know of, is Dolly Parton.

Dolly has the best life of anyone I've ever met. She is beautiful, healthy, talented, intuitive, funny and gets along with anybody from peasants to royalty. She feels comfortable within herself in any situation, and always looks at the positive rather than the negative. Dolly doesn't dwell on negatives, doesn't deal in fantasy, and lives in reality. She has maintained a childlike quality while being a mature, productive, professional person. She is amazing. I attribute that to her complete faith in God and herself. Her relationship with God is unwavering.

I remember the first time Dolly and I met. I was waiting for her outside the Beverly Hilton Hotel in my car, and when I saw her coming toward me I started laughing out loud because I couldn't believe my eyes. She was dressed as if she were on her way to the country music awards. She had *big* hair and was made up gorgeous, in this very fancy white dress with rhinestones and glittering jewelry. I didn't have time to be flattered, I just thought, "Oh my God, where the hell does she think we're going?" I was in jeans and a T-shirt, and we were going to have dinner at my house. When we got to my home, I gave her a pair of pants and a shirt to wear, which made me more comfortable.

Future

When I look at my future, I see a big question mark.* Isn't the future an unknown situation for everyone? I have my plans and God has his plans. And you know what? *His* plans are going to take precedence over mine.

I don't feel any anxiety about the coming millennium. I've heard all of the predictions about the "inevitable catastrophes" for both coasts, and I have homes near the water in Malibu and in New York, but it doesn't bother me. If it did, I suppose I wouldn't be in either place. Earthquakes, tornadoes or planes having a little bit of trouble don't

[*AUTHOR'S NOTE: *Sandy has recently been named chairman and CEO of Mirage Entertainment and Sports, Inc., a subsidiary of Mirage Resorts.*]

Photo by David Michalek
Sandy with Dolly Parton, 1997.

really bother me. It's not that I am not attached to this life; it's just that I feel that I am blessed by God.

If I could have anything that I do not yet have, it would be a life-time companion who I was madly in love with, who was madly in love with me. I'd also like to own a private plane to take me, my companion and my close friends on little trips to that remote little island we talked about earlier. God willing, that, too, will come to pass.

11

Wyland

Wyland Studios

Wyland painting bottlenose dolphins, Wilmington, Delaware.

Introduction

M any scientists feel that the last decade of the twentieth century may be the most important one in determining whether or not life will thrive on this planet. As thousands of species have become extinct in the last fifty years, the health of our seas is threatened more now than at any other time in history. But every crisis holds the seeds to its own solution, and Wyland is at the forefront of educating the masses about the urgency and necessity of cleaning up our act. His art, particularly his more than seventy Whaling Wall murals, on government buildings, clock towers, Olympic and aquatic attractions, and walls throughout the United States and the world, has inspired millions of people, transforming city views and forcing us to see the glory beneath our waters. Wyland's work takes us into the underwater domain, and next to his life-size portrayals of its inhabitants, we cannot help but feel humbled. To think that dolphins and whales are still slaughtered around the globe, and that our industrial and technological practices are increasingly wiping out the lives of these mammals and their habitats, makes his work of paramount importance.

It is always a pleasure to interview a person with such a profound sense of purpose. When Wyland was still a toddler, he searched for and found old house paint and carried it into his parents' bedroom, where his painting career began with the creation of a dinosaur mural on their headboard. Fortunately, his early teachers recognized Wyland's talent and fostered his creativity. When the kids in his high school were out partying, Wyland was locked in a makeshift studio, painting up to fourteen hours at a time, often throughout the night. It wasn't long before his murals adorned friends' vans and neighborhood garage doors, and his reputation began to spread beyond his hometown of Detroit.

Wyland always paints his murals for free, but the popularity of his work has resulted in a string of art galleries in Hawaii, California and Oregon, making for an extremely lucrative business. His creative endeavors are many: Time Life Books is releasing The Undersea World of Wyland, which includes photos of all of his paintings (with a foreword by one of the top marine scientists in the world, Dr. Sylvia Earle), and Health Communications is publishing Chicken Soup for the Ocean

Lover's Soul, *coauthored by Wyland. Several animated ocean cartoon series are in production, and the Discovery Channel is currently airing fourteen underwater specials entitled* Wyland's Two Worlds. *This prolific painter has been criticized by some who believe the myth that all artists should live a life of struggle, but he doesn't allow these detractors to stop him because he feels within him the urgent call of the ocean, which is far too powerful to ignore. Wyland feels that the spirits of those he paints literally speak to him, encouraging his work so that they will not be forgotten. His relentless drive to educate the masses about the beauty beneath our waters has inspired him to paint the largest mural or painting in the history of mankind, according to the* Guinness Book of World's Records. *The mural, in Long Beach, California, was completed in six days and required seven thousand gallons of paint. Covering three acres, it broke the world record by twenty-seven thousand square feet. When asked how he'll surpass that accomplishment, Wyland jokes that he'll have to paint the Great Wall of China.*

Another example of Wyland's bigger-than-life thinking, which may end up dwarfing his mural endeavors, is the Wyland Ocean Challenge of America. This three-part program is designed to educate students, create art and preserve the oceans, and will be initiated in 1998, the International Year of the Oceans. A challenge will go to every school in the nation (120,000 schools, private and public, from kindergarten to college), in which children will study the ocean and marine life, write essays, enter national art contests, and team up to paint an oceanic mural at their school. Wyland hopes this will result in over one hundred thousand murals and close to a million participants.

The challenge, which is dedicated to the memory of Jacques Cousteau (Wyland's hero), has been endorsed by the White House. Vice President Al Gore recently wrote to Wyland: "Your organization is making an invaluable contribution to the effort to promote environmental awareness among our youth, and to encourage them to continue in their own efforts." Senators and the United Nations Environmental Program are supporting this challenge [Wyland was just named 1998 Artist of the Year by the United Nations.] As one of the largest art and educational projects in history, it is being called Hands Across the Ocean. Wyland hopes to take the challenge to Japan, Russia and Canada in his efforts to inspire an entire generation.

Those of us who own Wyland's art or have been touched by his murals have no doubt that he has the power to awaken in us a passion to help our ocean brothers and sisters. We cannot look into the eyes of his creations without wondering what we can do as individuals. Ultimately, we will have to ask ourselves, as a collective, if we are willing to listen and act on what we can no longer ignore, thanks, in part, to Wyland's tireless efforts to save what we still have.

Wyland Studios

Whaling Wall XXXI, Southern California Edison Bldg. Redondo Beach, CA, 1991.

*   *   *   *

Happiness

I am very happy. I do what I love all of the time. I have never been unhappy. Ever. I don't believe in being unhappy. What for? My life has been pretty steady, consistently good. A well-balanced life.

If you are doing something that you love and are happy doing it, then you are already successful. The best thing is when you can integrate your passions and your hobbies into your job. It isn't a matter of being monetarily successful because that will come if you are doing what you love to do. Besides, if you love what you've chosen to do each day, happiness is pretty automatic.

Early Years

I was born with a severe clubfoot; I had eleven operations before I was seven years old, which affected my future in a great way. I appreciated early on how precious it was to be able to get into the water, because with a cast on every summer for six years, I was never allowed to swim. When my brothers and my friends ran into Cass Lake, I just sat and watched them, imagining in my mind what was under the surface. My imagination went wild, even though what I imagined then and what I paint now are worlds apart. When I was young, I thought there were all kinds of strange and ominous creatures under the surface, but when I finally got into the water, and later started diving, I found out that the most dangerous animal in the ocean is us. Man is the biggest monster.

I remember being four years old and looking under the kitchen sink for paint. It was very important to me to find some. I discovered several ugly beige colors, and a bit of a red, which wasn't much, but it was still paint. I was glad to have it because we were very poor. I was so little then that I could slide under the bed to paint my dinosaurs while Mom was at work. The quietness of being behind the bed board, just painting by myself, was very relaxing and peaceful. No one knew where I was. Mom found out later when we moved, by pulling the bed out from the wall. It was good stuff, I'd like to have one of those now. My aunt has one, but won't give it up.

My mom raised four boys by herself on welfare. It was bad—powdered milk and the whole bit. We were in the worst part of Detroit, living in uninsulated garages during the cold winters. One year we moved thirteen times—something about having four noisy and rowdy boys in one house. We kept getting in trouble and getting kicked out. We didn't know any better; we were just having fun.

Obstacles

I believe that everything happens for a reason. Nothing happens by accident. There was a reason I was born with a clubfoot; it helped me learn early how to work hard to overcome obstacles. As a result of having to overcome my disability, I went on to excel at sports, so I look at everything as a benefit. Another positive result of the surgeries was that I learned to appreciate the lakes, the streams and water in general.

When I grew up in Michigan, the Great Lakes were "dead." Over time, because of Jacques Cousteau and groups like Greenpeace getting the word out, the lakes are slowly coming back to life. My contribution has been with a paintbrush. Art is a powerful medium, and when you paint murals in public places, people have to become aware. They don't have a choice. Murals basically confront the passersby. People can choose not to go into a museum or gallery, but they cannot ignore a public mural that demands attention. That has been my whole point: If I can inspire the millions of people that encounter my murals over the years, then I can make an impact. And it's worked. Each year, one billion pairs of human eyes look at the *Whaling Walls*. It may be certain people over and over—say on a commute to work—but one billion impressions per year have got to have a positive effect. In Boston, 250,000 cars a day go by one of my walls. That's a quarter-million people in twenty-four hours; a tremendous amount. My whole intent from the start was to do a thirty-year tour of one hundred walls. This week, I'm off to do a seven-city, seven-mural Great Lakes tour, which will put me at seventy-six walls.

I'm just about to paint a giant wall near the Fox Theater and the Opera House in Detroit, which takes me full circle because that's where I grew up. There's a group of artists in Detroit who criticize me saying, "Why should he get to paint the best wall in Detroit?" [The wall has been completed since this interview and has received rave reviews.] The minute I announce my plans, a lot of people decide to do something. It was there for many years before I came along, so why didn't someone just do it? There are a lot of ugly walls in Detroit, as in every city, so go ahead! Some of these same artists started a bit of a controversy, saying that the ocean and whales are not appropriate for Michigan. But to me, it may be more important to paint marine life in that area because all rivers, lakes and oceans are connected. If you pollute any body of water, it will find its way to the sea. To a small mind, it may not be appropriate, but to an open mind, it's just the opposite. If you understand the bigger picture, which is what I paint, all life is connected.

I have dealt with harsh criticism of my work. A worldwide belief from long ago says to be a true artist, you have to be starving. And that belief does not just apply to painters. There are starving actors who don't like other actors who are doing well. I cannot let that mind-set affect me; I just keep moving forward. I use that negativity as my fuel and welcome the outrageous comments made by my critics because it's all part of the art. When Cristo [the conceptualist who uses the landscape as his medium] did his *Running Fence*, part of his art was the controversy and the craziness. I just have to accept that. You have to have thick skin to live your dreams.

It's easy to criticize, but it's harder to get out there and start doing something to help. I think the critics should quit talking and start doing. That's my advice. They sell more paintings for me anyhow—I should send them royalty checks! It's all a bit of a joke. Some people just cannot stand to see someone successful, but it is embarrassing that people would cut others down for their success. I am happy for the success of other artists and support other artists, even painting on the same canvases with those I admire. [Wyland often paints with other artists; he creates the underwater view, while another artist paints the above-water world.] People who cut down the work of artists don't deserve, in my opinion, to be successful. And most of them aren't. If they do end up making a lot of money, I'd bet they are unfulfilled in their life in some major way. If people want to criticize something, they should buy a mirror.

You can probably tell I'm in the trenches. I've heard everything over the years. A lot of my critics, once they actually come out and see what I do, are the first ones to commend it and say, "This is valid and important." There are a lot of critics who really don't know what I do, and how I feel about the work I'm doing. But the only ones I care about are the critics of tomorrow: I care a lot about what the children growing up now will think of me.

I admire people like Ted Danson and the late Lloyd Bridges. They didn't have to start the American Oceans Campaign or work for the conservation of our oceans. They could have sat in Hollywood and made movies for the rest of their lives. But each took a stand. I don't have to travel to the inner cities; I live in two of the most beautiful places in the world [Hawaii and Laguna Beach], but it's important to keep the balance and give back. That's what I believe has given me my success, and it's a lot more than monetary.

Drive

When I was young, I knew I would be an artist. I was a hard-core artist with a studio in our basement by the time I was in junior high. But I did try to get a normal job because I didn't know I could make a living painting. I got fired from three mediocre Detroit assembly-line jobs in a row and was told that I was a failure and would never make it in the working world, which helped foster the drive that I have. I came home from losing the third job, fixed up my studio in the basement, and knew I would have to make it work. I decided right then and there that I would develop a quality portfolio, get a scholarship [which he did, at the Center for Creative Studies in Detroit], and make it as an artist. My mom supported that dream, and my dad did, too. Dad and I are great friends, and he used to encourage my art by sitting and watching me paint.

Wyland and and his brother, Steve.

I'm the only artist in the family, unfortunately, but my older brother Steve used to paint. When we were kids, we entered a citywide art contest to clean up Detroit, and of course I was bragging, very confident, that I was going to win. Mom got a call telling her that her son won the art contest, and she thought it was me because my brother wasn't even an artist. They said, "No, *Steve* won." That again, gave me a lot more drive because I realized that no one was just going to hand things to me in life. I understood that I was going to have to work *hard*.

Influences

I had a teacher in first grade who really focused in on me. She showed me how to draw faces and figures, and told me that I was a good artist. She didn't spend any more than a half-hour with me, but because she was an artist, I believed her. Encouragement from someone you respect means a lot; I always remember what an impression it had on me. When I'm painting a wall and see the kids come out to watch, I come down and talk to them and draw with them and show them tips. I try to have little art supplies for them when I go on tour, and I feel it's important to spend time with the kids, telling them they are good artists. A lot of them are better than I was.

My mom found an article in the 1970s on Dennis Poosch, an airbrush master, who was better known at the time as "Shrunken Head." I went to Dennis and he literally took me under his wing as an apprentice. He not only showed me how to use an airbrush, but also how to paint with the big spray guns, and anything else I needed to create murals. We're still friends; he called me last week and volunteered to paint on the Detroit wall. Dennis is the one who showed me that I could make a living as an artist.

Jacques Cousteau, Lloyd Bridges and Dr. Roger Payne were three of my biggest ocean inspirations. And, of course, Greenpeace in the early 1970s. For younger generations who missed it, Lloyd Bridges was in a television series called "Sea Hunt," where he played a diver. I met him at the Biosphere, a few years ago, and I invited Lloyd and his son Beau to paint on my mural there. Lloyd took his brush and painted "Sea Hunt Lives" on my pants. It was so funny because the show had been off the air forever. [Lloyd dedicated Wyland's sixty-eighth wall and narrated Wyland's latest art video.]

Spirituality

I always felt protected by God as a child, and I still do. I *have* to feel protected because I do things that people shouldn't do: I dive two-hundred-plus feet into the ocean; I drive a Harley Davidson every day, and I hang two hundred feet in the air off the sides of buildings [over twenty stories up], so I have to have a lot of faith. Yes, I get scared. I'm afraid of heights—terrified—so I'm in the wrong business. I don't have wings, so when I get up there, I have major fear. I just focus on what I have to do and don't allow myself to think about it. One false move and I'm dead. The wall in Chicago I'm about to do— the Intercontinental—is twenty-six stories, and that will be my highest. I have to go up there.

I grew up in a Catholic family, so God was always very real to me. I don't go to church every Sunday, but I go to church every day in my own way. I pray all the time. You have to. I pray both out loud and silently, especially before I go to bed. That's my quiet time. Mostly my prayers are quiet, done in my own way. People ask me if I meditate formally and my answer is that I swim. Swimming, to me, is like being reborn. It's my discipline and my meditation. If I'm not in the ocean, I'm in a pool. I have to be in the water every day. Every single day. Being solar powered, I have to have sunlight, too. I don't mind a little rain, but I like it very sunny. I migrate with the whales, living in California in the summer, and then following them when they migrate back to Hawaii. If you see blowholes, throw me back in the water.

I'm connected with the ocean in a way I cannot explain, so I suppose it's very well possible that I was a whale or a dolphin (which, by the way, are small-toothed whales) in another life. I don't know. I was born under the water sign of Cancer, and water is just so much a part of who I am. [One of the cities Wyland calls home—Laguna Beach, California, where this interview took place—is also represented by the sign of Cancer.] When I'm diving, I'm much more comfortable down in the water than I am up here. I'd like to stay there. If I had a choice, I would stay down forever. It's incredible to be totally weightless and feel like you're flying under water. And the colors: There's so much to study. I'm really an explorer in my heart. I feel like a cross between Walt Disney and Jacques Cousteau. Art mixed with exploration.

Creativity

In school, I balanced my time between sports and art. I should have taken more business though. The art business is really hard. The school of hard knocks. When I first started, my work was seen as unusual.

Think about it—when did you start seeing whales and dolphins in art? Only in the last ten or fifteen years. Now there is a lot of duplication, but the history of marine art was whaling ships and man killing whales. Man was the dominant force. The depictions of whales used to be from dead whales that had washed up on shores, or from whales that had been killed. Their immense weight distorted their look, which meant that up until the early 1970s, the art was not very accurate. Larry Foster started doing scientifically accurate portraits of whales. I just bought one of his originals. But Larry never swam with them.

In 1980, I moved to Lahaina, Maui, and started studying humpback whales. Two researchers, Mark and Debbie Ferrari, who had been researching whales in Maui for years, came to my studio and said, "We like your art, but you need to go eye-to-eye with the whales." They invited me to be part of their research team and every year since, for eighteen years, I've been out there swimming right next to humpback whales, looking deep into their eyes. It changed the way I saw these beings because I started looking at them as individuals, not just general whales. I could see the individuation of their features, physical characteristics and personalities. Now for the first time, the art and the science were coming together. I also started working with John Ford, who does the orca studies off of Vancouver Island, and Mike Bigg and Grahm Ellis—all the best. These guys were really hard on me at first. They wanted me to be accurate. In fact, I invited Mike Bigg, the top orca researcher in the world, to come up and join me on the scaffolding with a piece of chalk, and he reshaped the dorsal fins and explained to me that there are transient and local orca pods. I became educated, and inspired them, too, as they realized that what I was doing could be a great vehicle for the science and study of whales.

I believe, in today's world, the artists and the scientists have to work together for the big picture. I'm trying to be a bridge, but it's tough because the science people want hard science and the artists want to be free. Somewhere in the middle is the common ground. I'm grateful that the trend now is to portray living whales. I call it marine-life art instead of marine art. Marine-life art celebrates the living whales and animals of the sea as it never has before.

Creativity is not always easy, even though the talent part appears to be God-given. One day, years ago, I came across a fantastic wall facing the coast of Lahaina, Maui, and I knew I had to paint it. Lahaina is the whaling capital of the United States: All of the whaling ships used to stop there, and now it's the whale-watching capital. It has a tremendous history of whaling and whale watching—past, present and future. So, I went to an old barnacle's office to get his permission; I showed him my work and explained to him that I wanted to paint the mural for the city, free of charge. This old guy (from the hysterical society) thought he owned the town and said to me: "No way, you'll never paint that wall. I run Front Street, and no one does anything here unless I approve it. Besides, it's not appropriate." I looked him in the eye and said, "I already painted it and there's nothing you can do about it." He got nervous and said, "What are you talking about?" thinking it was already done. "I've already painted it in my mind and there's nothing you can do to stop me." He asked me if I was serious and I said, "Yep."

I continued to ask the city of Lahaina for permission for nine years. Four years into it, I was walking with the landlord of the block, and as we faced the wall, I said, "Wouldn't that be a great wall for one of my murals?" He answered, "Yeah, that would be kind of nice," which I took as a yes. But because it wasn't the city's idea, they wouldn't allow it. The thing is, though, I'm young. I'm going to be here when those in power are gone, and when the new group comes in, they'll love the idea. With politics, one group always hates the other group. If one group doesn't like you, just wait a while until the new group comes in.

The only problem was that I had waited nine years, and, in this case, the old group was still in power. I was too impatient to wait any longer so, in other words, I don't always follow my own advice. I had just finished painting two murals in Kauai and had some paint left over. I don't like to waste paint, so I called my crew and said, "Send the paint over to Lahaina." They asked me why, and I told them not to worry about it. My intention was to wait for a full moon and paint the wall when everyone was asleep, but a totally dark night presented itself and I got anxious. At 3:00 A.M., I called my crew and said, "Let's go." There were five of us. I did the painting and they did the scaffolding.

It was a pitch-black Friday night. We didn't even have a flashlight, and we couldn't see a thing. Zero. I painted the whole wall from my mind's eye. I had looked at that forty-by-thirty-foot wall for so many years that I knew I could paint it blindfolded. Luckily, the police didn't stop us because no one knew we were there. When the sun started coming up, it looked great. It was a miracle. Pretty much finished by that time, I could have gone home. I had the choice to either run for it and let them figure out who did it later, or wait it out and eventually take them on. People started driving by, and the crowds were getting big. Everybody loved it; no one said a negative thing. Someone yelled, "Hey, there's a whale!" and I looked over my shoulder from painting the eye of the whale to see a humpback whale in the ocean with a perfect vantage point to see a likeness of himself

Wyland Studios   Wyland Studios

Before and after photos of the Maui Wall.

jumping across the wall. It was his usual view because I had painted a whale's-eye view of the west Maui mountains. This humpback came right near the wall, breaching completely out of the water to his tail. Once out of the water, he'd freeze, look at the wall, and come down as if he was celebrating with us. He looked exactly like the whale on the wall. It was spectacular! He must have breached forty times in a row. (Incidentally, many times when I've been painting a mural, I have turned around to see a whale or a dolphin watching me from the ocean.) The crowd was elated and, by this time, was getting enormous. I was milking it, just painting the details, laughing, and waiting to get abused by the city government.

Monday morning came—on Martin Luther King Jr.'s birthday—and we dedicated the wall to the city. I was waiting for everything to hit the fan, and all of a sudden the ripples came. The old barnacle had called the police to tell them to arrest me for painting the wall without a permit, but the police loved the mural and told him that was out of the question. Then the media shenanigans started: They spouted city government propaganda, making me look terrible by saying that I wasn't a local, that I was from Oahu, and so on.

The landlord called me up and said he really liked the mural, but that he was angry that the city was blackballing him, telling him that he would never be able to build even a shed if the mural wasn't removed. I started getting fined and they threatened to fine me one hundred dollars a day until it was removed. But their idea of removing it and mine were totally different. They wanted me to paint brown over it, but I had no intention of ruining the scene. I flew my contractor over and we took the paneling down, piece by piece, and put the whole thing in storage. Then we put up the same kind of paneling and painted it brown.

When the mural was gone, people in the town complained big time. They were really upset, but it was too late. It was apparent that we were never going to change the minds of the people in power. But you know? As artists and activists, sometimes you have to take the system on like that, otherwise it gets corrupt and smelly, like still water. It smells in Lahaina, but great people are coming into power, and the smelly ones are going away. At the appropriate time, I'm going to put it back up. As soon as that happens, we're going to have a big celebration. I guarantee it.

Miracle

I have had so many magical encounters diving in the ocean that it's hard to pick the most spectacular ones. I had a manatee encounter in Blue Springs, Florida, that was miraculous. A lot of people aren't familiar with this animal; they are referred to as "sea cows" because of their large size and gentle nature. I had never met a manatee before because they are so endangered. I was in Florida with Jimmy Buffett's people—Jimmy has done a lot of good work for this species and for the Everglades—and, at his invitation, I was doing a manatee mural at the main terminal of the Orlando airport to help raise awareness.

One afternoon, I wanted to go out and snorkel and get a feeling for the river and the brackish waters so that I could paint them later. I was told that the manatees probably wouldn't be out that late in the season, so I wasn't expecting to see anything. The water was actually pretty clear that day, and I was snorkeling when, all of a sudden, I looked, and coming through the water, I saw this strange-looking creature heading straight at me. Sure enough, as it got closer, it was a manatee. I almost bit a hole in my tongue, I was so excited. It was huge, probably fourteen-feet long, and it came right up to me. After looking me over, it left. That was enough for me. Even that small encounter made my day, believe me.

I swam up to the surface and I screamed to Jimmy Buffett's people on the shore. They were pointing and yelling back to me, and I thought they were trying to tell me she'd been there. I yelled back that I had seen her, too, and they yelled, "No, no, look!" I went back under, and there she was again—this time with her calf and three other adult manatees. The five of them encircled me and stayed

Wyland Studios

Wyland and Jimmy Buffet in front of manatees on Whaling Wall X, Orlando, Florida, 1986.

there for three hours. Nobody else wanted to go into the water because they said it was too cold, so it was just me with these amazing creatures. I was so happy to have my subject all around me. They hugged me by putting their flippers all around my body. I didn't have a camera, but I took it all in and can still recall their faces when I go to paint or sculpt them. I see the whole afternoon in slow motion, over and over.

The most moving thing was looking into the eyes of the mother. They resembled little black buttons, with a very old soul behind them. It was like being in the presence of an ancient person. I could tell that their reputation for being gentle was real, but there was more there. There was a consciousness in those eyes that I could never explain. I don't try and personify whales or dolphins, but it is hard in this case not to put it into human terms. She appeared to be the most ancient and gentle sage.

At times like these, I cannot help but feel that there is a reason I am given these encounters. It feels like I am meant to be shown these things because experiences like these are not common. I've had tremendous encounters with various marine life that I paint—orcas, humpbacks, sperm whales, sharks and giant manta rays—and I've never come close to being hurt. An orca could decide to open its mouth and chomp me up if it wanted to. In a second. But then again, I've never gone down there wearing a seal suit.

Passion

My first encounter with a humpback was awesome. I had only seen whales on television, but to be able to flip into 100-percent-visibility water for hundreds of feet, and to have whales that are sixty-five-feet long swim right over you, very curious to see you—looking right into your eyes—is incredible. Not only do you get the sense that they are looking right into your soul, but you feel that they are opening themselves up to you. I've touched wild orcas in the water and have had them swim right between my legs. Several times, mothers have allowed their calves to come between them and myself, as if they're saying, "Here's my baby." They must sense that there's no threat. But it may be something more. I don't want to get silly about it, but my experiences seem *so* big. One time, I swam into a group of whales too eagerly, and a mother just lifted her flipper real gently up over my head so that I could get by without bumping into her. I could fill volumes with my stories. It's as if they know that I'm trying to help them.

In one day last winter, I swam off the coast of Maui with forty individual humpbacks, and then went diving with turtles, octopuses and all kinds of fish. Later that day, my friends and I went down and swam with two different kinds of dolphins: bottlenose and spinners. To top it all off, on the last dive, in a secret spot off Maui, the most magical thing happened. I had been told that every day the giant manta rays come like clockwork at 4:30 P.M. to get cleaned by little cleaner fish. I had never seen this phenomenon before and half-thought my friends were making it up. We swam over and waited, and pretty soon, seven giant, sixteen-foot manta rays came in formation. We swam with them for about forty minutes. They didn't like bubbles, so we had to be careful not to blow too many, but they loved being touched and were very curious. They were awesome animals. I was amazed at their girth. In fact, I had to go home and fix one of my sculptures because the girth was too small.

I have swum with many sharks, too. The best experience I had was with blue-water sharks about twelve years ago. We were right here, between Catalina Island and San Clemente, about thirty miles out. I went with my attorneys because I knew I would be safe. They have professional courtesy: Sharks don't bite land sharks. Seriously though, we were having fun and I was kind of mocking the whole thing

Wyland Studios

Gray whales.

because I didn't see any sharks, and we were out there for about an hour. I was sitting in the back of the boat on a fake blow-up shark I had brought from my swimming pool. Suddenly real sharks started circling the boat and I said, "Pull me in." I'm not afraid of sharks, but I was a little uncomfortable sitting on my fake shark in the ocean, with my legs dangling off into the water. We had two shark cages, so we dove down into them and watched as the blue sharks and sea lions swam around us. Eventually, we got comfortable and swam out of the cages and when it appeared that the sharks were not going to bite us, we were able to touch their dorsal fins. After that was accepted, we started to ride them. It was so much fun; they seemed to enjoy our being there as much as we did.

Fame

I never feel guilty for my success. In America, in particular, everybody has an opportunity to do something they love to do and succeed. I'm not just talking about monetary goals either. Spiritually, too, anything is possible here. I came from one of the worst scenarios you can have. We didn't have a chance in the world to come out of our poverty in Detroit with a single parent. I did okay, so I believe that anyone else can, too. I believe we have to help others, though. I try to help people all of the time, as much as I do my nonhuman friends in the ocean, I just do it quietly. I don't like to make a big deal out of it. I help my family, my friends and people I don't know. I feel so fortunate to be able to do that. My whole family works for me now, and that's a good thing because when you achieve success, you need to have somebody watching your back.

My mother has always been very proud of anything my brothers and I did. Whether I made a touchdown, shot a basketball in the hoop or won the school high-jump record, my mom and dad [who lived elsewhere] were always proud. My whole family is proud, and I'm proud of them. It goes both ways. My family has contributed enormously to my success. What good would it be to be successful by yourself? Who would you share it with?

My fame is different than that of actors. People generally have a high regard for painters. They just acknowledge the work you do, and don't really bother you, or certainly don't mean to. The fans aren't screaming or crazy. I'm a bit of an entertainer in my own right, and my supporters are real nice and are happy to acknowledge the work. It's kind of nice.

My mailing list is 250,000 collectors in some form in all fifty states and forty countries. It's staggering that when we go out on tour, people come from all over the country. We had 40,000 people come out to the Portland, Maine, dedication. Imagine, who would think that anyone would come out and watch some young guy paint a wall?

Wyland Studios

Wyland with dolphin, "Nat," in Florida Keys.

Time and Energy

I would like to take a year off and experience all of the oceans of the world. I want to photograph and paint all the different species, capturing this time period. It would be a legacy for this millennium, like Curtis did for the Indian cultures in the 1800s.

Do I have all the energy I want? More than I need! It's phenomenal. My secret is iced tea. Lots of iced tea. No really, my whole family is highly motivated and has high energy. You know, when you do good things, I think the energy comes through you naturally. Conversely, when you do bad things, the energy gets sucked out of you. I think we're doing extraordinary things [Wyland is speaking of himself and his five hundred employees]. I'm really proud of this Ocean Challenge of America, and I think that gives me a lot of energy. I hop out of bed. I'm an artist with a porpoise.

When I think of my future, I see me finishing my one hundred murals. I see myself sculpting one hundred monumental life-size fountain marine-life sculptures. I'm going to be busy for a long time—I call that job security. It's my total passion. And it's challenging to be able to create these animals lifesize in different mediums. I'd like to do a show called "Wyland Life-Size" that travels to all of the natural history museums and inspires everyone. Whales are the living dinosaurs of today. If I can bring enough of these murals and sculptures into public places, people will want to get involved and protect them, just for their sheer beauty, if nothing else. I try not to just paint the great whales, but also their great spirits. They have an incredible consciousness, and are a symbol for the conservation for the oceans. They are reaching out to us, too, when really they don't have to. If a whale doesn't want you to see him, you won't.

Earth

I don't have any fear about the coming millennium. I'm pretty optimistic. I don't believe any of the doom-and-gloom theories. The kids coming up are going to change things and do it right. I'm going to help them, that's what I'm here for. We didn't know anything growing up about conservation, the environment or the fragility of the oceans. The kids now know more than we ever did. And, because some of them are better artists than me, I'm very optimistic.

This is a very important time. The environment is absolutely going to be the most important issue for the next millennium. The next wars will be over clean water. If I can inspire an entire generation with this challenge, that will be my legacy. That will be enough.

One of my favorite animals to paint is the baby seal. I think its cuteness and soulfulness may have saved it. They're coming back, but I hear the Canadian government is considering hunting the white coat again. It's a pretty sad situation. How could somebody hit a baby—any baby—over the head, and skin it alive in front of its own mother? That's one of the sickest things I've ever heard of. It's amazing what man can justify. There are a lot of sick things that man does, but this is one of the worst. People need to become more educated and more sensitive and have a higher regard for other life on this planet. I think we're getting there, but we have

Wyland Studios

Snow Pup, "Oil," 1990.

a lot more work to do. That's why people like me can't get lazy and stop. Just because I have a few critics, I'm going to stop? No way! I just get going harder.

It's going to take the commitment of a lot of people to turn things around. The people in this book are a good example. People who are willing to put in a lot of extra time to make changes because they care enough to work for the causes. Woody Harrelson is a great example. He's fearless! He didn't care one bit about his career when he spoke out against the Gulf War when everyone else was for it. He doesn't mind getting arrested if it means helping the old-growth forests. That takes a lot of strength. That's an actor with a backbone. I think people like us should all commend each other. Artists, actors, activists and environmentalists should work together instead of knocking each other down. Competition has got to end. It's embarrassing when one group knocks another group. We're all in the same boat here. Books like these are the discussions that have to happen, and I know how committed people like Woody and Keely are. Usually, it's the people

Wyland Sltudios

Honolulu, Hawaii.

who are doing all of the talking (criticizing) who are too busy to help out anyway.

We hear stories on National Public Radio of foreign countries dumping nuclear waste into the ocean, but it's the ones you don't hear about that are worse. The only way to stop the danger and ignorance is to educate every single kid growing up now. The only time there is no hope is when we don't do anything.

I'm married to my job right now. I haven't met the right whale yet. I've met all of the different species of whales, just not the right one.

WYLAND

12

Chris Chandler

Photo by Sandee Bartkowski, 1998

Introduction

Millions of boys in America grow up dreaming of playing football in the National Football League (NFL). Thousands play the position of quarterback in high schools across the country each year, and hundreds play it in college. But the opportunities for being a starting quarterback in the NFL diminish drastically, as only thirty spots exist in the professional arena. Chris Chandler has been one of those starting quarterbacks since his first year out of college, a major accomplishment in itself when you consider that approximately five hundred young men have come out of First-Division teams during his time in the league (not including many more from other colleges), hoping to take his place. The competition is mind-boggling. And yet, our media concentrates so much on winning, that unless you are Troy Aikman, Steve Young, John Elway or a handful of players fortunate enough to be on winning teams, you're not quite good enough. It is a trend, I believe, that is detrimental to the psyches of anyone hoping to succeed, because realistically there can be only a few at the very top of any field. That leaves a lot of room for major talent that often goes unheralded.

For a man officially ranked as one of the top five quarterbacks for most of the last four years and called "the most underrated quarterback in the NFL" by sports broadcaster and former coach of the Chicago Bears, Mike Ditka (November 1996 on NBC), this quiet personality consistently gains ground in talent, wisdom and experience. The cumulative effect of what Chris has learned in ten years of playing pro football makes him a force to be reckoned with. One of the reasons you have not heard more about him is that the teams he has led have not made the play-offs. Ironically, as I write this, Chris recently finished the 1997 season for the Atlanta Falcons ranked second in quarterback ratings behind Steve Young—an unexpected accomplishment because his offense was ranked near the bottom of the league. It is almost unheard of for a quarterback to have such strong numbers with a low offense rating, but Chris was an exception to the rule and, as a result, was invited to play in the 1998 Pro Bowl.

When Chris joined the Houston Oilers in 1995, they needed help. Their two wins to fourteen losses the year before made up the worst *record in the NFL. In spite of the odds, Chris made history against the Cincinnati Bengals when he received the best quarterback rating of any NFL player ever. In other words, no quarterback had ever played a better game. Although he was picked as the Miller Lite Player of the Week (statistics were a summation of the completed passes, touchdowns, yardage, percentage of interception rate, etc.), the Oilers still didn't command much national coverage. Chris played two seasons in Houston, but because of moves made by the front office in the drafting of a young quarterback, a trade was inevitable. Ball clubs throughout the league submitted their offers, and ESPN repeatedly called Chris the "best bargain in the NFL."*

Some of us who know and love Chris get frustrated by his disinterest in courting media relationships. We cringe as we watch some of the press misrepresent his shyness, calling him aloof and unapproachable. The bigger truth here is that Chris lives from a place of deep humility. He cares more about doing his job than being well known, or even well liked, and he has clearly defined priorities. When I asked him why he didn't have a publicist to give his statistics and accomplishments more nationwide acknowledgment, he looked stunned and told me simply, "I'm much too busy concentrating on my job to think of going on talk shows or blowing my own horn—that's not what this game is about."

There is a beautiful and inspirational story behind the surprisingly angelic face of Chris, who, in person, looks more like a model for a skin-care ad than a man on the front lines of a dangerous sport. Coming from a troubled childhood, with nine brothers and sisters, Chris learned early on to keep life as simple and as grounded as possible. He just doesn't see himself as someone who should get V.I.P. treatment. One afternoon, while Chris and I were driving together in Houston, a police car turned on its flashing lights and pulled up behind us. Chris's vehicle registration had not yet been renewed, and as we pulled to the side of the road, he was sure he was going to get a ticket. I said: "What are you thinking about? You're the quarterback for this city. The cop will see who you are, let you off the hook, and be happy to have met you." Chris thought I was indulging in wishful thinking, but just as I suspected, the policeman looked into his face and smiled. "Are you Chris Chandler?"

"Yes, I am."

"I'm sorry to bother you, sir, but your registration needs to be updated."
"Oh, yeah. I've been busy and I forgot. Do you know where the office is?"
The man gave us detailed directions, told Chris how much he
enjoyed his playing that year, and said good-bye. Chris was shocked.
He didn't seem to understand what he meant to the city, or how much
people enjoyed being in his presence. In his eyes, he's just a regular guy.
No big deal. I had to wait two years for this interview because of his
humility. Chris didn't seem to think he'd have anything to say that
would help others, but I knew otherwise. As the philosophy goes, often
the most silent have the most to share.

His wife, Diane Chandler, is one of the elements that makes Chris's
story so fascinating: Her father, John Brodie, was the legendary quarterback for the 49ers for seventeen years in the 1960s, 1970s and the
early 1980s. John was the highest-paid athlete in the NFL in 1966, and
ironically the two men share the number twelve. The resemblances
between them continue: John Brodie plays golf on the PGA's Senior
Tour, and Chris appears destined to do the same. It is not uncommon
for father- and son-in-law to be competing for first place in celebrity
tournaments. Diane cheers them on from the sidelines, awestruck at
how the hand of fate has merged her childhood and adult years.

One of the most noticeable traits about Chris is his common-sense
intelligence. He's quiet much of the time, but his mind is practical and
ever on the alert. His humor is the quick, semi-wicked brand that
catches friends and family members off guard. When I went
to start this interview, while Chris was still playing for the Oilers, I was
designated chef that night, and he and I drove to a funky little health-
food store to get dinner supplies. Chris had been teasing me since my
arrival about the fact that I had no luxuries living in the forest (saying
that my home was as close to camping as he'd ever want to come) and
found amusement in my rapture over his massive kitchen and walk-in
closet the size of my bedroom. I was no longer cooking on a camp stove
in my mountain home, but Chris remembered the days when I had
served him from its small burners.

The cashier asked me if I'd like a bag or a box for my groceries, and
I told her with great appreciation that I'd like a box. This was an
automatic response because after living in the snow and using a wood
stove for our sole source of heat, I had learned that cardboard from

boxes comes in handy when making fires. For anyone who hasn't had this experience, kindling catches quickly when placed on burning cardboard. We weren't in the snow, of course, but in an elite suburb of Houston. Charles Barkley lived a few miles away, and Warren Moon lived down the street. But I had gotten so used to requesting boxes in stores back home that my response was habitual. Chris, delighted, knew why I had opted for the box and said, "Well, since we have piped-in heat here, you could always use the box as a purse." His absurd comment was spoken in such a low-key fashion that I barely caught on, but when I did I could hardly stop laughing.

In all honesty, Chris is more of a lover than a fighter. I tease his wife that she'll have to be on the lookout after this book goes to print because I'm certain many women will wish they were in her shoes. It's a nice place to be. His commitment to his wife and his unwavering devotion to his children is enough to make most women sigh. In fact, Chris can get downright gushy. I remember one scene in Lake Tahoe at the Isuzu Golf Tournament that was particularly sentimental. Diane and I attend this yearly event together, keeping each other and the kids company while the men play the course. As we sat in the clubhouse one afternoon after the day's rounds were completed, we were surrounded on all sides by the biggest names in sports and broadcasting: John Elway, Charles Barkley, Michael Jordan, Matt Lauer and Bryant Gumbel to name a few. Chris knew them all, but he was too enamored of his baby girl, Ryann, to be sociable. He was absolutely unreachable, in a world of his own. As Chris gushed repetitive baby-talk utterances, those of us around him couldn't help but laugh at the sight. Here he was, a large man and a commanding presence, who didn't have the time of day for anyone *but his little girl. It was touching for me as a mother, to say the least. I knew that Chris was very happy to have been invited to this prestigious tournament, year after year, but clearly he was even happier with his immediate company. And the irony wasn't lost on me as I watched him carry his own purse that afternoon, in this case, a diaper bag.*

*   *   *   *

Happiness

Nothing in my life has ever made me as happy as watching my two little daughters. When Skye was born, a little over a year ago, Ryann was just fifteen months old. Seeing Skye's little face when she nursed, and watching her little jaw move up and down was just so amazing. Looking back, I never thought that having children would bring this type of all-consuming happiness. I knew I'd have kids, but I never knew I'd think about them all of the time or get completely immersed in watching them. Seeing little Ryann try to put her shoes on, and laughing as she falls over, are the dumb little moments that make life the best.

I could say that winning the Super Bowl would make me really happy, too, but that would be selling myself short to say that that would define my happiness. I've been working to win a Super Bowl for longer than anything else in my life, but now that I have a wonderful family, I see that no matter how long it takes me to get to that goal, it can't come close to the level of happiness I have at home. No matter how great a win like that would be, it would always fall short of what I consider this purest form of joy. I think ahead about when little Ryann starts skiing—watching that little bugger come down the hill. Life kind of revolves around those moments now. I always try to give back to them what they give to me. I'm probably no different than a lot of people my age who can look back and say, "I wish my childhood had been a little bit different." I want to make sure that I do everything for them. It makes me happy knowing that I'm making their childhood as perfect as it can be. My career is still very important, but it is not the all-consuming thing it once was. If you are happy in your life, as opposed to just in your career, you're career is going to happen. And, even if you lose your career, the happiness is still at home. If you think about it, when you're a parent, your family is your real career.

Vision

Up until I met Diane and got married, five years ago, getting on a winning team, going to the play-offs and winning a Super Bowl were the only things I cared about. There is still that part of me that finds that incredibly important, but it's been put in perspective, prioritized, and knocked down the chain of command. Ironically, I'm a better player with my new priorities. I've never played as well as I have the last couple of seasons. I was so consumed by the football side of my life that everything else suffered so much, ultimately causing the football side to suffer. I

Photo by Sandee Bartkowski

Ryann and Skye Chandler, 1997.

wasn't well-rounded. I'm not a square any longer, but I'm not quite a circle either. I'm rounding out as we speak. I think if you become consumed by anything, it can hurt the very thing you're going toward.

Sometimes when I'm playing golf, in a "little" money game with the guys, I try so hard to make the perfect shot that it doesn't happen as often as it does when I'm just playing by myself without caring about the outcome. When I'm out there by myself, enjoying the surroundings, I'm more into the process and not so concerned with the end result. Even though I still have the desire to have excellence happen, I'm detached from the outcome. On those days, it's easier to concentrate on what I'm doing and put my focus on just hitting the ball. There are no concerns about what others think, or about the "big prize." Those are the times I hit the best shots of my life and I think, "God, I'm going to do that this weekend," but then the same thing happens on Saturday with the guys.

With football, the temptation is to think, "I've got to get to the Super Bowl," but in reality, there is a whole lot of business to take care of before that. I have to worry about preparing for each game as well as the off-the-field stuff. When I was single and wanted to be the leader of the team to take us to the championships, my off-the-field activities led me down some negative roads. I didn't get in trouble with the law or anything, but I would stay out late and party. My lifestyle was not as healthy as it is today with my family, and I wasn't as focused. Now that I'm not putting so much pressure on the end result, and I'm more focused on the present, it seems that I'm doing a better job in every-thing. Being responsible for a family, I cannot do anything *but* focus. There isn't any time to waste when you're raising children. So, my priorities help me to know exactly where everything stands.

Family

I think about why Diane and I have such a good marriage, and the common denominator is that we have fun together. When you look at the people in your life, there are a lot of people you like, but may not have fun with. Then there are other people you tend to laugh with. Diane and I laugh a lot. I say dumb things, and she always laughs. Maybe she's just pretending, but we have a good time. Even when we're telling each other to "get off my case," we laugh. Sure we feel the occa-sional desire to be left alone, but it doesn't have to be a big deal.

Di and I met at a golf tournament. I walked into a party for the tour-nament and noticed her immediately. She was standing next to the late Bob Chandler [a receiver], so I thought she was his wife. She was working for the tournament and we kept running into each other and flirting. I found out that she was John Brodie's daughter, and I thought that if I met him we could have fun playing golf. Funny how the golf aspect meant a lot more to me than the fact that he was one of the best quarterbacks ever to play the game. Once you meet John, how-ever, that's a whole other book.

I found out that Diane wasn't Bob Chandler's wife and sent her flowers. She called to thank me and we started a phone relationship. Diane lived in San Diego and I was living and playing in Phoenix [for the Cardinals], so I started flying back and forth. It didn't take long for me to know that I wanted to marry her. But knowing that I wanted to and getting around to doing it were two different things.

Diane moved to Phoenix, and we had been living together for two months when her mom and dad came out. John asked, "So, you gonna marry her?" which totally shocked me because at the time I didn't know him very well. John is so blunt. He has a way of saying things for shock value. It was pretty funny. I had been thinking about how I would ask Diane to marry me, but I hadn't figured it out yet. I told John that I intended to ask her and realized then that I needed to get on with it. Before that, I had planned to be really romantic, but suddenly we were having coffee the next morning and I just blurted out, "Why don't we get married?" I joke with Di that being the ultimate romantic means *not* doing the usual gushy stuff.

One thing that's important for me to talk about is some of the media stereotypes about violence and infidelity among professional athletes. I can't speak for any other sport other than football, and for that matter I can only speak about people I know of. But of the married guys on the teams I've played on, I'm sure a percentage of them are not faithful to their wives; however, I'm not sure it's any different than for guys who work in offices every day. Football players are not on the road very much, it's not like the NBA. We fly into a city at five o'clock and have meetings and bed check at eleven. Even if guys wanted to fool around, it wouldn't be easy. But, even so, guys find the time to cheat if they want to. For a guy to say, "I don't want to cheat," for any reason other than he loves his wife (such as financial reasons), there is a chance he will. Or, "I don't want to cheat because God will get angry." Those are by-products that will happen, but they shouldn't be the reasons. Some guys will say they don't want to hit their wives. If it's

Photo by Sandee Bartkowski

Chris and Diane Chandler, 1998.

because they don't want to go to court, or they're afraid of the bad media press, then the marriage is on shaky ground. I wouldn't want to hit my wife because I love her and I don't want to hurt her. I would never want to cause Diane pain. To rationalize not cheating because you don't want to look bad is ridiculous. Being monogamous and faithful to Diane is all-important to me. My life was empty before her, and I would be a fool to ever jeopardize that.

Influences

I was fortunate in getting to know John Brodie. It turned out to be something I really needed. I've been able to gain a lot of wisdom from him. He's helped me to handle some of the situations that arise in the NFL—emotional and physical things that he had already gone through. He's helped me with my footwork, gaining better balance, and with the daily disciplines you constantly have to work on. It's easy once a long season goes by to get away from the fundamentals, but John reminds me to stay focused on the basics. I listen to him talk about what went through his mind when he was playing. So, knowing him has had a cumulative effect on my game. Hearing the same things at different times has rubbed off in a good way, and over time, John's attitude and mental toughness have sunk in, making me confident. I've assimilated his ideas in my own way. Football is much more a mental game than a physical one. Most quarterbacks in the NFL can throw the football. Most are pretty athletic. The difference is in decision making. The best quarterbacks are the smart ones, who can keep the game in perspective and not let it get too big mentally. When the game gets too big for a guy, his nerves can interfere. That used to happen for me when I was younger, but being in the league as long as I have, I've learned to get over those emotions. It took some time, but I reached a point where that doesn't happen anymore.

Photo by Sue Brodie

John Brodie and Chris, 1998 Tahoe, California.

Diane, too, has had a big impact on me because she's seen it all. For a woman, she has a good understanding of the game, and she makes me stand tough when I don't really feel like it. I am more complete and confident as a team leader and as a person with their influence. Diane and John showed me that it was okay to let out feelings that I had always had, but wasn't really confident expressing.

Early Years

I remember during the first part of kindergarten, the teacher had us go in a room to dribble balls for playtime. She told us to bounce them, and I did. Like crazy. I looked around and some of the other kids couldn't do it. Some bounced them off their feet, or fell down attempting to pick the ball up. I remember being surprised at how hard it was for some of them to do it, and I thought that I was pretty good in comparison. That was one of many experiences that confirmed for me that I would always play something. It was as simple as that. I wasn't thinking about a career at that age, as much as just having fun. Then, when I was ten years old, I played basketball in Little League, and I knew that I was a good athlete and I loved what I was doing. It just felt like something in the avenue of sports was what I would do for the rest of my life. Something inside of me always said, "Hey, don't worry about it, you're always going to play."

My brother Greg was ten years older than I and he was my mentor. Greg was the fifth child, and in a way he represented the missing side of my father, the guy I wished my dad had been more like. My dad was forty-five when I was born, and he didn't spend much time sprinting down the field with me. Greg played catch with me and took me golfing. I loved playing golf and went out and played on the course sunrise to sundown as a twelve-year-old in the summertime. Greg didn't mind hanging around with his little brother because he was also into sports and put a lot of his mind and being into athletics. He liked playing with me because I was good, and he taught me the mental side of sports at a young age. When I

Chris at three years old.

was thirteen years old, I didn't know how to concentrate. He said to me, "Do the coaches tell you how to concentrate?"

"Oh, yeah."

"What did they tell ya?"

"I don't know. They just tell me to concentrate on throwing the ball."

"Do you know how to concentrate?"

"No, I just do it."

So, until I was in college, Greg made a point to teach me how to concentrate at whatever I was doing. He told me how to stay focused, whether it was for practice or for a game. He taught me how to push worry out of my mind and not to be scatterbrained. And, how to focus on one thing at a time, staying in that second. He taught me how to visualize, imagining what I wanted to accomplish, which I still do. Greg told me how to see the ball before I threw it, not just right before, but the night before. I would lie in bed and think the game through, over and over. We only had a few plays, so it wasn't like now, where there are all sorts of situations that can come up. But, he taught me that visualizing was all part of the concentration. Sometimes I visualized something negative, and I'd have to cancel it. I'd think, "Where did that come from?" In hindsight, visualization probably worked for me because I was a first-team All-American with two other quarterbacks the year I got out of high school and I was given a full scholarship to Washington. I never asked Greg how he knew the stuff he told me. He was my big brother, he was a good ball player, and he was cool. I looked up to him and knew he knew how to do things. And, I think Greg and I both used sports as a way to stay out of our house.

My father was a heavy drinker at times. If he was getting bombed on a Monday, I knew Tuesday he'd be cool and Thursday I'd be fine. In other words, it was an every-other-night thing. He seemed to need that day to recover. On Wednesday and Friday, I didn't bring any friends over. I'd have to hide and stay out of his way. On some of those occasions, we'd have to put up with his tongue-lashings. My brother would ask me, "Is Dad drinking tonight?" That was the big question. So, it was easier being out playing sports than staying at home. I would think, *Hell, I'm not going home. I'll just stay here and keep shooting baskets or running down to the other end of the field.*

My buddies and I would play forever!

Looking back, my father was really proud of me and my talents, but he had a hard time expressing that. He never laid a hand on any of us when he was drinking, but the fear was always there during those times. It may actually have been better if he had slapped us around. Maybe it would have let off some tension, you know? I would go to bed all tense when he was drunk, wondering if he was going to come in and bother me. I got really scared. Scared shitless. When he wasn't drinking, he would be really cool sometimes. He was just a nice, good guy. It was kind of like a Dr. Jekyll and Mr. Hyde thing.

Now that I've had two kids, I can't imagine having ten like he did. I was number nine. My dad was an auto parts manager at Sears. With ten kids, the poor guy probably had stress oozing out of his pores. He was a very smart man. When he was watching football, he knew *everything*. He would do the *New York Times* crossword puzzle in the blink of an eye. Because he was scholastically very intelligent, with common sense, I thought it was tragic when he'd get stupid and vent his stress. I think having so many kids had a lot to do with it. One of my older brothers was always getting into trouble, and I know that was hard on him.

When I got into high school, my father stopped drinking. He had some kind of stomach pain and went to the hospital. The doctor couldn't find anything wrong with him, but my mother told the doctor to get on his case because he was drinking too much, so the doctor told him something that scared him and he never drank another drop. He started eating the heck out of ice cream, but no more alcohol.

The ice cream didn't make my father mean like the alcohol, but the emotions were still underlying. He physically stopped boozing, but I can't imagine that the pain went anywhere. I think it's possible that the discipline that the coaches saw in me was partially to get out of the energy of my house and just be on my own . . . free. But more than that, I think I had developed a kind of discipline, where I could spend hours and hours doing something, with focus, at a young age. Had my father come to grips, gotten counseling, and conquered his demons earlier, I still think I would have been focused with the same intensity, but maybe not. I don't know. That stuffed-away, repressed energy that I felt around the house was not nearly as much fun to be around as running stairs or doing something else as long as I could until I was told, "You've got to go home." I guess athletics became the theme for my life.

When I was a sophomore in high school, I knew that I would go to college and play football somewhere. I knew *I* was going to do that and *I* was going to make that happen. I had a really good year and had started getting letters from colleges. After my junior year I had gotten a ton of them, so that reinforced my certainty.

My mother died of breast cancer in 1984 when I was a freshman in college. I can remember going to the hospital with her when her cancer started getting bad. I watched her go through a lot, but she never complained. When I heard later about some of the tests she went through, I had no idea how much pain she must have been in. I'm sure that was for our sake. She didn't want us to worry or be affected by seeing how bad her disease had gotten, or how bad she felt. The night she died, I drove over from school and she said, "What are you doing here?" Even then, she played it off like we didn't have to come. Like what she was going through was no big deal. Diane tells me that I never complain when I'm injured, and I guess I got that from her. Mom was real mellow. I know I got my demeanor and my all-around laid-back attitude from Mom because my dad was high-strung. A high-tension guy.

I have felt many times that my mother helped things happen for me. The year after her death, in my first start against USC, there were four minutes left in the fourth quarter and we were down. We started from our two-yard line and began marching down the field. Somehow the ball got by the USC guys, we caught it, and then I threw a touchdown pass. I don't know if she was there, but the first thing I thought of was, "This is what Mom always wanted." She had been my biggest fan, and was awarded Mom of the Year for my senior year in high school. She made time to go to almost every game of my life, including away games, which wasn't easy with so many children to take care of. My dad got too nervous at games to watch. He'd go, but he had to get out of his seat and walk to the concession stand or watch from the tunnel. But Mom would sit tight.

I don't have my father's temper; I've gotten angry before but I've never gotten so angry that I would be afraid that I would hurt Diane or the girls. Mainly I just see that kind of anger as a waste of time.

That's where football is probably good for me. Working out for practice allows me to release a lot. Some guys never get the chance to do that, and maybe that's why they get dangerous. If I ever snapped, to the point where I got really mad and started throwing things, then it might be hard to stop. Almost like starting a job and wanting to finish it, but I've never gotten to that point. That's just not the way I do things.

Photo by Joanie Komura

Chris playing for the University of Washington.

After my mom died, I was able to take her strength and toughness and apply it to my own life. If I got tired, or I started to feel weak, I remembered all of the horrendous things she went through in the hospital and I would think, "What I'm feeling right now is nothing. If she could go through all of that, then I can go through an extra half-hour of this." Before my mother's illness, I never thought of her as being tough. She was always resourceful, finding ways to make dinner for all of us, or finding ways to fix a pair of socks that my three brothers had worn before me. She always made things right without much money, but I didn't see her as tough. I didn't realize then that going through childbirth ten times was enough to show strength.

Lifework

My career has been very up and down. I should say that it went up real fast, then down, and now it's up again. In my rookie year in 1988, I started for the Colts after the third game of the year. The starter, Gary Hogeboom, didn't play very well in the eyes of the coach. I didn't agree, and I thought the coach kind of scapegoated him, but for whatever reason, Gary was benched. Jack Trudeau, who was behind him, hurt his knee in the third week, so I came in right before half-time and played the rest of the game. It was pretty intense: The first pass I threw was a fifty-four-yard completion. I didn't know what I was doing, but I can still remember every minute. It was a Monday Night game and the old Cleveland stadium was rockin'. The coach had me start the next thirteen games and we won nine of them. As a rookie, I was in heaven. My feeling was that I would be playing for Indianapolis for the next fifteen years. But in the third game of the second year, against Atlanta, I blew my left knee out and sat out the rest of the season. Without warning, the Colts traded me to Tampa. I had never had a big injury before, and I was devastated. In high school and college, I had only had little things, nothing that took more than a few days to recover from. Getting traded was the first turbulence I felt in this league. In high school and college, I had played for the same teams for four years, learning about loyalty to the team. Here I was as a rookie, I had bought a house, and I was bleeding Indianapolis Blue. When they traded me I thought, "Wait a minute, how can you do that? How dare you?" That was my first taste of politics in this league. Right then and there, the game changed for me. It wasn't just about playing anymore; it became a business.

The year before I came into the league, in 1987, there was a strike. There was also one in 1982. I don't know what it was like before then, but I have to think that somewhere in that time frame the business end of playing became too important. When I was a rookie, guys were starting to make good money, but there was no free agency like there is now. Nowadays a guy who has been given a ton of money becomes untouchable. He is in a position of influence and power with his teammates and management. He has the loyalty of management because of the money invested in him. It seems that the less a team has

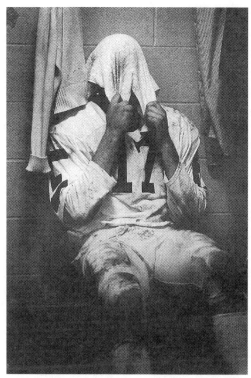

Photo by Rich Frishman

invested in a player, the less important he is regardless of whether he is a really good player or not. The loyalty isn't there like it was when my father-in-law was playing. On the other hand, the players don't give much loyalty back. It goes both ways. If you look at the better teams nowadays, they are the ones whose players have at least a degree of loyalty toward their team and vice-versa.

Winning makes for a better atmosphere. Teams like San Francisco, traditionally known as a great team to play for, are usually at the top by the end of the year. Or the Cowboys. Whenever you hear an interview with Troy Aikman, his focus is always on the team. And it has to be. There is never a quarterback worth anything whose focus isn't on the team. He won't be successful without that focus. What makes it difficult as a quarterback is if you give yourself to the guys on the team, making them the most important thing to you, and then you get treated unfairly by management. It's not pleasant, but you still have to give it your all. In those instances, I look to my teammates individually. I draw a very distinct line and stick with the group of guys who I play with. That's who you go out there for. It's a much more productive and better atmosphere if you're laying it on the line for the whole team, but if the management is trying to hurt you, or another group wants you out, you have to focus on the people who you believe in. It's a challenge as a quarterback because you have to give yourself to your teammates first, and then good things happen. When there's no loyalty expressed your way, it's real hard. One thing I learned when I got traded was that there is a definite line between players and management. There are two sides of the ball.

As far as I'm concerned, this is a player's league. You have to kind of watch who you trust, and I trust my players. It didn't used to be such big business. Guys used to stay with a team for their whole careers. Now it's gotten crazy. There are certain players who earn genuine respect, but there are so many egos. Everyone, from the front office to the players, has an ego. What I've found is the less energy you put into defending your ego, the better off you are.

One of the good things about having played on so many teams is that invariably wherever we play, I have friends to catch up with. There are a handful of guys that I am friends with in the league. When I see the guys I've spent my off-the-field time with, that's a lot of fun. An example for me would be Dwayne Bickett, who plays for Carolina. We played together at Indianapolis. We've played twice against each other, and it was very odd because I was concerned about him and wanted to see him play well, but of course, you still want to win. You always want to win. Winning is the priority.

Fame

The best aspect I can see about becoming famous is having the ability to help people. I don't think I've done much yet to help on a large scale, but I've always tried to help the people around me. If anything, maybe through this book and by my example, I can remind people to put their families first. I think if all of us men cherished our wives and nurtured our children, things wouldn't be so crazy. I guess growing up the way I did has made that really important to me. I can't think of anything more important. If we can't be happy and safe in our homes, we'll have no hope as a society.

Fame can help bring awareness. For example, I think Lyle Alzado helped the league when he came out and talked about his brain cancer caused by steroids. Other players who had heart problems because of steroids also became vocal and that sent a big message to the league, and beyond, that steroids were really bad. Now we're tested for steroids at the start of each year, with random tests all year long, even in the off-season. Same with cocaine and other drugs. There

Reprinted with permission from News America Publications, Inc., publisher of *TV Guide* magazine. Copyright Aug. 30–Sept. 5, 1997 News America Publications, Inc. TV Guide is a trademark of TV Guide Financial, Inc.

Chris Chandler, with Jamal Anderson and Coach Dan Reeves, on the cover of *TV Guide*, September 1997.

might be more guys doing it than I think, but I just don't see how a guy can play well and do drugs. I haven't seen a lot of drug use and I know that the people who have had the courage to share their addictive battles are greatly responsible for that.

Miracle

When I was around five years old, my family and I were on vacation at a river. My four brothers and a few of my sisters had walked ahead of me, across a shallow, wide stream, and they were all twenty yards away on the other side. I was a lot younger and smaller than they were and started walking across by myself. The water was getting really high and suddenly I stepped in a hole and it sucked me down. I didn't know how to swim and I knew right away that I was drowning. I'd manage to pop up a bit and see my brothers on the shore, but no one saw me. Then I'd go back down, fighting the water. I was totally alone. Then, somebody came out of nowhere and pulled me up. To this day, I remember just holding tight to this guy's neck until he placed me on my mother's lap. I grabbed her and just sat there. I wouldn't go in the water for years after that, but I have had a sense of being protected since then.

Spirituality

I pray, but the amount varies. Certainly I could do a better job at it. It's something I'm always working on. Most days I find some time to talk to God, but sometimes things happen to make it difficult to find the time. Wednesdays are real hard during the season because it's such a busy day and I don't have time to do a whole lot. Sundays I get so worked up for the game that it's all-consuming, but I don't feel guilty when I don't pray. Spiritually I feel very confident and give all of my thanks to God.

I wouldn't call what I do conventional. I don't go to church. I have always thought of my relationship with God as a close, personal thing. It's something I can share with other people, like with my wife, but I don't feel that I have to go to a place with others to have that one-on-one relationship. Churches are wonderful; I just don't spend my time going to them in order to be close to God.

I try to meditate. I don't know if my version of meditation is something that Guru Singh would call meditation, but I have a room upstairs that I often sit in for fifty minutes. Sometimes I fall asleep, but I don't think I sleep for very long. The hardest thing is to try to clear my mind and not let things get in there. I try to erase everything and then think of something that I want to happen, especially, during the season, before a game. I try to let a few good thoughts drift in there. So, sometimes I catch myself meditating with the intent to be successful, as opposed to meditating to get closer to God, which I know is the better reason. I don't think I'm being spiritually greedy, it's just that I'm attempting to use my meditation as a tool to uplift my life in all areas, career included. I start out visualizing and then sometimes I end up going to the void state, or to the gap, I think they call it. Whether you're praying or meditating, getting in touch with God is all that matters.

I'm told that when your mind is full of thoughts, it's like turbulent water and you could throw the Empire State Building in there and it wouldn't make a difference. But if your mind is calm, like a lake, then you could throw in the smallest pebble and create a wave. From what I understand, the only way you can create anything is to make your mind calm first. That is the point of meditation. Supposedly, we need to find the gaps between our thoughts, and the more we can widen the gaps, the better off we are. That's my goal: To be able to shut off everything so that I can go to those gaps and find God and myself, I guess. *The* self. From there, life becomes based on the self and not the ego. When I'm ego-driven, the true self isn't in control. Supposedly when we really know ourselves, we don't chase symbols like money, or anything else.

Sometimes, in a game, the exact thing happens that I've seen the night before in a visualization. It's hard to know the cause because a lot of times in football repetitive things happen. In those cases, I'm not sure if what I'm visualizing is a memory of something or a new creation. For instance, I remember throwing a route and having it completed for a touchdown that had already happened maybe three weeks before. I'm visualizing and also kind of remembering it, and the play happens again. Had I not meditated, the play still could have happened, but who knows? What I'm trying to do now is meditate or visualize about things that are not football-related. Like seeing Ryann on her first day of school. That is my new emphasis because those goals are more important in the long run than whether or not we run a 525 F Post Swing and I'm able to stick the post route in there. That has a sliver of importance, but not much overall.

Fear

Sometimes the media takes something that is happening and runs with it so out of control that a false image is painted. I think that has happened with me concerning injuries. In reality, I've gotten through most of my injuries very quickly and haven't missed nearly as many games as you would think by listening to the press. For whatever reason, I've gotten a reputation for being easily injured and that makes me nervous sometimes because it's not only not accurate, but it's a mind-set that is hard to shake. I've learned over the years to stop reading about myself and to just focus on what I need to do. That makes it easier.

It's frustrating when you know you can play through an injury, but the coach keeps you out for fear of your safety. I don't think anybody plays as well injured as they do healthy. Some guys play almost as well, some play half as well, and some guys play miserably. I think I play fairly well. Pain doesn't scare me. In football, a lot of times, it's not how well you play when you're injured, but just being out there.

Most of the time your team just wants to see you on the field.

My biggest fear has to do with people. People I can't trust scare me more than anything else. Not much else makes me insecure. I know how I like to treat people, and even though I may not be the biggest talker in the world, I still don't lie to anyone. It's awful when people lie to me or someone acts in a way that I didn't think they would, breaking the trust I had in them. Thinking that someone is on my side, thinking that they're my guy, and then having them change colors, is the worst. Maybe that's because it has happened to me in the NFL: thinking that I'm a Colt and that they love me, and then all of a sudden they don't anymore. Then to have it happen again in Tampa, and again in Phoenix. That's something I'm getting tired of. Like I said earlier, my father's personality could change radically toward me. So, this feeling that someone could just suddenly change without warning has probably been with me all of my life. Although there haven't been many times someone has really turned on me, it seems my guard is usually up.

Obstacles

I've been in the league for ten years, so somewhere between five hundred and eight hundred quarterbacks have wanted, in some respects, my job. Statistically I've been in the top ten of the thirty starters for sure, but I know I can play as good as anyone out there. All of the things that I've gone through would have exposed me before now if I was average. What I went through would have proven me to be a candle that blew out. But I was like one of those candles that blew out and then kept lighting back up. I would have never made it through those years of hell—two years in Tampa, one year with the Rams, three years in Phoenix, and two years with Houston— if I didn't have the talent. During my first year with the Oilers, the team was coming off a season where they had only won two games out of sixteen (1994). They changed their coaching staff, and got many new players, and together we went seven and nine that season. We had some good players on the team, and we were rebuilding, but they drafted a young quarterback to back me up and gave him a $30 million contract. Management wanted the future to be now.

I feel that I've had to earn everything I've gotten in this league, more than some of the other guys. Some guys, because of what they did in college, were drafted high, and sometimes, not always, that gives them more credit than they deserve. A good case against that would be Troy Aikman. Troy was the first pick in the draft, and he's played as good as anyone in the league. Much was given to him and expected of him, and he has more than lived up to it. He just plays good all the time. But there are other examples of guys who keep getting chances that they haven't earned. Because they were a first-round draft pick, with a lot invested in them, and media hype inventing an image, they're still getting credit for things they haven't done.

I can look at guys who've been in one spot, like John Elway in Denver, or Dan Marino in Miami, and these guys are great players. They deserve all of the respect and credit they are getting. Not only are they good, but they also earned it. Sometimes I still catch myself thinking, "God, if I hadn't blown out my knee, I could still be in Indianapolis." I have spent many nights lying awake in bed thinking that. But I let my mind think about that less as I get older. Sometimes I think that if I did have that kind of good fortune (of not being injured), with systems and teams built around me, I would have been a lot more fulfilled. But getting injured and having a team give up on me—and the roller-coaster ride of having to earn what I've got right now—has been kind of fun, too. Earning your way has its own rewards and builds character. Sure, there have been times when I've thought: "This is what the NFL is? This isn't very fun, getting screwed here, getting screwed there, maybe I should do something else and have more fun. I could be a CPA or an economist (because I was an economics major). I could just look at graphs all day." But I'm glad I stuck it out; it's been worth it.

And, when I look at my life, the rewards are obvious. I get to spend a lot of time with my family, more than most men do. I have several beautiful homes. My accountant says that we have enough money in the bank to last my family and I through the rest of our lives, even if I never did another thing. And all that from being able to play the game that I love. I know this is what I'm supposed to do. People ask me, "What are you going to do after football?" I can understand thinking about an afterlife, as many guys do, but I have no idea. This *is* what I do. I play football. I don't coach football or officiate football, I play it. I see myself playing for another eight years, at least, so I don't ever think about doing something else. Eight years is a long time.

Drives

Money is not and has never been a driving force for me. I feel completely financially secure. I can afford college for my kids if they want to go, and provide a roof over our heads, so with those two things taken care of, there really isn't a whole lot more to be concerned with. I always know that something is going to go right for me. I feel protected. I don't mean that I'll have Lear jets. My needs are pretty simple, and that makes me feel that we're at the point where everything is secure. There is no security in wanting all of the trappings. My friends don't live beyond their means either. You get some of that in my business. I see guys in the league who make more than I do, but some of them blow their money on all sorts of luxuries. That is pointless—again it's all about the ego. And it gets me from a personal, professional standpoint. Not from the standpoint of, "My life would be better if I had what he had," because it wouldn't. It would just be nice from the standpoint of professional respect to be making what they do.

Football attracts a violent type of person, without a doubt. There are crazy people in this game. They are so many big, strong, fast, wild guys. And, many of them are three hundred pounds, with only 15 percent body fat. With the speed, strength, power and violence guys play with nowadays, it gets insane. I'm in a position where I never give blows, but I get them. Every Monday, our linemen are sore.

I never look at the guys in the locker room and think, "He's angry because . . . and he's taking his anger out by playing football." Maybe that's the case, but I don't look beyond and wonder why. Now that you're asking me, I can't think of any of the guys I know real well who had good childhoods. How bad the childhoods were, I don't know. But I can say that out of the guys I know, the simple way to sum it up would be that their childhoods weren't good. Maybe that's part of the reason we took up the sport. I know, in my case, my drive to play and discipline myself, initially, was to have fun and feel free.

Guys who play golf since childhood have their more reserved country-club backgrounds. I have that side to me, too. It's a nice balance that I think is good to have for a quarterback. I can't go out and play my position angry, mean and out of control. The discipline of football helps my golf because when I'm in the middle of a stadium with sixty thousand people, and they're screaming for me and against me, I have learned to stay calm. As a quarterback, you have to be under control. Your emotions have to be intact. You can never lose your head or your temper, and you have to know so much about the game and key in on the defense. When you're in control of your mental abilities, not worried about the physical stuff, you'll play well. That just has to happen. There are times you drop back and run out of the pocket and someone says, "Hey, good job missing that guy." And you don't even remember seeing him, but something made you move. It may have been from the peripheral vision, something picks it up. You're so keyed in on something else, but physically, your deal just happens.

Future

My marriage has changed my life completely. Before I met Diane, I couldn't see a path for my life. I couldn't see an end, nothing down the road. Had I not gotten married, my life would have been this constant search for something, never knowing what I was missing. I felt like I was on a treadmill, each week was the week relived, over and over. Now I can see Diane and me goofing off with our girls for the next sixty-plus years. Once you have a reality that you're going to spend your life with a wife, raising kids—who will grow up and leave the nest someday—there is a plan. And that brings peace. Sometimes I look around the league and see players who are not committed to any woman, and I see that I was on that road. To be honest with you, when you are twenty-two, you think that's the greatest road there is. It's fun for a while being single because you don't know any better. There are a lot of opportunities.

The whole aging process doesn't scare me, except I'm hoping I can keep my hair. Diane is beautiful. When I first saw her, it was her physical beauty that attracted me, but as I got to know her, that became secondary. Some men worry that their wives may lose their looks with age. That never crosses my mind. It's not that I don't look at her and think she's beautiful, but I don't ever base my wanting to be with her on how she looks, so I don't ever think, "Someday if Diane gets fat, we're going to go on the *Jenny Jones* show and have it out." We were watching one of those shows the other day, and this guy said, "When I got married, my wife was fifty pounds less than she is now." The way Diane and I laugh together won't go away if she's old and wrinkled. Neither will our friendship. I'm in it for life—we're talking about many years from now, so I'll be old and wrinkled, too.

When I was little, I didn't see anything for my future, I just wanted to play. I knew I was going to be bouncing that ball forever. My focus was always on having fun and fortunately for me, being a stock-broker wasn't fun, or I'd be doing that. If that constituted playing in my mind, I would be sitting behind a desk. But playing to me meant sports. Fortunately it's been financially beneficial, too. And a lot of other things come with it, but it still boils down to the fact that I'm a football player and if I wasn't doing that, I wouldn't be doing anything but being a husband and a father. That's what makes it easy for me to keep going through all of the crud. I'm not going anywhere. I play football, and I play well. And I'm going to play it better every year. And when I do finally retire, I'll be spending my time with Di and our girls, skiing down the slopes.

13

Tatjana Patitz

Photo by Gilles Bensimone

Introduction

F or those who are not avid readers of fashion magazines, Tatjana is a European-born supermodel greatly responsible for helping to establish the acceptance of statuesque beauty in an industry once dominated by a standard of extreme thinness. Tatjana appeared on the scene at the same time as the likes of Cindy, Estelle and Frederique, and all were welcomed with open arms by millions of women throughout the world who could not identify with the rail-thin ideal.

Tatjana's goddesslike nature is immediately entrancing and the reason that some believe she has been at the top of her profession for over a decade (leading to movie roles in Rising Sun and Ready to Wear and perpetual commercials and television offers). With millions of gorgeous faces in the world, it takes something extra—in Tatjana's case, an extremely ethereal quality—to sustain supermodel success. We see many stunning women looking out at us from magazines and commercials; Tatjana's face is so compelling because she allows us to look in, as well, and truly see her. It is not often that a model's soul emerges from the pages of a high-fashion photo spread, but through her clear-eyed gaze at the camera, we catch a glimpse of the spirit behind her glamorous image.

Tatjana's home exhibits her love of nature and deeply grounded and mature personality. A description of her would not be complete without mentioning the uncommonly serene environment she has created for herself, her loved ones and her animals. I have never visited a home that so fully merges the essence of the spiritual with the natural beauty of the physical world, as does Tatjana's dreamlike retreat.

High in the hills of Malibu, overlooking the crashing surf and luxuriant springtime greenery of the California shoreline, sits her palace of sorts, a regally iron-gated world of imagination brought to reality. From the street, you see a Mediterranean mansion amidst a mini-jungle of lush foliage. Visible just inside the gates are a sports car and utility vehicle—epitomizing the two sides of this free spirit and avid camper. Five galloping dogs of different breeds bounce happily outside as large squawking parrots utter their joyful greetings. A first-timer to this place may think that the parrots are wild inhabitants of the surrounding vegetation, but instead finds them *living in the expansive living room. The home and grounds are a wonderland for animals, and their keeper is not unlike a modern-day Ms. Doctor Dolittle.*

The mistress of the house appears, and in the mystical glow of ocean-reflected light streaming in from above, Tatjana's eyes appear to be an extraordinary bright aquamarine. Her face, so unusually beautiful and almost fragile in this light, has the quality of being otherworldly; her accent—the combination of several European dialects—enhances the impression.

In Tatjana's presence, I am reminded of one of nature's gifts that is closest to her heart: dolphins. She carries a depth and ancient peacefulness combined with a warmth and playfulness that is associated with our relations of the sea. I find myself wondering if she was drawn to befriend these masters of the waters—spending a great deal of time swimming and being photographed with them all over the globe—because she is so much like them herself, or if doing so has in some way been a catalyst for the similarity.

Tatjana is intelligent, generous and peacefully self-reliant. Walking through her home, it appears as if she's taken her childhood fantasies and made them all come true. The many doors and windows are open, allowing freedom for the ocean breeze and the animals to move in and out. There seems to be little differentiation between the inside of the house and the outdoors, which was her intention. The towering windows arch high above our heads, each framed with sculptures of moons and stars, and the floors and countertops are inlaid with shells, stones and wildflowers, depicting Tatjana's love of all aspects of nature to the smallest detail. A hammock sways in the airy bedroom, the greenery just outside reflected in the floor-to-ceiling mirrors. Peace and tranquillity reign here.

Tatjana's life is charmed, there is no doubt. Her grace, goodness and spirituality embody a deep concern for all beings—from animals to children, and to the future generations of children. However, her journey has not been without poignant loss and struggle, and because of her openness and honesty, her stories are brutally candid. She fearlessly talks about what it is really like to work in the modeling industry, and about the wounds of a painful childhood that led to choices that nearly cost her her life.

With the amount of public recognition Tatjana enjoys, her depth of sharing is refreshing. More interested in speaking a truth that might encourage, uplift or inspire another soul, than protecting herself from invasion of her privacy or her vulnerabilities, this international beauty is a gift to us all. She has managed to hold on to her spiritual center in the midst of fame and greed, walking in modesty, humility and unpretentiousness. Tatjana hopes her revelations will help others to faithfully hold on to the good that they are, and to the greater good they can be, no matter what their walk in life.

*   *   *   *

Happiness

Happiness to me is being peaceful, where things in my life flow. A perfect day is one in which I take a few hours of solo time out for myself. When I am in a relationship, it is important for me to take time for that early in the day. Starting off each morning meditating and walking my dogs gives me the ability to think and feel complete within myself.

I have also found that the more disciplined I am, the happier I am. During the height of my modeling success, which came in the late 1980s, I was unorganized and undisciplined. That didn't seem to hinder me because I was one of the few voluptuous models who had broken through. When you are a novelty (as sexy womanly models were then) you can be irresponsible for a while, but my success wouldn't have lasted had I not changed. Success can happen overnight, but to keep it happening, hard work cannot be avoided. People tire of an unprofessional attitude, no matter how popular you are. Being disciplined in all areas—spiritually, mentally, physically and emotionally—helps me to be at peace. Then my life stays charmed.

Early Years

When I was a little girl, I loved hearing the story of how my parents met. I thought it was the most romantic story in the world: a case of two people falling in love and spending the rest of their lives together. Mom, who is Estonian, and Dad, who is German, met at a wine tasting in a bodega in Spain. Mom was a student traveling with a modern dance company and didn't have much money to buy food. She and her girlfriends were sitting at a table when a few of the guys my father was with went and asked them if they wanted to join their group for food. The women turned them down, but when they were asked a second time and their hunger had increased, the women agreed. Not for love, but for the stomach.

My parents started dating right away. Dad had to travel as a journalist, so he sent Mom letters. But another man who was in love with her stole them out of her post box. Mom would go to the same beach they used to visit together, hoping in vain to see him, and found out later that when she'd leave, he'd be visiting the area and arrive minutes afterward. In the meantime, her dance group moved from Barcelona to San Sebastian, and she had no way to tell my father about the move. One day he happened to go to San Sebastian for something and, walking down the street, they found each other. That was the night I was conceived.

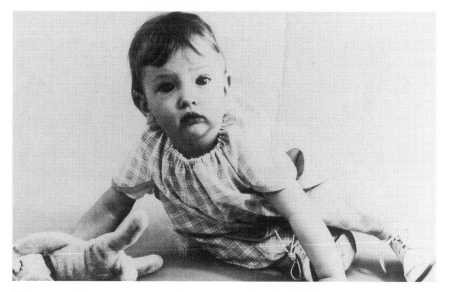

Tatjana, age 3.

As beautiful as this story has always been for me, in a way it is symbolic of how fate can be harsh. My parents' union was almost thwarted, and abandonment has been the key challenge in my life. I was separated from my parents for a year when I was young, and as a result, I had a sad childhood. I was born in Germany, but at five years old, I moved to Sweden to live with my grandmother because I couldn't stay in the public school I was attending. My teacher had singled me out amongst thirty kids to pick on; I was the only student she couldn't get to cry, and she hit me time and again. I remember vividly what she looked like. Because I had decided that she wouldn't break me, she hated me all the more. This woman did everything to make my life hell.

I was sent to the school psychologist, who gave me a piece of paper and told me to draw a picture of my family. I drew my parents as white sheep, my sister and brother as white lambs, and myself as a black sheep. So classic! Because I was the oldest child, and the only one in my family going to school, I felt completely alone and alienated. I was deeply insecure, and I didn't think I was special at all.

My mother took me out of school and Dad taught me at home, but my sister was a baby and it wasn't easy for them. They sent me to live with my grandmother until they could make the permanent move to Sweden a year later. Gram was kind and we became close, but being young, I didn't understand why I had to live with her. Children do not think logically, and I assumed that my parents didn't want me anymore. I thought my mother cared more for my brother, and my father cared more for my sister, making me the odd one out. My younger brother and I had been like two boys (I never wanted to be a part of anything girly), and being taken away from him was devastating. I never completely bonded with my family after that. The year felt like an eternity. I wanted to be special so badly and that need probably gave me the energy to succeed once I left home.

I still experience abandonment issues, and periodically the visions of leaving my family haunt me, but I believe the bad times were necessary for me to go through. It would be a waste of energy for me to regret anything, so I focus on the positives: These events helped mold me into an independent and strong person.

When my family arrived in Sweden, we were poor for awhile. I remember children teasing me because I wore the same clothes for days in a row. Ironically, I now wear clothing worth thousands of dollars for work. I don't remember thinking, "One day I'm going to dress nicely," but subconsciously those thoughts must have been there. I do remember deciding that I would travel a lot. My first priority became getting out of Sweden. My father said that I could travel alone if I made the money because he thought I'd never do it. But when I was fifteen, I saved up from working in pizza parlors and fish markets to go to Spain for the summer months. I rented a scooter and hung out on the beach and walked around a lot.

My father was a travel writer and we traveled a lot as children, so I was never afraid of the world. Going to new places was exciting for me. Dad was not confined to one country, and that is what I wanted.

Influences

The best thing my parents gave me was to be open with me. They provided a creatively free atmosphere for us to grow in, and they were not strong disciplinarians. When I consider what aspects of my childhood were charmed, one is that we were a literate family. My father read to us the great American books, especially the Mark Twain stories, and loved to teach us about poetry. That instilled in me an immense love of literature, which greatly enriches my life. I read everything from the serious writers to self-help spiritual books. My favorite poet is Goethe, and I reread Richard Bach's books every couple of years.

My father used to illustrate his travel books with paintings, and Mom, too, was a beautiful painter, so we were encouraged in the arts from all sides. Another aspect of my upbringing that brought some stability to my life was the fact that until we moved to Sweden, my mother was a full-time parent. After we moved, my father wrote at home, so he was always there for us.

Of the stresses we experienced as a family, the primary one had to do with money. My father had once made a good living selling his books in Germany but that changed somewhat in Sweden because he had to give up his job as a journalist. He became a freelance writer, which provided little at first. Most children have some idea of what they want to achieve when they get older and what they want to avoid; I used to see my parents argue over not having enough money, and decided early on that money would never hold me back. It became a matter of fact that I would have financial freedom; I never considered any other option. That attitude seemed to work well for me.

My parents also influenced me by teaching me and my siblings to love and take care of animals. They taught us that all animals have feelings and emotions, and they showed us how to rehabilitate any that were wounded. We brought home baby seagulls and fed them and nursed them back to health, even taking them on walks with us. We had crows, too, and many other wild birds in our garage. The sensitivity of both of my parents was one of the blessings of the way I was raised.

Horses were my first friends. My father put me in a horse-riding class in Germany, and I started hanging out at the stables and reading horse books. I began grooming horses for other people in exchange for lessons, and I fantasized, daydreamed, about being grown up. I wrote about an older girl and her horse and, like I had seen my father do, I illustrated the books with paintings. The girl and her horse had freedom and could go anywhere, like I wanted to be able to do. I was dying to leave everything I knew behind me. I still spend hours in the stable: riding, hosing the horses off afterward, drying them off, brushing them and making sure the stall is perfect. In recent years, I was more in a hurry to get away after I was finished riding, hiring others to complete the tasks for me, but now the whole process is a moving meditation.

When Christopher Reeve had his fall, even though it was a freak accident, I wouldn't get on my horses. I had just bought a magnificent Andalusian, who is calm and well balanced. He's white, with a mane down to his knees, and he dances like a feather, but I was afraid to ride him. If they're skittery at all, I don't get on them.

Photo by Sandra Johnson

Tatjana and her horse Cappy.

Lifework

I came to find the freedom I was searching for through modeling. Every once in a while, during my teens, I was approached by modeling scouts, and when I was fifteen, I was asked to enter Casablanca's "Look of the Year" contest in Sweden. I came in third and from there decided to move to Paris when I was seventeen. My father was supportive because he was independent early on and understood that his ways had rubbed off. For my mother, Paris was a more nerve-racking prospect. I was her young daughter, going off into a foreign land filled with unknowns. A seedy scene. When I look back, it's incredible how naive I was.

If I knew then what I know now about modeling, I would have been a veterinarian. At that point in my life, I was gullible and believed everybody for what they said. The negative things of the industry never hit me directly in the face; I was blessed enough to make it big fairly early, so the bad people couldn't get to me. The darkness was at a distance, but I saw it all around me. So many sharks, especially in Europe. Endless rich men after young innocent girls. Paris was dangerous; Italy was worse. America is different: Once you are in New York, you are away from most of the unsavory element. It is safer and more legitimate in America. I've met some highly questionable people in the movie industry here, but thank God now I can tell. I take one big look, a good look, and can feel who to avoid.

I went to a party recently that was so depressing, I couldn't get out of bed until 3:00 P.M. the next afternoon. There were many wealthy men with the sweetest young girls, all in their perfect outfits and perfect hairdos, waiting to get picked up, discovered or *anything*. The men used smooth pick-up lines that the girls will one day come to recognize as false because they will hear them hundreds of times. With experience, I pray they will be able to walk away.

I am so grateful that I had my parents' support when I started modeling. I was open with them and they always knew what was going on with me. My mother warned me about the types of people I would meet, and she and my father were always there to talk to. The hardest thing for me was learning who to trust. Fortunately, I had a booker named Scott who took care of me like a big brother. He sat me down for kitchen talks: "Now, listen to me. . . . You don't do this, you don't do that, be careful of this. . . ." He was my personal angel.

Photo by Sante D'Orazio

Tatjana with her mother, Anne Patitz.

I had been living in Paris for three months, when my agency booked me on a catalog shoot. My boyfriend at the time put me on the train to Brussels, which is where the location was scheduled, and I waited until he left and then jumped off the other side. I hid out in my girlfriend's apartment for three days, where I knew no one could find me. My agents were crazy looking for me, but I knew I could do better than catalogs. I pulled a similar stunt in Germany soon afterward, and my agency gave me a lecture about understanding the need to make money. I wasn't concerned with the money. I knew what I wanted, which was to be a big model in the magazines. The androgynous girls were in (like now), and voluptuous girls like me were not popular, but that all changed. The jobs came easily. First they were smaller jobs in *Elle* and the like, and then the covers. The most exciting part was when I started working with the great, famous photographers.

My agency thought I was a brat, but that did not upset me because I knew my career was in my hands. I am presently the same way with my acting career and turn down many offers because I only want to do projects that I love. I said no to a reading for a "Bond girl," choosing to act in an episode of *The Garry Shandling Show* instead, which was a blast. That, to me, is the kind of show I like to do.

Feeling that I deserve success in any area is important to me. I felt that I deserved to work on quality jobs, and that was what I was given. I have no trouble, emotionally, being paid huge sums of money. No guilt whatsoever. One thing I've come to realize is that a company using my image will make far more money than I will ever see. What I am paid, though large sums, are small drops of the total that companies make. Photographers, too, make much more than models.

I help my parents with my money, and it feels good to be able to do that. I bought them a house in France, and they are happy and in a comfortable place. It can get tricky, though, even nasty, dealing with family and money. I have gotten phone calls that make me feel like I am an ATM machine. People focus on the total sum that a contract pays, but after the agency takes their fee, and the government does the same, the total cuts in half right away. Taxes are incredible because I am still a German citizen. Despite the occasional awkwardness, though, I still love to help others, especially animals.

Some models complain that there is no meaning or spirituality in our work. Any job is only as good as the people within it, so in modeling it depends on who you work with. Working with photographers like Peter Lindbergh or Bruce Weber, who do creative editorial pieces—which is not a lot of money—is fulfilling because of the beauty that results. Each job involves creating a character, which is not unlike acting. That is why certain models are better than others—because of the emotions they are able to transmit. Anyone can look pretty. There are gorgeous girls who never make it as models because they are afraid to emote. When I look in the camera, I can see the picture being taken. I suppose that is where my sensitivity helps me. I become different characters by changing the way I move or dress—an innocent waif, a sexual diva or whatever the theme is about. I go with the look completely. It comes naturally to me, especially with a good photographer.

Photo by Peter Lindbergh

I still love what I do, except for ramp work, which is hell and often filled with drugs. (I was going to do the Paris shows this year, but decided to dedicate those

Modeling photo of Tatjana.

three months each year to acting. I believe in closing one door before another will open.) People think the drug era of modeling is over because the pill taking and drinking is not as prevalent. But now heavier drugs are the reality. Heroin and cocaine are widespread in modeling, more so than in the 1980s. The phase that is presently coming through, a result of the X-generation grunge influence, is extremely destructive. There is no resemblance to the 1960s seeking of spiritual realms through psychedelics; heroin is an escape and cocaine is the biggest ego booster out there. Cocaine is still big with models, especially the more successful ones because it gives them an edge and more energy so they can work harder. It also gives them self-confidence and makes them thinner, too. Even some designers are heavy users. It may not be out in the open anymore, like in the days of cocaine bowls at parties, but its effect is stronger and more underground.

I recently went to New York to do a show for Calvin Klein, and while I was in the hotel I got a phone call from an unknown caller. He asked me in a foreboding voice if I wanted some heroin. I hung up the phone and booked a flight home, once again reminded why I am focusing more on acting. And it's not just me who feels the disappointment of how things have changed. A lot of photographers talk about how bad the industry has gotten. We used to have fun; there used to be loyalty to quality people and pride in the work. It's all about money now. I just thank God I never got into heavy drugs. Smoking cigarettes is, unfortunately, the one bad habit I have. Everything in my life is good except for the fact that I still smoke.

When you look at magazines nowadays, the women don't look healthy. It seems to me that the industry is trying to be too futuristic, and, in that approach, the photographs are often disrespectful to nature and all that is natural. One thing I cannot understand is: Why is fur back? When I first started seeing the new fur campaigns, I was shocked. There are other ways to stay warm, for God's sake! Where is the responsibility?

I would not in a million years want to be a teenager in this day and age. I think the images of the waif-like women in magazines breed a lot of eating disorders in young girls. And women can't relate to these images either! It's why people look up to movie stars now more than models. Actresses are doing a lot of endorsements that used to be done by models.

Obstacles

After Paris I came to L.A., where I was completely out of control. I felt invincible because I was young and had started making great money. My parents used to worry about me, without communicating their fears, and all of their worry projected off on me. I became crazy and challenged destiny. I'm lucky to be alive.

I moved into the Chateau Marmont Hotel, which is where John Belushi died. The hotel doesn't exactly have healthy karma, and the months I lived there were the wildest of my life. I was too sensitive for the energy surrounding the locale, and if I had understood that, I could have removed myself. But instead I said, "I feel uncomfortable, I better have another drink." I rented a little Mercedes and blew money as fast as if I'd burned it. Somehow, nine years ago, I mellowed out big time. I had to—people were concerned about me because I would cancel jobs and sometimes not show up for bookings. My reputation was failing. Even now I hear rumors about myself that make me laugh. My wild ways live on in the minds of people who have nothing better to think about. Fortunately, I have moved forward.

I look at some of the things I used to do and realize that I had a guardian angel over my shoulder. I could have killed myself or someone else so many times, driving drunk. There were nights where I wouldn't remember getting home, yet my car would be parked outside my bedroom window. I would drive down Pacific Coast Highway with one eye closed so that the lines wouldn't blend in. When I look back, I don't think I was an alcoholic, but more a crazed teenager who was unable to deal with her life. I had always been incredibly shy, blushing at anything. Suddenly getting so much attention was hard for me to handle sober because I got anxiety attacks. I didn't have to go to recovery meetings to stop drinking; it was something I stopped easily because I felt awful and started breaking out in hives. I'm convinced that God gave them to me as a tool to wake me up. It worked. At first I thought they were flea bites. They showed up in Jamaica and on a job in Miami, eventually getting so severe that they were all over my arms and legs like blisters. I went to doctors and a tropical disease expert, but no one had any idea what they were. Finally, a dermatologist told me I had hives caused by stress.

My body was completely run-down. It may seem glamorous to fly all over the world, but it's exhausting. And, with people constantly touching you, telling you how to stand, sit and breathe, the taking leaves you completely empty. Even now, occasionally, someone will be pulling on my hair, and I won't feel myself anymore. That's when I take a break. The best thing I have found is to plan my schedule so that I have a balance of work and time off. Traveling on my own is not half as stressful as traveling with a group, so most of the time I try to meet the others at the location.

People often assume that if you are beautiful, life is automatically easier. But you know, it can really get a person into trouble. People go out of their way to be nice to you, but you never know what motives are behind their smiles. I've had to deal with some real creeps. Obviously, seeing the inside of a person is more important than the exterior, and that is why I started soul-searching. I needed to stop being dependent on what I looked like because the reality that I might look in the mirror at forty years old and be unhappy with what I saw scared me. I wanted to ensure that I didn't run to a plastic surgeon. When a person's spirit shines bright, everything else becomes irrelevant anyway. Vanity can ruin a person's soul.

Fears

Being insecure is my biggest fear outside of abandonment. I always felt tall and skinny as a child, and my height of five feet, eleven inches still makes me uncomfortable sometimes. I have to catch myself and not worry about living up to other people's expectations. Being judged scares me, so it is ironic that I would pick acting as my next career choice. Probably to help me get over my inhibitions. Sometimes I ask myself why I need to go through another insane business. The truth is that I love being different characters, and I'm addicted to the feeling of creating them.

When I first started my career, models who could be controlled were in high demand, so the more messed up the better, as long as you didn't talk about it. But, being wild helped my career in some sense because I was more fun to be around. I was up and giggly, going along with the partying. Even the wildest people thought I was crazy. (Now when I work with them, they think I've mellowed out beyond belief.)

One of the things that really taught me to own my own power was a turbulent relationship that, needless to say, didn't last very long. The man I was dating was a "crazymaker." One minute he was one way, the next minute he was the other. There was no harmony. What threw me off center was that I had been very independent before we met. He was so charming on the outside and said the right things, which taught me to watch a person's actions and not depend on his words.

I was already in the relationship too deeply when I realized that I was being emotionally and mentally abused. It was pointed out to me that he was a classic abuser: he would build me up by being so nice, giving me guilt presents and basically babying me. He would tell me that he couldn't live without me. Then, out of the blue, he'd tell me that I was worthless and verbally berate me. There was no middle ground. At the worst point, I believed him. I felt worthless. I felt ugly.

At first I took it all on, until I saw him treat other people the same way. It was then that I realized it was his incredible pain causing the problems, not mine. In hindsight, I'm grateful for this experience because it helped me let go of weaknesses within me that I had carried since my childhood. But it was not easy. I barely found the seed of strength within me to walk away, and I wasn't even financially dependent on this man. I shudder to think of how hard it must be for a woman to leave an abusive relationship when she has children and no means of supporting herself.

I have since learned that allowing an abuser to be abusive is much more damaging to the person giving the abuse than the one receiving it. If a person keeps getting away with destructive behavior, they are never forced to change the pattern that creates it. The partner becomes an enabler, similar to allowing an alcoholic to drink.

Fortunately, I am blessed with an independent nature, and I am increasingly comfortable by myself. I don't need a lot of things or situations to make me happy anymore. That is the good that came from my childhood, and other traumatic experiences throughout my life—a detachment that has served me. For instance, if modeling were to stop today, I'd be a little sad, and then I'd be on to the next thing. I am thankful it has been so good to me, but my job is not my life, and it does not define who I am.

Spirituality

When I was a girl, God was the Big Daddy in the sky on a cloud with a long gray beard. I went to Sunday school, but my parents didn't baptize us because they thought it important we pick what we wanted to practice for ourselves. I felt more scared of God than protected by him, but I feel protected now. My image of God is endless and has become more of a feeling than a picture.

Being spiritual to me means living a compassionate life. I consider the sensitivity my parents helped foster in me through art, literature and the care of animals to be one of my better characteristics. I can be overly sensitive at times, but I have learned to make that work to my benefit. It is wonderful for my creativity. It makes me vulnerable, which in the past hurt too much. The teachers in my life (except for the first one in Germany) told me that my sensitivity was more of a plus than anything else, and I have learned to use it in the creation of everything I do. I used it to design my home. I use it for my acting roles, for loving, and even for my spirituality. I think because of my sensitivity, which springs forth as creativity, I refuse to do what so many people do: I refuse to sell out.

One of my favorite books, which became a Gary Cooper movie, was *The Fountainhead.* The message was about integrity and art, and how certain people will do anything for success: They may build a bad building or do a bad job, strictly for the money. Then there are people who hold to their vision. I strive for my visions and that makes my life filled with magical experiences. If I had listened to my modeling agents when I first came to Paris, telling me to do bad jobs to make good money, perhaps I wouldn't have done so well. I think we are rewarded for having faith and believing we deserve to have the best in life. I believe I deserve God's blessings.

Fame

When I shine fully in my life, it is a great feeling. Success is contagious. I love feeling the ability to influence others to go for their dreams because I am living mine. At the same time, shining in this world breeds jealousy. There are some people who don't like to see others in a good place. I've had people not work with me because they felt too many things were going my way. The hardest thing for a jealous person to see is that I can be happy in spite of my success. I've had to distance myself from a few friends who say things like, "That's great but . . . ," always looking for the negative. As I move up in steps, some of the people around me take it personally and act differently. My success isn't personal about them at all. I've had to choose to gravitate toward people who empower me, and who allow me to empower them.

Fame is somewhat in our power to make of it what we want. If we take ourselves and our status seriously, we lose our roots, and most significantly, we forget that we are foremost spiritual beings who are all equal in the eyes of God. Anything we've been able to accomplish in life came from God, anyway. Some people who have a lot of money act as if they are special. That is ridiculous. I recently heard a man say, "I can get anything I want; I have more money than God." I wanted to tell him not to be so cocky. God can take away anything we have in an instant.

Being famous is a job in itself. It is a sacrifice to lose your anonymity. A high price. Still, much of it is up to the individual. There are famous people who are rarely seen or heard from, and every once in a while, they come out with whatever they do. You don't have to live "the scene." I try to keep the press away from me as much as possible. Some publicity is good for work, but not too much. Those are career decisions. There are also certain projects you choose to do to make a difference and help others, like this interview, for instance.

The criticism that stems from being well known can hurt, but in the end, modeling and acting are so physical that I cannot pay attention. All it does is make for insecurity and weakness. For a while, I was stressed about all of the skinny girls in my business. I am thin, but I am not a toothpick. Some are so skinny that their upper arms are as small as their wrists; they look half-dead without clothes on. Now I feel sorry for them.

Miracles

Looking back, my life has been charmed in that I was saved from danger so many times. Toward the end of my wild phase, I had a car accident driving to New Mexico with friends for the weekend. We blew a tire and my Jeep rolled over four times at seventy miles an hour, landing on the side of the freeway. As we were flipping, I saw my life pass before my eyes, literally. I saw, in clear detail, my childhood, parents, brother, sister and myself in different experiences, even my first day of school. Then I said, "This is not supposed to happen right now," and the visions stopped immediately. The car was upside down and the roll bar was half an inch from my head. My nose was bleeding, but basically my friends and I were all right. I could see little light bubbles everywhere—the kind you sometimes see in the daylight. However, it was night and they were much clearer than usual. I look for them now when I get afraid, especially when I board a plane. Somehow they remind me of being protected.

Probably the most significant miracle of my life has been my introduction to the world of dolphins. There have been so many blessings surrounding my friendship with these incredible beings, whom I didn't know anything about until I moved to Malibu. I kept seeing them in the water from my balcony, and when I rented the movie *The Big Blue,* that was it. I was hooked. I ran into someone who used to be a dolphin trainer, who led me to people in Hawaii, and from there the doors opened easily.

The first time I swam with captive dolphins was at the Marine Mammal Laboratory in Hawaii. The doctors there had me doing linguistic studies with the dolphins, and it was staggering how intelligent they were in person. They knew sign language and with certain tests I'd have to wear goggles because they could read my eyes. We would ask them yes and no questions about their environment and they would push on "yes" and "no" panels to answer us. It was mind boggling. At night, I watched them out in the ocean with their heads out of the water, staring at the stars. We all wondered what they were looking at, and if they could see and understand things we couldn't.

Swimming with these mammals is indescribable. They slow down to your speed, let you hold on to them, and when they know you can handle it, they pull you along. I don't think I had a total sense of dolphins until I swam with the wild ones. There is something that happens to captive dolphins, even if they're happy and well fed, because they are in a small, man-made area. Dolphins are such vast travelers and so highly communicative that being confined must be painful for them. They are one of the few species that can have more than one conversation at a time, talking with a dolphin next to them while simultaneously speaking with another one twenty miles away.

The most beautiful experience of my life was swimming with a wild female dolphin in the Bahamas. I found a piece of seaweed and she would take it in her mouth and go off with it, laying on her back so the seaweed went down her body. I'd take my bikini top off and she would grab it with her teeth and flip it back to me with her tail. Imagine . . . a wild dolphin. I was so high, I felt like I was on another planet. Holding on to a piling from a boat dock, she came up next to me, put her nose up to my heart, and let me stroke her entire body. Her skin was warm and felt like a wet suit—soft and strong. All muscle. The whole time she was communicating to me, making clicking noises over and over, sounding like a baby. It was so beautiful, I cried the whole time.

Afterward I dreamt about her for months. In the dreams, she and I swam together in clear rivers. The colors of the dream were in Technicolor, which makes me think that I was experiencing another dimension of some kind, because it was like nothing I had ever dreamt of before.

Soon, I had a reputation with photographers for swimming with dolphins, and they wanted to shoot me with them. One shoot was in Florida with Peter Lindbergh. When we arrived at our hotel, I went to sleep and had a dream that I was by a lake I had never seen. A female dolphin was out in the water, and two mermen [male mermaids] carried me out to meet her. The following morning, when Peter and I went to the shoot, we arrived at the same lake I had dreamt about the night before. In the water was the female dolphin from the dream, exactly, and two male ones.

Dolphins are flirtatious. The females flirt with male humans, and the male dolphins flirt with female humans. I have heard stories of female dolphins going out of their way to be mean to their male trainers' girlfriends: They splash and squawk at the women as they pass the tanks. The bonds trainers have with these mammals are typically much stronger than those made with other animals. It may be because of their psychic and intelligence abilities.

Once, a male dolphin took me way out in a lagoon and swam with me with what looked like sexy eyes. I was nervous to see what he was going to do because they have been reported to get sexual with humans. This particular one was gentle, but I knew of a male dolphin in Hawaii that was so sexual, no female human could swim with him. One woman did and he tried to have sex with her. We're talking about a foot-long you-know-what. And, he was so accurate in his attempts that he went straight for her reproductive parts. He was in his sexual prime—seven years old—which is puberty for them, so he was a bit frustrated. As a rule, dolphins have sex all day long; that's all they do besides eat and nap, so it can get interesting, to say the least.

Scientists believe that thirty million years ago, dolphins were land animals. When they are x-rayed, their pregnancies appear to be the same

Tatjana with a dolphin.

as humans—nine months. They nurse their young up until three or four years old, much like traditional native humans do, and on their flukes (hands) they have five digits that look like fingers. Their blowhole may have been a nose at one time, and eventually they took on an aerodynamic shape. No one understands why they went from land animals to the sea, but I would do anything in my power to help stop the destruction of this species.

Discipline

My spiritual disciplines are important to me, and my life definitely works better when I take time for myself. My ability to create money and other good things increases. Life stays charmed because all good things heighten. Even if it's just going for a walk and sitting under a tree, being in nature is essential for me. Taking time out to feel the beauty of the planet, which is easiest in the mornings, raises my mood and my level of peace. When I'm not at peace, I don't do as well at things because I get stressed out. That's when I take long aroma-therapy baths. (Relaxation is the gift I give myself because my business is so hectic.) I have noticed that even my ability to make money lessens when I stray from my spiritual practices.

I started taking yoga six years ago and fell in love with it from the start. It is my main form of exercise. I am a vegetarian and feel best when I eat a lot of raw foods, so I eat only fruit all morning long. For lunch I usually have pasta with vegetables, and for dinner the same or a salad. I use a little dairy on cereal, but not much. Luckily for me, I am not a sugar person and never have been. Sometimes I eat chocolate before my period, but I don't care much for cookies, cake or ice cream. I'm grateful not to have to fight with that. Pizza and pasta are my indulgences.

Earth

I have close friends in New Mexico, and when I take pleasure trips, I go there or to Montana. Being in both of those states rejuvenates my spirit and makes me strong. People always ask me why I don't move back to Europe. I love America. It is so vast here; there is so much land. I am inspired by large spaces of land and water. That is why I live next to the ocean. Seeing the old buildings of Europe triggers something uncomfortable in me, representing what I ran away from. America feels newer, fresher and more alive.

I get nervous when I think of the future of this planet. I make it a point not to watch the news or read much of the newspaper because I try not to pollute myself with all of the negative imagery the media feeds us day in and day out. You know, nature has a wonderful way of taking care of herself, and I try to remember that. When the intense rains come here to Southern California, I have to focus on the fact that there is a reason for all of it. In the springtime, I see how good those rains are. Everything is so green. Being in Malibu is a nightmare because we can't get in and out with the highway washing away, but it is only a logistical pain. I love the rain. It is the commotion of the people and news congregations that I mind. All they want to do is talk about how terrible everything is, and it isn't nearly as bad as the news portrays it. A few houses are lost, and if you focus on life strictly from a material standpoint, that is awful. But in the big picture, maybe those houses were not meant to be there. The whole aspect of the earth and what she is going through is far more important than our little wooden structures.

The only thing I want in life that I don't have is babies. I would love to have twins: a boy and a girl. Sometimes I see them in visions. First the girl and then the boy. A friend of mine was watching me with my horses one day and saw them, too, standing beside me. Recently, at the airport, a man said to me, "You have children, a boy and a girl, don't you?" We shall see. I never worry about being a good parent. Because of what I experienced as a child, I know that I will be devoted. I love my animals, so much so that I am always there for them. One of my horses got a viral infection and I almost took my sleeping bag and slept with him in the stall. I stayed with him until midnight each day, and as a result, I built stables at my house so that they are with me all the time.

Careerwise, I'd like to write screenplays and produce, eventually. But, I will fine-tune my acting first. Because that can only be done by doing it, maybe I'll stop turning down jobs. I want to be creative in life. Part of me wants to live on an island somewhere and be with dolphins—a hermit life, spent writing in quiet study. Another part of me wants to act and produce. I'm hoping I can do it all. That would be amazing.

My parents are living happily ever after together. I know now that all relationships are challenging, but I still believe in love. One day I'm going to be happily married with my girl and boy, riding horses and swimming with dolphins as a family. In there, too, will be fulfilling new career successes, but those details will just have to take care of themselves. My priority of the last few years has been to get healthy on all levels. I am reaping the rewards of a commitment to a lot of hard work, and I am appreciating the security of loving myself, my life, and trusting in others. These are the true blessings.

14

Arnold Palmer

Photo courtesy of Arnold Palmer Enterprises, 1998

Introduction

O ne of the things I learned working for celebrities is that the saying "it's all who you know" is based in truth. Well-known personalities are so busy juggling their own affairs that the
never-ending requests for interviews are, more often than not, completely ignored. This is especially the case when the celebrity wishes to
experience a normal and grounded life far removed from the press
and the social scene. When an unknown writer, like me, comes along
and solicits an interview, chances are that even if the celebrity finds
out about the request, the celebrity is likely in the process of writing his
or her own story. Such was the case with Arnold Palmer. When he is not
golfing, designing courses, flying airplanes, attending to his vast business
empire and spending time with his wife of forty-four years and their
children and grandchildren, he steals time to pen his own history.

So, when I had the original dream of this book and felt that it
needed to include Arnold (who, by the way, gets two book-interview
requests per day), I had a problem. Not only did I not know him, but
we lived on opposite coasts. The odds of becoming his professional dog-
walker were next to nil. So I prayed about it and waited. "Ask and ye
shall receive"—I made sure that God knew I was asking. Even though
interviewing the "Elvis of Golf," as my friends call him, was a dream
that would most likely go unrealized, I stayed optimistic. I couldn't
shake the image of Arnold as a masculine example of the charmed ideal.

Then I realized that I had a potential contact right under my nose—
John Brodie. John had played golf with Arnold for over thirty years, and
now they were regulars on the Senior Tour together. John was my best
friend Diane Chandler's father. But I was gun-shy. I had learned the hard
way that mixing business and friendship can be a very tricky thing. It
wasn't worth the risk of adding pressure to a friendship that had endured
since high school—one of the dearest and most sacred relationships of my
life. Not even for Arnold, a golf immortal and living legend.

A year after starting this book, however, Diane and her mother, Sue
Brodie, came up with an idea of their own: "Arnold Palmer would be
perfect for your book. Send us a letter for him, and we'll try to get it to
him personally." Sue carefully placed it in her suitcase and

hand-carried it into a barber shop at a tournament where Arnold was getting his hair cut. I guess she supposed that because he was sitting in the chair, he couldn't get up and walk away if he didn't appreciate the inconvenience. A few months went by, and I got a call: Arnold would do the interview. I was elated but cautious. As in any business, the deal isn't complete until it's completed. That was another hard lesson already learned. Months went by without any scheduled meeting, and then one evening, I heard the top news story blaring out from the television: "Arnold Palmer announced today that he has prostate cancer." More prayers and a lot more waiting. Two years after the delivery of the letter, I was driving a little rental car through the rain-slicked roads of Orlando, Florida, to the Bay Hill Club, one of the most stunning courses in the United States, where Arnold calls home.

I found a healthy and vibrant Arnold (in his late-sixties) when I arrived. Florida was experiencing tornado watches that day, and lucky for me, he was once again stuck in a chair, this time behind his beautiful cherrywood desk. With no hope of playing golf in such stormy weather, I had his gracious attention. We bonded over having lived the "hard life," he as a child and me, by choice, as an adult in the woods, and we laughed as we compared notes on how rain makes a heck of a lot of noise on the roof of an outhouse. Arnold told me how to shoot rabbits for food, as he had done as a boy, just in case I ran out of supplies living so far from civilization. I addressed him as "Mr. Palmer," but found out that he likes to be called "Arnie." He says that one of the worst things about having cancer was the way people stopped calling him Arnie and took to the more formal "Mr. Palmer." Strangers and friends alike had always called him Arnie, and he detested the formality that came with being ill. Thankfully, now that he is healthy and back on courses throughout the United States, fans once again blurt out his beloved nickname with gusto, relieved to see their hero back to his jovial and talented self.

I hope he will forgive me, but I must mention some of his accomplishments for anyone too young to know the details, or for the lone cave-dwelling hermit who may have recently emerged. Arnold was the Tiger Woods of his day, even bigger, if you can imagine that. Never before had state troopers been necessary to keep the peace on a golf course until Arnie came along. He was the John Wayne of sports in the

1950s and 1960s—the good guy who had pulled himself up by his golf-bag straps. Up until that time, golf had a reputation for being a sport for the conservative and wealthy. Not only did Arnie love to joke with as many people in the gallery as possible, but he was seen as one of them: a guy who had been born without the silver spoon and who had worked harder than anyone on the tour. Although he was raised on the border of a country club, Arnold was kept at arm's length from the very world he eventually conquered. He grew up on the outside looking in, something the fans could relate to. Arnie let them in, in droves, and they cheered when he was up and, in some cases, threw tantrums when he was down. His warm and sincere personality endeared him to millions of people throughout the world, many of whom still call themselves members of "Arnie's Army." These enthusiastic fan-club members are infamous for kicking Arnold's stray balls onto fairways during tournaments. It was a different era, a time when television was new and heroes were needed. Arnold was the chosen one.

Then came Jack Nicklaus, eleven years his junior. Jack's family was well-to-do. Jack was emotionally distant. Jack was heavy and often called names by the press, while Arnold was slim and handsome. And Jack was beating the beloved Arnie when no one else had. Arnie's Army was angry and vengeful, making Jack's playing time a punishing ordeal of name-calling and heckling. Jack became America's villain, but in spite of the public torment, the young Nicklaus stayed focused and disciplined, and eventually won the respect of the American people. And that was a good thing for golf in general because the public battle between them resulted in the longest-running athletic rivalry of all time and brought countless spectators and competitors to the sport.

Everything Arnie touched turned to gold and, because of his overwhelming popularity, people trusted him implicitly. So, Arnie and his business manager, Mark McCormack, invented the practice of product endorsement by a sports celebrity. Trustworthy names in sports had not yet been linked to selling products, but within a few years of this self-created trend, Arnie was endorsing everything from shaving cream to cars, becoming the top-grossing athlete for endorsement income for thirty years (until Michael Jordan broke his record in 1991).

Arnold has been written about for over forty years, and still he isn't comfortable with the praise, so I will sum this up before he wishes he

*had declined my interview request. His ninety-two professional cham-
pionships have led to honors for every award from* Sports Illustrated*'s
"Sportsman of the Year" to the 1960s Associated Press Poll's "Athlete of
the Decade." He won the Masters four times from 1958 through 1964,
the British Open in 1961 and 1962, and the U.S. Open in 1960.
Pulitzer Prize-nominated author Thomas Hauser has written one of
the best biographies I've ever read, entitled* Arnold Palmer: A Personal
Journey, *in case this leaves you wanting more.*

To date, I'm delighted to say that my friendships have all *been
enhanced by this fortunate meeting. The Brodies and the Chandlers
are my beloved warriors for risking their dear relationship with golf's
greatest legend by hooking us up. And I'm told that even Arnie says it
was a win-win experience. That may be a good thing to remember the
next time you question whether or not to put your neck on the line for
a friend.*

*   *   *   *

Happiness

Health is number one when it comes to happiness for me. If you're
healthy and your family is healthy, that is a pretty good start toward
happiness.

I have had all kinds of experiences with health. To begin with, my
father was a polio victim shortly after birth. Dad had a clubfoot and
was crippled from the knee down. I don't think unless you have that
happen to you, and it happens to a lot of people in the world, that
you can know the impact of being a cripple. You cannot envision or
feel what a person feels when that happens to him. What it did for my
father was that it drove him to strengthen himself in a lot of other
ways. In his arms, chest and body, he was very strong. He worked
very hard at being strong, but having a clubfoot also had a psychological effect on him. I suppose he had a defense that he set up in his
own mind to compensate for that.

As a golf professional, I was the National Chairman of the March of
Dimes Birth Defects Foundation for twenty years. Growing up and
seeing my father's disability contributed to my wanting to work with

the March of Dimes. Cancer, too, has touched my life several times now. I have a daughter who had breast cancer. She has been in total remission for seven years now, and she feels great. I just hope she stays great. Since I've had prostate cancer myself, I can say with experience that happiness, to me, equals health. I think of my grandchildren and my family, and I hope that they can enjoy good health throughout the years. It's very, very important.

After health, I suppose happiness means socially being able to do what you like to do, and of course, being able to follow your desires as far as your workplace is concerned. I've had all of those things. I'm a very happy person. I enjoy my family, my friends, and I enjoy my occupation. I look forward to getting up every day and going to work.

Passion

One of the things that has greatly enhanced my life is my love of flying airplanes. I have been flying for over forty years and continue to fly to work. It has been a passion of mine since I was little. I don't think you can ever know for sure as a child what your future will hold, but I pursued flying early because I liked it. When I was about ten years old, I had a good friend and one of the things we did together was build model airplanes. We spent months building a fairly large airplane, with a big, thick rubber band in it. It was quite extensive . . . I recall that very distinctly. We got it all finished and took it upstairs to the top of the house and put it out the window and watched it go down until it crashed. That was the beginning of my flying. So I suppose someday I might crash in an airplane. But I hope not!

I used to run out of our house, down the country-club road to the nearby airport, to listen to the pilots, who gathered around an old, potbellied stove. I loved watching the planes take off and land. I did this from a little boy upward. Still do. I was always curious about all aspects of flying. My questions to the pilots were always about the details of flying. In those days, the navigational aids were very limited and for the better part of any flight, most of the flying was visual. There was very little In the Clouds or IFR [instrument flight rules] as we know them now. Later in life, when I went to a golf tournament in one of my first trips in an airplane, I got violently scared and thought my life was over. I was sure that I was going to die. That's when I decided that what I had thought of as something that I wanted to do became more than just a desire to fly. My desire then shifted to becoming a pilot myself and to understanding what I was scared of. That doesn't mean that I am totally not afraid, even now. I think that I still have some apprehensions about flying, but I've got over fifteen thousand hours at the controls. I wouldn't say that I'm insecure about it, I just don't think that I know everything there is about the world of aviation, so I respect it and treat it with caution. I fly my own airplane when I travel or work. I've never had an accident, but I think if you fly as long as I have, you have things happen: I've lost engines and I've had mishaps over the years, but the experience and training that I've had have helped tremendously and saved my life, I suppose, on some occasions. But if you fly a lot, dangerous things are going to happen.

Photo courtesy of Arnold Palmer Enterprises, 1998

Arnold and his father, Deke (Deacon) Palmer, 1960s.

Early Years

My father was a tough taskmaster. I was raised under a pretty strict set of rules, but I can look back now and thank him for all of the discipline he gave me. And, good or bad, I give him a great deal of credit for whatever success I've had. My mother, on the other side of that coin, was the soft spot. She was the warm, caring person who kind of softened the blow from the harsh father teachings.

I was always in awe of my father. He was the one who introduced me to golf. He was the greenskeeper and club pro at the Latrobe Country Club in Pennsylvania, and he would take me around the golf course on his tractor. I started riding on his lap in the tractor when I was three years old. It was 1932, during the Great Depression, so it was a whole different lifestyle. We lived on the edge of the golf course and in those days, golf courses were not respected places to live. We lived very simply and had to do things to supplement the salary my father made. We raised pigs and chickens for food, right next to the maintenance building on the golf course, and had them butchered every fall. I had to pick the eggs every morning and slop the pigs. I also killed the chickens when it was time. I hated it when the pigs were shot because I was a kid and had helped to raise them. They were my friends. When they took the .22 and shot them and cut their throats and hung them up so they'd bleed, that was awfully hard on me.

We also hunted for food. I shot rabbits and pheasants and cleaned them. When we shot the rabbits, we used pellets, and then had to take the pellets out of the meat. Rabbits are fast, so if you shoot a rabbit, you have to try and shoot him in the head so you blow his head off. This probably isn't the kind of talk you'd expect from a golf professional, but if you want to be out in the rough, you have to be in the rough. We made it work.

We had a modern outhouse in those days, about fifty yards from the house. In the Depression, under President Roosevelt, WPA built outhouses out of wood. They had metal roofs, and when you were sitting under that roof in the rain, it was loud! I went to a two-room schoolhouse, with four grades in one room, and two teachers.

Even though my father was the golf pro at the club, he was not allowed in the clubhouse of the country club except on business. I thought we were treated a bit like second-class citizens. I could only play golf with the caddies, as long as I didn't get in the way with what was happening. My mother used to take me in the evenings to the golf course when everyone else was gone, and I'd play golf with her. There was probably something psychological about that that made me want to do things later that I wasn't allowed to do. For instance, I couldn't go to the country-club pool to swim. I had to swim in the stream that went by the edge of the golf course. My sister and I swam together and had as much fun as anyone else. Of course when I got a little older and realized what was happening, it was kind of fun because I figured out that we got to swim in the water *before* the kids at the country club did: They pumped the water from the stream up to the club. So life is all perspective, really. And I suppose to wind this story up, I should mention that I own the club now.

Photo courtesy of Arnold Palmer Enterprises, 1998

Arnold as a golfing beginner, with his sister, Lois Jean, holding the bag.

I have no resentment because a lot of the negative things that happened in the early days went away with time, obviously. When I was in high school, the members of the club used to take up little pots of funds for me so that I could play in golf tournaments. They'd give them to my father and say, "Here, let Arnie go play in the tournament." They were very nice. And, as life went on, some of those people became my very best friends.

When I was young, I never had a sense that I would be wealthy or well known. On that note, I suppose I'm a bit like my mother in that I'm a little bit financially insecure. It wouldn't matter how much money I had. I suppose somewhere there could be enough money for me, but I'm not sure that that would make me feel financially secure. I feel pretty secure about most things, but I inherited this financial insecurity from my mother and being a product of the Depression, seeing people lose their jobs and homes. Growing up in a steel town had an impact.

Vision

Because of the way I was raised, it is therefore very difficult for me to understand the wasteful lifestyles that we are accustomed to today. My wife and I are not extravagant. We've never been in debt and have never believed in spending money we didn't have.

My father taught me things that are not practiced much today. Things like manners. For instance, men used to remove their hats when they walked into a room, not just a room with women. In elevators also, men took their hats off.

When you're under cover, you don't need a hat. But today it's widely accepted to keep a hat on.

I think that people have been eccentric from the beginning of time in certain ways and in certain habits, but it's extremely difficult for me today to accept the things that we do that are not thoughtful of others. My father taught me to treat other people how I would like to be treated if I were sitting on the chair where you are. That is something I have really tried to do very hard, whether it be playing golf, flying or reading a book. Whatever I might be doing, I like to give the other person the benefit of the doubt and give him a chance to tell his story, too.

I don't think parents today spend as much time as they should teaching children what they should be teaching them: how to hold a knife and fork, how to eat, how not to talk with a full mouth. Good manners are things that should be *accepted*, but I'm also of the understanding, having been around a long time, that many parents weren't taught how to do these things, so it's pretty difficult for them to teach their children.

Spirituality

I don't know that there have been any miracles in my life. I would like to think that I would be able to live my life without miracles. That doesn't mean that I'm not very grateful for what my life has been. Maybe it's a miracle that I've been able to play golf as well as I have, and however that came about I'm most grateful for, but I don't think of life in terms of miracles. There's only one person who's ever created miracles and I don't think he's created a lot lately. I think he works all the time in different ways, but if he were creating miracles, I think we would know about it. We know about the ones he created in history.

My mother insisted that I go to church as a boy. We went pretty regularly, and when things got tough, I talked to God a lot. I suppose in some respect, I felt like God would look after me in a general sense. And that was the end of the deal. He gave me the skill, and then I'm on my own.

I'm not an overly religious person. I go to church with my wife occasionally, and I enjoy church. I ask for forgiveness and I thank God for what he does and what he has provided for me. Maybe he doesn't even know about the specifics of my life, but my life is good and I appreciate it. I'm not a person, however, who believes that when I go to hit a golf ball, I need to ask God to help me hit it. He put me here, and he gave me the opportunity to do it, and I take that opportunity. And that's all. Just the fact that he has allowed and given me the opportunity and the ability to take care of myself is all I want. If he chooses to see that I win, that's fine, but I don't ask him to help me win. I don't think God can help everybody who wants to go win golf tournaments.

Lifework

Jack Nicklaus and I have had a competitive rivalry for over forty years. I kept my eye on him after we met in 1956, and I knew that, with his talent, it was only a matter of time before his game would be a threat to mine. Our rivalry helped my game, and I think it helped the game of golf. I think it's been an asset to everyone involved: a spur that helped people appreciate the game more. I think that if Tiger Woods, for example, had someone who was a challenge to him, it would also help.

Photo courtesy of Arnold Palmer Enterprises, 1998

Arnold and Jack Nicklaus, early 1970s.

I've played golf with Tiger. He came to me for some personal advice before he turned pro, and I enjoy him as a young man. He's an intelligent young man, and he's got his focus in the right direction. Now all he needs to do is just carry it through. He needs to get on with living a twenty-three-year-old's life and enjoy it, and be careful not to get drawn up in the bright lights. We talked about it, and I think he understands that. It would be easy for him to lose his perspective and to lose his objectives. When you get the kind of acknowledgment he's getting, there is a great temptation to focus on that and lose your focus on the talent that got you to that place. I didn't really lose my focus, and I didn't wrestle with it much because I enjoyed the game so much. I still enjoy it, and one of my major thoughts during each day is still to play golf. I enjoy going out and playing, and I will continue to and hope that I can for as long as I live.

Sure it's frustrating that I can't hit scores as low as I used to! And I never stop trying. The other day I shot a sixty-seven. If I could do that every day and could continue to do that for another ten or twenty years, I would be fulfilled. I would be very happy.

Obstacles

You don't realize sometimes how close your friends really are until they die. One of my closest friends, who I met on the course, lived next door to Winnie and me in Latrobe. He and his wife raised their family there. He passed away recently. Same age as I am. I used to just pick up the phone; if he knew something that I didn't know, I just called him.

I've lost a lot of good friends. I lost a college roommate in an auto-mobile accident. His name was Buddy Worsham. His brother was the National Open champion in 1946, and because I graduated from high school in 1947, he had a big effect on me. Worsham's death affected my life in that it made me not appreciate school so much. We had been having a good time in college, playing golf together, and all of a sudden he wasn't there. I finished the semester that we were in at the time and left before my senior year was over and went into the service. His death was my excuse for leaving, but whether that was the whole story, in reality, I'm not sure.

I've had a lot of challenges in my career. There seems to be a sup-position in people's minds that I enjoyed being the underdog. The only reason that anyone ever wanted to be the underdog would be because they didn't want to be the top dog and be brought down. But, if I'm leading a golf tournament, I want to be leading when I'm finished. It's happened to me both ways: I have been in the lead and haven't won, and I suppose I've been more successful coming from behind. I've come from behind a lot, and certainly I've enjoyed that, but I didn't do that on purpose. I didn't get myself in arrears to put on a show. I got there because I didn't play well enough, or whatever, and I had the good fortune to play well when I needed to toward the end of a tour-nament. That was probably because I was scared I wasn't going to win.

One way I found to get out of any tight spot was to visualize my shots before they happened. I always try to do that. No one taught me how to do it; it was just one of the things I did on the practice tee as a boy, over and over. It came as second nature. I used to go play golf by myself and my imagination went crazy. I would imagine that I was in the National Open and I was playing against Ben Hogan or Sam Snead or Byron Nelson, and I needed a ten-foot putt to win. And I did it. I did it in my mind. And, sometimes I missed, but I always had that, or some objective, in my mind. I still imagine where I want my shots to go. When practicing, a lot of people just hit balls without any objective in their mind. As a result, they don't achieve their goals simply because they didn't have a clear goal. There are a lot of people I've known in the past, and particularly young players now, who put those objectives in their mind and then they practice and work toward those goals. I was fortunate that it was not something I had to work at.

Fame

I'm not sure what I would tell you about fame, or even what I know about fame. I know that people recognize me, and people thank me for a lot of things, whether it's telling them to have their PSA checked, or for providing some entertainment for them by watching me play golf. Some say that they're playing golf because I play golf, and because they love the game and it enriches their life, that pleases me. I consider all of that a privilege rather than an encumbrance. It's a privilege that I am fortunate enough to have been a part of good things for other people.

Being famous does have its uncomfortable aspects. There are times when I am embarrassed by some of the compliments. Some of the things that people say to me that are very flattering. For years, when people talked to me about endorsing a product or doing something in that vein, I would think of that and I couldn't even say Palmer. I couldn't say, "Palmer Golf Clubs." I was embarrassed. I was so in awe of people who had been-there-done-that that I just never thought about myself in terms of being somebody who others would be in awe of. Even now, after a lot of years, I suppose I look at it from a whole different perspective: It's not me, it's my name. Palmer is not really me; it's another thing or entity over there. [Arnold picks up the head of a golf club with his name engraved in the metal to emphasize his point.] The name is an entity that doesn't feel as personal as it did years ago. Even when I was at the height of my success, though, I didn't identify with the name because I was trying to establish myself and get to where I wanted to be.

The fans who cheer for me, on the other hand, do not embarrass me. It didn't even bother me at the height of the craze because I was trying to win and they were cheering for me to do that. That's like someone cheering for you to hit a home run when you're playing baseball. That's the way I accepted it. And it made me want to win all the more, no question about that. The "Army" [Arnie's army of fans, called the largest nonuniformed military organization in the world] formed relatively quickly when you think about it. It really happened during a series of Masters at Augusta that went from 1956 to 1958. The army from Fort Gordon, which is in Augusta, were the marshals who manned the scoreboards for the tournament. These young soldiers used to print signs when I went by that said, "Go Arnie, your army is in back of you." So they really started out as an army. In 1958, when I won the Masters, the newspapers picked it up and said, "Arnie's Army takes him on to victory."

Photo by Frank Christian, Historic Golf Prints, the Ron Watts Collection

Arnold's Masters victory at Augusta, 1964.

I would like to think that I've been able to help people through my fame. Just recently with the prostate situation I saw that. I mean, who would have given a damn if they didn't know who Arnold Palmer was if I said, "Go get your prostate checked." They would have said, "What do we care?" But the fact that fame got me to the point where they recognized who I was, did cause some men to go for the test. I've received thousands of letters from people thanking me for telling them to have their PSA checked. They thank me for saving them from the potential of dying of cancer. That has been the greatest personal benefit from going through this: being able to help people understand that it isn't necessarily doomsday when you have cancer. I've now had my own experience with cancer, as well as my daughter's experience to draw from. When I went to the Mayo Clinic to be operated on, my daughter went there with me. She insisted on going, which was pretty neat. I was with her, too, when she went through it. There wasn't much I could do except lend her moral support, but it was important to me to be there.

I've never wrestled with guilt over my success. That isn't something that I put in a category of things that I would concern myself with. I think that most people feel that they are successful. I try to encourage everyone to be tremendously successful, whether that person is my secretary or my manager or anyone else. It's to my best interest to have the people around me be successful. If they are, then they are doing a good job, and we're all successful for that reason.

Family

When I was a young man, I did all of the things that young men do. As I've said, my father was a great influence on me. I met my wife on a Tuesday and asked her to marry me on Saturday of the same week. We had great plans. I was going to be a Walker Cup player as an amateur in golf, and we were going to honeymoon in Europe. All great things. But I didn't have any money. I was working as a manufacturing rep in Cleveland, Ohio, and earning five hundred dollars a month and I was having trouble making that work. Like a lot of people, I was apprehensive about getting married because I didn't have much. I didn't have any real means for getting married and taking my wife to Europe as an amateur golfer. I may not be a genius, but I'm smart enough to know that you can keep borrowing only so long, and then you have to start paying it back. I realized that our plan wasn't going to work.

I was working up to telling my fiancée that we weren't going to have a big fancy wedding, and we weren't going to go to Europe on the Walker Cup Team. If we went, it was going to be sparingly and it was going to be tough. It was September when I realized all of this, and I told my father and my fiancée, Winifred, that I really thought that I should turn pro so that I could earn enough money to support the situation. They agreed, and I turned pro. Soon after, I signed a contract with Wilson Sporting Goods [that paid approximately five thousand dollars a year] in November and I went to play in a golf tournament in Miami, Florida, about the second week in December. I played horribly and missed the cut. I ran into a model who I knew from Chicago, and I told my father to head back to the hotel, and I took the model out. I didn't get back to the hotel until about four o'clock in the morning, and my father was waiting up for me.

He said, "Where the hell have you been?"

I replied, "Oh, I was upset about my golf and just went out and had a good time."

"Well, you're engaged!" he said. "Are you in love?"

I answered, "Yes."

"Then why don't you get your ass up there and get that girl and get married and get on with your golf?"

I asked him if he was serious, and when he said yes I said, "Okay pap, then how are you getting home? I'm going to take the car, marry Winifred, and get on with my life." So, that's exactly what I did. Dad got on an airplane and flew to Pittsburgh, and I got in my car and drove to Bethlehem and picked up Winnie, and we discussed the situation. We decided to elope, sneaking out the window so her parents couldn't stop us. (Her mother didn't mind, but her father was adamantly against it.) We went to my sister's house in Arlington, Virginia, and called her parents and told them we were going to get married and invited them to come to the wedding if they wanted to. My parents came, hers didn't.

It took a while, but her parents and I became friends. Winnie and

I lived in a tow-trailer behind our 1952 Ford for the first year on the tour, which my wife didn't like too much. She said she'd rather stay home while I toured, than live like that any longer. Fortunately, I made enough in prize money the next year that we didn't have to anymore.

Photo courtesy of Arnold Palmer Enterprises, 1998

Arnold, Winnie, their daughters and grandchildren.

Habits

Of course I have bad habits, but I'm certainly not going to share them here! Actually, two of my habits were quite public. Probably the worst habit I had in the past was smoking, but I quit twenty-seven years ago. And I smoked a lot! It was fairly easy to stop. I just decided to. And I was glad that I was able to because I knew it was possible that when I smoked on the golf course, I was influencing kids to smoke. That made it easier to quit: knowing that people watched what I was doing.

Another habit that has diminished with time is hitching up my pants. I guess that started when I was a boy because my mother was always telling me not to let my pants fall down. I used to have a thirty- to thirty-two-inch waist, and because my pants would slide down, I got in the habit of pulling them back up. I still hitch, but not as pronouncedly because my waist is so much bigger. They don't fall down anymore.

I still drink and I don't have any desire to quit that. I hope that I can control it, and I try to. But that's good enough for me.

Earth

If you read the future-oriented, exotic comic strips, you can learn a lot about what is coming in our future. Fifty years ago, during the Depression, if you looked at the comic strips you saw airplanes flying without propellers. You saw machines that flew through the air. This is a fact. This is what *Flash Gordon* and others carried. Everybody marveled at them and said, "It's just a comic strip, that's fiction. That'll never happen." But those planes and machines are exactly what we see in reality today. Even though it was a fictional comic strip from the past, we're living today the very things they foretold. And beyond, really. If you look at *Star Wars* now, you see fantastic machines and people living in space, and I believe that we'll be there before we know it. About fifty years from now, or less. Probably twenty-five years from now, we will be doing just what you see in fiction now. All of those spaceships you see in the movies will be an absolute cinch.

What the old comic strips (and every other futuristic movie) failed to do, and it's probably good they didn't, is tell you what will happen to the general population. They show you a lot, but they never show you the masses. They don't show the type of vehicles the average Joe is going to be using fifty years from now. They don't bring it into that perspective. Of course, anyone can take the future into their mind and formulate what they think will be in twenty-five to forty years. Whether it will be the Columbia spaceship they shoot off at Cape Kennedy or whether it will be an automobile in the desert going the speed of sound, those things will become commonplace. Airplanes will just take off from little runways or from standing positions and fly off into outer space.

I've seen a lot change in my lifetime. I don't know how much more I'll be allowed to see. I'm ready to die, but I don't want to because I've got a lot to do. If the plug was pulled and I couldn't do anything about it anyway, I'd accept it. I'd like to go peacefully, and I'd like to have played golf that day. My father played twenty-seven holes the day he passed away. I certainly don't want to be sick and unhealthy. I have said this many times and I will say it again: I want to live until I die. That's it.

Some people say that for the best athletes, God can actually shift balls in midair or change their course. I don't believe in that. I believe that you make it happen. There is no Great Spirit that moves balls. For instance, John Brodie was a great quarterback. He was great because he had a lot of talent, he had a lot of imagination and he made it work. His father visualized with him, which is very important. But did the ball suddenly shift because God told it to? No, not in my mind. God gives us the opportunity. We win or lose the game.

15

Robert A. Johnson

Photo by Russ Hopkins

Introduction

R obert A. Johnson has written some of the most respected works in
contemporary psychology, covering, among other topics, myth,
shadow work and gender studies. Whole shelves at bookstores are
devoted to his best-selling books, including He; She; We; Inner Work;
and Femininity Lost and Regained, and hours of college classes are
spent in analysis of his theories. I was first introduced to Robert's books
in my psychology classes at the University of Southern California,
where his writings were nearly as legendary, and certainly as
respected, as those of Freud or Erickson. I found it intriguing that the
ancient Old English and German meaning of his first name is "of shining fame," and his middle name, Alex, is from the Greek for "helper
and defender of mankind," making his universal appeal seem somewhat inevitable.

Robert's ability to inspire and educate on a grand scale was, in fact,
foretold in the 1940s by the famous East Indian spiritual teacher
Krishnamurti. After spending a year with Krishnamurti in Ojai,
California, the aging guru explained to Robert that he would grow to
be a world teacher and would be the one to carry on his life's work.
Robert, however, did not feel that calling and left the United States for
Europe. In 1949, the young Mr. Johnson was drawn to Switzerland to
study with Carl Jung, taking him into a life of celebrated work and
authorship as a Jungian analyst, not unlike what Krishnamurti had
foreseen years prior.

I had spoken to Robert on the phone only once before our interview.
By good fortune, a mutual friend had put us in contact, and our
meeting took place at Robert's beachside home in Southern California.
I didn't have much knowledge of his personal life before I arrived. Even
though Robert is a renowned author and lecturer, is published in
many languages, and has an extensive following, few people knew
anything of his personal life before he wrote his recent autobiography.
As a rule, he steers clear of the press. Robert is an intensely private and
humble man, living a near-monastic lifestyle. I knew that he almost
never gives interviews, and I was elated that in this case he was moved
to because, like his dear friend, the late Joseph Campbell, Robert feels

that our society is in great need of healthy role models and thoughtful discussion.

From the moment I entered Robert's house, I was overcome with the sense that I was in a sacred space, similar to the energy I've felt in ashrams, temples and churches. His environment was spotless and beautiful and, as I expected, he had few possessions. What he did have was of the highest quality: religious and cultural artifacts, simple furniture, books and an early seventeenth-century harpsichord that he had personally restored. Robert had prepared a pot of tea for our talk, and as we sat together, his demeanor never shifted from an even peacefulness, even when he laughed and made fun of himself or life in general.

I found Robert to be everything I envisioned he would be. Friends say that he truly lives what he teaches, and even suggest that he lives life completely present in each moment. Some call him a master, a title I'm sure that Robert would be very uncomfortable with, but one that I would hesitate to discount. I was surprised by the candor with which he spoke about his life and the deep insight he revealed about the person behind the great intellectual knowledge. Instead of masking his vulnerability, Robert explained how he carries an immense depth of emotion—something I wouldn't have guessed could live in the midst of such strong mental capabilities. As an action-oriented person, I found Robert's intense feeling-oriented view of life both foreign and intriguing. While a good portion of the people I've interviewed have had traumatic childhoods, Robert's early years could be seen as the most horrendous, undoubtedly shaping his rich sensitivity. But as Robert described how he once thought that the world would never be anything but a cold and lonely place, his story became brighter. Robert lived for years without relief from his personal agony until a magical event gave him the physical understanding that life was precious and held meaning. And the impact stays with him to this day. Through Robert's tales of suffering, I believe he gives hope to others still struggling.

One of the things that Robert feels impassioned about is how, through our modern-day, fast-paced lives, we have lost our ability to use ceremony and ritual to heal us. Robert calls our loss of contact with these old ways "psychological poverty." Our tribal ancestors honored the differing stages of life and, as the theory goes, suffered far less for doing so. Robert highly recommends the use of ritual to reduce stress, whether it be in the form of lighting a candle or incense, praying or burning old letters in a fire. These actions set us in a spiritual space, separating the sacred from the mundane, and allow us to feel the holiness of our existence in the divine connection. Another ancient practice that Robert uses to enhance, and even understand, life is the study of mythology. When I asked Robert to explain myth for those who are not familiar, he said, "That is difficult, but I would try by saying that mythology is really the condensed dreams of a society. A layout of the road map of the human psyche. Myths can be likened to the genetic structure, which informs our physical structure: Genes are physical and myth is the psychological parallel."

Again, like Joseph Campbell, Robert has the mysterious ability to understand the collective dreams and processes of society and, by using the past, brings them into profound clarity for modern man. Before the book Men Are from Mars, Women Are from Venus *reached widespread appeal with its common-sense approach to relationships, there were* He *and* She. *Having read them in my twenties, and then again following our interview, I found both books even more relevant and insightful today, over a decade later. Robert has been endowed with a great gift of understanding human nature and being able to convey timeless truths in words so beautiful and alive that they have a poetic resonance.*

When our interview was complete, Robert wanted to meet my husband and my son, so we walked out into the cool, starlit night together, where my family waited in the car. We promised to correspond during his trip to India, finishing follow-up questions by letter, and said our good-byes. As he turned for home and was just out of earshot, a sudden burst of tears erupted from my eyes, and I lowered my head into my hands and bawled for several minutes. Mark and Tosh were shocked, but they let me release without interruption until I had gained my composure. I cannot explain why I had the reaction that I did. I had never cried following an interview before that evening, and I haven't since. All I know is that I was overwhelmed with a sense of profound gratitude for our meeting. Feeling is, appropriately enough, the best mode in which to describe an experience with Robert, as that is the world in which he resides. I felt as if I had been in the presence of a superior being in some sense, even though I couldn't put my finger on why or how. One thing was clear: The helper and defender of mankind had moved me beyond everyday experience. Some things are indescribable and probably meant not to be defined, so I will start Robert's interview at this unfinished place: a place of unknowns, where anything—including magic—is possible, even likely.

*   *   *   *

Happiness

Happiness is doing the will of God, which can manifest in every area of life, including in our work. The best commentary I've found on happiness comes from Buddhism, which teaches that there is an appropriate thing to do, and only *one* appropriate thing to do, in any instant of time. There is never a choice. If you think there is a choice, according to Buddhism, you are in error because there is only one appropriate thing to do: that is, to do the will of God, which equals happiness.

Simply to be happy is the highest form of worship. I grew up in a Fundamentalist household, where I was forbidden to be happy. But I am living the will of God in my life, increasingly so. These are the happiest days of my life indeed, without any question. Which I didn't expect. I will be seventy-seven on my next birthday, and no one warned me that old age would be the happiest time. I feel good physically, but happiness is on all levels. I feel that I paid out the dark side of life first. This is not particularly happy language, but happiness came later in life for me. Most people do it in the reverse: They live off all of the brightness of life in their youth, and then sit around talking about what's escaped from them.

It is very interesting to observe the origin of the word *happy*, which is derived from the verb "to happen." Any Hindu will tell you that he's happy with whatever happens in his life, even if it's painful to him, because they are one and the same thing. But for most people, happiness is a fleeting matter. Rarely staying happy with any circumstance, people try to repeat their feelings later and wonder where they have gone.

Early Years

I came from a highly dysfunctional family, with a lot of anxiety and much loneliness. This is going to sound a bit dramatic, but it's all true: I'm an only child, with four parents and a childhood spent in the hospital. My grandmother was one of the four parents—the best of them. I don't remember ever thinking about having a sibling because it wasn't an option.

Robert as a boy.

I didn't have much of a fantasy life early on, nor did I show much promise as a child. What value I have now came out of the necessity of my life. Life was always harsh, but it got worse when I was in a dreadful accident when I was eleven. I was on roller skates on a sidewalk in Portland, Oregon, and was partway through a door leading to the local drugstore when two cars collided in the middle of the street and one of them jumped the curb and mashed me up against a brick wall. One leg was in the safety of the doorway and one was not, so only one leg was damaged. The blood vessels were torn, and thankfully, someone knew how to apply a tourniquet and saved my life on the spot.

In the middle of the night, lying in the hospital, the blood vessels that had been sutured back together broke loose inside the cast. I was bleeding to death and it didn't show. Vividly conscious, I knew I was dying and put all of my will against that. Suddenly I was dragged over a hump and down a tunnel into a place of absolute total beauty and happiness.

I went into the light that was everywhere, with indescribable celestial music playing. The feeling was one of absolute ecstatic glory that has dominated my life ever since. I've held everything else up to that experience, and because nothing can compare, it has been the main challenge of my life. It was an intense death and recovery experience, probably the biggest event of my life.

An alert nurse discovered the blood seeping through my cast and whisked me off to surgery. I was given blood transfusions immediately and was aware of being pulled back into my body. I didn't want to return and fought the pull back into the world as hard as I had fought against the dying process. I woke up in the surgery room with bright lights and men with face masks on, hurting like hell, constituting the major dichotomy of my life: I've seen what the next life is, and it's better than this one. It has thus been hard to convince me to do standard things here on the face of the earth, like going to school and working hard. I've seen better. But as I've gotten older, that glorious quality has slowly become less a matter of someplace else in some other time, suffusing more with my life now, here. The dichotomy is diminishing a lot, as a result of the hard inner work. All of the "fishing," as I call it.

My leg was subsequently amputated just below the knee. I was totally out of commission for one year following the accident, living mainly in the hospital. I went through crutches and prosthetics and hopping about. Then back to school again. I had been a poor student up until the accident. My parents got me a tutor at home during that difficult year, and partly because that tutor taught me how to study and partly because of the suffering of the hospital, surgeries, etc., I became a good student. I have found that suffering and consciousness are close to each other.

My mother was a very good person. She was an extroverted, sensation type in any language, and was so good with that. She was at her best when she had a mechanical or physical situation to deal with, and she got the best doctors and she encouraged me. Unfortunately, my mother didn't understand very much of anything else and got in my way very badly in the introverted or mystical side of my life. She tried to train me out of my sensitivity, forbidding it, because she didn't understand it and thought it was bad. I was a mystical child. After that kind of accident, who wouldn't be?

As I mentioned earlier, I had a good grandmother. I was raised chiefly by her; she was stern, but a kind and loving person, and I knew that she loved me even when I was in trouble. She was the most influential adult role model I had. My father was pretty much a washout. He was around, but he wasn't effective. He took refuge in an illness and really just waited his life out. He also was a good person, within the limits of his hypochondriacal nature.

By the time I was sixteen, both of my parents had lost me and didn't understand me. They did most of the wrong things with me, not maliciously, but in trying to train me into what they thought I ought to be. I lived with such a sense of inferiority (largely from my mismatch of typology with the family and society I was born into) and had great trouble imagining anything but total failure for myself. Any success I have is still a cause for astonishment for me.

At sixteen, I got my first job. It was a night job and was a grueling, terrible experience. I wasn't strong at the time but thought that if I didn't prove my manhood, I would die. One particular evening, I sank into depression and felt that the harshness of life would surely kill me if I didn't see something beautiful. I drove up into the hills to watch the sunrise, and hobbled out of my car. What I experienced saved my life. Suddenly life became magical. There are really no words to describe it, but I heard the sunrise, felt it, tasted it and smelled it. I felt as if I was experiencing heaven, and the celestial music was all around me and through me. Every faculty was flooded with a glorious meaningfulness. I was transfixed for over a half-hour. Unfortunately, the feeling didn't stay with me, but I never forgot it. In fact, it was almost my undoing because again, like the near-death experience when I was eleven, nothing held much meaning for me after that. The rest of my life has been devoted to recovering or restoring that sense of value and meaning.

These things do not leave you alone. Mostly they torture one early in one's life. If such a revelation comes too soon, and it is happening earlier and earlier in contemporary people's lives, it is an instant torture. If one's life is enjoyable, it seems to be handleable because a person knows that one day they will probably get there again and waiting is not so unbearable. For me, my life was so unpleasant that the result was a heavy loneliness. The early part of my life was unendurably lonely. I purposely picked lonely jobs, like being a forest-fire lookout in the mountains, because I was less lonely when I was alone. I liked being with my friends, but few could comprehend what I was talking about or needing. I didn't comprehend it either.

When I started learning about mythology, I found a story that explained what had happened to me. The myth of Parsifal, the Fisher King, and the search for the Holy Grail is one of the most precious legacies of Western culture, and after reading it, my life made more sense. Unfortunately, I had not yet heard the myth when I had my first Grail castle experience with the sunrise, and therefore had no idea what was happening to me. [The myth of Parsifal and the Holy Grail is long and detailed and can be understood fully in Robert's book, *He*. Parsifal is an innocent, who goes about the adventures and mishaps of life without a clue of any deeper meaning. He stumbles into the Grail castle—symbolized in this interview by Robert's sunrise experience—but loses it and is not able to get back to the castle until he has suffered many years. Eventually Parsifal gains enough wisdom to ask the right questions—"fishing"—and that leads him back into the castle, where he finds the golden chalice.] I went countless times to see the sunrise, but I was not able to hear the morning stars singing in unison as they had before. Life had no more meaning for ten years. It was actually a dangerous time for me. I wouldn't do anything. Why should I? I was almost immobilized with a crippling, excruciating loneliness that I could stand only when I was alone. So I backed off and spent a lot of time by myself. I functioned: I went to school and got straight As. My intelligence wasn't damaged, but any reason for doing those things was gone. There were no carrots in front of this donkey.

Many years later, Buddhism taught me some language for this: A person's first experience of the splendor of God is total suffering. If you survive (and many people crash under it), you slowly discover that what you had seen and suffered so severely under was the splendor of God. There is a wonderful quote from Einstein that I read midway through my life. I knew it was true, although it did nothing to make me feel better. More like rubbing salt in the wounds. Einstein said, "The solitude that was so painful in my youth has become the delight in my old age." That is what has happened to me. I simply had to stay with the loneliness until it transformed. The splendor of God was there all of the time, I just had to learn how to endure it.

The word *suffer* originally meant *to allow*. It is the suffering of life that makes for transformation. You gradually learn how to allow the splendor of God to be what it is. India has taught me much about this.

India, with its endless suffering, is also a place of profound peace. I have had the pleasure of knowing many peaceful people in India. Happy in spite of their dire poverty. A man named Selveraj, in particular. His wife died three years ago, and he and his ten-year-old son, Rama, make up one of the thin little families that live on the street in front of my guest house. When I wake up there, I find Selveraj and Rama wrapped up in their single blanket making a ragged bundle lying on the sidewalk. All of their possessions are within arm's reach and covered by a plastic tarp no larger than their own dimensions. Birth, death, cooking, eating and worship all go on in that small space jealously guarded from the hundred other people who would like to have that advantageous spot. Selveraj drives a rickshaw (owned by an entrepreneur) and takes me to the village I've been visiting for twenty years. He has a sense of goodness and gratitude about him that you rarely see in America.

I started playing the harpsichord immediately after my sunrise experience because so much of it appeared to me as music, and I was able to get closer to the vision of heaven I had experienced by way of music than I could in any other language, so I devoted myself to it. I was lucky with the teacher I found because she became my god-mother, which I needed very much. I had the good fortune and sense to adopt a godfather as well (they didn't know each other, except through me), and because I attached myself to these two role models, they finished raising me. I chose well.

My music teacher died when I was twenty-two years old, and I wasn't ready to let her go. That was the worst loss of my life. Funerals since then haven't been nearly as painful as that one. Like I said earlier, I tackled the tough stuff early. Actually, they tackled me. I had no choice. My godfather lived a long time. I was in my fifties when he died, and I was able to let him loose by that time.

I just published my autobiography with Harper & Row entitled *Balancing Heaven and Earth*. I wanted to call it *A Slender Thread* (although that title had a copyright) because all of the important things in my life have been slender threads, and were they slender! Like with my two godparents: I would not have survived if it had not been for those two people, and they fell into my life, so to speak, in the most fortuitous way. I have had a couple dozen events in my life that just happened to me. I just happened to meet somebody, get some money, to be invited somewhere, or just happened to have one leg in a doorway, and not the other. All of the important things of my life have happened that way.

Influences

I went to Ojai, California, in my early-twenties and lived with the spiritual teacher Krishnamurti for a year. I knew Beatrice Wood [chapter 5] there. She was nearly an old lady back in 1946! At least that was my perception at such a young age. Krishnamurti was a beautiful man. I loved him, but he was a poor teacher in general, specifically for me. He was a highly intelligent man, my present age when I was his neophyte student. To give him the best of the bargain, he would tell me what was true for him then, but it was not what I needed. I remembered what he said, and it is true for me now. But a good teacher sizes up his students and speaks their condition to the students. Krishnamurti didn't know how to do that. He was such an indescribable character. I'd ask him something, and he'd get a pained look on his aristocratic face and say, "No, no, no, no! You don't understand at all." And that was mostly what I got out of him. "Can't you understand? All you have to do is be aware. Is that too much?" He was just exasperated that I couldn't understand his seventy-five-year-old wisdom, which a twenty-two-year-old can't do, of course.

Krishnamurti told me that I was to be his successor. I wanted to be, but finally gathered up the courage to leave because I felt like I was going down a whirlpool: His was not the teaching I needed. I never quarreled with him. I loved the man and always intended to go back and tell him how much I loved him and what a wretched teacher he was. I was sorry when I heard that he had died, because I hadn't been back yet.

Soon after I left Ojai, I went to a Jungian analyst in Los Angeles who talked the language that was immediately applicable to me. It was pertinent and to the point, which isn't always pleasant, but necessary all the same. I don't know when I stopped being a patient and started being a student. So many Jungians came into their profession that way.

Meeting Carl Jung was another one of those slender threads. He gave me the information I needed, and I remembered it. I didn't go to Europe to see him; that is what I say now to make it sound reasonable. I went to Europe because I needed to go there. (Twenty or thirty years later, I went to India for the same reason.) I studied with Carl Jung at the C. G. Jung Institute in Zurich for a year—from 1948 to

1949—when I was twenty-five. He initially gave me about three hours of advice: what to do and what not to do. I trusted him completely, although I didn't accept all of what he said because some of it was so painful. For example, he told me to live alone for the rest of my life, point blank, over and over. It wasn't something he made up; rather it was a result of working with me on my dreams, which were all pointing in that direction. He didn't literally pound on the table to make sure I understood, but almost. My response was, "But I'm dying in aloneness." I tried to wriggle out of almost everything he said, but it simply was truth, so I adopted a conscious acceptance of his words. If I could have wriggled out of my fate, I would have. I tried so many times to escape the loneliness of my life, but there was no way out.

Robert as a young man in Zurich.

This brings up the whole idea of free will. Catholicism is very interesting in that respect: The church says that mankind has only one free will, whether to do or not do the will of God. And he has that free will. There have been some wise people in the church, but they talk in an old-fashioned language, which isn't very effective now.

Another blessed influence on my life, which originated from my time with Jung, was my friendship with Joseph Campbell. We were students together at the institute in Zurich. At that time he was an ardent Roman Catholic, though he was at odds with most of the institute's students who were inclined to think there was something wrong with you if you still put any credence in the church. Joseph would come to class early in the morning and in his deep, sonorous voice say, "My, but Mass was fine this morning!" This was my first sight of him.

I just did a documentary on Jung and the religious life that was originally scheduled to do with Bill Moyers, but he got sick and couldn't do it. So the documentary film is of Mary Woodman—probably the most famous Jungian woman alive—and me. We filmed it for PBS. Bill did such fine work and gained fame as the interviewer of Joseph Campbell, and I feel that in some ways I follow in Joseph's footsteps.

Spirituality

When I was a child, my grandmother was the religious head of our family. She was a Baptist and taught me the Fundamentalist view of God: white hair, white robes, thundering threats and retribution on mankind. Now, when people ask me what my concept of God is, I feel like a rabbit that has just been pinned down. But I have a good way out that comes from the medieval world: God is a circle whose center is everywhere and whose perimeter is nowhere. That blows up any definition. When I go to India, they speak of many gods. I see God as One, everywhere in everything. The Hindus are good at this: They say that man has two eyes, so he is likely to see things in duality, but really it is just One.

I've seen sacred tribal rituals that seem so hard to understand. One time in India I was allowed to witness a religious ritual where a cube of solidified camphor was put on a man's tongue and lighted as a sign of good faith for the uncomprehending foreigners. I was horrified to see my friend with a lighted cube of camphor drawn into his mouth, making for a wonderful-terrible moment when the light was shining through his white teeth just before the flame disappeared into his mouth. When my friend awoke from his trance, he had no recollection of what had gone on. I wondered why the display of fishhooks in his flesh, camphor burning on his tongue and the loss of ordinary consciousness. Why? What purpose could this possibly serve? To a Westerner, it seemed a fantastic but useless display of occult power at best, or a silly performance at worst. But soon I understood that the triumph of the spirit over flesh is exactly what primitive people need to counterbalance their earth-centered life. If wholeness is the great goal of human consciousness, then it would easily follow that earthbound people would need as dramatic a triumph of the spirit as they could find. I have been meditating ever since that probably we Westerners—more detached from the earthiness of life than any people in history—need earthing as desperately as those people need spiritualizing.

I am essentially a religious person: I've trained and worked as a psychologist, but I think I was taking refuge in the psychological world

Photo by Russ Hopkins

Robert's young friend in India before religious ceremony, 1996.

because the current religious world is in such chaos and turmoil. I wouldn't say, however, that I've always felt watched over, or protected by God, because sometimes what I've gone through has been very harsh. Like the accident. I got what I needed, but not what I wanted. The accident was my first touch of divinity: that's what it took. I didn't feel that I was being punished by God, nor did I have any kind of anger at God. Rather, I saw that God had revealed himself to me. If divinity had been trying to get my attention before that, in order to warn me, there was no way I could have noticed. Life was too harsh for me to notice subtleties. There is no place for sentimentality in this subject. People say that God is good and tempers the storms for the shorn lamb, and things like that. Well, he doesn't always. God kills sometimes.

I don't speak of past lives because that is not a language that works well for me. I hold that subject in abeyance: I don't know whether reincarnation is true or not. When I have such a past-life experience or memory, then I will believe. A family adopted me during my first trip to India and came up with an observation: "Of course, Robert has been in India many, many incarnations before. He committed some indiscretion last time and was banished to America for one incarnation. Now he's spending all of his time and money trying to get back home again." It's as good an explanation as I've found.

I love India. I go there each winter. India is where miracles happen for me. Of course, the most miraculous events of my life are deep within myself and inexpressible; but for something that can be discussed reasonably, the impact of India on this introverted-feeling type has been profound. To be among people who place feeling and relationship first on their list of priorities was a revelation to me. This would be my own list of values also, but I have grown up in a society and family where thinking and sensation were the most important. India has been like home to me in this respect. A true miracle!

I'm not a very courageous or adventurous person, but when I decided to travel to India for the first time, I packed up and went alone. I didn't know anyone there or have any idea where to go, and wonderful things happened. So, I've been going ever since. I have traveled a lot there, venturing off the beaten path, which is difficult and dangerous, and where one is most likely to get ill or run into the dark sides of the country. The first night in this foreign land, my second Grail castle experience happened. I arrived in New Delhi, beyond exhaustion. The trip had been a terribly long one. I had lost my luggage, and there were mobs of taxi drivers who, in the wee hours of the morning, fought for me, probably thinking that I was their last chance for a fare. When I got to my hotel, I looked out over the skyline of mosques, minarets and turrets, and as the sun rose, I had my Grail castle again, just as it had been over three decades before. I heard it, saw it and tasted it all over again. There is no translation to explain the glory of this ecstatic experience. It is not a rational thing. I find it fascinating that I had to be so utterly exhausted to experience it again, just as I was the first time. If you follow the myth of the Grail castle, you know that the second appearance stays with you. It is always within reach after that. I get work done and do my job, but the glory of that night is always near. The first time was a gift (given to most young men in some form), but the second had to be earned. Unfortunately, most men don't find it the second time and that emptiness shows in their faces and in the way men carry themselves. We have to fish for it, and by that I mean that we must work with our dreams, meditate, do our art or have meaning in our life. These are some of the ways to earn it.

India, with its many gods, has not cost me my Christianity. Rather, it has confirmed my Christianity: I grow more and more Catholic. I don't need to go to the Catholic Church and I'm not about to sign my name on the register and recite the creed, but by temperament and nature, I'm Catholic. I like the ritual of taking the wine and the Eucharist. It expresses better than any codified structure my feelings about reality. It speaks a language consistent with my temperament, more than the language of ideas.

Tools

It is a curious thing that I believe in ritual very strongly to help people gain strength and healing for themselves, and yet I don't like to partake in much ritual. To elaborate further, prescribed rituals don't seem to work well for most people anymore. However, a tailor-made ritual, for precisely the moment or situation, I love. I often teach people to bring their suffering, loneliness or their impossibilities into a ritual, to tailor-make right in the moment, for remarkable effects. I like ritual in that sense. I have a favorite ritual I do, but it is too private for me to share. For one of my other favorite rituals, I often light a brass lamp I have, which is adorned with Parvati, the Indian goddess, who holds a little pool of oil. I would advise people to go and devise their own. All ritual is a material expression of an interior fact. Light a candle, make an offering, plant a seed, feed somebody. These are outer expressions of what one experiences on the inside.

Believe it or not, watching football is a healthy form of ritual. Better still is to play it. Games release a great deal of suppressed energy. The Olympics, which are said to be seen by nearly half the world's people, are a great unifying force. This will have people puzzling for a long time: American people have chosen an out-of-round ball as a symbol of one of their favorite games [football]. Almost all other games in the world are played with round balls. This is the eccentric aspect of the American unconscious. Eccentric means out-of-round. I wouldn't say this is a bad thing, only an interesting thing.

Our national sport, baseball, is the only American game I have any knowledge of that goes counterclockwise. This speaks of the present century. Baseball was invented during the last century, but reached mass popularity within the last one hundred years. I think probably the most profound thing one can say, and we cannot go very far with this, is that God is now down and not up, counterclockwise and not clockwise anymore. God is feminine, no longer masculine. God is now dark, not light. God has changed within living memory. Churches talk about what was true historically, but not current with the nature of God now. It seems that they are stuck in the medieval language and struggling to find the modern language.

All of the great modern-day dreams of present-day people, almost exclusively, are down dreams. Our language and scriptures are all built on up: "I will lift up mine eyes unto the hills and ascend. . . ." Everyone knows that heaven is up, but the contemporary dreams are now down: "I was going down," or "I came down," or "I came out of a cave." God is now down. It takes a great reversal of attitudes to find the current face of God.

Fear

I have found that my fears do lessen with age. The remaining fears that are still with me are the fear of ill health and finding myself to be useless in a high-speed society. I never think that I've been through so much that nothing has the ability to hurt me again. I still get my feelings hurt very badly. I'm an introverted-feeling type, so feeling is my language. When I'm lecturing on this subject, I often startle people by saying, "Look, if you consent to have feelings, you consent to have your feelings hurt at least fifty times a day." That is largely why people set their feelings aside, because it is often painful. People hurt my feelings by snubbing me or getting sharp with me. I have ways of coping with that. Generally, people don't know if they've hurt me because I use high introversion—going within—to rise above those feelings. I also use courtesy.

I write about the importance of allowing ourselves to be irrational, spontaneous and crazy, but I don't believe in acting those things out. I don't have to get drunk and take LSD, but I'm fascinated with that world and those kinds of people. I have a high desire to go that way, but I also like the proportion and balance of my life. Anything that one adopts and identifies with instantly makes its opposite intensely attractive. You cannot live on the face of the earth without opinions or a lifestyle. I like my house to be clean and am not about to abandon that point of view, but it instantly constellates the opposite. I had a dream once about a beach bum, which is about as unlike my character as you can find. It was fascinating to me. Often the touch of one's opposite wakes us up, or jars us out of our one-sidedness. I'm neat and I'm clean and I'm courteous, so a beach bum fascinates me and scares me instantly. Carl Jung used to say, "Find out what a person fears most because that is where they'll develop next."

That is our shadow. We can have opinions, but it is best not to be rigid about them. I keep my world simple, but I don't fuss if things aren't the way I like them to be. India is incredibly dirty, but I'm all right when I'm there and stay clean if I can. The village I visit has no sense of hygiene and I cannot take food or drink from the village without severe danger of a dozen crippling illnesses. One day I found the exact description of the dilemma of a Westerner and an Indian in this respect: My Indian friend was worrying about the caste of the person who was pouring a drink for me while I was worrying about whether the water had been boiled or not. Contamination flies under many definitions!

Over the course of thirty-five years, I had two powerful dreams that involved the same symbols and characters. The first dream was so heavy that it literally took me three decades until I was able to find understanding through the second dream. Because I tend to spend a great deal of time alone, I am tempted to search for meaning and understanding in quiet places, like retreats or monasteries. The second dream had me enlightened on a crowded beach in Southern California, filled with all of the outward things I tend to disdain. But that's where the enlightenment came. Some things must be done in difficult circumstances, which was a joke on me, but again, the way it was supposed to be. Enlightenment is most likely to come in an unexpected place.

Family

I've never been married. I don't date in the usual sense of the word, but I have many close friends, so I am no longer isolated. The lonely part of my life is slowly completing. It is not a goal of mine to live a purely celibate lifestyle. I have not been married, that is true, but the desire to be has been there. For a long time, I was searching for the right person; I was hungry and lonely and feeling left out. I don't feel lonely or left out now because I have such good friends. I think I would be a good husband.

One of the great jokes of my life was that I went to India consciously to become spiritual. I presumed I would search out a teacher and devote myself to yoga, disciplining myself to be a good student. I planned to make my way to enlightenment there. India humanized me, however. It did not spiritualize me. India's gift to me was that I have been able to be closer to people. I go back for more and more and more.

People often ask me, "How do you know so much about femininity in your books—you haven't even had a wife?" My answer is that there are many forms of marriage. When a man searches inwardly, his search is for the feminine: the feminine principle or aspect of God. In monastic language, that is one of the forms of marriage. This is too intricate for the English language, really. I am constantly suffering with the paucity of interior terms that plagues our language. Sanskrit has ninety-six words for love. I need them.

Women are in better relationship with themselves and wiser in their feelings than men. A fifteen-year-old woman generally knows more about her feelings than a forty-five-year-old man. A while ago, it dawned on me what a man must look like through the eyes of a woman, and I was appalled. It is so ridiculous and fearful. Women have to be suspicious of any man who comes around the corner! In my last book, *Lying with the Heavenly Maiden* (the publisher put a jazzy cover on it, which embarrasses me), I speak about the various aspects of femininity that a man has to cope with, one way or another. Men are such characters. So often when a woman is being flirted with at a party, for instance, it is not so much sex the man wants so dearly, but rather Mom. If she looks in the male's eyes, a perceptive woman can see that he is in a five-year-old mode looking for his mother—or even deeper, the relationship with his inner femininity that he hasn't yet connected with. Men in this condition often look sad, and they are, because a female can never fulfill what he is really searching for.

Women are also much more in control of their moods. A woman tries different moods on to see which one she is going to wear. She will even change in midstream if that works for her. But men don't have that luxury. We have almost no control, whereas women are masters in the feeling department. Many problems arise when a woman assumes that a man has the same control. If there were one rule in marriage, my suggestion would be that the woman agree to withhold all judgment and criticism when her man is in a mood. Women don't like waiting until the man is ready to talk, but there is much wisdom in patience. If a man can remember that he's just having a mood attack, and nicely ask the woman to wait until he's through it, all would be much easier in male-female unions. We cannot live without mutual respect and nurturing service to each other.

Obstacles

Once one starts doing one's inner work, which is a necessary thing, horrendous things can happen. People ask, "Then why should I?" My answer to that is that worse things will happen if you don't. Bad things often happen when people do good work because when one turns around and looks at the accumulated shadow, it's a dangerous thing to do. The shadow is demanding to be looked at, but doesn't want to be at the same time. It's a little like arguing that you don't want to go to the hospital when you're sick because so many people die there. Yes, going to the hospital hurts, but if you're in need, it is still the sensible thing to do.

Doing our inner work allows us to gain insight into the conflicts and challenges that our lives represent. We can search the hidden depths of our own unconscious to find the strengths and resources that wait to be discovered there. The unconscious has developed a special language to use in dreams and imagination: It is the language of symbolism. That's why we have to spend time doing our inner work (interpreting our dreams and doing introspection), because these symbols are like a foreign language that takes time and commitment to understand. As Jung described, the inner life is the secret life we all lead. When we are in balance, the conscious mind and the unconscious live in relationship. There is a constant flow of energy and information between the two levels.

In our modern world, however, most forms of interaction with the unconscious that nourished our ancestors—dreams, visions, rituals and religious experiences—are dismissed by the modern mind as primitive or superstitious. We act as though the outer, material world is all-important, but the truth is that we must come face-to-face with the inner life or we will never be fulfilled. When we do not acknowledge this inner world, it eventually forces itself to the forefront in the form of neurosis, inner conflicts and psychological symptoms that demand our attention. We may find ourselves in the hospital, absolutely immobile. That may be the only way our subconscious can get us to take the time and energy to get the perspective we need to move forward. It is a rough way to do it, but sometimes it is the only way to get an active person to lie down.

Our society has become so off-balance. Even our clothes tell us that we are off track. By "dressing for success," our ties separate our heads from the rest of our bodies, thus symbolically cutting off sensation below our necks. It's no wonder that after the workday is through, we go wild, as all of that bottled-up energy looks for somewhere to go. Even so, when I am in formal situations, I always wear a tie. It is my announcement that I'm on-duty. I don't like them—they remind me of a noose around the neck—but when I'm on-duty, I'm not living my personal life, so it's okay. I taught at a graduate school one semester, and I arrived not knowing whether to wear my coat or not. I carried my coat inside and put it on the chair. You get judged very quickly by a group, especially graduate students. I started out and had been lecturing about twenty minutes when a big gruff voice from the back of the room said, "What you got the goddamn tie on for?" I looked to see a guy with big boots, his feet on top of the chair in front of him, so I saw more boots than face. I knew I was going to make it or break it with this group of people right there and I said, "This goddamn tie is to protect me from you." They all laughed, and I made it. That is what the tie is for: to make a delineation between me and a group of people, as far as personalities are concerned. It is not a personal matter. He understood that.

Habits

Do I have any habits I would like to conquer? Oh, yes. I had a wonderful time doing a lecture on any subject I wanted to at a Roman Catholic seminary. The devil got into me, and I'm not sure I've ever enjoyed myself more. I gave a lecture entitled, "Your Neurosis as a Low-Grade Religious Experience," and I had those kids absolutely in a riot. I said: "Your neurotic structure is your religious life not having found an adequate expression in your life. Not fitting into the old forms, it's making a form now. It's often clumsy and stupid, but a low-grade religious experience all the same." This big gawky kid jumped up and said, "You mean to tell me that things I do in bed at midnight, that I won't even take to my confessor, are a religious experience?" And I said, "You heard me." We had so much fun. The next day, the head of the seminary came and we had a profound discussion. He is now a Jungian analyst, married, with three kids. He heard something alive. That is where Carl Jung got me, so to speak, or where I became *his* man, when he said, "Your psychological problems and neurotic structure are your religious life in an inappropriate form." That is how I view bad habits. I don't believe we get rid of them, only put them in a greenhouse and see if we can't get to them in a better form.

A bad habit I have is that I am too shy and tend to leave people in a vacuum in ordinary conversation. I am the bane of hostesses in this regard. I also have a nasty streak in me on occasion. All of these habits weigh heavily on me, but guilt is a waste of time. I was weaned on guilt. Guilt is not a meaningful, useful or intelligent part of religious life. A friend of mine went to his Hindu teacher and confessed some dreadful thing he'd done. His teacher said, "Don't waste time on it; just don't do it again."

With time, I have purposefully moved a little bit toward a middle point. For instance, I've had to teach myself to pamper myself. My temperament tends to be too severe, especially on myself. I grew up during the Depression and saving money was pounded into me. I haven't had much money most of my life, so I needed to move my attitude away from harshness and severity. When my books and lectures got to earning me enough, I had to train myself to come to the middle place, and not always buy the cheapest thing on the shelf. In order to come off a one-sided point of view, I needed to rephrase my way of talking to myself. One of my favorite definitions is, "A heresy is a truth pushed too far." I was heretical when it came to money. Too cautious. I still don't spend a lot of money—someone had to shame me into buying some new clothes recently—but I'm better.

Creativity

I am devoted to my friends, and that is the chief motivation of my life. I don't consider that I have a lifework. My writings are just things to do, a gift I can give to my friends. If my friends are in trouble, or I can do something that would please them or lighten up their life, that is a delight to me. That is what I live for. I am not humble on purpose—that wouldn't be humility. It just makes sense. I do things for my friends, and that is what keeps me on the face of the earth. When I lecture (the books are merely a spin-off of that), I find somebody in the audience I like and then lecture to that person. You're not supposed to do that, but that is all that motivates me. I've always liked being one-on-one with people.

I never seem to have enough time. I face a stack of mail as high as my physical height every time I return from India. I sometimes go to a home I have in the desert and simply ignore time. That is easy for me to do.

Earth

The whole O. J. Simpson trial represented our collective shadow as a society. People got unbelievably caught up in the drama, which I found offensive, but not surprising. The trial turned into a circus and ceased being the trial of a man who did or didn't do something. In reality, it became a national rallying point.

I think, as a society, we are so out of balance that we become both offended and fascinated by anything dark. The Hoffman trial of the Lindbergh kidnapping happened in my lifetime, and in it, the people of the United States did about the same thing: they went wild and had to kill somebody. It is still not certain whether Hoffman kidnapped the child, but someone had to be hanged. The good of the O. J. trial was to show us that we have grown as a society—the mass demand for blood and retribution was averted this time. If the jury had found O. J. guilty, there would have been utter chaos and rioting and innocent people would have lost their lives. I am so glad the jury came up with what it did. I breathed a big sigh of relief. Whether he did the crime or not, you cannot go hang or jail somebody when the issues are bigger than any person. The people's lives that were spared because of the outcome are worth the level of injustice that may have occurred. We have to remember that God is the ultimate jury and will handle the details.

The issue of O. J.'s guilt, however, has to be worked out in the American psyche (which has been eased with the second trial). Spiritual ritual would help. I think we have come to the point where each individual person has to thrash out these dramas; it cannot be a collective movement or a mass matter anymore. The human race is in the process of coming out of the medieval world, and we can no longer do things in medieval ways. We all have to do our own inner work. For better or worse, we are all individuals now.

Dr. Jung once said that the best gift one can give to one's children (one's immediate world) or to the world in general is a "clean unconscious." That is to work out one's own problems and add no more to an already burdened world. The medieval world thought that the presence of a "clean" person (a saint) actually alleviated the darkness of the whole village or town. This was the origin of the great value put on relics. If you could not have a saint for the town you could at least have a piece of a saint, which was nearly as effective.

The village I have stayed at in India for the last twenty years is tiny . . . perhaps five hundred people live there. It is situated on the very edge of the ocean, ten miles north of the city of Pondicherry, a hundred miles south of Madras. This brings it well within the intensity of the tropics, and the village is thoroughly rooted in the medieval world. Except for the fact that the fishing nets are made of nylon instead of coconut fiber, little has changed in a thousand years. I have an involuntary fantasy that always grips my mind as I approach the village, that this is what would survive if India's attempt to be a modern nation should collapse. Without electricity and oil fuel, the urban parts of India would collapse in a month. Such a collapse is not unlikely, but the small villages—entirely independent of oil fuel or electricity— could survive. Fish from the sea and the generous coconut trees would make a simple living for such a village.

I expect that we will have huge cataclysms. I don't know if they will happen in my lifetime, but it doesn't matter to me now, I have lived enough. If I found out that I was going to die tomorrow, that would be all right with me. I have done everything I have wanted to do. That puts me in a peaceful place.*

> *"I take two steps forward and skid back three, but I'm making my way to heaven because I was headed in the wrong direction in the first place."*
>
> ROBERT A. JOHNSON

[*AUTHOR'S NOTE: *When I was in tenth grade, I was walking home from school one cold, clear day, when suddenly I looked up into the heavens and knew the secrets of the universe. In that moment, I felt as if I knew everything there was to know and thought, "My God, if I tell people this, the world will be forever happy." The feeling was glorious and profoundly simple. I was elated, but within a minute, all of the knowledge was gone. I have been waiting for that knowingness to return ever since. It wasn't until my interview with Robert that I had any outward validation for what I had experienced. Robert explained to me that because my life was so enjoyable at the time, waiting for the "splendor of God" to return was not unbearable, as it had been for him. I have come to believe over the years that I had touched the present moment so completely in that instant that I had merged with the Creator, which Robert concurred may be the best explanation.*]

16

Janet Yang

Photo by Dale Robinette

Introduction

J anet is a woman who represents what many believe is not achievable: She is a truly grounded, honest and gentle soul, who just happens to hold a major job in the movie industry. Janet made front-page news in the trades two years ago when she left her position as president of Oliver Stone's production company, Ixtlan, to partner with Lisa Henson (who left her position as president of Columbia Pictures) in what has been called the formation of the most powerful female production team ever.

Janet receives dozens of letters a month from people all over the world, many of them Asian-Americans, who admire her accomplishments and thank her for being a positive role model in a field where there are not many. Responsible for bringing the movie The Joy Luck Club to Ixtlan, and convincing Oliver Stone that it was a movie that "must be made," Janet communicated with the author, Amy Tan, before her book was even finished. Little did she know that it would turn out to be a bestseller, but Janet saw the potential of making the first American film to feature primarily Asian women and could feel a force outside of herself bring the project to fruition. The result was a movie that was far more successful than anyone had envisioned—a movie that has changed lives. Janet felt a similar bigger-than-life energy surrounding her acceptance of an Emmy in 1995 for producing her first television project, Indictment: The McMartin Trial, and again, in 1996, when the Golden Globes honored her with an award for the same TV movie. Awards, as an ego boost, mean little to Janet, but knowing that no other Asian woman had won an Emmy before brought a sense of purpose and accomplishment to her work that felt inspired by a higher source. What Janet has in common with most of the women in this book is a strong sense of her own destiny, which was gifted to her relatively early in life. Since its inception, Janet's career has appeared to be on a constant course of hit after hit. Every project she picks receives accolades and is of the highest quality. After producing the film The People vs. Larry Flynt, and seeing it nominated for five Golden Globes and two Oscars, it became clear to those of us watching Janet that she is a woman who knows how to align herself *with creative genius equal to her own, therefore increasing her talents to a dizzying degree.*

Mark and I met Janet through our mutual friend, Lauren Tom. Lauren is a wonderful actress who befriended Janet while filming The Joy Luck Club. *My husband and I were aimlessly wandering through the mountains of New Mexico one summer afternoon, looking for Guru Singh (who we were scheduled to meet at a Sikh prayer function), when we met Lauren, who was also looking for Guru. A friendship ensued, and soon we found ourselves in Lauren's L.A. kitchen, bonding with Janet Yang and her fiancé (now husband), Joe Bruggeman. Joe and Mark were L.A. bashing. The discussion started innocently enough, with references to the smog and overall tiring aspects of "living like rats," but quickly turned to the morose topics of riots, fires and killer quakes. Janet and I laughed about the absurdity that although we both loved our adventurous city-based careers, our men held quite the opposite viewpoint. As Mark and Joe talked of the "inevitable" landslides into the sea, Janet and I felt an immediate affinity for one another. We liked Los Angeles, loved it in fact, and our allegiance to the city that gave birth to our dreams was evident, in spite of the caustic and comical comments swirling around us.*

As our friendship evolved, Mark and I made a road trip to Janet and Joe's second home, not far from us, in Boulder, Colorado. This was our first "big chill" weekend together and, as we sat on their balcony overlooking a lush meadow and rolling hills, Janet and I couldn't hide the fact that we, too, were more at peace in Mother Nature. As Sting and Pavarotti serenaded us from the living-room speakers, shooting stars put on a veritable show of celebration late into the night, as if all was well with the world.

I didn't know at the time that the whole topic of finding one's home had been a significant dilemma in Janet's life (and even more of an issue now that she was about to be married), a challenge actually echoed in her parents' lives. Janet's mother and father came to America as students from China, only to find that while they were in the United States their country was taken over by the Communists. Unable to return home to their families for over two decades, until President Nixon developed history-making relations with China, Janet's parents struggled for years with the question of where to call home. After graduating from Brown University, Janet decided to live in China and connect with the heritage she had never known growing up.

While in Asia, Janet became fluent in Mandarin and worked in the Chinese publishing industry. She was inspired by Chinese films; having been raised in America, with limited Chinese role models depicted in the movies, Janet was astounded by the variety of roles played by Chinese actors. Unlike the stereotypical Asian roles she was used to, Janet witnessed Asian actors playing the gamut of roles from lawyers to lovers, giving her a view of her heritage to which she had never been exposed. After returning to America, her emotional ties to China continued to mature. Once Janet completed business school at Columbia University, she spent the second half of the 1980s traveling back and forth to China distributing Chinese films. She was then hired by Universal Studios to sell American films to China, which led to a dream job: helping to set up the production of Empire of the Sun *with Steven Spielberg. Her love of two countries and two cultures made her the perfect liaison between the Chinese government and Steven's production team. Being in the right place at the right time, in an area where her skills were unique and invaluable, set in motion the attainment of countless goals.*

Janet is a treasure. Having watched her at work on several movie sets, I'm always awed by her calm and peaceful way of handling intense pressure. No matter what the energy of the set, she brings a sense of relief to the tensest egos. Her dark eyes sparkle, and her frequent laugh lights up any room. At Janet and Joe's wedding, James Woods stood up and gave a hilarious and lengthy speech about how Janet has a miraculous ability of getting people to do things against their will, without even knowing they've been strong-armed (in his case, acting in a movie that he didn't initially want to do). James had worked with Janet on several movies and is still confounded by her quiet power, calling her an "immovable force with a smile." It was through Janet that I met Woody Harrelson, and I wonder if Woody ended up doing the interview for this book because of her influence. He seemed willing enough on his own, but I imagine that if he was tempted to stall, or run away from my deep inquiries altogether, all Janet had to do was give him one of her genuinely loving looks (that somehow translates to, "Do it or else, buddy.") and he was sunk.

Obviously, to hold such a high-level position in Hollywood, working with the biggest names in the business, Janet is no wilting flower. But it seems that she has an exceptional talent for staying soft, loving and feminine while swimming in the shark pool. No doubt she's got to swim right alongside the big boys, but her essence appears to stay intact throughout the process. Janet walks a powerful and purposeful path. Her steps are easy and light, but when she looks back, there's no denying how far she's come. There is an uncommon strength in those quiet steps that enabled her to create a job for herself at Ixtlan, which led to her becoming producing partners with Oliver Stone, one of Hollywood's most creative forces. For all of the rumors and speculation about this intimidating man, Oliver gave Janet immense creative freedom, something for which she is forever grateful. Even after leaving Ixtlan, they continue to honor and support one another.

I imagine there isn't anything this woman can't do. She exudes the belief that with the right frame of mind, it is possible to "have it all" in life. The only thing she did not have, up until now, was a child. Janet wanted to have a well-rounded life, and prioritized putting herself in a position of power before getting pregnant. Now that she works for herself, Janet is able to have the baby she has been hoping for (as I write this, she is seven months pregnant) while continuing to maintain the career that has brought her so much fulfillment. And at forty-one, she is inspiring for anyone daring to dream of themselves in an environment where there are few role models to emulate. If Janet ever wants to get a plaque for her desk, my suggestion is this: "Limitations of race or gender need not apply here."

*　　*　　*　　*

Happiness

I am happiest in a harmonious atmosphere, whether it be in the natural environment, a spiritual setting, or in working with people. I think it's partially why I like the work that I do, because in making movies, I can sometimes achieve that. There is a sense of bonding making a film, where the group has a shared sensibility. Something happens on the set of a movie, where all of the players understand that they are creating something greater than themselves, something that will resonate with other people. It's that feeling of resonance that makes me happy.

Early Years

Emotionally, my childhood was very mixed. I have an older brother and sister, so I was the youngest. I remember distinct times when I was happy, but perhaps even more times when I wasn't. Again, I was happy when I felt secure with friends or with family, when there was a lightheartedness or an absence of tension. Our home could be tense when I heard my parents bickering or when my brother, who had a bad temper, was upset. For me, sometimes I felt that there was too much busyness and rigidity in our home.

I grew up in Long Island, in a mostly Jewish neighborhood. My father was an engineer and my mother worked for the United Nations from the late 1940s until the 1970s. My mother's job was very influential in terms of my whole perspective on having a career. Mom was a statistician in the cost-of-living section. I used to visit her at work and loved her work environment: people from so many different cultures—many in their national garb—in the same place. It was a big building that represented the world as an international body, and there was something formidable about the United Nations to me. I was very proud of my mother. I remember when our school took a trip to the United Nations. My mother walked down the stairs toward our class and I thought, "That's my mom."

Coming from China, I think it must have been a big thing for my mom to be able to work there, especially given the circumstances. Both of my parents came over during a time when China was war-torn and full of strife on many levels. There had been civil wars and World War II. My parents had lived through a lot of turmoil and instability. When they arrived in the United States, they were very poor. Because they came only to study, without the intention of staying, they brought very little with them. Just the bare minimum—a few photos and necessities. The Communists came into power in China while they were here, and many people thought it wouldn't last. It was shocking for many Chinese, especially for the intellectual class that my parents were from, because the Communist party was largely made up of peasants, with whom they didn't usually have a lot of contact. I interviewed a lot of my parents' friends for a thesis I did in college about their experiences. They felt that Communism was a fairly alien movement for them. A lot of Communists were related in some fashion to the Kuomintang Party, which had been overthrown and fled to Taiwan.

All of the Chinese abroad had a tough reality to face: Should they go back or should they stay? If they went back, they knew they may never get out. All of my parents' relatives had recommended that they *not* go back right away. No one was sure how the communist situation would play out. I never met any of my grandparents. My father's mother died when he was here in the States. Same with my mother's parents. There is a lot of speculation that my mother's father was forced to commit suicide because he was a landowner. He was basically killed, but it was called a suicide—a common practice during the Cultural Revolution. There was so much political strife over many, many decades in China. It seemed that everybody suffered because of it, one way or another. People were separated from their spouses and children, and there were many suicides and murders.

I did not know my history as a little girl. I know it now because I actively sought out the stories of my family. My parents did not want to talk about it. They purposely kept these stories from us. We lived a fairly conventional life, with my parents being the strong authority figures. I didn't feel strong as a child or as an adolescent, but I think I became strong once I started digging through my history. Before that, I was unsure of myself and it felt as if there was a lot I didn't know, whether it was an emotional undercurrent in our family, or the whole history of suffering that preceded me. What I consider the very humanizing factors about my parents were not discussed. There was so much that I didn't understand, and I was weighed down by my questions. I was a God-seeker and asked my parents to take me to church. I was looking for answers and I felt troubled, anxious and not fully present much of the time. I was surrounded by a cloud of uncertainty.

Spirituality

The search for my concept of God was confusing because most of my friends went to Hebrew school. They celebrated Yom Kippur and

Rosh Hashanah, and they had bar mitzvahs and bas mitzvahs. I knew I wasn't Jewish. But I wasn't sure what I was. I thought most Americans were Jewish. I didn't know until later that most weren't. It's funny that I ended up in Hollywood, maybe so I could feel at home again.

I knew that Christianity was the other possibility if you weren't

Jewish. Although we had no particular religious upbringing as kids, there were influences. Because my mother worked for the United Nations, she retained her Chinese citizenship for many years and we were considered a family living abroad. The United Nations, therefore, provided for our education and allowed us to bring a nanny over from our "home country." They all tended to be Buddhist. Most working-class people in China were Buddhist. I recently bought a tape that triggered

Janet's parents, Yang Tien-Yi and Tsien Chung-Tzu, 1948.

many childhood memories; it was a Buddhist chant, "Amitofa" from China that I had heard so frequently growing up. While it seemed alien at the time, it obviously stayed in my consciousness. I had thought of the chant periodically throughout the years, but didn't make much of it until just two years ago when I reconnected with it. It's so beautiful, and I chant it now. Funny how those things work through your system. It's interesting to me how much has come full circle. I'm kind of jumping ahead, but one of the main miracles of my life is watching things come full circle. I feel like there are no pieces left scattered, although growing up, all the pieces seemed like loose ends. I couldn't connect anything. As I'm getting older, they're all connecting.

In my attempt to find God, I went to the closest church to our house, which happened to be Baptist. I went every Sunday from about third through sixth grade, which amazes me because I loved to sleep in. My parents woke me up, dropped me off, and went back home. I didn't know how extreme the Baptists were because I had no religious context to compare them to. The main thing I remember was how the people in the church seemed different. More soft-spoken than the people I knew. The girls wore nylon stockings, and I thought that was so grown-up and unusual. Week after week, people got up and gave their testimonies about how they found Jesus, or how Jesus found them. They expressed how they'd be walking through the grocery store, and Jesus would tap them on the shoulder. People would get up with such confidence and relate their miraculous encounters. I thought, "Wow, how cool!" For years, I lived in anticipation of Jesus tapping me on the shoulder and my being able to finally embrace him. I waited and waited. I would repeat, "The Lord is my shepherd," waiting and hoping.

Jesus never came to me. Eventually, I just gave up and thought, "This is not happening." I was disappointed and thought, "I guess I'm not one of the chosen ones." I thought that if I just found Jesus, I would be happy. There is still a part of me that wants to find the shortcuts. My husband accuses me of that. I do believe there are moments when we have epiphanies, and God knows I can't get enough of them, but you can't live for the epiphanies. What I'm learning is to live for whatever moment is happening, no matter how mundane it may seem. But there is definitely a part of me attracted to the big breakthroughs.

Sometimes I have epiphanies and can see the bigger picture. Even if I'm having a disagreement with someone, part of me is engaged and part of me sees beyond what appears to be happening. I guess I am always looking for those kinds of dynamics and universal truths. That's where I can see the connections and why things may be happening. I'm fascinated by the little I know about quantum physics, about how so much of reality is influenced by our belief systems. It's very fulfilling to see the deeper picture.

Miracle

In February 1972, Nixon and Kissinger made their historic visit to China. When Nixon came back, one of the key messages from the

Chinese government was, "We invite all overseas Chinese to come back to China. Please visit your Motherland and see your relatives." Since the 1950s, no one was allowed to do that. China had been completely closed off to outsiders. My mother's words, "I'm going," changed my life. My father said, "Are you sure you want to go?" We were all petrified because this was "Red China" and the sense was that we might be put in prison and never get out. China has changed so drastically in the last ten or twenty years, it is difficult to imagine that at that time it was considered a monstrous place. We had heard that many people were being randomly killed, and there was no rhyme or reason to it. I had been brought up as a 1950s baby: we had air raids because we were afraid the Communists were going to bomb us. Americans had been greatly influenced by the McCarthy era and Communists were seen as *the* big, bad evil. Personally, we couldn't resist because "they" were our relatives.

My mother had no doubts about going back. She and my father had actually fought for years about whether to return and live in China. For ten years, my parents didn't buy any new furniture because they felt they were just in the United States temporarily and that they could go home any day. I was born in 1956, which was a pivotal year in China. The country was doing relatively well; for the first time in years, people weren't begging in the streets and things were really coming together. The feeling was, "Wow, maybe this regime is going to take care of the people after all." In 1956, something happened that was frightening to people like my parents: the Hundred Flowers Campaign. Mao felt that there was a lot of dissent going on and said, "Okay everybody, just speak up and criticize the government." The expression used was, "Let a hundred flowers bloom, let a hundred schools of thought contend." People started gradually printing editorials in newspapers and putting up posters on the walls. Debates were held on the weaknesses of communist society. It got out of hand, and a lot of people were arrested and persecuted. Mao must have been afraid and probably thought he had to show who was boss. Political scientists tried to figure out if it had been a ploy from the start, an effort to weed out the bad elements. I had just been born and my parents finally stopped arguing about whether to go back and live. After Nixon's visit, however, mainland China was considered the real

China again, and once the opportunity arose to visit, my mother felt compelled to go.

My father was afraid that if we all went to China together, we could disappear and nobody would be able to get us out. So we decided to split up the family. My mother and I went first, and then my father went with my sister and my brother. I was fifteen when my mother and I went, and we were among the first overseas private citizens to go over. Up until then, I had next to no awareness of China, the way my parents grew up, or who my relatives were. I had never even seen their pictures. The visit totally changed my life for so many reasons. It was one of the best things I've ever done. I was at a very impressionable age. I wasn't very political, but the times were, and my classmates had been talking about the Cambodian-Laotian issue and the Vietnam War. People were carrying little red books and China was emerging as this odd place, kind of frightening on the one hand, but intriguing, too, as the counterculture identified with it.

I had lived my life in a middle-class world of the Jewish community on Long Island. I was practically the only Asian in all of my schools growing up. In elementary school, I was the *only* one and then in junior high there was one other Chinese girl. Like me, she had long hair and was tall and thin and people used to mix us up. It would drive me crazy because I thought she was a nerd. I had never been around many Asians, and my whole identity was *not* Chinese. When I went to China, I looked like one of them, but I felt so different. I remember crossing the border by foot and facing rows and rows of military officials. During most of our trip, I was dependent on my mother for translating. I had heard Mandarin around the house, but I couldn't speak it very well. They separated us and put me in a room and started interrogating me. I was petrified and barely understood what they were saying. Eventually, they let my mother come in to help. They asked me, "Is there a lot of prejudice in America? Are you treated badly?" I gave these kinds of nebulous replies like, "Yeah, well there's definitely some discrimination, but it doesn't affect me much."

In every way, China was a new experience. This was the first time I had ever been in a country that was extremely poor. Like nothing I'd ever seen. Most people didn't have hot running water or electricity and were living ten people to a room and killing chickens on the street for food. In addition, having never experienced that level of social and political rigidity, censorship or lack of privacy, it was a shock. We had to talk to our relatives in whispers because they were afraid the rooms were being bugged and we were being followed throughout our stay.

China was still in the middle of the Cultural Revolution. The years 1966 to 1976 were the most extreme leftist period. They had very limited reading materials; everything was revolutionary. All of the music and culture was strictly limited and enforced. Propaganda blared out over the loudspeakers everywhere we went, and there was a total worshiping of Mao. The Communists had made a regular practice of going through everyone's homes and ransacking and confiscating people's things. Anything that was old or foreign was taken, such as antique furniture or Beethoven music. Religion was totally gone by then, and even family bonding was not seen as a good thing. What we learned was that they had made our relatives suffer because my parents were living abroad. They found any excuse to punish people. My mother had been accused of being a spy because she worked for the United Nations and we had traveled frequently to Taiwan through the United Nations. Because she had that reputation, all of her relatives suffered from guilt by association. Many were locked up, sent to the countryside, and forced to live in pig sheds while they worked the land. You can't even begin to imagine. And my parents had had no idea until we heard the stories firsthand.

Obviously, the Communists kept good track of everything because before my mother and I arrived, all of my relatives' belongings had been returned. Jewelry and pictures at first and eventually land and homes were given back. A few people even got better housing. The government put on a good face for our visit. The neighborhoods were cleaned up for our arrival, and a few of our relatives were able to get transferred out of their country jobs and go back into the city, which was a big deal. People used to wait for ten or twenty years to go back to where they were from. They called it *hukou*—where you're assigned to live and work. People had no choice in the matter and had to sit and wait. Thank God our visit benefited them.

Everyone in the different villages we visited were hyper-aware that we were there. They were very guarded; I wasn't even allowed to take pictures. So much of their system at the time was based on gossip. You couldn't get away with *anything*. Everybody was watching everybody else. The officials barely had to watch over people because neighbors, even your own children, would turn you in. During the revolution, children persecuted their parents and students persecuted their teachers because the youth were targeted to help fight "evil." Children and teens did a lot of the dirty work. They were told that evil might be lurking in their own families, with their parents' old feudal-like ideas. So, whole armies of youth were marching through the streets. They were the most feared group and primarily were the ones ransacking the homes.

I met most of my relatives at our first stop in Canton. There were thirty people there, and it was like looking at a huge gene pool. My mother was bawling. Her father had just died, probably killed because he was a landowner. I remember sitting in a hotel room, and my mother was crying because she wanted to go see her father's ashes, and her brothers were begging her not to go because there was no grave, and they thought it would be too painful. My mother experienced so much loss. Her older sister had died giving birth. I feel like I know this beautiful woman I had never met. I've seen pictures of her; she had a really tragic life. It's an interesting story because it shows the fate of these two sisters. Talk about a charmed life—I think my mother has had a charmed life. Her sister was placed in an arranged marriage at a young age by her parents. She had no desire to be in the marriage and was very unhappy. She was artistic and musical, and several years into the marriage, she met a man who was also married. They fell desperately in love, but divorce was almost unheard of at the time. By conventional standards, her husband was a good catch, and she would have been thought of as spoiled to leave him. She saw her lover illicitly, and they were ostracized by society because they couldn't hide their love. After years and years, they were both able to get divorced, but even then they hardly saw each other. He was sent off to work, and she was, too. Finally, they were able to be married, and she got pregnant right away. He was then sent off to the hinterland, which is inland. Most people like to be by the coasts, which is where the cities are, with a lot more opportunities. She had the child, and her husband came back to visit. She got pregnant right away again, and again he was sent away. They had hardly spent any time together, and when she was giving birth to the second child, she died. Shortly after that, he died, rumor has it of a broken heart. Their son and daughter were left with no parents, and my mother's family took them in.

These children, now adults, were amongst the relatives meeting us. For years, my mother had been dying to get them out of China, and I was recently able to help my female cousin get out. She and her husband and son are now living with me.

When we were in China, I sensed a great deal of fear in the eyes of my relatives. They were afraid to meet us because they knew what a big thing it was—good and bad. On the one hand, we could help them so much, but on the other hand, they could get in even worse trouble if they said the wrong thing, or if my mother turned out to really be a spy. Most didn't really believe she was a spy, but some may have had lingering doubts, so thoroughly brainwashed were they. There was a sense of desperation with their lives and fascination with ours. They went through my toiletry bag and were in awe of the different things they had never seen before, such as a shower cap and my contact lenses. They exemplified every degree of emotion, from greed to total unconditional selflessness. In the case of my orphaned cousins, who were used to not having anything, they insisted on hand-washing our clothes. There were the cousins who boldly declared, "Mao is a bad egg." Then there were those who were afraid to say anything. Most people just shrugged their shoulders in acceptance when we would probe why things seemed so irrational. In America, you get the sense that things work. There are reasons why most things happen. Here was a country where there seemed to be no easy explanations.

I was approached in my travels by a man who was leading a group of Canadian Chinese through China. Canada had established travel there many years before the United States did. He started in on me and said, "You are Chinese. You *have* to get with it and be more political and Chinese-identified. You cannot deny it anymore." He was like an evangelist, and I was so scared of what he was saying, but it touched something in me. I sensed that there was an element of truth to what he was saying, even though I was very turned off by his delivery. That time had seen the birth of what we now know to be a multiethnic, affirmative action, back-to-your-roots movement. And I was taken by it. I would talk to my relatives and open up their texts that said "Down with American imperialists," calling us "paper tigers," which was a metaphor for a threat without substance. I saw so many paradoxes. While they were learning to hate America, they were simultaneously totally fascinated with anything American. Again, nothing made sense.

Influences

I came back to America and finished high school. One of the effects of coming back was that I became almost dangerously thin. I was so turned off by food and consumption and materialism because I had just seen so much deprivation. I felt guilty for having so much. Anything excessive or vulgar was too much for me. China had had a very profound influence. The high school I went to was a boarding school, called Phillips Exeter Academy. It had the highest academic rating of any high school in the United States. Up until that year, it had been an all-boys school for one hundred years. My parents were impressed with the school, and my class was the first that allowed girls. In old Chinese society, if you had a good education you had everything: power, wealth, respect. At the last minute, my mother didn't want me to go, but my father said, "She must go, it's the best school in the country." I was the only girl in most of my small classes, which only had twelve students. This was my first encounter with the preppie, Ivy League, male-oriented, WASPy, success-oriented, New England, Old-World way of looking at the world.

The best thing about Exeter was the mix of students. There were obviously a lot of rich kids whose ancestors had been going to Exeter for five generations, but the school also has a huge endowment and many kids from Harlem went there, too. This was the first time I went to school with other Asian students. One of the students while I was there was actually a prince from Thailand. We also had Olympic skaters. People who excelled in all fields. We had brilliant concert pianists, and kids would literally be composing symphonies in high school! There were students who were writing novels and plays. And, lots of nerds. We called them the "briefcase gang." I was friends with a brilliant cartoonist. He was the son of a senator, and he hardly ever bathed and wore a tuxedo all the time. There were so many eccentric people. It was a very fertile environment, although I don't know if I recognized it as such for me at the time because I felt so ordinary and diminutive amongst these brilliant kids. What it did do was get me comfortable being around people who are at the top of their fields.

All of the students lived in a little New Hampshire town, away from our parents. There were a lot of daredevils and extremists, and the amount of drugs was shocking to me. It was a good thing I was there, though, because I was such an adolescent! I'm glad that I saved my parents from having to deal with me during that time because it might have damaged our relationship had I been living at home. I was so rebellious, a "nego," which meant that I was negative and cynical. Very down on the Establishment. All of my anxieties seemed to revolve around peer pressure.

After high school, I went to Brown University for two years, but I was very restless. I wanted to learn more about China and study the language. My parents were worried because I had no idea what I wanted to do with my life. There was so much pressure to find a major. All I knew was that China kept whispering to me. I would find myself thinking about it and wondering about it, reading anything I could about life there. It felt like a great magnet was leading me toward it. I started studying Chinese, but Harvard had a lot more Chinese classes, so I ended up going there for two years as a visiting student. I was becoming obsessed with China. One of my teachers was from China, and before I left Harvard I said, "Please, if you can think of *any* way for me to work in China, let me know."

My first job out of college was working for a magazine called *Book Digest*. It doesn't exist anymore, but it was a great opportunity to work in publishing. We excerpted books, so I got to read a lot of books and meet many authors. I learned the publishing world quickly, and I loved it.

Several months into the job, I got a letter from my Harvard teacher, who said, "There is an opening in China at a place called the Foreign Languages Press, and they want someone who has publishing experience and who will help them edit their works in English." They wanted a Chinese-American who could live amongst the Chinese and not have to be treated as a "foreign expert" with a lot of privilege, and not have to be paid too much. I started corresponding with them and got the job. The company published books and magazines for export. With the "normalization of relations," which had taken effect in 1979, a lot of things suddenly became operative. Official diplomatic ties enabled the United States to open up an embassy and I was in the first wave of journalists, diplomats and exchange students allowed to live for a period in China.

I lived there for almost a year and a half. It was the most incredible experience of my life up until then. I learned how to speak Mandarin fluently. Amazingly, I had no problem blending in, but I was struggling with my identity. It was the strangest thing for me because people kept thinking I was Chinese. I was confused and felt so alien. I remember so many times being refused entry into a hotel or the embassy saying, "I'm an American, don't you understand? Here's my American passport," but they didn't believe me because I looked Chinese. If I was speaking English, they thought I had learned it. If I was with an American, they thought I was an interpreter. So many times I'd go to the Peking Hotel, which was the main hotel at the time, and finally manage to convince the guards outside the gate that I was an American, only to be halfway through the lobby when another guard would come running after me. This was the first time I truly experienced overt discrimination against Chinese, and in their own country to boot! I would get so angry, so confused and so hurt. And then I'd watch them treat foreigners completely differently. If I was seen with a man, I was glared at with the obvious subtext, "There's a local girl trying to sleep her way out of China. What a slut." I became so utterly self-conscious of how I was being perceived. If I was wearing my American clothes, people would say, "There's a Chinese person trying to look foreign." But all I had were foreign clothes. I'd want to go to the hotels to take baths, because we didn't have hot running water where I was living. I'd want to go see my friends who were Americans like myself, but who were working in a different capacity, like for a newspaper or for a bank. Sometimes I just wanted to have a glass of orange juice or buy something nice from one of the hotels. The difficulties of getting in were so exhausting. It seemed as if there were so many different kinds of cages holding me back. I felt like I was escaping from one cage to go into another. Even the hotels were a kind of cage.

When I first arrived, I was with a tall American friend of mine named Frank, who was about as American as you could get. He wore a cowboy hat and cowboy boots and was a student at Beijing University. Frank spoke perfect colloquial Chinese. We went to Tiananmen Square, the staging ground for large public events, because they were having a huge celebration to pay respects to some of the Communist leaders. There were mobs and mobs of people who came in organized groups; then there were the stragglers who weren't part of any group, like people who were out of work, or students. You cannot imagine how many people there were. Frank started casually goofing around with some kids, using Beijing slang, and they thought he was hilarious. People started circling around us and soon there was a mob of people. The mob got bigger and people were yelling, "Sing us a song!" Soon the mob got huge and people started throwing themselves at us. We ended up on our hands and knees on the ground and the crowd of hundreds was about to crush us to death. I have never been so scared. The mob was swaying and was so dense that we couldn't move. Luckily, a policeman came, and the crowd slowly moved away. Frank and I started walking and then running out of the square as fast as we could and sought sanctuary in the Peking Hotel. From that point on, the police followed me throughout the rest of the day. They waited outside of the hotel, followed me to another hotel, and then to a dance that night. They followed me home to my work unit, and Monday morning, they showed up again and said, "We want to arrest that girl." They thought I was a local Chinese person, but my Chinese coworkers explained that I was American and that I worked there.

I suddenly realized the gravity of my situation. I had been naive up until then and hadn't realized I'd been so conspicuous. I couldn't be seen with foreigners, yet, if I was with Chinese, they were scared of me because I was a foreigner. At that time, it was not good to be seen with foreigners if you were Chinese. I felt all the traps of identity, which in retrospect has been a big gift. It's been about shedding all those things. Because of the system, I was just not going to fit in anywhere. In America, you can fit in anywhere. The traps are more psychological. There are people out there who have prejudices, but there are no institutionalized boundaries. In the past, I was often amazed that I was in the circles I was in because there was a part of my mind that felt like I didn't belong. I never felt like one of "them." My whole life, until recently, I've felt like there's a club and I don't belong. You watch television and Chinese are not represented. You watch movies and people who look like me are not seen. *The Joy Luck Club* was amazing for me in the sense that it broke through those boundaries. It taught me that just because something has not happened before doesn't mean it cannot happen.

The Joy Luck Club was the first movie ever made by an American Hollywood studio with a primarily Asian cast. And so many of those actors have gone on to do great projects. When I lived in China, one of the things that struck me was watching television and movies. After 1981, a whole new crop of filmmakers was coming out with Chinese films that weren't just pure propaganda. They had taken the technology they already had, and instead of using it for propaganda, they started creating art. There was something very liberating about being in China and seeing a movie—even though they weren't always very good movies—with every imaginable personality type and line of work represented. And they were *all* Chinese. I didn't realize that I had been trapped by my own thinking. It's hard to imagine how varied China is. You cannot even begin to generalize about what Chinese people are. In my mind, I had been fighting the image of Chinese being nerds or the underclass, so it was liberating for me to see the varied reality.

On a more micro level, my mother was a strong influence for me. I'm certain that while I was growing up I identified primarily with her. I saw her more clearly, bonded with her more, and felt that I understood her better than my father. She was dynamic and outgoing and took a more obvious or active interest in me. As I look back, I saw my father as a shadowy figure. Today, however, my father has come into clear focus as a human being. He is very dear to me. During my growing years, he was traditional in terms of societal expectations. He believed that if I went to the right school, I'd get the right job. His notion of society was very structured, and granted, in his day, all you needed were the "right" credentials. Both of my parents were very concerned with status, but if they had been truly traditional they probably wouldn't have expected their daughters to work at all. Because they were semitraditional, they had a puritanical work ethic and expected as much from their daughters as they did from their son, so it's no surprise to me that I'm so career-oriented and that my older sister is a lawyer.

My father was an engineer, and he had a hard time getting a job in this country. There was a lot of prejudice against Chinese and Communists during the whole Red scare. I read a letter he wrote to a company that was building the ventilation system for the United Nations and it said, "I must work for you, for nothing, because this is one way I can indirectly help my Motherland." He told them that he eventually wanted to go back to his country, but that while he was here he wanted to contribute. So he was taken on at the company, for no salary, and then after a short time, they gave him a little paycheck. My father worked his way up and eventually became a vice president of the company. Later, he bought out the partners and then went on to sell the company, which was a major business coup for him.

I never imagined that I wouldn't work. It was a nonissue. I realize how blessed I was in that way, because for so many women, the issue of working or not working is a real psychological struggle, especially during the feminist revolution.

Family

Growing up, I never thought I would get married. I just didn't see the attraction or why anyone would want to spend the rest of her life with one man. Now I realize you can still have a lot of freedom in a relationship. For instance, the freedom to go inside more. I'm a Cancer, but I never felt like one because we are supposed to be such homebodies. People would come to my place and be shocked to find a lack of furniture or food in the refrigerator. Only in the last several years have I finally experienced what people call "domestic bliss." I feel I have much more potential as a human being and a citizen of the world because I am much more fulfilled in my personal life.

For the first time in my life, rather than feeling that I'm between

worlds, what used to seem like disparate strands have been organi-
cally integrated. We are bringing a child into the world who will be
clearly influenced by both East and West. Our wedding, too, was an
interesting blend of different cultures and generations celebrating
together. As I've gotten older, I've grown to appreciate my parents and
their friends more and more. I see how much we have in common.
That's a big part of the integration I feel.

There are different
theories on what
makes relationships
work and the one that
seems applicable to
Joe and me is that
opposites attract. We
complement each
other. The things that
Joe is good at are very
different from the
things I am good at.
Therefore, our world
feels bigger and there
is a sense of expan-
sion that comes from
our being together.
Joe is a big champion
of individualism and

Photo by Tom Rasalovich

Janet and her husband, Joe Bruggeman, 1997.

is very self-motivated. He operates better when he's clear of distractions, whereas I work best with a lot of different people and elements.
I put my energy into trying to bring out the best in people, and to create a stimulating and creative environment to work in. I have to bug
Joe to return his phone calls. Part of the work I do honors the individual's vision, but at the same time, nothing happens without team
effort. It's an odd balancing act.

Life with Joe is definitely more stable and rich. He is interested in
who I am, not in what I do. There is no possibility that he has a hidden agenda, which would be very easy for someone to have, without
even realizing it. He's much more interested in the world at large than

in my business. I think he sees me more for who I am—the stuff underneath—than other people do. He doesn't see me for what I can do for him, or what I can do in general. That's so valuable to me.

Even when I wasn't sure if I would ever marry, I always had a notion that I wanted to have children. Inside I feel like a kid, and I connect with children easily. I started seriously thinking about having a baby when I was thirty-three. I had been with a man for seven years, and when we ended, I went through a little crisis because I had thought we were going to have children together. Looking back, I'm glad we didn't work out, but at the time you can never know that. I was having a tough time in my work at Universal because I didn't like working for a corporation. I started questioning everything. I knew I needed to get more in touch with my feminine side and gain some self-awareness. It was to the point where I hadn't yet learned how to be a woman. I had never thought of myself as ambitious, but other people who were watching me did. I didn't have a conscious goal to get ahead, but I was so passionate about my work that I threw myself into it with everything I had. My hunger and desire to travel, especially to China, were fulfilled through my work. I felt so privileged that my work had been tailored to my life, and I just ate it up. So many doors had opened up at the right time in the right place, and I was saying "yes" to all of the opportunities. It was then that I realized that I needed to go inside more, and that was the beginning of a more spiritual period for me. In that period, I started panicking about not being a mother. I was more worried about having a baby than I have been in the last few years because in my mind thirty-three was old. It's funny how mind-sets change. Our sense of possibilities change. In retrospect, if I had had a child, I don't think I would have ended up working for Oliver Stone. It would have been too much of a full-time commitment, for no other reason than I wouldn't have been available to make myself be hired.

I'm only a handful of months away from having my baby. Joe and I had talked about having a child for a while, and with us, things took a long time to prepare psychologically, but then everything happened so quickly. We've been together almost four years, but in the last six months we got married, bought a house and now we're pregnant. It's a life change I was obviously ready for, and I really like home life a lot. It helps me be more balanced, and I'm told that having children balances life even more, which I'm already feeling. It feels like a big opening.

Lifework

In 1989, I put myself in front of Oliver and said, "Hire me." My boyfriend at the time, Justin, and I were living in New York. Justin had made a number of documentaries, and I think that's why I fell in love with him because he was always going off to far-flung places. He made a movie in Cambodia with the Khmer Rouge, and then he made another film in the Golden Triangle about the big drug warlord who lives in Burma. Justin had spent a lot of time in Thailand and Southeast Asia. He was intelligent, dignified and European-bred. I was attracted to the image of him and the fabulous things he was doing, as I didn't yet have a sense of what I wanted to do with my life.

Oliver had just written the movie *Year of the Dragon,* which was about Chinese drug warlords. Oliver had contacted Justin because he wanted to know what it was like filming in Thailand. They became friendly, and Oliver and his wife invited us to dinner. We were to meet in a restaurant in SoHo. I came by myself and walked into the restaurant and Oliver, who didn't know who I was, ran up to me and said, "Oh my God, you should try out for our movie. You'd be perfect for the lead." I said, "I'm not an actress." He told me to call the director and gave me his number. Oliver and I became fast friends. At the time, I was organizing Chinese film festivals, bringing films over from China, and Oliver was very interested in the Chinese cinema. We stayed friends over the years and when he made *Born on the Fourth of July* at Universal, I was still working there so we were in touch. He became a loyal friend. I recognized his very powerful energy, even though he wasn't a big deal at the time. Oliver was a genius writer who had won an Academy Award with *Midnight Express,* but he hadn't yet made a big splash as a director.

After I received my MBA from Columbia, I went to work in San Francisco, heading a small company that imported films from China. I was sharing an office with Wayne Wang, the director, who was a spokesperson for the Chinese-American community. It was particularly ironic because *Year of the Dragon* had just come out, and the

Chinese-American community lambasted it. Wayne was at the forefront of this public outcry against Oliver, for having written such an
"irresponsible" movie about Chinese-Americans. Oliver came to the
office one day, and they thought I was dating him, which was not the
case (and never has been), but I liked Oliver and we began to hang
out while we were in the city. Once again it seemed that my whole
life was betwixt and between. I've often felt like this bridge between
East and West, between Americans and Chinese, and between this faction and that faction. In this instance, I felt caught between Oliver and
Wayne. Just another example of my mixed identity. Oliver represented
the white man's irresponsibility, the Establishment. Here was yet
another Hollywood movie that had exploited Asian-Americans. Wayne
represented the victimization of minorities.

In retrospect, everything Oliver was saying in that movie was true,
and Wayne would be the first to admit it. These things exist. There are
such things as Chinese warlords who deal in drugs. I understood both
sides. When there is a very limited number of film projects with Asians
in them, there are so many expectations that those projects will represent only the positive.

After Oliver made *Platoon,* and it did very well, he was offered a
first-look production deal at a studio where he would take the movies
he was interested in making. I had heard about it through Justin, and

Courtesty of Manifest Film Co., 1998

Janet, Steven Spielberg and director, Xie Jin, during the
making of *Empire of the Sun,* Shanghai, China, 1986.

they were talking on
the phone one day,
and I said, "Let me
talk to him." I got on
the phone and said,
"Oliver, you've got to
hire me." He told me
to come in to talk to
him about it and that
we'd go have lunch.
When we met, I
think I was a little
over the top. I said,
"Oliver,   there's   a

feeding frenzy of scripts out there, and you're going to need someone to help you." I was already working as a production executive (at Universal) and had worked on Steven Spielberg's *Empire of the Sun,* so I didn't know much, but I knew what he needed. Oliver's deal was not only to direct movies, but to produce them as well. I said, "Oliver, you need someone to help you. How can you single-handedly read all of these scripts and call people back, etc. You really need help!" He had been operating up until then with just one assistant, which was pretty amazing. After lunch, he told me to write a letter to him, laying it all out, which I did. He said, "Okay, let's put you on trial."

My title was vice president of production at Ixtlan. It was a new company that no one knew anything about. One of the things I told myself, and continued to tell myself throughout my working with Oliver was, "Stay calm, he's just a person." There was a part of me that was excited and in awe of him. I was so hungry to get to work. It was the same thing when I worked with Steven Spielberg. "Stay calm, he's just another person." Especially in the movie business, there is so much hype around certain celebrities, it's easy to let your mind run wild. For me, at that point in my life, there was one huge opportunity after another, and it wasn't slowing down.

During the first month I was at Ixtlan, I got a call one day from an agent who said, "I represent Carlos Castaneda. We were wondering if you'd like to get together and meet." I knew that the name Ixtlan had come from the book *Journey to Ixtlan,* by Carlos. Oliver had read that book and many others by the same author, and I had read his work also. This was another example of "Stay calm, he's just another person." Carlos was such a mystical and legendary man and had helped change so many lives. I went to Oliver and told him that Carlos wanted to meet us. He so revered this person that I think he was a little nervous that he would disappoint Carlos, by maybe promising a movie and then not being able to follow through or something. I said, "No, I think it's just a meeting of the minds. I don't think he's expecting anything." We all got together in Santa Monica and had an interesting talk. Carlos was very accessible and friendly.

As Carlos tells the story, when I walked in the room, he saw my energy, which is what he deals in—the world of energy. He knew

right away that I had to work with him because he saw in me somebody who was very clear in half of my body, and the other part of me
was what he calls covered in fuzz, like static. From that point on, for
the next several years of my life, I took his classes two or three times
a week. It was a lot of physical movements, like Kung Fu, that would
allow us to have sorcerous experiences to help create an energetic
mass within our systems so we could go into the dream state. He
called it sorcery, which is the manipulation of energy. This work was
extremely influential for me and colored everything I was going
through at the time. I was very conflicted, because again, I felt this
strange mismatch of the world I was entering and the world I was
from. Carlos totally embraced me into his world and I thought, "My
God, this must be happening for a reason." He had very strong opinions about life and what was right for me and took a strong interest
in my spiritual growth. I realized then that I must be destined to be
around men with very strong opinions! When I look back, I think it is
possible that I was looking for a father figure. I know that my ten-
dency growing up was to have really close girlfriends, but when boys
came into my life, I became sort of obsessed and girlfriends dropped
away. I had a lot of male friends and most of the people in my high
school were males, so other than a few close girlfriends, I put a lot of
my energy into boys. Same with college. I feel more balanced now
because my girlfriends are so important to me, but it took a while for
me to work that out. It's weird to see this so clearly now because I
wouldn't have then, but I was defining myself by the people around
me. I felt like I had to conform to another world other than my own.

Carlos created a strange dichotomy in my life. He was the first
person to get me to understand that everything in life is an illusion and
all essentially bullshit. That was a pretty rocking notion because I was
at an age where I had put everything into the physical world. It took
me years to learn to resolve the dichotomy between my spiritual life
and my desire to create in the outside world and learn how to dis-
mantle the importance of the physical world. I couldn't know at first
what else to rely on but the world I knew. When you're first going
through that process, you really need to rely on someone or something, and I relied on Carlos to show me the way. I felt uncomfortable
on my own, and sometimes I felt uncomfortable with him. But I still

felt like he knew the truth, and I needed to find out what the truth was and do whatever was necessary to get to the truth.

Carlos showed me so many things, and some of them seem so obvious, but they had a big impact. For instance, kinesiology, or muscle testing. If you don't know anything about this and suddenly you're shown what teas and foods are bad for you by the reaction of your own muscles, that is a phenomenal experience. This was the first time I started seeing chiropractors, herbalists, acupuncturists and doctors who practiced Eastern medicine. A whole new world was starting to open up to me, and it was a little scary because it was so new.

It seems that in my life, when there are changes, everything happens at once. I had just broken up with Justin, I was in this new job, had moved, and now I was working with Carlos. Carlos was the first person to kind of jolt me into a whole other reality. At the time, Oliver was making *The Doors*. My parents hadn't seen any of his movies and didn't know who he was. They said, "Oh, what's he making now?" I didn't exactly brag about this 1960s, drug- and sex-ridden movie.

The first two movies I brought to Ixtlan that were made were two smaller movies: *South Central* and *ZebraHead*. I was proud when they both got great reviews. I found the financing to get them made and produced them. There are different people and companies who finance movies, and you just have to keep convincing them that it's worth it. It's hard work. The whole Hollywood system is difficult for people to understand. A movie itself may or may not make money, but individuals involved make money. In fact, most movies don't make money in the traditional sense. Very few do. With certain "hits," after you deduct all of the expenses, the interest and fees, they are still not officially "profitable." There is something called the back end, where you supposedly get a percentage of profits, but since there are no "profits," there is no back end. It's all a myth. Unless the movie cost so little money that it can't be padded. To avoid not getting their share, actors just ask for big money up front. That's one of the things that's driving the price of movies up because people think, "Well, we're never going to see the back end, so we might as well get as much as we can from the front end." It's a vicious cycle, because the more movies cost, the more people don't see the back end. DreamWorks is apparently trying to institute an equitable accounting system where each movie really does matter and people can see the back end. My belief is that if everybody took a little less in the beginning, there might be a chance to see some at the back end. Periodically, a movie is made that way, but it's very hard to convince people to do that.

To go back a bit, I was in New York when some publishers had just bought Amy Tan's novel, *The Joy Luck Club,* for some record sum of money. I got in touch with Amy, who started sending me chapters. I was still working at Universal Studios and I said to her, "I don't think I have the power to get this off the ground, but I really would love to help you in any way I can." I submitted it to the one place where I had some influence, Amblin (Steven Spielberg's company), and they had just finished *Empire of the Sun* and kind of had the attitude that they had just done their China movie. Even though many people really liked the book, no one would make the movie. It kept getting submitted with different writers, directors and producers and people kept hovering over the project, year in, year out, but nobody bought it.

When I joined Oliver, several people came to me that I had had relationships with, knowing that I was running Ixtlan. I had much more influence than I had as one of twelve executives at a studio. Key projects came in at that point, some of which I'm still hoping to make, which just goes to show how long things take. When I first read the *Joy Luck* script, I cried my eyes out. I saw Oliver right away and tearily said, "Oh, Oliver, you're going to *die*, I love this. I love it. It's so good." He said, "If you like it, go ahead." That's what he always said, "If you like it, go ahead, you have my blessing." Oliver is great that way because he knows it takes passion and commitment to make a movie. With his name and my work, he knew we'd get a lot done. We were a good team and he trusted in my intuition. Oliver recognized that it was a good script and his wife, Elizabeth, had read the book and absolutely loved it. Ironically, Wayne Wang directed it. Talk about full circle!

Producing was tricky for Oliver, because when he produces a movie, he's risking his reputation, which is a lot. His name is a valuable commodity to put on the line, and that is an ongoing issue for him. There are no guarantees of success and Oliver had mixed feelings about producing in the first place, and about what kinds of movies to produce. Nobody ever knows what will succeed. It's all a crapshoot. Oliver is a director and writer first of all, used to having total control over his projects. He simply will never be as interested in someone else's project as he is in his own, which is natural. However, to be a really good producer you have to be highly dedicated. Once you say that you'll produce someone's

Photos by Patrick Markey

Janet and author, Amy Tan, on the set of *Joy Luck Club*, San Francisco, 1993.

movie, they can be really demanding and rightly so. They want you to get out there and hustle, sell, make the calls and leave no stone unturned. You have to call every actor who's a possibility and do all that you can to get the movie made. Eventually, I established my own reputation, and I think people came to trust me, but in the beginning the biggest thing going for me was that I was the only person who could legitimately use Oliver's name.

The one thing that I had to battle a lot early on was Oliver's discouragement. If we had hired a writer to do a script and the script came in that wasn't great, he would get let down. I explained to him the developmental process that takes a lot of work. For a long time, Oliver had been a nobody, and he couldn't sell a project. Then all of a sudden he became a big shot, and everybody would do anything he wanted. He never experienced the middle ground of how you work at something, nurture it and make it better. He is a writer and wants to be left alone to write, so he wasn't used to soliciting other people's opinions. I learned that often it was a good idea not to show him scripts for three or four drafts and then he'd say, "Wow, this is really good." So I stopped telling him bad news and only told him the good news so that he wouldn't get discouraged.

Joy Luck put Oliver and me on the map as producers. A lot of this industry is about proving how strong you are. We were able to make a ground-breaking movie. For the first time, a lot of people took me seriously in my own right and stopped seeing me as some D [development] Girl for Oliver. I had my own taste and could clearly influence Oliver. His name helped sell the movie, although it was not the kind of movie he was typically associated with.

The whole experience changed my life. Even reading the book changed my life, because I had never thought that anybody could describe in words the very intimate and uniquely personal experiences I had had. I thought that I was the only person in the whole world going through these things, but I came to find that not only were many other people experiencing these feelings, but that someone could actually put them all into words. It was an amazing time for me because it was a confluence of so many things. It was a major reward to realize that my personal and professional lives could be so integrated. I had always seen movies as something "out there," and had been trying to learn what "they" wanted to watch and what "they" wanted to make. I never really thought that it could be so personal and fulfilling. It taught me a lot about holding a vision; I figured that if I felt so strongly about something, there were other people out there who would also feel strongly. It was a validation that it was possible to go against convention, and it gave me a sense of my own power within the industry to have been able to do something that broke so many rules. *Joy Luck* broke every rule in the book. It was not white to start with. It was not male. It did not have a conventional story structure. People talk endlessly about the three-act story structure: what page the first act ends on, what page the climax is on and so on. It's endless. We defied the norm totally, and nobody could believe it.

With more success, Oliver seemed to get more comfortable producing. I became president in 1993. *Joy Luck* had just come out and after we were in Telluride, Colorado, opening up the movie, we went to China for the first international film festival in Shanghai. Oliver was invited to be a jury member, and they had a whole retrospective of his works. He was thrilled to go because he loves Asia. We spent a lot of time together, and I asked him then if I could be president of Ixtlan.

Although I felt a little bit aggressive asking to be president, I wasn't even as close to aggressive as some of the people who later came on board. One man was hired later and got more money and perks than I did because he simply asked. He would shove things under Oliver's nose, demanding attention. I used to think, "Unless I absolutely need to, I'm not going to bother Oliver." That attitude may not have been the most advantageous, but I wasn't comfortable any other

Courtesy of Manifest Film Co, 1998

Janet, Joan Chen, Oliver Stone, Elizabeth Stone and Dr. Chris Renna, Thailand, 1993.

way. I find that I often hold back in relationships, for the sake of the relationship. Some people will say that's why I survived with Oliver so long. I was more concerned with the longevity of our working relationship than always having to get my way. I chose my battles wisely. And he really did leave me alone. I could probably have gotten more if I had pushed harder, but I didn't feel like I absolutely had to or that it would have been worth it.

Joy Luck did very well. It was never going to compete with *Die Hard,* but people were shocked that it did so well. We spent only ten million to make it, but we earned almost forty domestically. If you can make three to four times what a movie costs, that's fantastic. Asian women had never been the leads in a Hollywood movie, and many movies were spawned from that. It was the beginning of a string of women's movies. A lot of people said that *Little Women* and movies like that were able to come out because of the success of *Joy Luck.* It helped solidify an Asian-American consciousness. It wasn't my doing; it was a phenomenon. When things get done that have never been achieved before, it changes people's perceptions. I saw so many things that the movie gave birth to.

Vision

I've always felt a particular responsibility to do good work because of the influence this work has. There has to be a line between art and politics. If I made my decisions based on what I thought other people would like me to do, it wouldn't work. I have to just feel it or not. I've read scripts that I thought were very politically correct and technically were great, but I didn't feel it. I've learned to make the separation and go with my feelings.

When I was working with Steven Spielberg in China, I thought, "This is the culmination of my life work and it doesn't get any better than this." When I was living in China, I thought, "It doesn't get better than this." And then after *Joy Luck* came out, I thought the same thing. I've stopped saying that because it keeps getting better. People ask me what it felt like to win an Emmy, and I have to say honestly that it almost felt like nothing. The only reason I cared about it was so that people could see an Asian woman walk up on stage. I didn't think that had ever happened before. I don't think there had ever been an Asian person to ever win an Emmy or an Oscar. I wanted to win for the symbol of it. I mean, it's all an illusion anyway. I didn't feel like it was me winning, but something happening out there. It didn't make me feel better or worse as a person. What's so funny is that when we got the nomination, everyone was congratulating us, but Oliver was worried that it was going to go to my head. He said, "I hope you don't think it means anything. Your lawyer better not call up asking for more money." He had seen that Hollywood has a way of developing huge egos as it tends to be very self-congratulatory, and he didn't want it to be a big deal for me. He didn't go, and because the Emmys weren't aired on television until after the live program, I called him from the post-Emmy party and said, "Guess what, I have something for you." He said, "What?" "It's an Emmy." He was excited, but we both felt it was important not to get too caught up in the hype around us. Joe was actually more excited than I was. When I came down from the stage with the Emmy, he was crying. It was so cute!

Joey realized that for his family and his friends this was a big deal. As the people in my office tell it, they were all screaming. And if I had been watching it for Oliver, I would have been screaming, too. There's something about what television does. The power of the medium is so great. The power of all of the people watching the same thing at the same time is magical. The way they work the lights and the music and the anticipation . . . we're all programmed to get excited over things that happen on television. When you're actually there, it's long. The most fun thing about that night was the ride over, drinking champagne in the stretch limo. You know, you can never know when you're doing a project whether it will be big. At a certain point in the work, you feel like you're just being lifted up by some benevolent force. All of the good that's happening around you is really out of your control, and you feel like you're mostly a vehicle. At that point, so much energy has been infused into it, it almost feels as if it goes by itself. Carlos told me that his goal was to amass enough energy so that he could do really important things with intent. And that's what winning the Emmy felt like to me. I, and a lot of people, had put so much energy into the work that there was enough momentum and it just took off.

Future

I am grateful that I'm now in a position to make my own films, and I'm looking forward to doing just that, while raising my baby. I had been thinking for a while that it would be great to be out on my own with a partner, but I hadn't identified anyone, except Lisa Henson, the president of Columbia Pictures. But Lisa had been president for three years and I thought she would be there for another five or ten more years. What I didn't know at the time was that her contract was about to be up, and she was in the middle of figuring out whether or not to renew it. Joey kept saying to me, "Why don't you at least ask her?" and I'd say, "No, it's way too early, I'm sure she wouldn't leave the studio." Lisa and I had known each other for years, and we had just worked very closely on *The People vs. Larry Flynt* together. We talked about three times a day during the filming, and I found that we had a good collaborative relationship and good communication. We felt like a team. A lot of people say horrible things about their studio experiences, but I've never had a bad studio experience, this one included. One evening, we were all having dinner together and Joe said, "Janet thinks that you would make good partners." Lisa surprised me and said that she had given some thought to going out on her own as well.

One thing led to another, and Lisa mentioned to her superiors at Columbia that she and I were thinking of starting a partnership. They

Photo by Sidney Baldwin

Janet and Woody Harrelson, on the set of *The People vs. Larry Flynt*, 1996.

responded really well and immediately offered us a generous producing deal. Studios have deals with various producers, directors and writers. They offered us offices on their lot, which is a good way to attract material to the studio because having producers on the lot brings in good material and ultimately leads to getting movies made. It was strange because, as usual, it all happened so quickly. Joe and I were at a film festival in the Czech Republic. After that, we took a trip to Belgium to a little town called Brugge, which is the town where Joe's ancestors came from. It all happened while we were on vacation. Lisa was on jury duty that week, and Oliver was in Greece, so from these three distant locations we worked it all out. Once the offer came through from Columbia, it all happened very quickly. I had considered some other possibilities, like going up north and working with Francis Ford Coppola's company, but this opportunity felt the best. Lisa and I opened an office on the Sony lot, which owns Columbia and Tristar. I felt very comfortable going there because I liked everyone I had gotten to know working on *Flynt,* from the people in the marketing department to people in distribution and business affairs. It all just felt right. We have a wonderful bungalow, right in the middle of the lot. Peter Guber and Francis Coppola both used it at one time, and neither one of us on our own would have gotten that space because of the way it's laid out, but it's perfect for us because we wanted to share an office. In fact, we even share a desk.

I don't really think about the different categories of life anymore, and yet people inevitably thrust them upon me. I just did a panel at the Santa Barbara film festival on women directors and we spent half the time discussing whether it was even healthy to keep marginalizing women by labeling them as "women directors." Inevitably I'm always asked to speak on behalf of Asian-Americans. I don't mind it, but sometimes it feels a little unauthentic because although being Asian is so much a part of me, it's an integrated part, and I no longer know how to separate it out. For instance, I have no idea what it's like to be a white man. My life experiences have been infused so much with being Asian that in my adult life I've stopped trying to hide from that. The identity thing is not an issue for me anymore. In general, I feel more integrated, and I don't feel a conscious effort to blend in. I don't think about the notion of belonging anymore. I just recently heard an excellent tape, about the chakras of the body, by Caroline Myss. The first chakra, the tribal chakra, deals with the strong need to belong, but as you move up the chakras, life becomes more about finding your own level of consciousness. The need to belong dissipates. Does anyone feel like they belong? I just don't think of "belonging" as a desirable thing anymore. Even if there is a club that I can't join, I'm too busy doing what I love to mind.

Woody Harrelson

Photo by Sidney Baldwin

Woody on the set of *HiLo Country*.

Introduction

While traveling with Janet Yang in June of 1995, I had a fortuitous encounter with Woody Harrelson when we arrived at Oliver Stone's horse ranch the same afternoon. Surrounding the house were thousands of acres of rolling grassland, and from the front porch, where our conversation began, the snow-covered peaks of the Rocky Mountains seemed nearly within grasp from our bird's-eye view of the Colorado landscape below. The setting sun added a surreal quality to the panoramic beauty.

Throughout our conversation, Woody's eyes were mesmerizing. Bright and vivid blue, they seemed to dance with the joy of living. Much has been written of these eyes. Oliver Stone says that he sees violence in them, but one could easily disagree. Intensity, yes. Hidden secrets, likely. But violence, no. Not in the eyes I've seen. And yet, Woody himself admits to his dichotomous nature—the yin and yang living and expressing themselves simultaneously.

As we made our way to a roaring campfire, it seemed natural in this setting to engage in philosophical conversation. Woody's reflections were learned and somewhat controversial. We did not agree on all topics, but in time arrived at a place of mutual respect for the underlying workings of each other's individual opinions. I knew then that I wanted to ask Woody for an interview because even though he held dearly many spiritual beliefs and practices expressed by others for this book, I had a sense that he would articulate unique viewpoints, those of a man who answers to his own callings, regardless of what people around him deem right or wrong.

Of the traits Woody's friends are so attracted to are his truthfulness and his passion for the environment. People may not agree with his beliefs or his actions, but few of his stature appear to be as courageous when faced with opposition. For instance, caught up in the energy of an antiwar rally prior to the bombing of Iraq by U.S. troops in 1991, Woody publicly expressed repulsion about the war effort—as one may recall, a highly opposed view during the height of American patriotism. Even after receiving hate mail for his position, Woody continued to speak out against the atrocities occurring halfway across the globe, *regardless of what effect his stance would have on his career. In an open letter to the IRS, Woody opposed our government's way of doing business and he refuses to pay a portion of his taxes each year. In the summer of 1996, in another act of defiance against the bureaucracy, Woody was arrested at a hemp legalization rally in Kentucky, where he had planted hemp seeds (not the marijuana variety) in an effort to bring attention to the benefits of this alternative fiber. Woody's most recent public demonstration landed him in jail, where he was charged with scaling the Golden Gate Bridge and bringing traffic to a halt as he and eight others hung a banner educating passersby about the planned destruction of one of California's last old-growth redwood forests.*

Woody's two children by his former assistant are another example of a man living in opposition with social mores. Once outspoken in his lack of beliefs in or desire for monogamy, Woody now wrestles with a growing spiritual outlook and the reality that his relationships still do not conform to any particular mold. After having children, Woody believed that he could be a fully present and adoring parent without having to be married to their mother; however, as committed as he is to fighting for his environmental convictions, Woody was frustrated by his inability to commit to her, or any woman. Just recently he and Laura surprised everyone by holding a marriage ceremony in Costa Rica. True to form, no legal papers were signed, but Woody thinks that affairs of the heart need not be governed by institutions.

Considering his troubled beginnings, it is inspiring that Woody has achieved as much fulfillment as he has. Growing up in Texas and Ohio, Woody was only seven when he heard on the car radio that his father had been imprisoned for life for killing a federal judge. Having a parent on the FBI's most-wanted list for over a year generated his insecurity about the future, and may have been a catalyst that helped shape the environmental activist he has become. Woody cannot ignore the reality that without a healthy planet—our true caretaker—we all face an uncertain future.

With the success of Indecent Proposal, White Men Can't Jump, Natural Born Killers, *and his Oscar nomination for his portrayal of* Larry Flynt *in* The People vs. Larry Flynt, *Woody's career is thriving, but a growing dissatisfaction toward outward success causes him to find deeper peace by embracing the spiritual side of life. Woody's diet, for example, is extremely disciplined, consisting of almost 80 percent raw fruits and vegetables, made easier in the fertile lands of his Costa Rica home. He avoids eating animal products, and every six weeks takes one week off to fast, even during his daily, strenuous yoga practice.*

Photo by Sidney Baldwin

Woody holding hemp fibers.

Woody's thoughts continually return to the bigger picture, and his interests and actions are increasingly global: In addition to writing songs about the environment and helping animal-rights groups, Woody educates others about the benefits of hemp through his co-ownership of a factory that processes the tree-saving fiber. Woody's wearing of the clothing he manufactures doesn't hurt business either: Whether he's sporting hemp yoga-wear or formal attire, the packaging, like the man, is conscious, yet defiant and untamed.

*   *   *   *

Happiness

Happiness is being truly relaxed. I've been one of those guys maniacally in pursuit of happiness for years and years and years. Ever since I can remember. Happiness has always been a goal for me, which is ironic because it's not a place to be. Larry Flynt said that "happiness is not a goal, it's a mode of transportation." A way to travel.

I think a lot of people have the thought that happiness is this elusive thing that's outside of themselves. Most people are in constant pursuit of it. I've been to India, Africa, Macchu Pichu, everywhere, looking for that all-elusive thing which amounts to taking a deep breath wherever I am sitting and just chilling the fuck out. That's all it is—knowing how to relax. All of the frequent flier miles just to learn that!

Family

One morning I was riding in the car with Deni, my daughter, and Laura [Deni's mother] was driving. Deni was three years old, and I did something with her that I had never done before: I started explaining to her that the human body emits electricity. I told her to put her hand next to mine, with an inch in between our hands so we weren't touching. As Laura's speeding through traffic, and Deni and I were both seat-belted next to each other in our two-seater Miata, Deni's holding her little hand up to mine. I told her to feel the pulse of energy between our hands and showed her how to get a feel for it by moving her hand a bit toward mine and then away from mine. During the whole twenty-five-minute drive from Beverly Hills to Santa Monica we were doing this. She was totally enthralled by the process. I told Deni to breathe deeply and she was doing really well holding her hand there and feeling the pulse of energy. I was feeling it too, which generated as heat. The whole experience was amazing to me because Deni is so young, but seems to be evolved in a way that I only dream of.

When we pulled up at our destination, a yoga class, I picked Deni up to say good-bye and she was a different person suddenly. She is normally so full of life and always very energized and talkative, but she was in another zone—another hemisphere. She had focused so deeply that she appeared to be in an alpha state. I said her name and she could barely look up at me, which if you knew Deni is totally unlike her. What I thought of as a cool little game to teach her about energy, she took to the cosmos. For her to get that relaxed from just deep breathing and focusing on the energy of her body was incredible. It relaxed me also, which was funny to me. Here we were taking a few deep breaths in the car on the way to a yoga class that was supposedly going to *really* relax me.

Being a parent has been profound for me. I think whenever you experience something akin to unconditional love, it is going to change you somehow. And, by the way, when Deni was first born, I didn't feel total unconditional love for her—there were definite conditions to it. I found that we were each defining our space. Imagine, vying for space with a three-week-old, or a two-month-old. Most people don't talk of this as a reality: vying for space with a baby. People without children often assume that because you are family, you will have this incredible bond, but that bond develops over time, or it doesn't.

I don't know if Deni's mother and I will get married. [This part of the interview was completed before the Costa Rica ceremony.] We are so much like a family, but that would take us to a deeper level. I have never been a big advocate of monogamy, but my opinions and attitudes are shifting a lot. I very much admired the love my character felt for Demi Moore's character in *Indecent Proposal*. I was just thinking today that there would be nothing better than to really be able to show that kind of love. I really love Laura, but she shows it all the time, continuously. Me, I throw it in every once in a while. Sometimes I don't know what it is that has made me such a stoic kind of cut-off guy..

I wish I could say that I'm a better person because of my daughter [This interview with Woody took place over a two-and-a-half-year period. This section was recorded before the birth of his second daughter, Zoe.] I wish I could out-and-out lie in this case. But, when I'm with her I'm the best person I can be, and when I'm away from her, I'm still the same old asshole, I guess.

Obstacles

I'm not really an asshole, but I've realized that I have a certain arrogance that is not in keeping with my essence—the real me. I'm not yet comfortable using the word *arrogant*. It must be one of my shadow words—one of those qualities I hate so much in other people because I hate it within myself. I said to a friend of mine a couple of years ago that someone had had the audacity to call me arrogant, and by my friend's reaction, I was led to think immediately, "My God, I am arrogant." But, prior to that, I had never realized it.

I know arrogance is a family trait that I inherited. My father is arrogant, and he would be the first to agree with me on that. There is an aspect of this inherited personality that sometimes causes me to be arrogant without even knowing. This is not a result of fame, as some might think, but a trait that has always been a part of my makeup. It is time for me to let go of this aspect of myself, and one way to do that is to realize how it has served me in the past. In a weird way, it helped me get where I am. I remember when I lived in New York and went through seventeen jobs in one year. A coworker would say to me, "Someone threw up over at table three, go clean it up," and I'd say: "You go clean it up. I'm not cleaning up that shit." My arrogance helped me to get where I am because I couldn't keep another job. Acting is the only job that tolerates that attitude. I thank God I never got successful waiting tables because it can be a good wage, especially in New York, where it would have been easy to get complacent.

Courtesy of Diane Harrelson

I would say also that confidence and arrogance often go hand-in-hand. I know I have a certain confidence in my abilities. Believing in yourself in a deeper way is the most important component to material success, and certainly the most important component to spiritual success. This reminds me of something Teddy Roosevelt said, "Whether you think you can or think you can't, you're right."

Drive

I have always had a real strong personal drive. A sense of really wanting to succeed. It's both an effective thing to visualize what you want and go after it and get it, but at the same time, I find it's a destructive thing in that you become too future-oriented, making it hard to be present. I've noticed that when I hang out with really successful people, a lot of times they're not present when they're talking. Their minds are elsewhere.

What I want more than anything—beyond whatever success is—is to be present in whatever I am doing. Success to me does not equal money. The ideal success to me is being happy. Being a true success is being here and now, present in everything I'm doing. I think I'm doing pretty well with that.

Fame

I spoke with Shirley MacLaine for a few hours once when we sat next to each other on a plane. It was incredible. She was cool. She thinks that very often famous people live with a raw dissatisfaction in the midst of what looks like a perfect life, and I think that's a good description.

To go for fame is a wrong reason in and of itself. You don't even know the Pandora's box you're opening up. The need to go for fame is to want to be accepted on a really big level. Prior to that, you want to be accepted by everyone around you. I definitely had a desire to be accepted on a large scale. I don't understand some celebrities who say they didn't intend or want to be famous. Maybe that happens sometimes, in a case where some guy goes and pulls somebody out of a burning building and his photo is in the paper the next day, but most people who become famous wanted it badly. As for actors, if you don't want fame, you can be a theater actor somewhere, just doing plays. That is a far different scale than being a movie star.

The desire and drive for fame has shifted for me. The vehicle and form of fame are still present, but it lacks substance and is hollow in my life. It doesn't feel right. Being wildly ambitious does not feel right. Now my lawyers and agents caution me against wanting to do artsy films. They tell me I'm not thinking enough about being commercial. After *Money Train,* I realized that I cannot do these films that everybody tells me will be good for me. My heart has to be in a project for it to be fulfilling. As much as Wesley Snipes and I tried to improve things for that movie, it never became a story worth caring about, which is a frequent by-product of focusing on commercial results.

Earth

I really ingest the world problems a lot. It makes me crazy sometimes being so concerned with environmental issues. The way I see it, the primary reason people are suffering is because we are completely out of balance with nature. We have a dysfunctional relationship with the planet. People for years and years lived without money, they didn't have a symbol called currency. Now, everything from architecture to making paper from trees is creating nightmares for urban America. All I can do is try to do something.

I went to see the Headwaters redwood forest in Northern California because I heard the trees were being sold and they needed help. The battle cry right now is to save the sixty thousand acres of forest owned by a man named Charles Hurwitz. I spent the night among the redwoods there. It was magical, so beautiful. People say that once you walk amongst the ancient redwoods, which in that area were between a thousand and two thousand years old, you will always be attached to them. I believe that's true. Although I had been in forests, I had never been in a redwood forest. It was a great experience. I was awestruck by their sheer magnificence and beauty.

A lot of the most magnificent trees were marked with blue paint, signifying which ones were to be cut down. The area I was in no longer exists today. It was completely destroyed. Over half of the sixty thousand acres is stump fields now, heavily logged. Another 30 to 40 percent has been partially logged. The buyers go for the big ones. For the guy doing the cutting, this is in his best interest because he gets paid in terms of quantity of wood cut. A lot of ancient trees go down, and even the smaller trees are often killed because when the big trees are taken down, their huge mass kills the trees in their path. It's devastating to see. To me, if there is anything that's sacred, it's these trees. They are arguably the most beautiful and largest creatures on the planet.

Unfortunately, they don't seem to have any rights. They don't speak English and they aren't white. Their bark is red, just like the red-skinned people who used to live on this continent, who were also almost destroyed.

Hurwitz, who owns this forest, also owns Pacific Lumber. When he was asked, "Have you ever seen the redwood forest?" he supposedly said, "I don't need to see it, I own it." People like him are automatons, total robots. "I must make money, I must make money. Money, money, money, money." His most famous quote came after he bought the lumber company. He was taped in Scotia, addressing his new employees of the Pacific Lumber Company in 1986: "The Golden Rule is: He who has the gold rules." Basically, he's cutting the forest down as fast as he can.

A twenty-four-year-old woman, Julia Butterfly, has been living 180

Photo by Eric Slomanson

"Luna," Julia's tree home.

feet up, in a redwood tree named "Luna" on Hurwitz's land. She's been up there for 211 days and counting. Luna is two hundred feet tall, so she's almost at the top. Julia's home is a platform, without sides. If that weren't dangerous enough, the tree she's in overlooks a four-hundred-foot drop. Julia's attracted a lot of attention, as her story has inspired people all over the world. Julia had been in a head-on collision in a car crash that almost took her life. She had massive head injuries and was paralyzed for a year. When she came out of rehab, she decided to do something meaningful with her life and was called to help the redwoods. She went to the forest base camp of activists, who were closing up their sixty-nine day tree sit with the onset of winter. Determined to do her part, she volunteered to go up. It was December 10, and she sat through all the El Niño storms and torrential rains. Winds up to one hundred miles per hour ripped her tarps to shreds.

There were people next to Julia in other trees, but the loggers climbed those trees and forced the people out. The branches on Julia's tree are structured so that it is much too difficult to climb for the loggers, so through a series of circumstances, Julia remains the last person out there. If the loggers could have, they would have cut off all her supplies and arrested her by now. At first she was trespassing, but the Pacific Lumber Company ultimately said on CNN and in the *New York Times* that Julia has permission to stay in the tree. I think they were trying to tone down the media spectacle of it all and reduce the confrontational aspects. They hope she'll just get tired. People assume she must get lonely, but she's got a cell phone and a constant stream of visitors. A movie crew has come up to film, and *Time, People,* the *Los Angeles Times,* the *London Times* and many other news organizations have been up there.

The trees that remain very close to her are still standing, which is really important because those trees are holding up the hillside. Of the many reasons she's up there, probably the primary reason is that the area she's in is very prone to mud slides. About one hundred yards from where she's sitting, high up on the mountain, a mud slide originated from a neighboring clear-cut and, like a tidal wave, mud destroyed the town of Stafford below. Julia is sitting in the tree known as Luna, the Stafford Giant. The roots of a redwood tree only go six feet deep; that's why they usually fall down when they die. Really, the whole hillside could come down with her in the tree at any time. Enough trees have been left around it to hopefully hold up the hillside, but the ground has been saturated this year, so she's engaged in a life-threatening activity. Everyone is aware of the danger, which is why there is so much respect for her.

Even amongst the redwoods that are being saved, many are dying because they don't like the elements. When they are thinned out and roads and highways are built through them, they become exposed to rain, wind, vibrations, car exhaust, soil compaction and so on, and they don't do well. Before 1850, there used to be 2 million acres of redwood forest. Since then, one million, nine hundred thousand have been logged. So, less than 5 percent are left. Some of those acres have grown back, only to be logged again.

It's not common knowledge these days what the primary functions of trees really are. The most important thing a tree does is store water. It sucks up water during the rainy season and then it lets that water out during the dry season so that the creeks, rivers, lakes and wells remain full. One of the most common complaints from logging is that people's wells dry up. The rivers, creeks and lakes dry up as well.

Probably the second most valuable role trees play is weather modification. They attract rain and moisture.

Photo by Eric Slomanson

Julia Butterfly in "Luna," an ancient redwood to be cut by Pacific Lumber Co.

Redwoods get 50 percent of their water from fog. If there are no trees to catch the fog, the fog just rolls in and rolls out without condensing to the ground. Activists will sit in trees and when the fog rolls in, they get drenched. At the same time, only ten feet away at the start of a clear-cut, the ground stays dry. Trees cool the land twenty to thirty degrees. So in an urban area, the temperature may be one hundred degrees, but if you walk one mile away into an old-growth tree park, the temperature will be seventy-five degrees.

When the sun hits a forest, the heat is absorbed and converted into various forms of energy by growing plants. If the forest isn't there, the heat is reflected back into the atmosphere, making the atmosphere warmer. We've all heard of global warming, and this is one of the causes. The sheer loss of shade alone has major effects on the climate.

I could go on and on, and obviously there isn't enough time here, but I'll mention that another big adverse effect of cutting trees is the loss of fish. Trees provide the creeks with shade for the fish. No tree, no fish. Water temperatures become deadly. Salmon, for example, cannot live in temperatures above sixty-eight degrees. Take the shade away, you've got dead fish. Without the trees, the soil goes down to the creeks and the rivers, and the fish can't breathe because their habitats are filled with dirt. The mudslides are constant. These are the things we don't think about when we grow up and live in an industrial society.

Julia's doing her part to try and save a few trees, but who knows what she'll be able to accomplish? One evening, a bunch of us were sitting around a campfire on Hurwitz's land. I said, "I don't know, there's something missing, there's got to be a better action." A girl said, "Why don't we scale the Golden Gate Bridge?" I said, "Good idea!" A lot of people would have heard that and said, "No way, that's crazy!" but this group of activists are so cool. Activists to me are the ultimate modern-day heroes. They just sat around and started talking in real, concrete, physical terms how it could be done. They knew of other attempts that had failed in the not-too-distant past, and they were talking about why they had failed. It was amazing to see it all go into action. I've spent more time with activists since then and they never cease to amaze me.

On a movie set, you see people who have all of these different specialties. When something goes wrong, they run in and—boom!—they fix it. That's what these guys were like, only they had a wide range of talents. They could scale anything, from a tree to a building. They are capable of a million and one things, and almost all of them are extraordinary athletes. [Woody is also an incredible athlete. I've seen him do dangerous acrobatics on a trampoline, ride a horse at the

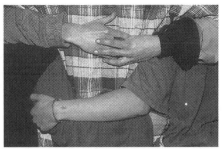

Photo by Eric Slomanson/ZUMA

Activists join together.

speed of the wind, fall into splits and play a mean game of basketball, affirming for me that white men really *can* jump.]

Photo by Eric Slomanson/ZUMA

Woody climbing the Golden Gate Bridge.

Climbing the bridge was kind of scary. You've got to believe in the safety of your lines, but they were thin little lines and it was so high up. I don't have many regrets because it brought a lot of attention to the redwoods. But we were vilified, particularly locally, because of the traffic situation that resulted. The one regret I have about the climb is that there was a lack of communication. On our

way up, the cops called up; we had radios and ways of keeping in touch with the ground. The cops wanted to talk, to try and get us to come down. We were on our way up, and the weight of the huge banner—which said "Hurwitz, aren't ancient redwoods more precious than

Photo by Eric Slomanson/ZUMA

The arrest.

gold?"—was extreme. The guy who was carrying it was having a little trouble. The cops said, "We're going to block off traffic." My thought was, "Okay, they've got to do what they've got to do, and we've got to do what we've got to do." But I wish I had gotten on the horn and said, "Hey, don't do that. We'll be down as soon as we get this banner unfurled."

It was a classic example of the need for a little communication. I think if I had talked to them, the cops wouldn't have closed off the lanes. They knew as soon as they started blocking off the lanes, the motorists would be screaming at us and we'd see the traffic. It was a pretty clever way to do it. So, at least in San Francisco, a lot of people couldn't see the forest for the traffic. But overall, I'm really happy to have been a part of it. Even with all the media attention, the forest is still being destroyed. When I went up there recently, it was akin to being at Gettysburg the morning after, with stumps and dead trees everywhere.

When I was young, I had a strong affinity for nature, animals and insects. I now see the same affinity through Deni. She's obsessed with nature. She loves to take walks, chase butterflies and explore it all. We've spent a lot of time in Central America and that's probably helped. I feel that I'm fighting for both of my daughters' rights to enjoy what older generations took for granted. Trees represent life. Without them, we don't have life. God knows an old radical like myself won't last long, but my kids and their kids will be here and they deserve the same rights we were given.

There is no reason to kill so many trees. Until the late 1800s, 90 percent of paper came from hemp. Hemp is one of the strongest natural fibers known to man. It is criminal to use trees when other, more renewable fibers can be used instead. It only takes between three and four months for a hemp plant to grow to maturity (ten to fifteen feet high). Paper is a major source of wood pulp. Hemp paper is not only stronger, but it lasts longer. If it were grown in bulk, it would be far less costly to produce than tree fiber. Even at this point, there are four companies producing hemp office paper in North America and the price has been going down for years [see contact page for consumer information].

I went up to a meeting once in San Francisco, and a man came up to me who owned a tree farm. He had hundreds of thousands of trees on his plantation. They were being grown for paper and for other products. Yet he couldn't sell his trees because the trees from our national forests are being given away at bargain-basement prices, subsidized by the government.

When I first found out about the selling off of our national forests, I went on *Larry King* and did my best to publicize it. At that time there were six million acres in Montana we were trying to save, much of it probably cut down by now.* I wanted to bring attention to them, but I realized that I also had to offer a solution. Hemp was my solution. In 1932, *Popular Mechanics* magazine stated that there were twenty-five thousand different uses for hemp. It is the most versatile plant on the planet, but our society is paranoid and has outlawed it because it looks like a flower that makes you feel euphoric. Now, we can't have that! We can't use a cousin of the euphoria flower. You know, sometimes you've got to laugh to keep from crying.

I believe that personal transformation equals planetary transformation. Even though I'm working to produce hemp and I'm not paying part of my taxes out of protest at the way this government does business subsidizing the timber, petroleum, nuclear war and pesticide industries, the main thing I need to do is a personal transformation, and that's only going to come by learning to relax.

[*AUTHOR'S NOTE: *According to Darryl Cherney, a friend of Woody's who is a redwood activist for Earth First Redwood Action Team, there is hope. Darryl believes that the 1960s brought a great spiritual awakening (helped in large part by the popularity of the Beatles), that resulted in widespread acceptance of yoga, Eastern philosophy, feminism, vegetarianism and many other positive influences. A major consciousness shift occurred, resulting in giant ripples that affect the environment to the present day. "It's really hard to kill a planet," says Darryl. "Although we've experienced the end of life as we know it in many ways, the Earth is resilient and able to heal itself. There is a strong possibility that if we stop our destructive ways now, the planet's own self-correcting healing systems could kick in enough to make the environment healthy again." Darryl sees the battle to save the planet as a race. "There's a point where we won't be able to undo the damage already done. Some feel that we've surpassed the point of no return, but no one knows for sure. It's worth fighting for our planet. The trees can still grow back. Where there's life, there's hope."*]